DRAWING NEAR
to the HEART *of* GOD

DRAWING NEAR
to the HEART of GOD

A Year of Devotions from a Rich Tradition

Compiled by
Mark and Donna Kelderman

Reformation Heritage Books
Grand Rapids, Michigan

Drawing Near to the Heart of God
© 2022 by Mark and Donna Kelderman

Reformation Heritage Books
3070 29th St. SE
Grand Rapids, MI 49512
616-977-0889
orders@heritagebooks.org
www.heritagebooks.org

Scripture taken from the King James Version. In the public domain.

Italics in Scripture have been added for emphasis.

Printed in the United States of America
22 23 24 25 26 27/10 9 8 7 6 5 4 3 2 1

Library of Congress Cataloging-in-Publication Data

Names: Kelderman, Mark, compiler. | Kelderman, Donna, compiler.
Title: Drawing near to the heart of God : a year of devotions from a rich tradition /
    compiled by Mark and Donna Kelderman.
Description: Grand Rapids, Michigan : Reformation Heritage Books, [2022] |
    Includes index.
Identifiers: LCCN 2022022540 (print) | LCCN 2022022541 (ebook) | ISBN
    9781601789594 (hardback) | ISBN 9781601789600 (epub)
Subjects: LCSH: Devotional calendars.
Classification: LCC BV4810 .K44 2022 (print) | LCC BV4810 (ebook) | DDC
    242/.2--dc23/eng/20220711
LC record available at https://lccn.loc.gov/2022022540
LC ebook record available at https://lccn.loc.gov/2022022541

For additional Reformed literature, request a free book list from Reformation Heritage Books at the above regular or email address.

Preface

One of the daily challenges people face is the uncertainty of this world as we observe pandemics, wars, financial woes, and society's attacks on the truth of God's Word. We take vacations and go on retreats seeking peace and rest. Despite all our attempts, though, it seems that unrest and uncertainty are increasing, impacting our personal lives as well as our relationships. We continue to experience anxiety, tension, and brokenness. You probably find that the question "Where can I find peace and rest?" frequently arises in your heart.

Horatius Bonar writes, "Every trouble, comes fragrant with blessing. It is a new opportunity of getting nearer God and learning more of His love." In Matthew 11:28–30 Jesus says, "Come unto me, all ye that labour and are heavy laden, and I will give you rest. Take my yoke upon you, and learn of me; for I am meek and lowly in heart: and ye shall find rest unto your souls. For my yoke is easy, and my burden is light." True rest is found in Christ alone. Therefore, as we take up His yoke and burden and draw near to the heart of God, we find rest, as Bonar points out.

Drawing Near to the Heart of God is a devotional compiled during a time of personal uncertainty because of ongoing health difficulties. One day while I was grieving over an increased loss of physical abilities, a dear friend urged me to use the abilities I do have to compile a companion devotional to my earlier one, *Seasons of the Heart*. Over the next two years my own soul profited while working on this project in the midst of suffering pain and afflictions. My dear husband came alongside me and wrote the thought to ponder for each day. He also gave me much encouragement.

The themes woven throughout this devotional include repentance and humility before God, using our time well, living godly in our relationships, understanding the value of our soul, living our lives for God's honor and glory, and suffering.

A theology of suffering is generally missing in our culture today, even in the church. While I was researching this book, I found a common thread emerging in the writings of these twelve authors: the theme of suffering and afflictions. Suffering should not discourage us, for Christ Himself said that all Christians must take up their cross. The Lord doesn't say *if*, but "*when* thou passest through the waters, I *will* be with thee; and through the rivers, they shall not overflow thee: when thou walkest through the fire, thou shalt not be burned; neither shall the flame kindle upon thee. For I *am* the LORD thy God" (Isa. 43:2–3). God has laid on each one of us the precise burden He wants us to carry so that we learn to lean hard on Him and His grace. Most of the authors of these devotionals suffered persecution, the death of their children or spouse, or the disappointment of their own personal weaknesses, and yet they kept their focus on their God.

Let the Bible and these writings demonstrate to you the truth of Romans 8:28, for then we will believe that everything we experience in life, even the challenges in our personal lives and relationships, are designed by God to serve His transforming process of making us more like Christ.

Spend quiet time each day in reading and prayer with the aim of directing your heart—either for the first time or by renewal—closer to the heart of God. It is our prayer that this devotional may profit you in your personal quiet time, in reading and discussing with your spouse, or during family devotions. Let the words of these godly men who have trodden the path before us be used as a cordial to draw us closer to the heart of God.

There is a place of quiet rest,
　Near to the heart of God,
A place where sin cannot molest,
　Near to the heart of God.

There is a place of comfort sweet,
　Near to the heart of God,
A place where we our Savior meet,
　Near to the heart of God.

There is a place of full release,
　Near to the heart of God,
A place where all is joy and peace,
　Near to the heart of God.

O Jesus, blest Redeemer,
　Sent from the heart of God,
Hold us, who wait before Thee,
　Near to the heart of God.
　　　　　　　　—McAfee

JANUARY

◆

What is your hope about your soul?

—J. C. RYLE

What Is Your Hope?

For what is a man profited, if he shall gain the whole world, and lose his own soul? or what shall a man give in exchange for his soul?
—MATTHEW 16:26

What is your own hope about your soul? I do not ask out of idle curiosity. I ask it as an ambassador for Christ and as a friend to your best interests. I ask it in order to stir up self-inquiry and promote your spiritual welfare. I ask, What is your hope about your soul? I do not want to know whether you go to church; there will be no account of this in heaven. I do not want to know whether you approve of the gospel and think it very right and proper that people should have their religion and say their prayers. All this is beside the mark; it is not the point. The point I want you to look at is this: What is your own hope about your soul?

It matters nothing what your relatives think. It matters nothing what the rest of the church or town approve. The account of God will not be taken by towns, or by churches, or by families. Each must stand separately and answer for himself. Every one of us shall give account of himself to God (Rom. 14:12). What will be your plea? What is your hope about your soul?

Time is short and is passing quickly away. Yet a few years, and we shall be dead and gone. The trees perhaps are cut down out of which our coffins will be made.... Eternity draws near. There ought to be no trifling. What, what is your hope for your soul?

Another world will soon begin. Trade, politics, money, land, cottages, palaces, eating, drinking, dressing, reading, hunting...will soon be at an end forever. There will remain nothing but a heaven for some, and a hell for others. What, what is your hope about your soul?

—J. C. RYLE

◆ *What are you seeking to gain in this life? What is the price of your soul?*

Complete in Him

And ye are complete in him.
—COLOSSIANS 2:10

D o you realize the preciousness of this truth, that to be "in Christ" is to have everything the soul can require in time and throughout eternity? This is the only real wealth. Earthly possessions pass away. Fame, riches, honor—all these are but gilded toys; but this is the pearl of great price, the treasure above all treasures, the enduring inheritance. To be "in Christ" is to "have happiness and heaven." He is essential to every soul, and where He is, the root of everything else that is required is there too. Therefore, there is "no condemnation to them which are in Christ Jesus" (Rom. 8:1). The Son of God became the Son of Man that He might make us the sons of God forever. By His dying He destroyed death, and by His rising to life again, He restored us to everlasting life.

No wonder the apostle, when contemplating this wondrous truth, should exclaim, "Ye are complete in him" (Col. 2:10). Yes, believers are complete. They have a fullness in Christ which nothing can exhaust, a love which passes knowledge, a strength which is omnipotent, and a faithfulness which cannot be questioned. The more they dwell upon it, the deeper becomes the conviction of their own weakness and Christ's sufficiency—their own emptiness and His fullness, their own ignorance and His wisdom, their own utter inability to keep the path of duty, and their daily, hourly need of Christ to animate, sustain, and guide them. *"Ye are complete in him."*

This lesson is frequently realized to the believer. By painful and pressing trials, by reverses and misfortunes, by humiliating defeats in the conflict against temptation, he is reminded that in him "dwelleth no good thing," that his own strength is weakness (Rom. 7:18). He is driven away from self and from all confidence in flesh, to Him who alone can guide and sustain him. And this is the secret of all Christian progress: more earnestness in prayer for supplies of grace. And such supplies of grace will ever be found sufficient.

—ASHTON OXENDEN

◆ *Consider the ways in which God has been teaching you the lessons of decreasing in self and how you are growing in dependence on Christ.*

The Christian's Resolutions

*When thou vowest a vow unto God, defer not to pay it; for he
hath no pleasure in fools: pay that which thou hast vowed.*
—ECCLESIASTES 5:4

When you read the writings of David, you see how often and how
solemnly he resolves to love, pray, praise, and obey the Lord. Could
he have been so eminent a servant of the Lord if he had not been so fully
determined in his mind? As far as reason and Scripture speak on this subject,
they require the following rules:

1. Our resolutions should not be unwisely or quickly taken but well
thought out. It is a snare to a man after vows to make inquiry. God abhors
all false pretenses and empty resolutions.

2. Beware of limiting your resolutions of consecration to God. Some are
ready to give God only lip service. Others seem ready to serve Him secretly,
but they are not ready to live out their confession before the world. Some
are willing to change for a time but not ready to serve God all their lives,
yea, to all eternity. Others wish to have certain sins exempt. They think it's
a small matter. Reader, deal not so with God. Give Him all; for after all it is
but little you can do for Him, who has done so much for you.

3. In all your resolutions, keep your eye on the person, work, grace,
example, sufferings, righteousness, power, and intercession of Christ. Without Him you can do nothing. His blood can cleanse, but nothing else can
wash away the stain of sin.

4. Lastly, never forget your dependence upon the power of the Spirit. He
is the anointing oil with which humble souls are made kings and priests unto
God. We can feel blind, but the Holy Spirit is the eye salve to open blind eyes.
We can be sad and despondent in good things, but He is the oil of gladness to
the saints. So, let the words of your resolutions be few but specific.

> Here, Lord, I give myself away,
> 'Tis all that I can do.

—WILLIAM PLUMER

♦ *"As he thinketh in his heart, so is he" (Prov. 23:7). What are your resolutions for this year? Are you living up to those you have previously made?*

Pressing On

I press toward the mark for the prize of the
high calling of God in Christ Jesus.
—PHILIPPIANS 3:14

Believers, if you wish to have an increase in happiness in Christ's service, strive every year to grow in grace. Beware of standing still. The holiest Christians are always the happiest. Let your aim be every year to be more holy, to know more, to feel more, to see more of the fullness of Christ. Rest not upon old grace. Do not be content with the degree of holiness you have already reached. Search the Scriptures more earnestly. Pray more fervently. Hate sin more. Mortify self-will more. Become more humble the older you get. Seek more direct, personal communion with the Lord Jesus. Strive to be more like Enoch, daily walking with God. Keep your conscience clear of little sins. Grieve not the Spirit. Avoid arguing and debating about the minor matters of religion. Lay more firm hold upon those great truths, without which no man can be saved. Remember and practice these things, and you will be happier.

If you would have an increase of happiness in Christ's service, labor every year to be more thankful. Pray that you may know more and more what it is to "rejoice in the Lord" (Phil. 4:4). Learn to have a deeper sense of your own wretched sinfulness and corruption, and to be more deeply grateful that, by the grace of God, you are what you are. Alas, there is too much complaining and too little thanksgiving among the people of God. There is too much murmuring and poring over the things that we do not have. There is too little praising and blessing for the many undeserved mercies that we have. May God pour out upon us a greater spirit of thankfulness and praise.

—J. C. RYLE

◆ *What area do you most need to grow in grace? Pray for the Holy Spirit's help as you press toward the mark.*

Praying Together

O come, let us worship and bow down:
let us kneel before the LORD our maker.
—PSALM 95:6

When a husband and wife are happily partakers of the same faith, it seems expedient for their mutual good that, besides private devotions and joining in family prayer, they should pray together. They have many wants, mercies, and concerns in common with each other and different from the rest of the family. The manner in which they should spend their time in this joint exercise cannot be prescribed by a third person; yet I will venture to suggest one thing. I believe that it would profit much for their comfort to pray alternately, not only the husband with and for the wife, but the wife with and for her husband. The Spirit of God, by the apostle, has expressly restrained women from praying in public worship; but I believe the practice I am speaking of can in no way interfere with that restriction. I judge it to be equally right and proper for either of them to pray with the other when in private prayer together. Nor do I find anything in Saint Paul's writings to alter my thinking; if he had been a married man, he would, though an apostle, have been glad of the prayers of his wife.

Happy is that family where the worship of God is constantly and conscientiously maintained. Such houses are temples where the Lord dwells, and castles garrisoned by a divine power. I do not say that by honoring God in your house you will escape a share in the trials due to the uncertain state of things. A measure of trials is necessary for the exercise and manifestation of your graces, to give you a more convincing proof of the truth and sweetness of the promises made in a time of affliction, to mortify sin and to wean you more effectually from the world. But this I will confidently say, that the Lord will both honor and comfort those who so honor Him.

—JOHN NEWTON

◆ *Is it your practice to pray with your spouse? If not, consider beginning this wonderful practice today.*

Alone with Your God

And when he had sent the multitudes away, he went up into a mountain apart to pray: and when the evening was come, he was there alone.
—MATTHEW 14:23

To the true Christian, the dearest spot on earth will be his Father's house, that hallowed place "where prayer is wont to be made." We cannot, however, be always in God's house. But there is another place where we may continually resort for prayer; *our own closet.* "Thou, when thou prayest, enter into thy closet," says our Lord (Matt. 6:6). This is the place where a devout Christian will often be found. He wishes to be sometimes alone with God, and to "pray to [his] Father which is in secret" (v. 6). What blessings are to be found in drawing near to God in private!

"If you can," says one, "secure five minutes in the day *alone with your God.*" But if you live in a crowd, get it in the quiet chamber of your own heart. A young sailor boy was remarked for his serenity and presence of mind in his first battle. "How was it, my boy," the mate asked, "that you were ready for everything, and yet as quiet as if by your mother's fireside?" "Because," said he, "I was *alone with my God* for an hour before the fight began."

Are you a man of business? You have need every now and then to get a sight of your heavenly Father, or this world will soon obtain possession of your heart. Are you a care-worn mother? Are you full of thought and anxiety about your family? Go often into your secret chamber and tell your troubles to Him who knows them all and can sustain you under them. Are you a working man, toiling for your very life? Look up to your heavenly friend; He can make your labor sweet. Are you young and healthy, in the prime of your early days? Get aside from your young companions now and then; go up to your bedroom, and acknowledge all your follies and sins, and ask Jesus to be with you and to bless you.

In short, if you wish to be in earnest about your soul, you will feel the comfort of resorting to God's house and also the preciousness of closet prayer.

—ASHTON OXENDEN

◆ *Consider the value of having a prayer closet. How can you also foster having times of prayer throughout the day?*

A Holy and Useful Life

Walk in wisdom toward them that are without, redeeming the time.
—COLOSSIANS 4:5

If we would aim at a holy and useful life, let us learn to redeem time. "I am large about redeeming time," says Richard Baxter in the preface to his *Christian Directory*, "because therein the sum of a holy obedient life is included." Let us redeem the time because the days are evil (Eph. 5:16; Col. 4:5). A wasted life is the result of unredeemed time. Unfocused working, impulsive giving, fitful planning, irregular reading, ill-assorted hours, perfunctory or unpunctual execution of business, hurry and bustle, loitering and unreadiness—these, and such like, are the things which take out the whole essence and power from life, which hinder holiness, and which eat like a canker into our moral being. These make success and progress an impossibility, either in regard to ourselves or others. There need not be routine, but there must be regularity; there ought not to be mechanical stiffness, but there must be order; there may not be haste, but there must be no trifling with our own time or that of others. "Whatsoever thy hand findeth to do, do it with thy might" (Eccl. 9:10).

If the thing is worth doing at all it is worth doing well, and in little things as well as great, we must show that we are in earnest. There must be no idling, but a girding up of the loins, a running the race with patience, the warring of a good warfare, steadfastness, and perseverance, "always abounding in the work of the Lord" (1 Cor. 15:58). The flowers are constant in their growing; the stars are constant in their courses; the rivers are constant in their flowing; they lose not time. So must our life be. Not one of fits and starts or random impulses; not one of levity or inconstancy or fickle scheming, but steady and resolute. Christians who know their earthly mission have their eye upon the heavenly goal.

—HORATIUS BONAR

◆ *Is there some area of your life that can be better spent for Christ? Ask someone close to you about their perception of your use of time. Listen carefully and seek to help each other.*

A Happy Christian Home

Come, ye children, hearken unto me:
I will teach you the fear of the LORD.

—PSALM 34:11

This book may, perhaps, fall into the hands of some Christian parent. What deeply interesting and affecting duties you have to discharge—to order your household in the fear of the Lord and to bring up your children for Him! But it must not be enough for me merely to hint at these important duties. Remember your position is a most responsible one. Every child is a precious talent committed to your care. See that you employ it, as one who must give an account. Endeavor to be a spiritual as well as a natural parent to your children; to take more care to get a portion for their souls in heaven than to make provision for their bodies on earth.

What a difference there is in family circles and how much of that difference may depend on the parent! Think of that family at Nazareth of which Jesus was a member. What a happy home it must have been. And if we were only more like Him, how many happy homes would there be in our own land! "But there are, we fear," observes a Christian writer, "many unhappy homes, many wretched homes—more by far than is generally supposed. And what is the cure for this? The presence of Jesus. Let Him into your houses to dwell with you, and…He will turn your homes into little Edens. He will heal your divisions; He will banish sadness and sorrow; He will cement you into one holy, happy family and then will be realized all that imagination ever conceived of the charms of home. He would fain enter into our homes if we would let Him. Believe me, it is His presence that sanctifies and sweetens domestic life. Without this it is a poor thing. Many fine things have been said of domestic bliss; but rest assured that the presence and love of Jesus is the sweetest drop in the cup, and that without this it will speedily turn into gall and wormwood."

—ASHTON OXENDEN

♦*Are you conscientiously making Christ the center of your family life? Pray that the Lord will bless your home with spiritual conversations about Jesus.*

Christ's Sensitiveness to Desertion

When they were alone, he expounded all things to his disciples.
—MARK 4:34

Is the way God is leading you, my reader, a way of loneliness? Is your path shaded with grief, solitary with desertion? Have friends and family forsaken you? You are not all alone! Your mind needed the teaching of solitude, your heart the discipline of separation; and so Christ allured you into this wilderness that He might instruct, sanctify, and comfort you.

It is in the calmer quietude of separation, alone with God, that divine truth is often the best studied and understood. We read of Christ that, "when they were *alone*, he expounded all things to his disciples" (Mark 4:34). The Word of God, ever precious and instructive, is never so much so as when the circumstances that exile us from man shut us up exclusively and entirely to its study with God. How instructive, consolatory, and precious then grows this divine book. The mystery of providence helps to explain the mysteries of revelation; the bitterness of sorrow draws forth the sweetness of the divine promises; the crushed hopes of earth brings the soul into a closer realization of the assured hope of heaven; and the wintry chill and gloom of adversity makes us acquainted with the Brother born for it.

Who can describe the precious, soothing, and sustaining power of God's Word in the severest, extreme circumstance of tragedy, loneliness, and despair? How beautifully adapted, then, is the *sympathy* of Christ to seasons of desertion and loneliness. Did Christ know what it was to be alone—to be unfriended and deserted? Was He abandoned and forsaken in sorrow, all divine and human consolation for a time suspended? Then Christ is with you in your present condition. You have Jesus side by side with you in the shaded path you tread. He is with you, the companion of your loneliness, the sharer of your grief, softening, sweetening, sanctifying it, deepening, and maturing His work of grace in your soul, and by putting far from you lover and friend, drawing you all the closer to Himself.

—OCTAVIUS WINSLOW

◆ *Have you suffered the loss of a close companion? Has it been a reminder to you that Jesus is your true source of comfort and joy?*

Profiting from Bible Reading

But his delight is in the law of the LORD; and in
his law doth he meditate day and night.

—PSALM 1:2

L et me give some advice for those who are beginning to read their Bible more earnestly. Begin reading your Bible this very day. The way to do a thing is to do it, and the way to read the Bible is to actually read it. It is not meaning, or wishing, or resolving, or intending, or thinking about it, which will advance you one step. You must positively read. There is no royal road in this matter, any more than in the matter of prayer. If you cannot read yourself, have someone read to you. But one way or another, through eyes or ears, the words of Scripture must pass before your mind.

Read the Bible with an earnest desire to understand it. Think not for a moment that the greatest purpose is to read a certain number of chapters and that it matters not whether you understand it or not. Settle it in your mind as a general principle that a Bible not understood is a Bible that does no good. Say to yourself often as you read, "What is this all about?" Dig for the meaning like a man digging for gold. Work hard, and do not give up the work in a hurry.

Read the Bible with much reverence. Say to your soul whenever you open your Bible, "O my soul, you are going to read a message from God." The sentences of judges and the speeches of kings are received with awe and respect. How much more reverence is due to the words of the Judge of Judges and King of Kings! Enter therefore into the spirit of Moses on Mount Horeb, and "put off thy shoes from off thy feet, for the place whereon thou standest is holy ground" (Ex. 3:5).

—J. C. RYLE

◆ *Consider your current habit of Bible reading. How could meditating on what you read help you profit from the Word?*

Our God Reigns

*Be still, and know that I am God: I will be exalted among
the heathen, I will be exalted in the earth.*

—PSALM 46:10

When we read the history of ages past and consider our ever-changing world; when we study man and understand a small portion of the passions and contending interests which shake the fabric of society—how comforting is this all-gracious declaration: "Be still, and know that I am God" (Ps. 46:10).

The political world, like the air and sea that surround us, is ever changing; but the happy believer finds his rest in God. In our day the human mind seems to be advancing in a most remarkable manner. Knowledge is diffusing its light in every direction, and the intellectual powers continue to develop; the ancient boundaries are no longer limited or controlled. The Christian world is all awake to the spiritual and moral decline of mankind and is laboring to spread the sacred truths of revelation, which alone can raise up our fallen race.

The enemies of the gospel and of social order are alike awake to their deeds of darkness. There is an evident struggle between light and darkness. The struggle may be violent, but the believer hears the cheering voice from heaven, which dissipates every rising fear: "Be still, and know that I am God."

Dear Christian, rejoice that the Lord reigns! He can calm the rough surges of the mind. He can bid the inward tempest cease. He can pour an enlivening ray upon the drooping heart and cause a sweet serenity and peace to reign within. Trust in the Lord at all times. Be still, and know that He is God.

There is something peculiarly soothing to the heart of a Christian to know that He who rules over all, in whose hands are the destinies of the nations, and who guides the minutest concerns of family and individuals, is his Father and his friend. The more we know of God, of His power, wisdom, love, faithfulness, and truth, the more we shall bow before His throne in humble adoration and filial confidence and love.

—THOMAS READE

◆*Amid our present cultural warfare, can you be still and know that God
reigns? Meditate on God's power, wisdom, love, and faithfulness. Pray for
a heart filled with calm stillness.*

The Call to Be Happy

Rejoice evermore. —1 THESSALONIANS 5:16

The religion of Christ is no gloomy thing. It gives a brightness and a reality to all our earthly ties. It makes us better parents, more loving spouses, more dutiful children, more affectionate siblings. God never intended that it should break these earthly bonds but rather strengthen them. He will never blame us for loving our relations too much, but for loving *Him* too little.

Seek to be happy *for your own sake*. What a bright coloring it will give to your whole life. Seek to be happy *for the sake of others*. Will it not act as a charm to draw them also into the path which you have found so sweet? Seek to be happy *for your Savior's sake*, for so you will be honoring Him and bring glory to His cause.

Would you be a happy Christian? Then *live much* on Christ. Realize His presence. Think of Him as your heavenly friend. Hold intercourse with Him as your daily and hourly companion. This is the only true home for the believing heart. Nothing less will satisfy and fill it. You are weak; but here is your strength. Even the feeble ivy is strong and able to climb high when it clings to the sturdy tree; and so will you be, if you lay hold of Him who is able to bear you up. "In the LORD have I righteousness and strength" (Isa. 45:24). Live in humble, admiring, self-forgetting fellowship with Him.

Be a *holy* Christian. Is there a child in any family who seems to be happier than the rest? It is the one who is ever desiring to obey his parents and delighting to please them. And so, the child of God, who loves his heavenly Father, and walks in His holy ways, enjoys a happiness which the world could never give him.

Be a *thankful* Christian. Few think enough of their mercies. We are apt to take them too much as a matter of course. We ask eagerly for blessings, but when they come, we feel little or no thankfulness. We receive the gifts, but forget to give thanks to the almighty Giver. Let us be full of thankfulness and hope.

—ASHTON OXENDEN

◆ *What does it look like to be a happy Christian? How would it be winsome to the lost?*

Examine Yourselves

Examine yourselves, whether ye be in the faith; prove your own selves.
—2 CORINTHIANS 13:5

If the first duty of the Christian be charity, then without it, all our works are worth nothing. If faith working by love is the only saving faith, how important Paul's admonition is to the Corinthian church, and to all the churches of Christ! "Examine yourselves, whether ye be in the faith; prove your own selves" (2 Cor. 13:5).

The great design of divine revelation is to make us acquainted with God and ourselves. This knowledge is intimately connected with our well-being, both now and for eternity. Faith in a revealed Savior purifies the heart. Love to a crucified Redeemer produces universal obedience. As self-examination is needed daily, the Christian reader will often ask his heart questions as these:

- Have my thoughts been mostly engaged this day about God or the world?
- Have I carefully taken every opportunity to meditate on Christ and His precious salvation?
- While laboring in my lawful calling, have I labored to keep my heart from a growing attachment to earthly things by frequent and fervent prayers and desires after spiritual-mindedness which is life and peace?
- Have I this day been troubled with *evil thoughts*? What reception did they meet with? Did I indulge or instantly resist them? Were they pleasing or bitter to my soul?
- Have I this day been blessed, through grace, with *holy thoughts*? Did I cherish them and pray for their continuance and carefully avoid whatever might cause these sweet influences of the Spirit to be withdrawn?
- Do I feel myself daily more humbled under a growing conviction of my own sinfulness? And does a sense of my unworthiness make me more patient and meeker under provocations?
- Do I feel *self* being more annihilated, the fleshly desires more subdued, and all my affections more spiritual than they once were?
- Is Christ becoming more precious to my heart and more lovely in my eyes? Have I a clearer view of His person and offices and a more experiential acquaintance with Him as my advocate with the Father?

—THOMAS READE

◆ *Reread each of these questions with a prayer for the Spirit to give you honesty and repentance.*

What Is Faith?

Believe on the Lord Jesus Christ, and
thou shalt be saved, and thy house.

—ACTS 16:31

Faith in the Lord Jesus Christ is a wholehearted persuasion that He is the Son of God, the Savior of men, the only hope of lost sinners, and one very able to take our souls into His hands and keep us from the evil that is in the world. The seat of faith is not in the brain but in the heart. "For," says Paul, "with the heart man believeth unto righteousness" (Rom. 10:10). In genuine faith the mind does indeed assent to the truth, but the heart consents to it. When we truly believe in Jesus, we heartily rely on Him and on Him alone for salvation.

He who so embraces Christ and relies on Him shall be saved. So say the Scriptures in many places, "Abraham believed God, and it was accounted to him for righteousness" (Gal. 3:6). "The just shall live by faith" (Rom. 1:17; Gal. 3:11). Our text says, "Believe on the Lord Jesus Christ, and thou shalt be saved" (Acts 16:31). It is only by faith that we can become members of God's family. "Ye are all the children of God by faith in Christ Jesus" (Gal. 3:26). All who thus receive the Savior have been born again. "Whosoever believeth that Jesus is the Christ is born of God" (1 John 5:1). Such a faith will purify the heart, will cure the love of sin, and destroy the habit of sinning. This is the great work to be accomplished in the case of fallen men.

This faith in Christ warms up the cold heart of man. It works by love. It takes away the hatred of the natural heart to things. It makes Christ precious to the soul. Millions have gladly died for Him. It quenches the fiery darts of the wicked one. When temptations fall thick and fast on one who has lively faith, they have not power to hurt him. By faith we also gain the victory over the world; it opens our view to the unseen world and shows us glory beyond this life, the only glory worth setting our hearts upon.

—WILLIAM PLUMER

◆ *In what ways will faith change you? How can you receive greater assurance of faith? Is it your prayer, "Lord, increase our faith"?*

Our Willing God

For I have no pleasure in the death of him that dieth, saith the
Lord GOD: wherefore turn yourselves, and live ye.
—EZEKIEL 18:32

Y ou that have a fearful heart see the willingness of God to save sinners.
For if God the Father had not been very willing, He would never have
allowed His own only Son to suffer so greatly for their salvation. What could
be more repulsive to the heart of a tender father than to put his own, only,
and obedient son to death? It goes against the heart of a tender father to see
his child die. "Let me not see the death of the child," said Hagar. "And she sat
down over against him, and lift up her voice, and wept" (Gen. 21:16). But to
lay His own hands upon Him, in reference to His death—this is grief beyond
all expression; yet this God the Father did, for He bruised His Son, He put
Him to grief, He smote Him, and He laid upon Him the iniquities of us all.
Surely, if God the Father had not been infinitely willing to save sinners, He
would never have done such a thing; and if Christ Himself were not willing,
He would never have suffered such difficult things for salvation. What is not
a woman willing to do for her child, whom she had a sore travail for? Christ's
travail was a sore travail; surely therefore, He is infinitely willing to save sinners, and if God the Father is willing, and Christ is willing, then why should
not every poor, doubting soul say, "Lord, I believe; help thou mine unbelief"
(Mark 9:24)? I once doubted His love, because I doubted His willingness to
save such as I am. Often I have put an *if* on His willingness, saying with the
leper, "Lord, if thou wilt, thou canst make me clean" (Matt. 8:2). But now I
see He is willing to save sinners; why should I then doubt again?

Upon this account, all poor sinners may be encouraged to come to
Christ; for if Christ came down from heaven for you, will He refuse you
when you come to Him? If He suffered such hard and bitter things for sinners, do you think He will cast them out that come to Him? He will not.
What great encouragement does this doctrine proclaim to all sinners to
come to Christ. —WILLIAM BRIDGE

◆ *Have you fled to Christ, the willing Savior of sinners? Are you fleeing con-*
tinually to Him for all that you need? Is He not just as willing to help you
as to save you?

A Life Ruled by Love

By this shall all men know that ye are my disciples,
if ye have love one to another.

—JOHN 13:35

There is a truth about love. Love never knows when it has done enough. It knows no such thing as too much. Men say, "Why do we need to be so strict as to walk carefully? Why do we need to be so holy?" This is a base kind of reasoning. Is this as becomes the gospel? If you were touched by love, then you would never think that you had done enough for God. You would rather think, *If I had ten thousand, thousand times more strength than I have, Lord, Thou art worthy of it all. Whatever I have, whatever I am, whatever I can do, Thou art worthy of it all.*

Never stand arguing why this or that is too much, or is the thing a good thing. Love never thinks anything as too much. We know that love cannot bear with dishonor done unto those that we love. If anyone wrongs someone that we love, if our hearts are filled with love, we do not know how to bear it. It strikes us in the apple of our eye. That is a conversation that becomes the gospel. When we see the name of God dishonored, our hearts rise more against anything that is done against God than it does against anything that is done against us.

Love makes us delight in the presence of those that we love. So that's a conversation that becomes the gospel, when we manifest that there is nothing in the world that we delight in more than to be in the presence of our Beloved. Oh, to be always with God in the arms of Christ is our heaven on earth! The main thing in the gospel is declaring the love of God. Therefore, Christians who would live as becomes the gospel must live so as touched by love.

—JEREMIAH BURROUGHS

◆ *Can a person love another or God too much? If not, why would we ask ourselves if we've done enough? Where is the limit of how much is required of me in loving either God or one another?*

Christ All in All

Christic is all, and in all.
—COLOSSIANS 3:11

C hrist is a supreme good. Put what you will in the balance with Christ; He does infinitely outweigh it. Is life sweet? Christ is better. He is the life of the soul (Col. 3:4); His lovingkindness is better than life (Ps. 63:3). Are relations sweet? Christ is better. He is the "friend that sticketh closer than a brother" (Prov. 18:24).

Christ is a sufficient good. He who has Christ needs no more; just as he who has the ocean needs not the cistern. If one had a manuscript that contained all manner of learning in it, having all the arts and sciences, he need look in no other book; so he that has Christ needs look no further. Christ gives grace and glory (Ps. 84:11). The one to cleanse us; the other to crown us.

Christ is a suitable good. In Him dwells all fullness (Col. 1:19). He is whatever the soul can desire. Christ is beauty to adorn, gold to enrich, balm to heal, bread to strengthen, wine to comfort, salvation to crown. If we are in danger, Christ is a shield; and if we are disconsolate, He is a sun; for He has enough in His wardrobe abundantly to furnish the soul.

Christ is a sanctifying good. He makes every situation happy to us. He sweetens all our comforts, and sanctifies all our crosses.

Christ sweetens all our comforts for He turns them into blessings. Health is blessed, estate is blessed, relations are blessed. Christ's love is as the pouring of sweet water on flowers, which makes them cast a more fragrant perfume. A wicked man cannot have that comfort in outward things which a godly man has; for though he may possess more, he enjoys less. He who has Christ may say, "This mercy is reached to me by the hand of my Savior. This is a love-token from Him, an earnest of glory."

—THOMAS WATSON

◆ *Think about what Christ's "good" looks like in your life. How can you enjoy Him more?*

Cheering Words for the Anxious

Be careful for nothing; but in every thing by prayer and supplication
with thanksgiving let your requests be made known unto God.

—PHILIPPIANS 4:6

C hristian reader, behold, your privilege: "Be careful for nothing." When any trial comes upon you which would fill you with anxiety, do not grapple with it in your own strength or lean to your own understanding. Trust in the Lord with all your heart; go by earnest prayer to the Father of mercies; implore Him to direct and overrule for good the cloud that you so much dread; and then, calmly, leave at His feet the burden of your fears. Do this with thankfulness that you have such a God who cares for you and on whom you have boldly cast all your cares. While you acknowledge Him in all your ways, God will direct your paths and either support you under or deliver you out of all your troubles.

How sweet is the voice of mercy speaking peace to the troubled heart, "Blessed is the man that trusteth in the LORD, and whose hope the LORD is. For he shall be as a tree planted by the waters, and that spreadeth out her roots by the river, and shall not see when heat cometh, but her leaf shall be green; and shall not be careful in the year of drought, neither shall cease from yielding fruit" (Jer. 17:7–8).

Suffering believer, cast your burden on the Lord. How quieting are the words of Jesus: "Take therefore no thought for the morrow: for the morrow shall take thought for the things of itself. Sufficient unto the day is the evil thereof.… Let not your heart be troubled.… Neither be ye of doubtful mind" (Matt. 6:34; John 14:1; Luke 12:29).

Happy is that soul whose hopes are firmly anchored on the promises of Christ. We live far below our privileges. Had we more faith and spiritual mindedness, we would have more strength and joy in every trial; our moderation would be known to all men; our conversation would be without covetousness, for we would be content with such things as we have.

—THOMAS READE

◆ *What things are you anxious about? Why are you anxious? Think about*
encouraging promises of God's Word.

The End and Object of the Christian's Life

I have created him for my glory.
—ISAIAH 43:7

Let me put this matter before you in such a way that you may act upon it. I will offer you some directions and mention some ways in which you may glorify God.

1. Try to wean yourself from all *self*-glorifying. Even when there is grace in the heart, we have need to be on our guard. Self is forever endeavoring to get the upper hand. The old Adam, our old nature, is constantly striving to exalt itself. Like Diotrephes, we "love to have the pre-eminence." We are continually wishing to be something more than Christ would have us to be. Oh, let us curb this desire and be willing to be nothing for Christ's sake.

2. Set God's glory distinctly before you in all you do. I am to glorify God; this is the great end I am to live for. Perhaps we have never thought of this. Perhaps we have never done a single thing in our whole lives from this grand and glorious motive. We have acted often from a desire to do what is right, from a sense of duty, or from a feeling of kindness and love, or from a wish to be useful. But how seldom have we done a thing from a simple desire to glorify God! And yet this is the highest and most blessed motive from which a Christian can act. This is doing as Christ did and feeling as He felt.

3. Endeavor to honor God by *the holiness of your life*. Nothing brings such dishonor to the gospel, and nothing leads to such contempt for the truth, as the unholy lives of His professing people. And, on the other hand, nothing is so pleasing to Him and brings such honor to His name and cause as the holy lives of His followers.

We Christians are called with a *holy* calling. We are called to be like Jesus—holy, harmless, undefiled, and separate from sinners.

—ASHTON OXENDEN

♦ *Many of the saints of old made resolutions in order to focus their minds more on serving the Lord. List some resolutions you would make to help you live a more God-glorifying life.*

Our Gentle Shepherd

He shall feed his flock like a shepherd: he shall
gather the lambs with his arm, and carry them in his bosom,
and shall gently lead those that are with young.

—ISAIAH 40:11

What a help heavenward, what strength and heart-cheer, will you find in believing this truth—the gentleness of Christ! Never doubt, never question, never reject it. It is an ingredient in every cup you drink, it is light in every cloud you behold, it is an accent in every voice you hear of Christ's dealings, leading, and teachings. He is—He must be—gentle. He is not only gentle, but He is gentleness. Gentleness is His nature because love is His essence. The heart of Christ is such that it cannot be otherwise than gentle in its every feeling.

The physician is not less kind because he prescribes a nauseous remedy, nor the surgeon less feeling because he makes a deep incision, nor the parent less loving because he uses the rod. Nor is your Lord less so because the way by which He leads, and the discipline by which He sanctifies, and the method by which He instructs you may for a moment veil the reality, light, and comfort of this truth: He "shall gently lead those that are with young" (Isa. 40:11). Lest we should be weary, He will not overdrive us; lest we should faint, He leads us by springs of water; lest our soul should be discouraged by reason of the way, He causes us to lie down beneath the shadow of the Rock that is higher than we (Ps. 61:2).

If this be so, then yield yourself to the Lord's leading. Be satisfied that He is leading you by the right way homeward. Do not distrust His wisdom, nor question His love, nor fret, murmur, and rebel that the way is not exactly just as you would have chosen. Be sure of this: it is the right way. And if it is one of self-denial, one of difficulty and of cloud, yet it is the way home.

—OCTAVIUS WINSLOW

◆*What a glorious Shepherd we have! How does Winslow's advice help you today? Are you able to see the Shepherd's hand in the things He leads you through?*

Walking in the Spirit

If we live in the Spirit, let us also walk in the Spirit.
—GALATIANS 5:25

If God has been merciful to you in giving you another spirit, improve this mercy. Show in all your ways that you are acted upon by another spirit. Let the renewed spirit guide you; let the beauty and excellency of it become evident. "If we live in the Spirit, let us also walk in the Spirit," said the apostle (Gal. 5:25). "The works of the flesh are manifest" (v. 19). Why should not the spirit be so too? God has beautified your spirits with His own image. In this He has honored you that you might honor Him in showing forth the beauty and excellency of His image by your life. He has made you a "peculiar people" to the end that you might show forth the virtues of Him who has "called you out of darkness into his marvellous light" (1 Peter 2:9).

It is a dishonor to a parent, or any special friend, to hang his picture in some dark corner, in some obscure, contemptible place. It is expected we should make it conspicuous, that we should hang it in the prominent place to show that we rejoice in it as a loving reminder to us. It is a great evil to obscure the graces of God's Spirit, to keep the work of God hidden in our spirits in which He has revealed the glory of His image to the end that He might be glorified in us before men and angels.

If God has shone upon your spirits by His grace, let your lights shine before men that the world may see there are men of other spirits who can do such things as they cannot.

—JEREMIAH BURROUGHS

◆ *Do others see evidence of a renewed spirit in you? Ask someone close to you whether you are increasingly displaying the character of God in your words and actions. Be thankful when it is present, and seek grace to walk more in the Spirit.*

A Heavenward Focus (1)

But seek ye first the kingdom of God, and his righteousness;
and all these things shall be added unto you.

—MATTHEW 6:33

Work to obtain such a disposition of mind that you may choose heaven for your inheritance and home, and may earnestly long for it, and be willing to exchange this world and all its enjoyments for heaven. Labor to have your heart taken up so much about heaven and heavenly enjoyments that you may rejoice when God calls you to leave your best earthly friends and comforts for heaven, there to enjoy God and Christ.

Be persuaded to travel in the way that leads to heaven—holiness, self-denial, mortification, obedience to all the commands of God, following Christ's example—in the way of a heavenly life, or imitation of the saints and angels in heaven. Let it be your daily work, from morning till night, and continue to the end; let nothing stop or discourage you or turn you aside from this way. Let all other concerns be subordinated to this. The world is not your abiding place; the future world is to be your everlasting abode; and the enjoyments and concerns of this world are given entirely to another.

Consider how worthy heaven is that your life should be wholly spent as a journey toward it. To what better purpose can you spend your life? What better end can you propose to your journey than to obtain heaven? You are placed in this world with a choice given you, that you may travel which way you please; and one way leads to heaven. All people have a purpose in life. Some mainly seek worldly things; they spend their days in such pursuits. But is not heaven—where is fullness of joy forever—much more worthy to be sought after by you? How can you better use your strength, your finances, and spend your days than in traveling the road which leads to the everlasting enjoyment of God; to His glorious presence; to the new Jerusalem; to the heavenly Mount Zion; where all your desires will be filled, and no danger of ever losing your happiness? No man is at home in this world, whether he choose heaven or not; here he is but a transient person. Where can you choose your home better than in heaven?

—JONATHAN EDWARDS

◆ *Is heaven your anticipated home? What can you show as evidence that you believe this to be so?*

A Heavenward Focus (2)

But seek ye first the kingdom of God, and his righteousness;
and all these things shall be added unto you.
—MATTHEW 6:33

Consider that this is the way to have death comfortable to us; to spend our lives only journeying toward heaven is the way to be free from bondage and to have the prospect and forethought of a comfortable death. Does the traveler think of his journey's end with fear and terror? Is it terrible to think that he is almost at his journey's end? Were the children of Israel sorry, after forty years' travel in the wilderness, when they had almost entered Canaan? This is the way to be able to part with the world without grief. Does it grieve the traveler, when he has gotten home, to lay down his staff and load of provisions that he had to sustain him by the way?

Consider that no more of your life will be pleasant to think of when you come to die than has been spent traveling in the way that leads to heaven. If you have spent none of your life this way, your whole life will be terrible to you to think of, unless you die under some great delusion. You will see then that all your life that has been spent otherwise is lost and see the vanity of all other aims. The thought of what you here possessed and enjoyed will not be pleasant to you unless you think also that you have subordinated them to this purpose.

Consider that those who are willing to spend their lives as a journey toward heaven may have heaven. Heaven, however high and glorious, is attainable for such poor worthless creatures as we are. We may reach heaven, which is the dwelling-place of the Son of God and the glorious presence of the great Jehovah.

Consider that if our lives are not a journey toward heaven, they will be a journey to hell. All mankind goes to either of the two places when they depart out of this world: the one is heaven, where a small number in comparison travel; the other is hell, where the bulk of mankind throng. And one or other of these must be our final destination.

—JONATHAN EDWARDS

◆ *How can we be heavenly minded without losing sight of being what we are called to be here and now? If you are not journeying toward heaven, give yourself no rest until you are on the right path.*

Let Your Light Shine

Ye are the light of the world. A city that is set on an hill cannot be hid.
—MATTHEW 5:14

If Jesus actually lives with you, other people will be sure to notice. When Jesus went into the borders of Tyre and Sidon, He could not be hid. If you travel through a certain district in southern France in lavender time, you are sure to know that it is lavender country by the sweet fragrance in the air. Christ is always self-revealing. No genuine Christian will ever desire to conceal Him; he could not even if he would. Many absurd things have been written about "secret hopes," but, my friend, if nobody in this world, not even your most intimate friend, suspects that you are a Christian, I do not believe that you are one.

If Jesus dwells in our hearts, we should be carrying Him with us. "Let your light so *shine* before men," that they may recognize that Jesus is within you (Matt. 5:16). Show your Christlike kindnesses to people while they are living, and do not take it out in heaping flowers on their coffins. I have sometimes thought when I looked at memorials, if these silent lips could speak, they would wish that a few more flowers of love had sweetened their hard, weary lives!

Carry Christ with you to your unconverted friends. If you win their respect for you and get a hold on them, you can talk to them about their souls; tell them what Christ has done for you, and, as it were, add your knock to His knock at their heart's door. Reverently be it said, the Christ in you will appeal to them through you. Here lies the only real power of which any Christian has with the sinning and suffering people around him.

—THEODORE CUYLER

♦ *What ways you are reflecting Christ and in what ways do you need to improve?*

The School of Sanctified Trial

I will not leave you comfortless. —JOHN 14:18

Trial is precious because *it increases the preciousness of Christ*. It is in adversity that human friendship is tested. When the wintry blast sweeps by, when riches vanish, and health fails, and position lowers, and popularity wanes, and influence lessens, then the summer birds of earthly friendship expand their wings and seek a warmer climate. The same test that proves the hollowness of the world's affection and constancy confirms the believer in the reality, power, and preciousness of the friendship of Jesus. To know fully what Christ is, we must know something of adversity. We must be tried, tempted, and oppressed; we must taste the bitterness of sorrow, feel the pressure of want, tread the path of solitude, and often be brought to the end of our own strength and of human sympathy and counsel.

Jesus shines the brightest to faith's eye when all things are dark and dreary. And when others have left our side, their patience wearied, their sympathy exhausted, their counsel baffled, their affections chilled; *then* Christ approaches and takes the vacant place. He sits at our side, speaks peace to our troubled heart, soothes our sorrows, guides our judgment, and bids us "fear not."

Beloved reader, when has Christ appeared nearest and most precious to your soul? Has it not been in seasons when you have stood most in need of His guiding counsel and of His soothing love? In the region of your heart's sinfulness, you have learned the value, completeness, and preciousness of His atoning work and finished salvation. But the tender, loving, sympathetic part of His nature you have been brought to experience only in the school of sanctified trial. How precious does trial make Him! Into what sacred intimacy and close fellowship and conscious nearness has it brought you. Shrink not from nor rebel against that which makes you more intimately acquainted with your best friend—the tender, sympathizing one, the Beloved of your soul. You will know more of Jesus in one sanctified trial than in wading through a library of books or in listening to a lifetime of sermons.

—OCTAVIUS WINSLOW

◆ *Has Christ brought you through trials to better acquaint you with Himself? Thank Him. Are you in a trial? Cling to Him more tightly, knowing He sympathizes with you!*

Do Something for God

Now therefore, O God, strengthen my hands.
—NEHEMIAH 6:9

You were neither born nor reborn for yourselves alone. You may not be able to do much, but do something; work while it is day. You may not be able to give much, but give something, according to your ability, remembering that the Lord loves a cheerful giver. Take heed, and beware of covetousness; for the love of money is the root of all evil. Whenever worldliness comes in, in any shape, whether it be love of money or love of pleasure, you cease to be faithful to Christ and are trying to serve both God and mammon.

Do something, then, for God, while time lasts. It may not be long; for the day goes away, and the shadows of the evening are stretched out. Do something every day. Work, and throw your heart into the work. Work joyfully and with a right goodwill. As men who love both their work and their boss. Be not weary in well-doing. Work, and work in faith. Work in love and patience and hope. Don't shrink from hard labor or unpleasant duties or a situation which is difficult for your flesh and blood. "Endure hardness, as a good soldier of Jesus Christ" (2 Tim. 2:3). "Be ye steadfast, unmoveable, always abounding in the work of the Lord" (1 Cor. 15:58). Don't fold your hands and lay aside your tools. Don't give way to slothfulness and flesh-pleasing, saying to yourselves, "I can get to heaven without working."

Your gifts may be small, your time not much, your opportunities few; but work, and do it quietly, without bustle or self-importance; not as pleasing men, but pleasing God; not seeking the honor which cometh from men, but that which comes from God. The day of honor is coming, and the Master's "well done" will make up for all the hardship and labor here.

—HORATIUS BONAR

◆ *God said, "Them that honour me I will honour" (1 Sam. 2:30). How are you laboring to honor Him? Is there any excuse which needs to be renounced so that you may labor more diligently?*

Seeing the Sinfulness of Sin

The law is holy, and the commandment holy, and just, and good.
Was then that which is good made death unto me? God forbid. But sin,
that it might appear sin, working death in me by that which is good;
that sin by the commandment might become exceeding sinful.

—ROMANS 7:12–13

As you wish to have the character of a child of God, work more and more to see the sinfulness of sin. Look much upon Christ crucified. Christ on the cross is a glass wherein you may see the sinfulness of sin.

Labor more and more to walk in the presence of God, in the light of God's countenance. Just as you see little specs of dust when the sun shines into a room, so you see little sins when God shines into your heart. The beams of God's countenance discover sin and the sinfulness of it.

Labor more and more to examine your own souls. Be in private examination, for it is rare to find a growing Christian that is little in private examination. Likewise, it is rare to find a proud man that is in much examination.

Take as much effort to keep the sense of sin upon your heart as when finding it; some work to get themselves into a good frame but take no effort to keep themselves in it. In case you find any particular sin, study it, consider the circumstances around it, and impress it upon your own soul. Be sure you judge sin as the Scripture judges it and not as men judge it. The Scripture judges sin by the consequences as our Savior Jesus Christ says, "I was an hungred, and ye gave me no meat: I was thirsty, and ye gave me no drink…naked, and ye clothed me not." How so? "Inasmuch as ye did it not to one of the least of these, ye did it not to me" (Matt. 25:42–43, 45).

If you desire to see the sinfulness of sin, then look at the commandments as great things. The more important the commandments of God are to you, the greater sin will appear to you. Never think anything small between God and you; there is nothing small between God and us, for God is an infinite God.

—WILLIAM BRIDGE

◆ *How much time do you spend in self-examination? While it is true that*
we are to take ten looks to Christ for every look within, do not allow this to
excuse a lack of proper examination.

Living as Covenant People

And he said, LORD God of Israel, there is no God like thee, in heaven above, or on earth beneath, who keepest covenant and mercy with thy servants that walk before thee with all their heart.

—1 KINGS 8:23

If you have tasted of the covenant mercy of God, you should walk and live as a people in covenant with God. As you differ from others in respect to dignity, so you must in conduct.

You must love this God. God's love to you calls for love. It is a free love. Why should God pass by others and take you into a league of friendship with Himself? In the law, God passed by the lion and the eagle and chose the dove; so He passes by the noble and mighty. It is a full love. When God takes you into covenant, you are His Hephzibah; His delight is in you (Isa. 62:4). He gives you the key of all His treasure. He heaps pearls upon you. He settles heaven and earth upon you and says, "All I have is thine." And does this not call for love in return? Who can tread upon these hot coals and His heart not burn in love to God?

You must walk holily. The covenant has made you a royal nation; therefore be a holy people. Shine as lights in the world; live as earthly angels. God has taken you into covenant, that you and He may have communion together; and what is it that keeps up your communion with God but holiness.

You must walk thankfully (Ps. 103:1). God is your God in covenant; He has done more for you than if He had made you ride upon the high places of the earth and given you crowns and scepters. Take the cup of salvation and bless the Lord! Eternity will be little enough to praise Him. Musicians love to play their music where there is the loudest sound; and God loves to bestow His mercies where He may have the loudest praises. You have angels' reward; do angels' work. Begin that work of praise here, which you hope to be always doing in heaven.

—THOMAS WATSON

◆ *What does it mean to be in covenant with God? Does the way you live reflect that great honor?*

Unbroken Fellowship

Yet the LORD will command his lovingkindness in the day time, and in the night his song shall be with me, and my prayer unto the God of my life.
—PSALM 42:8

F ew things tend more to deaden the soul, to harden the heart, to drive out spirituality than cold, formal prayer. It will eat as a canker. Dread it and shun it. Do not mock God by asking what you don't want or by pretending to desire what you don't care for.

Be much alone with God. Do not put Him off with a few minutes in the morning and evening. Take time to get thoroughly acquainted. Talk over everything with Him. Unburden yourself to Him wholly—every thought, feeling, wish, plan, doubt. He wants communication with His people; shall His creatures not want communication with Him? He wants not merely to be on "good terms" with you, if one may use man's phrase, but to be *intimate*. Would you decline the intimacy and be satisfied with mere acquaintance? Would you be intimate with the world, with your spouse, with friends, with neighbors, with politicians but not with God? That would look ill indeed. Such folly to prefer the clay to the potter, the marble to the sculptor, this little earth and its lesser creatures to the mighty Maker of the universe, the great "all, and in all" (Col. 3:11)!

Do not shrink from being alone. Much of a true man's life must be so spent. Much private fellowship with God will give you sevenfold success. Pray much if you would work much; and if you want to work more, pray more. Luther used to say when great business came upon him, "I must pray *more* today." Be like him in the day of work or trial. Do not think that mere *working* will keep you right or set you right. Work will do nothing for you till *you have gone to God for a working heart.*

—HORATIUS BONAR

♦*In what ways are you stirred by this meditation to resolve to pray? Confess your shortcomings and ask God to teach you the value of an intimate prayer life.*

Are You Willing to Sacrifice All for Christ?

For the which cause I also suffer these things: nevertheless I am not ashamed: for I know whom I have believed, and am persuaded that he is able to keep that which I have committed unto him against that day.

—2 TIMOTHY 1:12

A real decision for the Redeemer cannot exist without some sacrifice, as a term of discipleship. The sacrifices expected and endured are various. Some are called to conscientiously defend the faith even in the face of hostility from those most loved, respected, and cherished. Against him are father, mother, brother, sister, wife, husband, child—ties of affection which bind the heart so closely to the family table and the home. The pang of separation from these, who can estimate? The deep, lone grief, who can describe? Yet the Savior has said, "He that loveth father or mother more than me is not worthy of me: and he that loveth son or daughter more than me is not worthy of me" (Matt. 10:37).

Other saints are called to abandon their worldly interests, renounce their earthly property, exclude themselves from the means of acquiring distinction, rank, honor, and wealth, and to link themselves with poverty and toil and want, facing the reproach of friends, shattered hopes, disappointed wishes, and ruined expectations. This is nothing more than Jesus foretold.

For whom are you enduring and suffering and sacrificing all this? For Jesus! For Him who, though He was rich, for your sakes became poor, that you through His poverty might be rich. For Him who was not ashamed to call you His brother, but bowed His godhead to your nature, and on your behalf became a man of sorrows and acquainted with grief. For Him who, while working out your righteousness by His life of unwearied and perfect obedience, could say, "Foxes have holes, and the birds of the air have nests; but the Son of man hath not where to lay his head" (Matt. 8:20). For Him who gave His back to the smiter, His cheek to them that plucked off the hair, who sorrowed in Gethsemane, was mocked and buffeted and spit upon, who bore the full weight of sin and the curse...and then bowed His head and died.

—OCTAVIUS WINSLOW

♦ *What has been the cost of confessing Christ? Has He not been better to you than all those things? What encouragement do you glean from the last paragraph of this meditation?*

Short Views

Take therefore no thought for the morrow: for the morrow shall take thought for the things of itself. Sufficient unto the day is the evil thereof.
—MATTHEW 6:34

The man who is climbing the Alps must not look too far ahead, or it will tire him; he must not look back, or he gets dizzy; he has but to follow his guide and to set his foot on the right spot before him. This is the way you and I must let Christ lead, and have Him so close to us also that it will be but a short view to behold. Sometimes young Christians say to me, "I am afraid to make a public confession of Christ, I may not hold out." They have nothing to do with holding out; it is simply their duty to hold on. When future trials and perils come, their Master will give them help for the hour, if they only make sure that they are His. The short view they need to take is a close, clear view of their own spiritual wants, and a distinct view of Jesus as ever at hand to meet those wants. Some of us, at the beginning of a year's work, are tempted to overload ourselves with the anticipation of how much we must do; we need not worry if we will only remember that during the whole year there will be only one working day, and that is today. Sufficient to each day is the labor thereof.

Let us take short views. Let us not climb the high wall till we get to it, or fight the battle till it opens, or shed tears over sorrows that may never come, or lose the joys and blessing that we have by the sinful fear that God will take them away from us. We need all our strength and all the grace God can give us for today's burdens and today's battle. Tomorrow belongs to our heavenly Father: I would not know its secrets if I could. It is far better to know whom we trust and that He is able to keep all we commit to Him until the last great day (2 Tim. 1:12).

—THEODORE CUYLER

◆ *In what ways are you looking into the future instead of trusting God? How does the verse, "My grace is sufficient for thee" (2 Cor. 12:9) relate to today's reading and your previous answer?*

FEBRUARY

◆

God calls us to be holy. He becomes
our God to make us like Himself.

—HORATIUS BONAR

Christian Joy

This is the day which the LORD hath made;
we will rejoice and be glad in it.
—PSALM 118:24

Christian, if you desire to "rejoice in the Lord," you must live near to the throne of grace; you must pray for a more lively faith in the efficacy and power of vital godliness, to cheer the heart in the darkest and dreariest hour. Remember, it is God's will that you should be happy and cheerful every day, that you should find joy in everything around you, a pure, sinless, increasing joy; and that you should pass through all life's fluctuations rejoicing in the love of Christ and in the hope of glory. Strive, then, to live up to your privileges, to rise to all the joy that is set before you, and to shed on all around the bright and cheering rays of true religion. Tell those in the world, and let them see by your example and spirit, that Christianity is *not* the gloomy thing *they* imagine, that a life of holiness is a life of real happiness, of happiness for this life and for eternity.

But tell them there is something gloomy: the *joy* which blazes for a moment like a dazzling meteor and then vanishes forever; the hopes which are dependent on worldly possessions and worldly pleasures, and which made him who had experienced them all cry out in the anguish of disappointment, "Vanity of vanities; all is vanity" (Eccl. 1:2). Tell them it is a gloomy thing to be drawing near to the grave with *no hope* of heaven.

Be it yours to retain the possession of your joy by abiding in your Savior's love, by living daily upon His fullness, resting beneath His shadow, lovingly obeying all His commands, submissively receiving all His chastenings, joyfully welcoming all His rebukes, and unhesitatingly following all His leadings. Glorify Him in mercy and in trial, in health and in sickness, in prosperity and adversity until that blessed hour when He will take you home, and you will "drink of the river of [His] pleasures" and partake of joys which are at God's right hand for evermore (Pss. 36:8; 16:11).

—ASHTON OXENDEN

◆*Are you living in Christian joy? If not, why? How can you be more joyful?*

Short Petitions in the Face of Temptations

Attend unto my cry; for I am brought very low.
—PSALM 142:6

Prayer is always necessary but is especially so in a time of temptation. It is hard to come boldly that we may obtain help in time of need, but however difficult it is, it must be attempted. By not praying, we give the enemy the greatest encouragement possible; for then he sees that his temptations have the effect which he intends by them, to intercept us from our stronghold. When our Lord was in agony, He prayed most earnestly; the fervor of His prayer increased with the distress of His soul. We would be happy if we could always imitate Him in this; but too often temptations and difficulties, instead of rousing our desire to pray, dishearten and weaken us, so that our cries are the faintest when we stand most in need of assistance. But as long as prayer is set aside, our burden is increased. And if Satan cannot make us stop praying, he will repeatedly try to weary us by working on the legality which cleaves so close to our heart.

Satan is a hard taskmaster when he interferes in the performance of our spiritual duties. This he does more frequently than we think of; for he can, if it serves his purpose, appear as an angel of light. When the soul is in a tempest and attempts to pray, he will suggest that prayer on these occasions should be protracted to such a length and performed with such steadiness, but it is found to be at that season quite impracticable. Such constrained efforts are wearisome, and from the manner of the performance, he takes occasion to fix fresh guilt upon the conscience.

Short, frequent, and fervent petitions, which will almost necessarily arise from what is felt when temptation is intense, are what is most needed. We need not add to the burden by tasking ourselves beyond our power as if we expect to be heard for our much speaking. Blessed be God that we fight with an enemy already vanquished by our Lord, and that we have a sure promise of victory.

—JOHN NEWTON

◆ *Are you discouraged in prayer? How can short, urgent cries to God in our daily activities be more effective than prolonged prayers which leave us feeling we still have not prayed enough?*

Rest for the Journey

And he said unto them, Come ye yourselves apart
into a desert place, and rest a while.

—MARK 6:31

In our march heavenward the Master has kindly provided some welcome spots for the refreshment of our souls. But they are only halting places. We come sometimes to an *Elim* with its "twelve wells of water, and three-score and ten palm trees" (Ex. 15:27)—a delightful spot to sit down and cool off, and partake of the manna and the King's pleasant fruits. Yet it is not Canaan, and we must up and march again. Elijah could not spend all his life under the juniper tree. Jesus invited His disciples to go "into a desert place, and rest a while" (Mark 6:31). It was only for a little while. Calvary was just ahead for Him, and the Pentecostal baptism of blessed toil for them.

God is very wise and very kind in providing scenes and hours of sweet refreshment during this life of varied temptations, toils, and trials. They take the tire out of us, cheer us up, and give us Eshcol clusters that taste of the promised land (Num. 13:23–24). Lest we should settle down with the idea that these are our abiding places, God is evermore rousing us up with the call, "Arise ye, and depart; for this is not your rest" (Mic. 2:10).

That rest is for us a little further away. Heaven will not be an idle holiday or an everlasting concert of sacred song. There will be no lack of work there. Instead of a holy lounging place, heaven will be a scene of such constant, pure, inspiring, blissful, and unwearying activity, which the Word of God describes as a perfect rest. Not an aching heart or a tearstained eye or a tired foot forever and ever more!

—THEODORE CUYLER

◆ *How can you help one another keep the eternal perspective? How can we be thankful for periods of rest but also not settle down there without pressing on in our Christian race?*

Encouragement against Doubt and Fears

*My flesh and my heart faileth: but God is the strength
of my heart, and my portion for ever.*

—PSALM 73:26

The Christian calling, like many others, is easy and clear in theory but not without care and difficulty in practice. Things appear quite different when felt experientially than they appear when read in a book. Sailors may learn about the art of navigation from a book, but when they come to sea, with their heads full of rules and without experience, they find that the art is only to be thoroughly learned upon the spot. So, to renounce self, to live upon Jesus, to walk with God, to overcome the world, to hope against hope, to trust the Lord when we cannot trace Him, and to know that our duty and privilege consist in these things may be readily acknowledged or quickly learned; but upon repeated trial we find that saying and doing are two different things.

We think at the start that we have sat down and counted the cost; but our views are so superficial at first that we have reason to correct our estimate daily. For every day shows us some new thing in our heart or some new turn in the management of the war against us which we were not aware of; and upon these accounts, discouragements may arise so high as to bring us to the very point of throwing down our arms and making either a tame surrender or a shameful flight. So it would be with us to surrender if the Lord of hosts were not on our side. But if He is the Captain of our salvation, if His eye is upon us, His arm stretched out around us, and His ear open to our cry, and if He has engaged to teach our hands to war and our fingers to fight and to cover our heads in the day of battle, then we need not fear, though a host rise up against us; but, lifting up our banner in His name, let us go forth conquering and to conquer.

—JOHN NEWTON

◆ *What is your experience with regard to knowing a spiritual truth in your minds but finding it challenging to lay hold of that truth when in a trial?*

Gradual Growth

For I am the LORD your God: ye shall therefore
sanctify yourselves, and ye shall be holy; for I am holy.
—LEVITICUS 11:44

God calls us to be holy. He becomes our God to make us like Himself. He calls us to be partakers of the divine nature, having escaped the corruption that is in the world through lust. He expects that we should represent Him among fellow Christians by our resemblance to Himself. The carrying out of this holiness is His own work by the operation of His Spirit. Whether our perfection in holiness is gradual or instantaneous is determined solely by His Word and not by any ideas of our own. That God *could* make each soul perfect the moment he believes, we admit; that He may have wise reasons for not doing this, wise reasons for *gradual growth*, will not be denied.

Gradual growth is the law of all things here—man, animals, trees, and flowers—so that unless we had some notable example in Scripture of a sinless man or of miraculous and instantaneous perfection by an act of faith, we are not willing to accept the theory of instantaneous sinlessness, as that to which we are called in believing.

Yet God expects us to grow in *unlikeness* to this world and in *likeness* to that world which is to come. He expects us to follow Him who did not sin, even though the attainment of perfection should not be in a day or a year but the growth of a lifetime. It is for want of daily *growth*, not for want of complete and constant sinlessness, that God so often challenges His own.

Let us grow daily and hourly. Let us grow down; let us grow up. Let us strike our roots deeper; let us spread out our branches more widely. Let us not only "blossom and bud," but let us bring forth fruit, ripe and plentiful, on every bough. "Herein is my Father glorified, that ye bear much fruit; so shall ye be my disciples" (John 15:8).

—HORATIUS BONAR

◆*Are you growing? Ask someone close to you to help you honestly assess.*
Do not be discouraged by gradual progress, but allow evidences of grace to
encourage you to continue to grow.

Love—the Christian's Mainspring

We love him, because he first loved us.
—1 JOHN 4:19

The Christian's enjoyment of God may not be always the same. Sometimes it may be greater, and sometimes less. Sometimes his heart may be warmer toward God than at other times. But as the needle of the compass, when moved, ever turns to one particular point and there fixes itself, so is God the one great object of attraction to the believer. There he finds a resting place, and there alone does he love to dwell. The best of earthly things he cannot enjoy apart from God. He only enjoys them, as he enjoys God in them. Even spiritual gifts alone will not satisfy him; he wants *the Giver*, as well as the *gifts*. He desires Christ's presence, as well as His ordinances. He knows that *the Fountain* is fuller than the stream, and *the Sun itself* more glorious than its rays.

This is a heavenly feeling indeed, and only grace can produce it within us. God Himself must plant this love in the barren soil of our hearts. He must "shed [it] abroad in our hearts by the Holy Ghost" (Rom. 5:5).

How is it that we see some Christians working so hard for Christ and serving Him so faithfully and happily? Their zeal never appears to flag; the fire within them never seems to cool. Let the watch you wear serve to answer the question. How are the hands ever moving and the little wheels always doing their work? What puts it all in motion? Look closely, and you will discover a strong but almost unseen spring that sets it all going. Take away that mainspring and the watch is useless. So there is something, too, within the Christian which secretly moves his heart, his affections, and his desires. Love is the Christian's mainspring. "We love him, because he first loved us" (1 John 4:19). "The love of Christ constraineth us" (2 Cor. 5:14).

Ask God, then, to endue you with this holy principle of love. Pray that you may love Him, not *sometimes*, but *always*; not a *little*, but *with the whole heart*. Let your love be firm and constant—not coming and returning like the tide, but flowing on like a river, with a full and even course.

—ASHTON OXENDEN

◆ *Consider the great love which Jesus has for His own, and let this stir your hearts to greater love and service.*

A Fixed Heart

My heart is fixed, O God, my heart is fixed: I will sing and give praise.
—PSALM 57:7

A contented Christian carries heaven about him; for what is heaven but that sweet repose and full contentment that the soul shall have in God? In contentment there is the first fruit of heaven. There are two things in a contented spirit which make it like heaven.

1. God is there. Something of God is to be seen in the contented heart. A discontented Christian is like a rough, tempestuous sea; when the water is rough, you can see nothing there, but when it is smooth and serene, then you can see your face in the water (Prov. 27:19). When the heart rages through discontent, it is like a rough sea; you can see nothing there but passion and murmuring; there is nothing of God, nothing of heaven in that heart. But a contented heart is like the sea when it is smooth and calm, there is a face shining there; you may see something of Christ in that heart, a representation of all the graces.

2. Rest is there. What a Sabbath is kept in a contented heart. What a heaven. A contented Christian is like Noah in the ark; though the ark were tossed with waves, Noah could sit and sing in the ark. The soul that is entered into the ark of contentment sits quiet and sails above all the waves of trouble; he can sing in this spiritual ark. When we meet with motion and change in those around us, a contented spirit is not stirred or moved out of its center. The sails of a mill move with the wind, but the mill itself stands still—an emblem of contentment. When our outward estate moves with the wind of providence, yet the heart is settled through holy contentment. And when others are like quicksilver, shaking and trembling through disquiet, the contented Christian can say as David, "My heart is fixed, O God, my heart is fixed" (Ps. 57:7). What is this but a part of heaven?

—THOMAS WATSON

♦ *Have you experienced heaven in your soul? Be content and meditate on the fact that, if you have fled to Christ by faith, He dwells within you by His Spirit who bears witness with our spirit that we are the children of God.*

Christ's Heart of Love

Yea, I have loved thee with an everlasting love:
therefore with lovingkindness have I drawn thee.

—JEREMIAH 31:3

Believer, live not without a deep, constant realization of your precious-ness to Christ and of the depths, tenderness, and constancy of the love He bears toward you. All your holiness, happiness, and comfort come from believing this fact, that you are precious to the heart of Jesus. Let your faith grasp it, amid the various phases and changes of your Christian life, and it will be as a sweet flowing stream, gliding and sparkling by your side all through the sandy desert, giving swiftness to your feet in travel, strength to your hand in labor, soothing, reviving, and refreshment to your heart when sad or faint and weary.

The Holy Spirit, testifying to your soul of the love of the Savior, requires removal of all that constraint, shyness, and following of Him at a distance, which characterizes so many of His disciples. Be assured of your personal interest in Christ, your place in His affections, of your home and sanctuary in His heart, and no act of obedience, of love, or of service on your part will be too costly. Apart from all that He has done and is doing now, Jesus challenges our admiration and affection. His personal worth, His official work, His glory, and His government all demand our highest honor. This He receives from the angels, who having not sinned need no repentance, and having not fallen need no Savior; and this He will receive in that day when to Him every knee shall bow and every tongue shall confess; how much more is He worthy of it from those whom He has redeemed with His most precious blood!

Reader, has your eye seen His beauty? Has your heart bowed before the cross? Have you fallen at His feet? Have you crowned Him Lord and King of your soul? What is Christ to you—despised, hated, and rejected, or adored, loved, and welcomed?

—OCTAVIUS WINSLOW

♦ *Meditate on the love of the triune God toward sinners. Consider especially*
the love of Christ in His humiliation and exaltation, His active and passive
obedience, and His being God and man.

Help and Deliverance

Whereby are given unto us exceeding great and precious promises.
—2 PETER 1:4

The humble but unshaken confidence is the soul of prayer. So come to the throne of grace, pleading the exceeding great and precious promises of your God, and you will never be sent away empty. "Put me in remembrance," says God, "let us plead together: declare thou, that thou mayest be justified" (Isa. 43:26). Whatever be the blessing you desire, or the help you stand in need of, put your heavenly Father in remembrance of the promise, by which He has insured it to you. It is His own direction and therefore cannot be unavailing.

Do you desire to have the guardian care of Him who slumbers not nor sleeps? Remind the Lord that He has said, "He shall give his angels charge over thee, to keep thee in all thy ways" (Ps. 91:11). Do you long for a companion who will lead you heavenward? The promise is, "My presence shall go with thee, and I will give thee rest" (Ex. 33:14). Do you ask for forgiveness? Take with you the words, "Though your sins be as scarlet, they shall be as white as snow; though they be red like crimson, they shall be as wool" (Isa. 1:18). Do you seek acceptance? He has declared, "Him that cometh to me I will in no wise cast out" (John 6:37). Happy is it for the Christian when he can faithfully plead, and contentedly repose his soul, on such promises as these; he will have no cause for alarm. "When the enemy shall come in like a flood, the Spirit of the LORD shall lift up a standard against him" (Isa. 59:19).

Learn, Christian, where you ought to go with all your difficulties—to the throne of grace. There you are sure of *help* and *deliverance*. It is to the true Christian the citadel where he will always find a protector to aid and a home where there is always a Father to listen to him. "I must tell this to my God," said a Christian slave, while writhing under the lash of a cruel taskmaster. There was no one else who could hear or help him. How many are the crosses of the Christian, which ought only to be told to this never-failing friend!

—ASHTON OXENDEN

◆*Are you carrying crosses that are known to no one? Take them to the Lord in prayer knowing that "He hears the needy when they cry, He saves their souls when death draws nigh."*

Avoid Every Sin

Can a man take fire in his bosom, and his clothes not be burned?
—PROVERBS 6:27

Men have gone into a fiery furnace and have come out without having their hair singed or the smell of fire on them, but no man ever lay down with a sin in his bosom and arose without a stain on his soul. One cannot touch tar without getting black stains.

We should keep from all sin because sin in its nature and its effects is so dreadful. It wrings from the soul every sigh sent up from earth or hell. It has dug every grave and built every prison and every tomb. It has filled earth and hell with woes and wailings. It makes war on God. If it could, it would dethrone Him. It is the real cause of all disorder, violence, and confusion in the human race. It is easy for men to think too much of the evil of poverty or sickness; but no man thinks sin worse than it is.

If a man does not abstain from sin, it clearly proves that he is in league with sin and that his heart goes out after it. The sow proves her swinish nature by loving to wallow in the mire. There was never a wolf that did not love blood. It is the wicked that do wickedly.

He who toys with sin will have an unhappy life. There are some men who seem to be always sinning and repenting. Of course, their repentance is not genuine, or they would cease to commit such sin. It is sad to see husband and wife pouting and quarrelling one hour, however loving they may be the next. Their conscience and their life are constantly at war. They have no settled peace. Their prospects are dark and gloomy. Only those who abstain from the appearance of evil and sin prove themselves to be real Christians.

—WILLIAM PLUMER

◆ *Consider how even the smallest sin is like picking a fight with God.*

A Forgiving Heart

*And be ye kind one to another, tenderhearted, forgiving
one another, even as God for Christ's sake hath forgiven you.*
—EPHESIANS 4:32

Those whom God pardons and forgives, He puts in a merciful frame of heart to forgive others and that upon divine grounds. Many will forgive, but it is only how the ungodly forgive each other. It is a shame that many who profess themselves as Christians do not even go so far. You must forgive in a spiritual way, for that is the way that accompanies pardon of sin, to forgive because I have had more forgiven. Someone has offended me, but how much more have I offended the Lord? And if the Lord forgives me, ought not I to forgive others?

The one in the gospel who had so many talents forgiven him and afterward went and took his brother by the throat, how ill the Lord took it, that having been forgiven so much that he would then take from his brother the utmost farthing? Has God forgiven you your sin, which, had He not, it would have everlastingly chained you in torments, and will you not forgive? As it is an evidence, so it is a duty and a part of prayer in the example of the Lord's Prayer. Matthew 6:12 says, "Forgive us our debts, as we forgive our debtors." And in another place, it says, "Forgive us our sins; for we also forgive" (Luke 11:4).

Therefore, you can have no evidence that God has forgiven your iniquities and pardoned your trespasses unless others are in your thoughts forgiven too. I might have given many Scriptures, but I mention it as a duty that you who have any knowledge of your sin having been pardoned would make this a ground to forgive your brother. Say, "Alas, poor wretch, has God forgiven me? Was there ever such a distance between my brother and me as there was between God and me? And has God forgiven, and shall not I forgive my brother?" It is impossible that a soul should be made acquainted with the rich mercy of God in the forgiveness of their sin and not have a meek spirit to forgive his brother.

—JEREMIAH BURROUGHS

◆*Have you forgiven those who have offended you? Is there someone that
you need to forgive today in your heart and be ready to forgive when they
ask you? Or maybe you should go to the person who offended you and
seek reconciliation.*

Faith versus Assurance

I know that my redeemer liveth. —JOB 19:25

It is important to keep in view the distinction between faith and assurance. It explains things which a seeker after truth sometimes finds hard to understand.

Faith is the root, and assurance is the flower. Doubtless you can never have the flower without the root; but it is no less certain you may have the root and not the flower.

Faith is that poor trembling woman who came behind Jesus in the press and touched the hem of His garment (Mark 5:27). Assurance is Stephen standing calmly in the midst of his murderers and saying, "I see the heavens opened, and the Son of man standing on the right hand of God" (Acts 7:56).

Faith is the penitent thief, crying, "Lord, remember me" (Luke 23:42). Assurance is Job, sitting in the dust, covered with sores, and saying, "I know that my redeemer liveth" (Job 19:25). "Though he slay me, yet will I trust in him" (13:15).

Faith is Peter's drowning cry, as he began to sink: "Lord, save me" (Matt. 14:30). Assurance is that same Peter declaring before the council, "This is the stone which was set at nought of you builders, which is become the head of the corner. Neither is there salvation in any other: for there is none other name under heaven given among men, whereby we must be saved" (Acts 4:11–12).

Faith is life. How great the blessing! And yet life may be weak, sickly, unhealthy, painful, trying, anxious, worn, burdensome, joyless, smileless to the very end. Assurance is more than life. It is health, strength, power, vigor, activity, energy, manliness, beauty. Reader, it is not a question of saved or not saved that lies before us but of privilege or no privilege. It is not a question of peace or no peace but of great peace or little peace.

He that has faith does well. They are safe. They are washed. They are justified. They are beyond the power of hell. Satan, with all his malice, shall never pluck them out of Christ's hand. But he that has assurance does far better, sees more, feels more, knows more, enjoys more, has more days like those spoken of in Deuteronomy: "the days of heaven upon the earth" (11:21).

—J. C. RYLE

◆*Do you have assurance of your salvation?*

The Service of Christ Is Easy

And walk in love, as Christ also hath loved us,
and hath given himself for us.
—EPHESIANS 5:2

Those who bear the yoke of Christ act from a principle which makes all things easy. This is love. It is said of Jacob that when he served a hard master seven years for Rachel, they seemed to him but a few days for the love which he had for her. And many of you find it easy to do much for your spouse, parents, children, and friends because you love them. But there is no love like that which a redeemed sinner bears to Him who "loved us, and washed us from our sins in his own blood" (Rev. 1:5).

Love produces the greatest effects when it is mutual. We are willing to do and suffer much to gain the affection of a person we regard, though we are not sure of success; but when the affection is reciprocal, it adds strength to every motive. The believer does not love uncertainly; he knows that Jesus loved him first, loved him when he was in a state of enmity, and that nothing but the manifestation and power of this love could have taught his hard, unfeeling heart to love Him whom he never saw before. This love, therefore, gives encouragement in service.

Love does what it can and is sorry it cannot do more. We seldom think much either of time, discomforts, or expense when the heart is warmly engaged. The world, who understands not this heartfelt spring of true religion, thinks it is strange that the believer will not live as worldly as them. They wonder what pleasure they can find in secret prayer, in reading and hearing the Word of God. They pity the person who has a melancholy day and advise him not to take things too far. But the believer can say, "The love of Christ constrains me." The worldling's passion is the same as theirs, which makes his pursuit no less uniform and abiding; but the objects are as different as light from darkness. They love the perishing pleasures of sin, ungodly friends, and the praise of men; but he loves Jesus.

—JOHN NEWTON

◆ *Try to explain how love motivates you to serve. Are you fully engaged in His service?*

A Loving, Affectionate Friend

And to know the love of Christ, which passeth knowledge,
that ye might be filled with all the fulness of God.

—EPHESIANS 3:19

Do you want a loving and affectionate friend? Such a friend is Jesus Christ. Love shines forth in His dealings with sinners after they have believed in Him and become His friends. He is very patient with them, though their actions are often very trying and provoking. He is never tired of hearing their complaints, however often they may come to Him. He sympathizes deeply in all their sorrows. He knows what pain is. He is acquainted with grief. In all their afflictions He is afflicted. He never allows them to be tempted above what they are able to bear. He supplies them with the daily grace for their daily conflict. Their weak services are acceptable to Him. He is as well pleased with them as a parent is with his child's attempts to talk and walk. He has caused it to be written in His book that "the LORD taketh pleasure in his people" and "the LORD taketh pleasure in them that fear him" (Pss. 149:4; 147:11).

Reader, there is no love on earth that can be named together with this love. We love those in whom we see something that deserves our affection, or those who are our flesh and bone; the Lord Jesus loves sinners in whom there is no good thing. We love those from whom we get some return for our affection; the Lord Jesus loves those who can do little or nothing for Him compared with what He does for them. We love where we can give some reason for loving; the great friend of sinners draws His reasons out of His own everlasting compassion. His love is purely self-sacrificial, purely unselfish, purely free. Never, never was there so truly loving a friend as Jesus Christ.

—J. C. RYLE

◆*Do you know and rejoice in the unfailing love of Christ?*

Rejected by Friends

For it was not an enemy that reproached me; then I could have borne it:
neither was it he that hated me that did magnify himself against me;
then I would have hid myself from him: But it was thou,
a man mine equal, my guide, and mine acquaintance.

—PSALM 55:12–13

It is sad when a friend is like a brook in the summer; the traveler being parched with heat comes to the brook hoping to refresh himself, but the brook is dried up. You are not alone. Others of the saints have been betrayed by friends; and when they have leaned on them, they have been as a foot out of joint. This was true in the type David—"It was not an enemy that reproached me.... But it was thou, a man mine equal, my guide, and mine acquaintance. We took sweet counsel together" (Ps. 55:12–14)—and in the antitype Christ, who was betrayed by a friend. Why should we think it strange to have the same measure dealt out to us as Jesus Christ had? "The disciple is not above his master" (Luke 6:40).

A Christian may often see his sin in his punishment. Have not you dealt treacherously with God? How often you have grieved the Comforter, broken your vows, and through unbelief sided with Satan against God! How often you have abused love, taking the jewels of God's mercies, and making a golden calf of them, serving your own lusts! How often you have made the free grace of God, which should have been a bolt to keep out sin, a key to open the door to it. These wounds the Lord received in the house of His friends. Look upon the unkindness of your friend and mourn for your own unkindness against God. Shall a Christian condemn in another that which he has been guilty of himself?

Has your friend proved treacherous? Perhaps you put too much confidence in him. Perhaps you put more trust in your friend than you did dare to put in God. Friends are as brittle glasses; we may use them, but if we lean too hard on them, they will break. You have a friend in heaven who will never fail you. "There is a friend," says Solomon, "that sticketh closer than a brother" (Prov. 18:24).

—THOMAS WATSON

◆ *Do you have a friend in whom you trust—your spouse or another?*
Thank God for good friends, but beware not to put more trust in them
than in Christ.

The Most Delightful Love in the World

Who shall separate us from the love of Christ?
—ROMANS 8:35

The love of Christ is far more pleasant than any other love. Christ is far more amiable than any other object in the world. For:

1. No other love is so pure, heavenly, and divine a nature as the love of Christ is; and therefore, no other love can raise such a divine and exalted pleasure.

2. All that love Christ are certain they are loved. The pleasure of love is to be loved again. If love is not mutual, it is a torment and not a pleasure; but he that knows he loves Christ, knows Christ loves him with a love far higher and dearer.

3. Nothing can deprive those that love Christ either of present communion with or future enjoyment of Him. It is not so in other kinds of love; they are full of perplexities for fear of being deprived of enjoyment. There are a thousand events which may spoil it, and death certainly will separate them; but Christ will be enjoyed to all eternity, and all the world can't hinder it. Christ will receive them into His closest embrace, and in His arms shall they rest forevermore.

4. The union between Christ and those that love Him is closer, and the communion more intimate, than between any other lovers. Believers have the pleasure to think that He who they love has also loved them so much as to receive them so near to Himself as to make them His bone and flesh. The believer is joined to Christ and is become one with Him. How must this be to those who love Him in truth! Love naturally desires a close and inseparable union and intimate communion, but there is no such intimate conversation between any other lovers as between Christ and the Christian.

5. There is no love so advantageous as the love to Christ and therefore none so pleasant. Love is sweet when the ones loving each other enjoy one another in prosperous circumstances. Christ is already crowned with glory, and He will crown those that love Him with glory, too, so that they shall together eternally be in the greatest glory.

—JONATHAN EDWARDS

♦ *Do you love Christ? Take a few minutes to meditate on that and what the implications of your answer are.*

Our Burdens

Call upon me in the day of trouble: I will deliver thee.
—PSALM 50:15

How shall we live as we carry our burdens? Cast them on the Lord, and He shall sustain you. You cannot carry them alone. Roll them over on the arm of God. Do this by faith—faith in God's Word, faith in God's Son. Faith in the Lord Jesus is the only cure for heart troubles. By faith in the Lord Jesus, all the guilt of sin is taken away, its sting removed, and its power destroyed. This faith must be exercised in prayer. Call upon the Lord in the day of trouble, and He will deliver you, and you shall glorify Him. Millions of times have the poor and needy cried for help, and they have gotten all they asked.

One of the greatest errors is that when our burdens do not seem to be very heavy, we try to carry them ourselves. John Newton tells of one who seemed to react properly when a great affliction came upon him but lost his temper when a careless servant broke a piece of pottery. I have seen one who seemed to have a gentle disposition when God took away a dear child but spoke unadvisedly when the clerk charged too much for a bundle of paper. Cast all your burdens on the Lord. Any one of them will be too much for you if God leaves you to yourself. Your strength is weakness. You cannot sustain yourself. You have no might to do good.

The Word says, "He shall sustain thee" (Ps. 55:22). It does not say He will take away the burden, but God will sustain His people in all their trials. God's people have found this true in every age. David said, "It is good for me that I have been afflicted" (119:71). Micah said, "When I sit in darkness, the LORD shall be a light unto me" (Mic. 7:8). Finally, Jesus said, "Peace I leave with you, my peace I give unto you.... Let not your heart be troubled, neither let it be afraid" (John 14:27).

—WILLIAM PLUMER

◆ *Bring your present burdens to Christ in prayer, trusting in His love and care.*

When Self Is Renounced

*And have put on the new man, which is renewed in knowledge
after the image of him that created him.*
—COLOSSIANS 3:10

The constraining love of Christ has a direct and marvelous tendency—in proportion to the measure of faith—to mortify *self*, which for a time is our focus and by which we are too much biased after we know the Lord. But as grace prevails, self is renounced. We feel that we are not our own, that we are bought with a price, and that it is our duty, honor, and happiness to be the servants of God and of the Lord Jesus Christ. To devote our soul and body, every talent, power, and faculty, to the service of His cause and will; to let our light shine to the praise of His grace; to place our highest joy in thinking of His adorable perfectness; to rejoice even in tribulations and distresses, in reproaches and infirmities, if the power of Christ rests upon us and is magnified in us; to be content, even glad, to be nothing that He may be all in all; to obey Him in face of opposition or threats of men; to trust Him though all outward appearances seem against us; to rejoice in Him, though we have nothing else to rejoice in; to live above the world and to have our conversation in heaven—this is the prize, the mark of our high calling to which we are encouraged with a holy ambition continually to desire. It is true, we still fall short, and we will find that when we would do good, evil is present with us. But the attempt is glorious and shall not be wholly in vain. He that gives us *to will,* will enable us to perform with growing success and teach us to profit even by our mistakes and imperfections.

O blessed Christian that so fears the Lord, that delights in His Word, and derives his principles, motives, and consolations from that unfailing source of light and strength. He shall be like a tree planted by the rivers of water, whose leaf is always green and fruit abundant.

—JOHN NEWTON

◆*Describe how you have found the Word of God to be a help in
renouncing self.*

Be Honest before God and Man

And why beholdest thou the mote that is in thy brother's eye,
but perceivest not the beam that is in thine own eye?
—LUKE 6:41

If we would but faithfully judge ourselves, we should be spared the pain of divine chastisements. But we are not faithful to our own souls. We deal with a slack hand in things pertaining to our own sins, and let things go unreproved and uncondemned in ourselves which we are sharp enough to see and rebuke in others. Deal honestly with every part of your daily life, regarding duty, trial, sacrifice, self-denial, or forbearance with others. Beware of *one-sidedness* or self-partiality—in truth, in experience, or in action. Remember that all things have two sides; a tender conscience and a well-balanced mind will deal with both. Deal honestly with conscience in all things, small and great, spiritual or temporal; deal honestly with the church of God and with the brethren; deal honestly with God—Father, Son, and Spirit.

It is strange that in spiritual things we should try to cheat *ourselves* as well as others; yet it is so. We are unwilling to take the worst view of our own case; to think evil of ourselves; to act the stern censor in regard to our own omissions and commissions. We have few excuses for others, many for ourselves; evils that seem monstrous in others are trifles in us. When looking at others, we use a microscope; at ourselves, we either shut our eyes or put on a veil. This dishonest dealing is very pernicious; this "covering of sin" is destructive both of peace as well as progress. And when we remember that all dishonest dealing with ourselves is in reality dishonest dealing with God, the evil is seen to be more hateful and more inexcusable (Hos. 11:12). Be honest and upright before God and man, with your own conscience, with the blood of sprinkling, and with that law which is "holy, and just, and good" (Rom. 7:12). Don't flatter your own heart, nor tell a lie to conscience, nor think to deceive God.

—HORATIUS BONAR

♦*Take a few moments and lay your heart bare before God, asking if you magnify the faults of others and minimize your own.*

True Courage

The LORD is on my side; I will not fear.
—PSALM 118:6

To be a Christian is to be of a noble disposition because Christianity gives true courage and fortitude to the mind. Courage is by the consent of mankind reckoned as one necessary qualification of a noble mind, and cowardice is looked upon as meanness of spirit. But it is the Christian, and the Christian only, that is endowed with true courage and fortitude. Courage may be defined as a strength of mind that enables and prompts someone to do what he should do without being hindered or impeded by fear. Wicked men do not have this courage; they are afraid to do what they should do. Their fear has such power on them that it takes away their strength; it confounds them. They are afraid to do what God and nature and the good of mankind and their own interest requires of them. They are so cowardly that they are afraid to do what is necessary for them to escape their own destruction and to obtain their own happiness. They are afraid to engage in religion; they are afraid of hurting themselves and bringing affliction on themselves; they are afraid of being reproached by their companions, afraid of the laughter of fools. They fear where no fear is. "The wicked flee when no man pursueth" (Prov. 28:1).

But the Christian is not so. Their hearts are filled with a holy courage and resolution. They are not scared by such scarecrows as terrify the wicked. They are not afraid of doing that which is their duty to do, and that which is proper they should do. They are not frightened by the thoughts of self-denial and suffering. They are not afraid of reproaches; they are not frightened from living a Christian life because they are laughed at by others. They are not afraid of persecution. They have such courage and resolution that they can overcome the world with all its terrors and cruelties. Such courage as this is Christian courage, which far exceeds the courage of renowned heroes. Christian courage is the only true courage.

—JONATHAN EDWARDS

◆*What do you think of Edwards's definition of courage, and how would you gauge your own courage?*

The Christian Race

Let us lay aside every weight, and the sin which doth so easily beset us,
and let us run with patience the race that is set before us.
—HEBREWS 12:1

Let us consider the apostle's advice to "lay aside every weight." By this he means that we must give up everything which is really hurtful to our souls. We must act like men who throw off all their long and flowing garments, which are a hindrance, when about to try their speed in running. We must cast away everything which hinders us upon our road toward heaven—the lust of the flesh, pleasures, honors, the spirit of lukewarmness and carelessness, and indifference about the things of God. All must be rooted out and forsaken if we are eager for the prize. We must mortify the deeds of the body. We must crucify the affection for this world. We must look well to our habits and desires and work, and if we find anything coming in as a stumbling block between ourselves and salvation, we must be ready to lay it aside as if it were a millstone about our necks, although it cost us as much pain as cutting off a hand or plucking out a right eye. Away with everything which keeps us back. Our feet are slow at the very best, and we have a long course to run; we cannot afford to carry weight if we are really contending for everlasting life.

But above all we must take heed that we lay aside the sin which most easily besets us, the sin which from our age, habit, taste, disposition, or feelings possesses the greatest power over us. I know of two sins which try the most advanced Christians even to the end, and these are pride and unbelief—pride in our own difference from others, pride in our reputation as Christians, pride in our spiritual attainment, and unbelief about our own sinfulness, about God's wisdom, about God's mercy. Oh, they are heavy burdens and sorely do they keep us back.

—J. C. RYLE

♦ *In what ways do you exhibit the sins of pride and unbelief? Practically, how can you overcome these sins?*

Your Life Speaks

Let your light so shine before men, that they may see your good works,
and glorify your Father which is in heaven.

—MATTHEW 5:16

Our Lord was not ashamed of *the opinion of the world*. It had its views of Christ, its opinion of His character and conduct. And although there were occasions when Christ manifested an interest in the popular sentiment concerning Himself—"Whom do men say that I am?" (Mark 8:27)—teaching that His disciples may not be wholly indifferent to the sentiment of others, yet, whatever that opinion was, He never for one moment allowed it so to influence or control Him as to deviate one hair's breadth from the strictest, straightest line of duty, integrity, and love.

Every believer, however limited and sheltered from the human eye his walk of life, will create a public sentiment respecting his individual self. His family, his friends, his neighbors will form their opinion of his character, actions, and life. Few pass through this life incognito to eternity; few glide through the world unseen, unnoticed, unfelt. To this we cannot be nor ought to be wholly indifferent. Each individual Christian especially should live for an object. He should live to make his talents, influence, and example have impact upon the present and eternal well-being of all with whom he comes in contact. As a "light" he is to shine; as "salt" he is to influence; as a "witness" he is to testify for Christ.

In a world like this, where there is so much evil to correct, so much temptation to resist, so much sorrow to soothe, so much want to supply, so much misery to counteract, so much ignorance to instruct, so much good to be done, none need be all day idle, dreaming away existence, vegetating in selfishness, and living for man—but rather laboring for God. Oh, be an earnest, active Christian; be up and doing. Life is too real, too solemn, too responsible for sluggishness, inactivity, and selfishness.

—OCTAVIUS WINSLOW

♦ *Examine your past day, week, and month as to how your time has been spent for the Savior. Confess where you have been negligent in living for Him, and be stirred to live more each day for Him.*

The Rod of Love

And whether we be afflicted, it is for your consolation and salvation.
—2 CORINTHIANS 1:6

Often nothing but adversity will do for us. We need to be stripped of every earthly portion, that we may seek entirely our portion in Jehovah Himself. We need to be turned out of a home on earth that we may seek a home in heaven. Earth's music is too seducing and takes away our relish for a new song. God must either hush it or take us apart into a desert place, that we may no longer be led captive by it but that we may have our ear open only to the heavenly melody. We cannot be trusted with too full a cup or too pleasant a resting place. We abuse everything that God has given us and prove ourselves not trustworthy as to any one of them.

Some God cannot trust with health; they need sickness to keep them low and make them walk softly all their days. Others He cannot trust with prosperity; they need adversity to humble them, lest like Jeshurun, they should "wax fat and kick" (see Deut. 32:15). Others He cannot trust with riches; they must be kept poor, lest covetousness should spring up and pierce them through with many sorrows. Others He cannot trust with friends; they make idols of them, they give their hearts to them, and this interferes with the claims of Jehovah to have us altogether as His own.

But still in all God deals with us as with the members of His own family. Never for a moment does He lose sight of this. Neither should we. So that when trials overtake us, when we are so "judged," we should feel that we are "chastened of the Lord, that we should not be condemned with the world" (1 Cor. 11:32); we should learn not merely to submit to the rod but to kiss and welcome it, not merely to acquiesce in chastisement but to "glory in tribulations also: knowing that tribulation worketh patience; and patience, experience; and experience, hope; and hope maketh not ashamed" (Rom. 5:3–5). We should learn not merely to praise God *in* affliction but to praise Him *for* it.

—HORATIUS BONAR

◆ *Is there something in your life that God may not be entrusting you with because He knows what is best for you? Reread Romans 5:3–5 and consider how this is being fulfilled in you.*

United to Christ

Therefore being justified by faith, we have peace
with God through our Lord Jesus Christ.

—ROMANS 5:1

Faith is a grace produced in the heart of a sinner through the power of the Holy Ghost; being emptied of all thought of his own righteousness and strength, he is enabled to look to Christ. He flies to Him as his hiding place, relies on Him for the remission of sins, for righteousness to justify him in the sight of God, for strength to follow after holiness, to encounter spiritual enemies, and for eternal life when his labors of love are ended. By faith he trusts in Christ as his Priest, receives Him as his Prophet, and submits to Him as his King while with adoring gratitude he gives all glory to the Savior who is over all, God blessed forever.

Such is the preciousness of saving faith which draws all its strength from the fullness of Christ, which receives from Him pardon with one hand and holiness with the other, both being equally the design of His mediatorial work, and equally the desire of every newborn soul. Hope anchors the trembling sinner—plagued by inward fears—upon Christ the Rock of Ages, while faith, fixing its eye upon the atonement of Jesus, produces a great peace.

Is this your experience? Are you united to Christ by faith? If so, then the joy of the Lord is your strength, and the love of Christ obliges you to make a full surrender of yourself to Him. To you to live is Christ and to die is gain.

What a rich provision has a God of love made for His church. The blessed truths are revealed to our minds; the sweetest consolations are revealed to our hearts; the purest instructions are given to us for our guidance through life. These blessings are inseparable in the experience of every true believer.

—THOMAS READE

◆*Are you rejoicing in Christ alone? Does what He has done for you fill your soul? What do you need to surrender to Him in response to what He has done for you?*

All to the Glory of God

Whether therefore ye eat, or drink, or whatsoever ye do,
do all to the glory of God.
—1 CORINTHIANS 10:31

Do we live to the world, or do we live to God? Has the world the victory in our hearts over all principles of goodness? Which do we choose: to be rich or to be holy; to feed sumptuously to please ourselves with food or to feed on Jesus Christ, the bread that came down from heaven, the heavenly food; to have our bodies finely arrayed or our souls clothed with meekness and humility and the righteousness of Christ; to dwell in beautiful homes or to have our souls made the temples of the Holy Ghost?

We ought to consider our thoughts. How are the faculties of our souls chiefly employed? Are our thoughts and affections mainly thinking about earthly things, about what we shall eat and drink and how we will be clothed? Are our minds set chiefly on vanities and trifles that are of little profit or advantage? Do we allow our thoughts to rove to the ends of the earth? Do we give our thoughts the reins to go where they incline, sometimes after objects of the lusts of our flesh; sometimes after the objects of covetousness and the lusts of the eye; sometimes after the objects of ambitious desires and haughty expectations led and governed by the pride of life; and at other times about things of no advantage or importance? Or do we restrain them and keep them mainly exercised on heavenly objects?

We ought to consider our words. Words commonly follow thoughts: if our thoughts are much upon religion, certainly our tongues will be apt sometimes to be upon the same subject; but if our thoughts are mostly vain, our words will be likewise vain and to little purpose.

Thoughts, words, and actions all go together. We ought also to consider the nature of our actions with respect to God: whether they are done in His service and to His glory; whether all that we do is part of the work that God has appointed for us and commanded, for everything that we do that is not part of God's service is part of the devil's service.

—JONATHAN EDWARDS

◆ *What are the chief objects of your thoughts, words, and actions? Look deeply into your heart. Are you focused on this world or living to God's glory?*

Christian Prudence

In all thy ways acknowledge him, and he shall direct thy paths.

—PROVERBS 3:6

To combine zeal with prudence is indeed difficult. There is often too much self in our zeal, and too much of the fear of man in our prudence. Prudence is a word much abused; but there is a heavenly wisdom, which the Lord has promised to give to those who humbly wait upon Him for it. It does not consist in forming a bundle of rules and principles, but in a spiritual taste and discernment, derived from an experiential knowledge of the truth and of the heart of man, as described in the Word of God; and its exercise consists much in a simple dependence upon the Lord, to guide and prompt us in every decision.

We seldom act wrong when we truly depend upon Him and can cease from leaning on our own understanding. When the heart is in a right frame, and His Word dwells richly in us, there is a kind of immediate perception of what is proper for us to do in present circumstances, without much painful inquiry; a light shines before us upon the path of duty; and if He permits us in such a spirit to make some mistakes, He will also teach us to profit by them, and our reflections upon what was wrong will make us act more wisely the next time.

At best we must always expect to meet with new proofs of our own weakness and insufficiency; otherwise, how should we be kept humble or know how to prize the liberty He allows us of coming to the throne of grace for fresh forgiveness and direction every day? But if He enables us to walk before Him with a single eye, He will graciously accept our desire of serving Him better if we could, and His blessing will make our feeble endeavors in some degree successful, even as at the same time we see defects and evils in our best services sufficient to make us ashamed of them.

—JOHN NEWTON

◆ *What is Christian prudence, and how should we exercise it?*

Holiness and Consistency of Character

See then that ye walk circumspectly, not as fools, but as wise.
—EPHESIANS 5:15

Words often have but little effect, however well spoken; but a holy life is a most powerful preacher. Let it be seen by those around you that religion has a firm hold of you; that you are living under its constraining power; and that in all you do and say, it is the one mainspring that moves you.

We little know what a wholesome influence a holy walk may have upon others. The example and influence of a good man may influence the lives and conduct of hundreds, while one ungodly man in a house or in a church may do untold harm and may ruin many souls.

For instance, a man may be going to do something wrong when he meets a friend whom he knows to be a religious person. Not a word may pass between them, and yet the very sight of his neighbor may lead the man to think of better things, and he may change his intentions.

Have you not sometimes felt that to be in the company of a holy servant of God only for a few minutes, though not one word may be spoken directly to you, has led you to go away thoughtful? There was something about his Christian bearing which made you feel self-condemned. So, when we little know it, or intend it ourselves, we are continually influencing one another, either for good or for evil.

See then how useful you *may* be in your daily walk. You may be in a very humble station of life; you may have little or no learning; you may have no particular gift of speech; and yet you may be a blessing to those among whom you mix. Your light may shine without your knowing it; your life may speak when your tongue is silent. If you are living to Christ, you are a daily and hourly witness to the fact that there is a power in religion which can make a man a blessing in this world of sin and sorrow.

—ASHTON OXENDEN

◆ *How have the lives of other Christians had an effect on you? Resolve to live so that those around you will be impacted for God's glory.*

The Law of Liberty

The creature itself also shall be delivered from the bondage of corruption into the glorious liberty of the children of God.
—ROMANS 8:21

When we come to understand the meaning and value of the work upon the cross, when we accept what God has declared concerning all who believe His testimony to that work, the burden drops, and we enter into liberty. With that liberty comes holiness. We seek henceforth conformity to Him who has set us free and who bids us follow Him in the path of conformity to the Father's will. With that holiness comes love—love to Him who has brought our souls out of prison by going into prison for us. With that love comes zeal—the zeal of Him who followed after His lost ones till He had recovered them, and the zeal of him who said, "The zeal of thine house hath eaten me up" (Ps. 69:9). With this love and zeal there comes self-denial—the self-denial of Him who "pleased not himself," who lived on earth solely for others; though rich, for our sakes becoming poor (Rom. 15:3; 2 Cor. 8:9).

Of all this, be it ever remembered that the root is "peace with God through our Lord Jesus Christ" (Rom. 5:1), and that this peace comes from the knowledge of the peacemaking blood, the blood of the one divine peace offering, whom to know is peace! It is out of the sacrificial blood that we extract the peace which is the beginning of all service, all religion, all uprightness of walk. "No condemnation" commences the life of freedom and self-denial and zeal (8:1). We cease to know the law as our enemy and begin to know it as our friend; for that which is "holy, and just, and good" must ever be our delight, our joy, our guide (7:12). "I *delight* in the *law* of God after the inward man" is one of our truest watchwords (v. 22); for we are set free from the law in order that we might *delight* in the *law*, and in order that "the righteousness of the *law* might be *fulfilled* in us" (8:4).

—HORATIUS BONAR

◆ *Does God's law have a place in the Christian life? Is the law your delight, and do you know the liberty with which Christ sets a person free?*

The Proper Balance

Neither murmur ye.
—1 CORINTHIANS 10:10

An aggravation of the sin of murmuring is when we murmur about small things. I remember reading in Seneca that he had this comparison, which is a good one, to set out the great evil of murmuring over smaller afflictions. "Suppose a man has a very nice house to live in, and he has beautiful orchards and gardens surrounded with beautiful trees for decoration. If this man would now murmur because the wind blows a few leaves off his trees, what a most unreasonable thing it would be, for him to be weeping and wringing his hands over the loss of a few leaves when he has plenty of all kinds of fruit. So, it is with many," says Seneca, "though they have many comforts about them, yet some little things, the blowing off of a few leaves, is enough to disquiet them." It was a great evil that when Ahab had a kingdom, the lack of his neighbor's vineyard had such power to upset him. So, for us to murmur—not because we don't have something we need, but because we don't have what we possibly could have—this is a very great sin.

Suppose God gives a woman a child who has a perfectly formed body, a child who is very beautiful, with great gifts, intellect, and memory, but maybe there is a wart growing on the finger of the child, and she murmurs at it that it is such an affliction to her. She is so taken up with it that she forgets to give thanks to God for her child, and all the goodness of God to her in the child is swallowed up in that. Would you not say that this was foolishness and a very great evil in this woman to do so? Likewise, our afflictions, if weighed rightly, are but such small things in comparison to our mercies.

—JEREMIAH BURROUGHS

♦ *Make a list of the great mercies God has shown you, and then compare them with the things you perhaps complain about which are comparatively small.*

MARCH

◆

*Christian, be it yours to regard it as your
highest and holiest and dearest privilege that
you are permitted to draw near to God.*

—ASHTON OXENDEN

The Enjoyment of God

I will love thee, O LORD. —PSALM 18:1

The happiness of society, and the enjoyment of friends, is one of the highest types of pleasures, next to the pleasures of religion. If that is so sweet, how inexpressibly sweet and delightful it must be to enjoy this God, who is infinitely more excellent, more lovely, than the most perfect of our fellow creatures. There is inexpressibly more pleasure and delight in the enjoyment of God than in the enjoyment of the most excellent, dear friends upon earth.

1. God is every way transcendently more amiable than the most perfect and lovely of all our fellow creatures. If men take great delight and pleasure in seeing and enjoying the perfections and beauties of their friends, with what delights, with what sweet rapture will the sweet glories and beauties of the blessed God be beheld and enjoyed!

2. God loves those that He admits to the enjoyment of Him with far greater love than the highest love of fellow creatures.

3. Those that enjoy God shall love Him with transcendently greater love than it is possible to love the loveliest creature, so that the love will be mutual; the glorified saint shall be completely transformed to love God, and shall be completely transformed to joy at the thought of God so dearly loving him.

4. The glorified saint shall be more closely united to God than ever the best friends are united here in this world. They shall be received into the closest union with God; we represent it by "being embraced in God's arms," but that is too faint a shadow to represent the close union that there will be; the very soul of the saint shall be united to God, and God shall be in them, in their very souls, by His glorious presence.

5. They shall more fully enjoy God than the nearest friends. The enjoyment of friends is not full and satisfying. It is frequently interrupted; but it is not so with respect to God and the glorified saint, but the enjoyment will be entire, to the full satisfaction of the soul, and it shall be constant and without interruption.

—JONATHAN EDWARDS

◆ *This is the chief end of man: to know God and enjoy Him forever. How can you enjoy Him better even now?*

Family Prayer

For I know him, that he will command his children and his household after him, and they shall keep the way of the LORD.

—GENESIS 18:19

One of the plainest marks of a godly household is the use of family prayer. If you wish well to your children and those under your roof, you will pray *for* them. And you will do more; you will pray *with* them.

Family prayer is *your duty*. No one can be a Christian parent who neglects it. What would you think of a father or a mother who refused to clothe and feed their children? You would certainly call them very cruel. But remember, your children have souls as well as bodies; and I am sure, if you feel a concern for your own soul, you will feel concerned for theirs also. Yes, their souls are very precious.

If you really want your children to turn out well, and to become the servants of Christ, you cannot begin too early to train them up "in the nurture and admonition of the Lord" (Eph. 6:4). Let them see that *you* honor God yourselves. Gather them around you morning and evening, or at least once a day, and then commend them to His fatherly care. Ask for a blessing, not on yourselves only, but on your family also. Bring before God not merely your own private wants but those of your household. This was Abraham's practice; and God said of him, "I know him, that he will command his children and his household after him, and they shall keep the way of the LORD" (Gen. 18:19). A good man used to say, "A family without prayer is like a house without a roof, exposed to all the injuries of the weather and to every storm that blows."

What a happy sight is a truly Christian household! There may be great poverty there, but still there is contentment. There may be sickness and trials there, yet there is peace. The hand of death may be there, but there is cheerful submission. Your home, my dear friend, may be poor, and your furniture scanty, but if Christ is there, all will be well. If the voice of prayer and praise is heard in it, then God's blessing will be felt.

—ASHTON OXENDEN

◆*Are you praying with your children and teaching them to pray in their own childlike way? How can you teach them how to pray without quenching the childlike simplicity with which they pray?*

The Believer's Joy

Thou hast made known to me the ways of life;
thou shalt make me full of joy with thy countenance.
—ACTS 2:28

Has a believer enjoyment in life? Is he void of all rational delights because he makes the Lord his portion? It would be an impeachment of the good of God to suppose His service a mere Egyptian bondage.

The true believer in Jesus has the sweetest enjoyment of life. He can eat his food with singleness of heart, praising God. He can taste the sweetness of Christian friendship and family life; he can enjoy all the endearing charities of husband, father, brother. He can feel his heart sympathizing toward the poor and find his joy in speaking words of comfort to the troubled heart. He can delight in all the beauties of natural scenery and appreciate all the charms of sound philosophy. He can rejoice in every opening prospect for the extension of the Redeemer's kingdom through institutions devised by Christian wisdom and conducted in Christian simplicity. He can weep in his best moments over the ruins of the fall, not only as felt in his own heart, but as beheld in the abject condition of millions of people. He can rejoice with those who rejoice and weep with those who weep (Rom. 12:15).

Then, can such a man be miserable? Can such a man be destitute of sources of real enjoyment? He lives by faith; he longs for heaven; he desires to be daily conformed to Jesus and to glorify Him more, whether it be by life or death. To him to live is Christ and to die is gain. Such is the character of the converted sinner. Oh! How precious, how divine, how rare a character!

"Lord, impart this grace unto me, who am less than the least of all Thy mercies, until faith shall end in the glorious fruition of Thyself in Thy everlasting kingdom of light and glory."

—THOMAS READE

◆ *Pray, expanding on the final prayer sentence. Take each thought and word of this prayer, and lay it before the throne of grace.*

He Leadeth Me

Thus saith the LORD, thy Redeemer, the Holy One of Israel;
I am the LORD thy God which teacheth thee to profit,
which leadeth thee by the way that thou shouldest go.

—ISAIAH 48:17

The Lord is truer in His friendship than a brother, more pitiful than a father, more loving than a mother, more gentle than a woman. He doesn't afflict willingly. Nor does the Lord ever lead me other than wisely. He makes no mistakes. He knows the way I ought to go. He knows how much sweet and how much bitter are best for me. He understands me fully. He knows my spirit would fail before Him if I were dealt with severely. Oh, how He mingles mercy with judgment!

True, He often leads me in a mysterious way. I don't see the end from the beginning. I cannot see afar off. If I perfectly comprehended all God's ways, I think I should be capable of guiding myself, at least to some extent. When all His waves and billows go over me, how can I tell anything? Would Jacob or Joseph or Bunyan have chosen the way the Lord led them? Have not the saints long been crying, "O Lord, how long?" But He never does wrong. He leads in the paths of righteousness (Ps. 23:3). "Righteousness and judgment are the habitation of his throne" (97:2). In review of all the past, I can truly say, "Thou hast dealt well with thy servant, O LORD.... I know... that thou in faithfulness hast afflicted me" (119:65, 75).

Then He leads me always: in prosperity and in adversity; in joy and in sorrow; when alone and when surrounded by others. If He left me even for an hour, I should be lost. When I sleep Thou, Lord, keep vigil over me. When I awake I am still with Thee. On the land and on the sea, I am kept by the mighty power of God. He leadeth me, and I will trust Him.

—WILLIAM PLUMER

◆*Reflect on how the Lord has led you. Were you always able to see what He was doing in your life when it happened, or did that come afterward? How can you take courage from how He has dealt with you in the past to press on in your present trial?*

The Training of the Will

For whosoever shall do the will of God,
the same is my brother, and my sister, and mother.
—MARK 3:35

The will is the seat of rebelliousness. Here the warfare is carried on. "The flesh lusteth against the Spirit, and the Spirit against the flesh" (Gal. 5:17). At conversion the will is bent in the right direction, but it is still crooked and rigid. Rebelliousness is still there. Prosperous days may sometimes hide it so that we are almost unconscious of its strength. But it still exists. Furnace heat is needed for softening and strengthening it. No milder remedy will do. "It requires," says a suffering saint, "all the energy of God to bend my will to His." Yet it must be done. The will is the soul's stronghold; therefore, it is the will that God seems so specially to aim at in chastisement. Fire after fire He kindles in order to soften it; and blow after blow He brings down on it to straighten it. He rests not till He has made it thoroughly flexible and hammered out of it the many remnants of self which it contains. He will not stay His hand till He has thoroughly marred our self-formed plans and shown us the folly of our self-chosen ways.

This is especially the case in long continued trials; either when these come stroke after stroke in sad succession, or when one fearful stroke has left behind its consequences which years perhaps will not fully unfold. The bending and straightening of the will is often a long process, during which the soul has to pass through waters deep and many, through fires hot and ever kindling up anew. Prolonged trials seem especially aimed at the will. Its perversity and stiffness can only be driven out of it by a long succession of trials. It is only by degrees that it becomes truly pliable and is brought into harmony with the will of God. We can cut off an unseemly branch; but to properly bend the tree requires time and tireless applications for months or years. So our will must give way. However proud, however forward, it must bend. God will not leave it till He has made it one with His own.

—HORATIUS BONAR

◆ *Is your will being shaped and formed to be like His? Where do you find*
that you still want your own way? How can you overcome this?

Little Faith Strengthened

And he said unto them, Why are ye so fearful?
how is it that ye have no faith?
—MARK 4:40

Would you like to feel the everlasting arms around you and to hear the voice of Jesus daily drawing nigh to your soul and saying, "I am thy salvation" (Ps. 35:3)? Would you like to be a useful laborer in the vineyard in your day and generation? Would you be known of all as a bold, firm, decided, single-eyed, uncompromising follower of Christ? Would you be eminently spiritually minded and holy? I doubt not some readers will say, "These are the very things our hearts desire. We long for them. We pant after them, but they seem far from us."

Has it never struck you that your neglect of assurance may possibly be the main secret of all your failures, that the low measure of faith which satisfies you may be the cause of your low sense of peace? Can you think it a strange thing that your graces are faint and languishing, when faith, the root and mother of them all, is allowed to remain feeble and weak?

Take my advice this day. Seek an increase of faith. Seek an assured hope of salvation like the apostle Paul's. Seek to obtain a simple, childlike confidence in God's promises. Seek to be able to say, "I know whom I have believed: I am persuaded that He is mine and I am His" (see 2 Tim. 1:12; Song 2:16).

You have very likely tried other ways and methods, and completely failed. Change your plan. Lay aside your doubts. Lean more entirely on the Lord's arm. Begin with implicit trusting. Cast aside your faithless backwardness and take the Lord at His word. Come and roll yourself, your soul, and your sins upon your gracious Savoir. Begin with simple believing, and all other things will soon be added to you.

—J. C. RYLE

◆ *Do you have doubts and fears that need to be laid aside? What is hindering you from a greater assured hope?*

A Gracious Invitation

Draw nigh to God, and he will draw nigh to you.
—JAMES 4:8

God is everywhere, and where He is there is a prayer-hearing and prayer-answering God. Surrounded with this gracious, loving presence, the Christian may fear no danger. His every petition is heard—his every cry for help enters into the ears of the Lord God of Sabaoth. "The LORD is nigh unto them that are of a broken heart; and saveth such as be of a contrite spirit" (Ps. 34:18). "And it shall come to pass, that before they call, I will answer; and while they are yet speaking, I will hear" (Isa. 65:24).

Christian, be it yours to regard it as your highest and holiest and dearest privilege that you are permitted to draw near to God. Pray that He would *stand by you* in every difficulty, that He would draw you by the cords of love and keep you ever near Him, so that you may continually enjoy, in your journey through life, the consciousness of His love, His friendship, His guardian care. Go forth to your life duties believing that He is at your right hand, and you shall not be greatly moved. Let thoughts of His goodness, His mercy, His love and faithfulness and watchful care mingle with all your thoughts, and be thankful for all His benefits.

Cultivate a spirit of earnest devotedness to your Father's will, patiently do and endure whatever He appoints, and rest assured He will give strength according to your day. He will "shew [you] the path of life," and He will at length give you to realize in your blessed experience that in His "presence is fulness of joy; at [His] right hand there are pleasures for evermore" (Ps. 16:11).

Almighty God, Father of our Lord Jesus Christ, we humble ourselves before Thee, confessing that we are not worthy of the least of all Thy mercies. We adore Thee as the Father of lights, from whom cometh down every good and every perfect gift. And ascribing no worth or excellence to ourselves, we would, as long as we live, render unto Thee due praise and unceasing thanks for Thine unmerited goodness.
—ASHTON OXENDEN

◆*How do you draw near to God? Are you convinced that if you draw near to God, He will draw near to you? Meditate on the magnitude of this promise.*

The Christian Warfare

He giveth power to the faint; and to them that have
no might he increaseth strength.

—ISAIAH 40:29

Dear friend, your welfare I rejoice in; your warfare I understand something of. Saint Paul describes his own case in a few words: "without were fightings, within were fears" (2 Cor. 7:5). Does not this encompass all you would say? How are you to know experientially either your own weakness or the power, wisdom, and grace of God, but by frequent and various trials? How are the graces of patience, resignation, meekness, and faith to be discovered and increased except by exercise? The Lord has chosen, called, and armed us for the fight, and shall we wish to be excused? Shall we not rather rejoice that we have the honor to appear in such a cause, under such a Captain, such a banner, and in such company? A complete suit of armor is provided, weapons not to be resisted, and precious balm to heal us if haply we receive a wound, and precious ointment to revive us when we are in danger of fainting.

Further, we are assured of the victory beforehand. What a crown is prepared for every conqueror, which Jesus, the righteous Judge, the gracious Savior, shall place upon every faithful head with His own hand! Then let us not be weary and faint, for in due season we shall reap. The time is short; yet a little while and the struggle of indwelling sin and the contradiction of surrounding sinners shall be known no more You are blessed because you hunger and thirst after righteousness. He whose name is Amen has said you shall be filled.

To claim the promise is to make it our own; yet we must practice submission not only in temporal but spiritual things. We should be ashamed and grieved at our slow progress, yet we must not expect to receive everything at once but wait for a gradual increase, nor forget to be thankful for what we deem little in comparison to the much we suppose others have received. A little grace, a spark of true love to God, a grain of faith, though small as a mustard-seed, is worth a thousand worlds.

—JOHN NEWTON

◆ *Name some of the encouragements Newton sought to convey to a friend in*
this letter. What are some things you could say to friends to encourage them?

A Close Union

I am in my Father, and ye in me, and I in you.
— JOHN 14:20

A close union made between Christ and the soul is a great mystery of godliness. When God comes to forgive sin, the way God works is this: He brings a man into such a close union with His own Son so that you become one with Him; yea, to be one with Christ so that no two things in the world are joined together as you and Christ are. The soul that God pardons, He does it in this way; it is not simply that you have sinned and I will pardon you; there is no such slight business in a sinner's pardon. No, for when God forgives you, He makes you one with His own Son so that no two things in the world are as close together as you and Christ are. Therefore, the Scripture expresses it by the union of a branch and root, and the body and its members. That is a near union of flesh and bones in one body, so also the union between man and wife; but the union between Christ and a justified soul is nearer than any of these.

There is one expression in Scripture that Christ uses in John 14:20, "Ye in Me, and I in you." There are no two things so closely united. Though the members are in the body, the body is not in the members; though the branch is in the root, the root cannot be in the branch. But the union between Christ and us is Christ in us and we in Him. "He that is joined unto the Lord is one spirit" (1 Cor. 6:17). It is a spiritual union, and the union of spiritual things is the nearest that can be.

Now, blessed is the man whose sins are forgiven because, by this means, God brings the soul and Christ into such a near union that all natural unions are but dark shadows of it.

—JEREMIAH BURROUGHS

◆ *Reflect on union with Christ. If you are not in union with Christ, what does that mean?*

Looking unto Jesus

Looking unto Jesus the author and finisher of our faith;
who for the joy that was set before him endured the cross, despising
the shame, and is set down at the right hand of the throne of God.

—HEBREWS 12:2

Where are the men and women who are running the race and struggling toward the heavenly Jerusalem? Do not think that you have anything which makes your journey more difficult than others'; the saints at God's right hand were perfected through sufferings; and you must run with patience. Millions have gone safe through, and so shall you.

Beware of cumbering yourselves with any weight of earthly chances; examine your hearts closely and purge out each besetting sin with a godly, prayerful jealousy. Remember that blessed rule, "looking unto Jesus." Peter did run well for a time when he left the ship to walk upon the sea to Jesus, but when he saw the waves and storm, he was afraid and began to sink. So many a person sets out courageously, but after a while corruptions rise high within, corruptions are strong without, the eye is drawn away from Jesus, the devil gets an advantage, and the soul begins to sink.

Oh, keep your eye steadily fixed on Christ, and when you go through fire and water, they shall not hurt you. Are you tempted? Look unto Jesus. Are you afflicted? Look unto Jesus. Do all speak evil of you? Look unto Jesus. Do you feel cold, dull, backsliding? Look unto Jesus. Never say, "I will heal myself and then look unto Jesus; I will get into a good state of mind and then take comfort in my beloved." It is the very delusion of Satan. Whether you are weak or strong, in the valley or on the mount, in sickness or in health, in sorrow or in joy, in going out or in coming in, in youth or in old age, in riches or in poverty, in life or in death, let this be your motto and your guide—looking unto Jesus.

—J. C. RYLE

◆*How well are you running at present? Be encouraged to ever look to Jesus*
and tell Him all your needs.

A Contented Christian

But godliness with contentment is great gain.
—1 TIMOTHY 6:6

A contented Christian can turn himself to anything when in either want or plenty. Sadly, the children of Israel knew neither how to abound nor yet how to want. When they were in want, they murmured, "Can God prepare a table in the wilderness?" and when they ate and were filled, then they lifted up the heel. Paul, however, knew how to manage every estate; he could be either high or low; he was, in this sense a universalist—he could do anything that God would have him. If he were in prosperity, he knew how to be thankful; if in adversity, he knew how to be patient; he was neither lifted up with the one nor cast down with the other: he could carry a greater sail or lesser.

So a contented Christian knows how to turn himself to any condition. There are some who can be contented in some state but not in every state. They can be content in a wealthy state when they have the streams of milk and honey; while God's candle shines upon their head, they are content; but if the wind turn and be against them, they are discontented. While they have a silver crutch to lean on, they are content; but if God breaks this crutch, they are discontented; but Paul had learned in every estate to carry himself with calmness of mind.

A contented Christian does not try to choose his cross but leaves God to choose for him; he is content both for the kind and the duration. He lets God apply what medicine He pleases and lets it lie on as long as it will. He knows when it has finished its cure, God will take it off again. In a word, a contented Christian being sweetly captivated under the authority of God's Word desires to be wholly at God's disposal and is willing to live in that sphere and climate where God has set him.

—THOMAS WATSON

◆ *Are you learning by experience to be thankful in prosperity, patient in adversity, and hopeful for the future?*

Giving Ourselves to God

I beseech you therefore, brethren, by the mercies of God,
that ye present your bodies a living sacrifice, holy, acceptable
unto God, which is your reasonable service.

—ROMANS 12:1

If we pretend to give ourselves to God, we must give ourselves to Him entirely and wholly and heartily. God will not accept any if we keep back a part. The flesh, the world, and the devil are God's most irreconcilable enemies. There is no such thing as belonging to God and to His enemies or belonging partly to God and partly to His enemies; we cannot serve God and mammon, but we must give ourselves altogether to God or else belong altogether to His adversaries.

If we would offer ourselves to God, we must renounce the flesh: that slothfulness, that love to ease and pleasure—which makes us hard to set about religion in good earnest, which makes us hate to leave sin and to deny ourselves—must be renounced and parted with. We must give ourselves away from ourselves, and never more challenge any right to ourselves to please ourselves, other than as we please God. We must no more challenge any right to these understandings, these wills, affections, bodies, or these senses. We must look upon these as entirely belonging to God and altogether His own; and going forward we give ourselves to God. We must no more, till we die, expect to gratify any of our lusts, no more to gratify the flesh and any of its appetites, but must take our eternal leave of them.

The world must be renounced. We must take our hearts off from worldly pomp, show, or prosperity, and no more set our hearts on them, or to pride ourselves in the possession and enjoyment of them, or to be overanxious about them. World glory, worldly pleasure, and worldly riches must all be renounced at once.

We must renounce the devil and resolve no longer to serve him, as we have done in time past; no more to listen to him, however he tempts us, whatever allurements he sets before us, or whatever difficulties he presents to scare us from our duty. This is the most difficult part of this great and necessary duty of giving ourselves to God.

—JONATHAN EDWARDS

◆ *Is there any area of your life that you are holding back from wholehearted devotion to the Lord? Make it a point to renounce these things.*

Joy in Possessing Christ

I will be glad and rejoice in thee.
—PSALM 9:2

All joy apart from Christ is but the inspiration of the wind. The man who seeks the element of joy in anything apart from Christ is building upon that which has no foundation. It is a false, spurious, fatal joy; a joy which will prove but as the crackling of thorns under a pot. But, dear reader, we hope and speak better things of you. You have found Christ, or rather, Christ has found you, and you have in Him the substance, the essence, the fullness of all holy joy. You possess in Christ a divine Redeemer, a loving friend, a sympathizing brother, an ever-interceding Intercessor, and a powerful Advocate. His presence is with you always; truly this is the grounds for the deepest, holiest joy.

Friend, we realize too little and too imperfectly what we possess in possessing Christ. Throw into one scale all the good of the world—its rank, honors, wealth, pleasures; all the kindness, sympathy, and the power of the creatures and of all creatures. Place in the other scale Christ—Christ as your Savior, Christ as your friend, Christ as your portion, Christ as your all. Which sinks, and which rises? Again, cast into one scale poverty, sickness, affliction of every kind, sorrow of every form—the adversity that swept from your affluence or the grief that tore from you a loved one. Place Jesus in the other—Jesus in His ceaseless love, Jesus in His human sympathy, Jesus in His boundless fullness, Jesus in bearing you upon His heart in heaven and receiving you into His grace on earth—and then what should be the nature, the depth, the music of your joy. Be joyful, then, believer in Jesus. There breathes not a being in the universe—tried, tempted, sad though you are—who has greater reason to be joyful than you. Rejoice, then, in what Christ is in Himself, in His preciousness and fullness. Rejoice in what Christ is to you and rejoice in what you are to Christ.

—OCTAVIUS WINSLOW

◆*Meditate for a few moments on Christ. Think about what He means to you and what He has done for and in you. Does not your heart burn within you when you consider Him?*

You Are Not Your Own

And that he died for all, that they which live should not henceforth live unto themselves, but unto him which died for them, and rose again.

—2 CORINTHIANS 5:15

Our love, if it is a true love, will be sure to produce obedience, and devotedness, and submission to God's will. We should feel that our little short life may well be spent in His service and to His glory. "Ye are not your own," says the apostle. "For ye are bought with a price: therefore glorify God in your body, and in your spirit, which are God's" (1 Cor. 6:19–20). We are not sent into this world, as many seem to think, merely to eat and drink, and get our living, and pass our time as may be most pleasing to ourselves. We are sent here for a great work—to obtain salvation for our souls, to glorify our Lord, and to serve Him in our day and generation. Christ has laid down His life for us; and in return for so vast a benefit, we should give our lives to Him.

Most of us in these days are called not to any one great act of heroism or self-sacrifice; but Christ calls us to a life of active daily duty, and in such a life we may best glorify Him. But how difficult to live such a life! To carry out the humble duties of each day with cheerfulness and contentment—to keep up the warmth of our piety amid the cold and deadening cares and occupations of the world—to do everything as for God, and to have a high and holy end before us, even in our lowliest toils—this needs a faith as strong as that of a man who dies with the song of martyrdom on his lips. Truly it is a great thing to love Christ so dearly as to be ready to *die* for Him; but it is often a thing not less great to be ready to take up our daily cross and to *live* for Him.

If you are a true Christian, then, you will *love God* and *live unto Him.* And remember this—you cannot live to God in the world, unless you live much *with* Him apart from the world.

—ASHTON OXENDEN

◆ *The other side of this equation is that we must die to ourselves so that we might live more for God. In what ways do you need to die to yourself? Ask someone close to you what things need to be put to death in you?*

Living Near to God

Thou art near, O LORD.
—PSALM 119:151

Jesus Christ by His atoning blood not only brings us into reconciliation with God but also into close fellowship and communion with Him. We are no longer aliens and outcasts but are received into God's household. We become members of His family with a right to all the privileges of His children. God gives us a home and graciously says to us: "I will be your Father, and ye shall be My sons and daughters." The peace, the joy, the sweetness, the purity, and the power of every Christian depends, in a great measure, upon his or her *living near to God.*

We are too apt to think of God as dwelling at an infinite distance from us—as a Father in heaven, and not as a Father close by our side. We are surrounded by Him. God is so close to us that He is always within speaking distance. A Christian's prayer is not a message sent to a distant throne; it is his intimate prayer with one near at hand. Faith reverently and lovingly talks with God; breathes confession of sin into His ear; tells Him its secrets and bare your whole soul to Him.

In perplexity, in trouble we want a helper near at hand. Abraham Lincoln once said, "I have been driven many times to my knees by the overwhelming conviction that I had nowhere else to go. My own wisdom and that of all about me seem insufficient for that day." What this noble president often felt amid his agonizing pressures and perplexities, we have felt in life's darkest hours. The true prayer of the true Christian is a breathing of the heart's desires right into an ear that is close by. And that ear is never deaf to the prayer of faith.

—THEODORE CUYLER

◆*Recall what God says about His nearness to His people—He loves them with an everlasting love, they are seated with Him in heavenly places, risen with Christ, united to Him, etc. How does this comfort you and draw you nearer to Him?*

The Truly Blessed

Behold, that thus shall the man be blessed that feareth the LORD.
—PSALM 128:4

There are those who have found happiness and are truly blessed. These the Scripture calls blessed, and they are blessed indeed. Consider:

1. The Scripture calls them blessed that have their sins pardoned. "Blessed is he whose transgression is forgiven, whose sin is covered" (Ps. 32:1).

2. The Scripture calls them blessed who the Lord teaches the mysteries of His kingdom. "Blessed is the man whom thou…teachest him out of thy law" (Ps. 94:12).

3. The Scripture calls them blessed that wait at the door of wisdom and are made wise thereby. "Blessed is the man that heareth me, watching daily at my gates, waiting at the posts of my doors" (Prov. 8:34). "Happy is the man that findeth wisdom, and the man that getteth understanding" (3:13).

4. The Scripture calls them blessed that are of a meek, humble, and pure spirit. "Blessed are the poor in spirit…. Blessed are the meek…. Blessed are the pure in heart" (Matt. 5:3, 5, 8).

5. The Scripture calls them blessed that walk in God's ways and not in the ways of the world. Psalm 1:1–2 says, "Blessed is the man that walketh not in the counsel of the ungodly, nor standeth in the way of sinners, nor sitteth in the seat of the scornful. But his delight is in the law of the LORD; and in his law doth he meditate day and night."

6. The Scripture calls them blessed that suffer for Christ, His way, truth, and name. "Blessed are ye, when men shall revile you, and persecute you… for my sake" (Matt. 5:11).

7. The Scripture calls them blessed that consider the poor saints and people of God, who have bowels of love and compassion. "Blessed is he that considereth the poor" (Ps. 41:1).

8. The Scripture calls them blessed that die in the Lord and that are found to be faithful and wise servants when Christ comes. "Blessed are the dead which die in the Lord" (Rev. 14:13). "Blessed is that servant, whom his lord when he cometh shall find so doing" (Matt. 24:46).

—WILLIAM BRIDGE

◆*Are you blessed? If so, how can you be a blessing to others around you?*

Why God Pardons Sinners

But to him that worketh not, but believeth on him that justifieth
the ungodly, his faith is counted for righteousness.

—ROMANS 4:5

God does not pardon because a sinner has his heart changed already, but that he might be changed. And so the pardons of God differ from all other pardons. A prince pardons a criminal, or a father a child, upon what terms? A prince would expect his subject should be changed as far as he can discern, and a father (though never so tender) will not pardon a child unless he comes in and shows a change in his disobedient spirit, and then he pardons.

God does not pardon because we are changed, but that we might be changed. His pardon comes first. Romans 4:5 may encourage any poor soul, who is troubled for sin, to come and lay hold upon God's mercy in Christ. When God justifies a sinner, He looks upon him as ungodly. He does not wait until the sinner is made godly and then justifies him, as a prince waits until a criminal's heart is changed and he becomes a loyal subject and then pardons. God is not so in justifying souls. He justifies the ungodly. One who is ungodly and comes to Him, He justifies. This is a mighty argument. I say it because I would teach people that, notwithstanding any sin or guilt that lies upon their spirit, yet they have liberty to come and lay hold upon Christ for justification.

Do not say, "I am ungodly. I am a great sinner and have a wicked heart. I do not find my nature changed and, therefore, how dare I lay hold upon God's grace for mercy and pardon?" You may do just that, because God justifies the ungodly. Though your nature is not changed and sanctified, as you say, you may lay hold of God's grace for justification that you may be sanctified—not only pardoned but sanctified. Come with your heart affected by this truth, and close with the grace of God, that you may be sanctified as well as pardoned.

—JEREMIAH BURROUGHS

◆ *Why is it dangerous for a sinner to wait for change in their life before flee-*
ing to Christ? Why are we prone not to come to God unless we have cleaned
up ourselves first?

A Delightful Exercise

But thou, when thou prayest, enter into thy closet, and
when thou hast shut thy door, pray to thy Father which is in secret;
and thy Father which seeth in secret shall reward thee openly.

—MATTHEW 6:6

Prayer is like our food. The *natural* life is weak and ready to faint if we eat only a little and have no appetite; the *spiritual* life declines when we have no hearty desire to pray and are not bothered with this decay. One would say they cannot give themselves a heart to pray. No—nor can you do anything that is right. God tells us, He will fulfill the desires of them that call upon Him.

How encouraging then are the promises of Jesus! "When thou prayest, enter into thy closet, and when thou hast shut thy door, pray to thy Father which is in secret; and thy Father which seeth in secret shall reward thee openly" (Matt. 6:6). See how a blessing is pronounced on secret prayer. If they who fear the Lord talk often to one another, how much more will they delight to hold communion with their heavenly Father through the Son of His love?

Christian reader, is prayer the delightful exercise of your soul? Are your refreshments sought for, and found, at the throne of grace? Do you have access by faith in the blood of Jesus, to the Father of mercies, through the power of the Holy Ghost?

Value a throne of grace. Cherish the Spirit; prize the privilege of prayer. It is the first evidence of the beginning of a religious life, and the last act of the expiring believer. To the true believer, prayer is a precious privilege. At the mercy seat, sprinkled with the blood of Jesus, he pours out his heart, makes known his wants, and is given renewed strength to perform his duties. There he lays his burden at his Savior's feet, and there he is filled with peace and joy.

—THOMAS READE

◆ *This delightful exercise of prayer can at times become a struggle.*
Read 1 Peter 3:7. In what ways can our prayers be hindered in our
relationships or marriage?

Improving the Use of Our Tongue

*Teach me, and I will hold my tongue: and cause
me to understand wherein I have erred.*

—JOB 6:24

If you would not sin in your tongue, call to mind how you have formerly offended in your tongue, and that will make you more watchful for the future. Have not you spoken words that have savored of discontent or envy? Have not you been guilty of censuring and slandering? Have not you been disgusted with passion? Hath not your tongue outrun your discretion? Have not you spoken words that you have been sorry for afterward, and which have caused either shame or tears?

O, observe former failings, how you have sinned in your tongue, and that will be a good help for the future! David certainly made a critical observation upon some of his words, wherein he had offended—words of pride—"In my prosperity I said, I shall never be moved" (Ps. 30:6). And "I said in my haste, All men are liars" (116:11). David may have thought, "Even Samuel and all the prophets who promised me the kingdom, they are all liars; and I shall die before I can come to enjoy it." David, having observed how he had offended in his tongue, is more careful of his words and made a strict vow with himself, that he would look better to them. "I said, I will take heed to my ways, that I sin not with my tongue" (39:1).

Look to the former slips of your tongue, and how you have by your words provoked God, and that will be a good means to make you more cautious for the future. A mariner that hath touched upon a rock and been almost cast away will be more careful how he comes there again.

—THOMAS WATSON

◆ *Consider as well when someone's tongue has offended you and the sting you felt. Are you using your tongue in your relationships for building up and encouragement or for breaking down?*

Our Daily Cross

For my yoke is easy, and my burden is light.
—MATTHEW 11:30

There is often in the experience of many the burden of some heavy daily cross. A personal grief, a trial in relationships, or a family death is the weight they bear, perhaps without relief. Is it not a burden to have a wounded spirit? Is it no burden to nurse a sorrow which surpasses all human sympathy, which because of its profound depth and sacredness allows no others to share it? Is it no burden to stand up alone for Jesus and His truth in the family, with whom we have the closest bonds of nature and concerning them we must exclaim, "I am become a stranger unto my brethren, and an alien unto my mother's children" (Ps. 69:8), in whom your spiritual joy awakens no response, and your spiritual sorrow no sympathy?

But what a privilege and honor to endure reproach and separation, alienated affection, studied neglect, and relentless persecution for Christ's sake. "And on him they laid the cross, that he might bear it after Jesus" (Luke 23:26). Tried, persecuted disciple, "unto you it is given in the behalf of Christ, not only to believe on him, but also to suffer for his sake" (Phil. 1:29). Unto you Jesus has laid the burden, the sweet precious burden, of His cross, that you might bear it after Him. Did any burden speak such honor, bring such rest, secure such a crown so bright, or lead to such glory and blessedness? "Whosoever shall confess me before men, him shall the Son of man also confess before the angels of God" (Luke 12:8).

Lord, make Thyself more precious to my heart, then will Thy burden be light, Thy yoke easier, shame for Thee will be sweeter, and Thy cross, crude and heavy though it be, will become increasingly my joy, my glory, and my boast.

—OCTAVIUS WINSLOW

◆ *Why do our crosses seem too heavy to bear? How does seeing the preciousness of Christ make it more bearable?*

The Believer's Privileges

The secret of the LORD is with them that fear him;
and he will shew them his covenant.
—PSALM 25:14

The secret of the Lord is with them that fear Him. He deals familiarly with them. He calls them not servants only but friends; and He treats them as friends. He affords them more than promises; for He opens to them the plan of His great designs from everlasting to everlasting; shows them the strong foundations and inviolable securities of His favor toward them, the height, and depth, and length, and breadth of His love, which passeth knowledge, and the unsearchable riches of His grace.

He instructs them in the mysterious conduct of His providence, the reasons and ends of all His dispensations in which they are concerned; and solves a thousand hard questions to their satisfaction, which are inexplicable to the natural wisdom of man.

He teaches them likewise the beauty of His precepts, the path of their duty, and the nature of their warfare. He acquaints them with the plots of their enemies, the snares and dangers they are exposed to, and the best methods of avoiding them.

And He permits and enables them to acquaint Him with all their cares, fears, wants, and troubles, with more freedom than they can bare their hearts to their nearest earthly friends. His ear is always open to them; He is never weary of hearing their complaints and answering their petitions. The men of the world would account it a high honor and privilege to have an unrestrained liberty of access to an earthly king; but what words can express the privilege and honor of believers, who, whenever they please, have audience of the King of Kings, whose compassion, mercy, and power are, like His majesty, infinite?

—JOHN NEWTON

♦*List some of the attributes of our God. How are they encouraging to you?*
Let the meditation of His character give you much hope and comfort.

Strength for the Day

And the LORD, he it is that doth go before thee; he will be with thee,
he will not fail thee, neither forsake thee: fear not, neither be dismayed.

—DEUTERONOMY 31:8

We may be sure that our blessed Lord knew what was in man when He gave so much space in His sermon to this one tormenting sin and repeated six times over His entreaties to avoid it. Worry is not only a sin against God; it is a sin against ourselves. It sometimes amounts to a slow suicide. Thousands have shortened their lives by it, and millions have made their lives bitter by dropping this gall into their souls every day. Honest work very seldom hurts us; it is worry that kills. I have a perfect right to ask God for a strength equal to the day, but I have no right to ask Him for one extra ounce of strength for tomorrow's burden. When tomorrow comes, grace will come with it, sufficient for the tasks, the trials, or the troubles. God never built a Christian strong enough to stand the strain of present duties and all the tons of tomorrow's duties and sufferings piled upon the top of them. Paul himself would have broken down.

There is only one practical remedy for this deadly sin of anxiety, and that is to take close looks. Faith is content to live "from hand to mouth," enjoying each blessing from God as it comes. This perverse spirit of worry runs off and gathers some anticipated troubles and throws them into the cup of mercies and turns them to vinegar. My friend, if you have enough money today for your daily needs and something for God's treasury, don't torment yourself that you will get into the almshouse. If your children gather around your table, enjoy them, train them, and entrust them to God without racking yourself with a dread of them dying of some disease, or of the older ones being ill-married or causing disgrace. Faith carries present loads and meets present assaults and feeds on present promises, and commits the future to a faithful God.

—THEODORE CUYLER

◆*Can you name one day in which you turned to God and He did not sustain*
you? Look back over your life and thank God for all the ways that He has
carried you through, trusting Him for the future.

Love the Brethren

We know that we have passed from death unto life,
because we love the brethren.

—1 JOHN 3:14

Toward your fellow Christians you have a special duty. "Love the brethren" is the apostle's precept. It was said of the early Christians, even by the heathen, "See how these Christians love one another." They are God's people; they belong to Christ; and if you love *Him*, you will love *them* also. This special love toward the children of God is a mark which always belongs to His family: "We know," says the apostle, "that we have passed from death unto life, because we love the brethren" (1 John 3:14).

Learn to bear with the faults and failings of your fellow Christian. They are not perfect, they have many infirmities, and remember how great, how many, are your own. Never be jealous of them if they are preferred before you or are more noticed than yourself. When you hear a Christian brother or sister highly spoken of, it should give you real pleasure; and instead of thrusting in a word by way of lessening the praise bestowed upon them, you should rejoice that they are honored.

Again, never try to exalt yourself above others. It was the sin of Diotrephes that "he loved to have the pre-eminence." How much more Christlike it is to be willing to take the lower place and to esteem others "better than [yourself]" (Phil. 2:3), being "kindly affectioned one to another with brotherly love; in honour preferring one another" (Rom. 12:10). Show your brethren kindness for Christ's sake. Is it not written, "Whosoever shall give to drink unto one of these little ones a cup of cold water only in the name of a disciple, verily I say unto you, he shall in no wise lose his reward" (Matt. 10:42)? And again, "Let us do good unto all men, especially unto them who are of the household of faith" (Gal. 6:10).

—ASHTON OXENDEN

♦ *If you are a believer, do you think more of the family of God to which you belong or of your earthly family? Think of ways you could minister to your local church family better.*

The Providence of God

The lot is cast into the lap; but the
whole disposing thereof is of the LORD.
—PROVERBS 16:33

As Christians we must learn quietly to submit to divine providence. Do not murmur at the things that are ordered by divine wisdom. We may no more find fault with the works of providence than we may with the works of creation. It is a sin as much to quarrel with God's providence as to deny His providence. If men do not act as we would have them, they shall act as God would have them. His providence is His master wheel that turns these lesser wheels, and God will bring His glory out of all at last. "I was dumb, I opened not my mouth; because thou didst it" (Ps. 39:9). It may be that sometimes we think we could order things better if we had the government of the world in our hand; but alas! Should we be left to our own choice, we should choose those things that are hurtful for us. David earnestly desired the life of his child, which was the fruit of his sin, but had the child lived, it would have been a perpetual monument of his shame. Let us be content that God should rule the world; learn to acquiesce in His will and submit to His providence. Does any affliction befall you? Remember God sees it as that which is fit for you, or it would not come. Your clothes cannot be so fit for you as your crosses. God's providence may sometimes be secret, but it is always wise; and though we may not be silent under God's dishonor, yet we should learn to be silent under His displeasure.

You that are Christians, believe that all God's providence shall be for your good at last. The providences of God are sometimes dark, and our eyes dim, and we can hardly tell what to make of them; but when we cannot unriddle providence, let us believe that it will work together for the good of the elect (Rom. 8:28).

—THOMAS WATSON

◆ *How should we view providential crosses in our lives? Have you ever experienced that God worked those things out for your good? Share this with others, to God's glory.*

A Sign of Spiritual Life

Behold, he prayeth. —ACTS 9:11

An unhumbled heart cannot delight in prayer. A proud man may love to preach, for he is flattered by the attention of his hearers. A proud person may take pleasure in giving alms, for he thereby gains the praise of his fellow men. But a proud person cannot love prayer. For in prayer man is nothing; God is all. In prayer we are not givers but receivers; not full but empty; not as those that can do great things but as those that can do nothing but as God enables them.

Dear reader, I want you to look closely into your own heart to see how it has been with you. Think of the prayers you offered up this very morning and are going to offer up tonight. What are they? Perhaps nothing more than so many words correctly uttered by the tongue, but the heart has no part in them.

Now, if your conscience whispers to you that there has been something wrong in your prayers or that perhaps they have been no prayers at all, it is well to have made the discovery. Better it is to know that our prayers are worthless than to go on deceiving ourselves and supposing that all is right with God.

But I earnestly desire that you become from this time *a really praying person.* Until we begin to draw near to God in earnest, there can be no spiritual life in us. If the body does not breathe, we are certain that it cannot be alive. And so, too, with the soul. When it does not pray, we know that it is dead, for prayer is its very breath.

Be assured that God's people are always *a praying people.* This is one of the most certain marks by which His children may be known. One who has learned to pray as he ought has found out the secret of a godly life. We may grow rich without prayer. We may live long without prayer. We may get through the world without prayer. But never, never shall we reach heaven without it.

—ASHTON OXENDEN

◆ *What does it mean to really pray in our prayers? Can you relate to this meditation? What do you see as a solution to not simply praying and forgetting what you have prayed?*

Thy Will, Not Mine

*And Jesus said unto them, Ye shall indeed
drink of the cup that I drink of.*
—MARK 10:39

Child of suffering and of sorrow, it may *not* be the will of God that your request for your trial to pass should be granted. That cup from which you shrink is not possible to pass. You need to drink and drain it as did He, but His words shall strengthen and aid you: "Thy will, not mine be done." It is in clinging by faith through the deep waters we reach the firmest footing, and in climbing the difficult mountain we reach the highest, brightest, holiest elevation in our Christianity which is the complete absorption of our will to God's will. Great trials make great saints. The most deeply afflicted are the most deeply sanctified. It was not until our blessed Lord first pressed the cup to His lips that the conflict and the triumph of the will took place. "Let this cup pass from me.... Thy will be done" (Matt. 26:39, 42).

What a holy, practical lesson may we learn. Does Christ so sympathize with us? Does the Lord know our weak frames and remember that we are dust? Then let us go forward in perfect sympathy with Christ in everything that relates to His truth, His kingdom, and His people. He is unworthy of a love so self-sacrificing, of a sympathy so encircling, who does not feel himself one with and identifies with Christ in everything.

Embraced by such a love, let us melt into the profound realization that it was for us Christ sighed, wept, bled, and suffered; and standing before that awful scene, let us resolve that the sins which crucified Him once shall not crucify Him again. Let the death our Savior died for sins be our death unto sin, and that going forward we will be Christ's true disciples, Christ's faithful followers. You will learn, then, to sympathize with the suffering members of Christ's body. Soothed by such a sympathy as His, your own sympathy will flow forth in its tenderness toward all who through the weakness and infirmity of the flesh are shrinking from or are drinking the cup of suffering.

—OCTAVIUS WINSLOW

♦ *Think of someone near you who needs comfort. What can you do to comfort them with the comfort with which you have been comforted by God?*

The New Life

A new heart also will I give you, and a
new spirit will I put within you.
—EZEKIEL 36:26

It is to a new life that God is calling us, not to some new steps in life, some new habits or ways or motives or prospects, but to *a new life*.

To produce this new life, the eternal Son of God took flesh, died and was buried, and rose again. It was not life-producing life, a lower life rising into a higher, but life rooting itself in its opposite, life wrought out of death, by the death of "the Prince of life" (Acts 3:15). Of the new creation, as of the old, He is the author.

For the working out of this, the Holy Spirit came down in power, entering men's souls and dwelling there, that out of the old He might bring forth the new.

That which God calls new must be so. For the Bible means what it says, as being, of all books, not only the truest in thought, but the most accurate in speech. Great then and authentic must be that "new thing in the earth" (Jer. 31:22), which God creates, to which He calls us, and which He brings about by such stupendous means and at such a cost. Most hateful also must that old life of ours be to Him, when, in order to abolish it, He delivered up His Son; and most dear must we be in His sight when, in order to rescue us from the old life and make us partakers of the new, He brings forth all the divine resources of love and power and wisdom to meet the demands of a case which would otherwise have been wholly desperate.

The man from whom the old life has gone out, and into whom the new life has come, is still the same person. The same being that was once "under the law" is now "under grace" (Rom. 6:14). His features and limbs are still the same; his intellect, imagination, capacities, and responsibilities are still the same. Yet "old things are passed away; behold, all things are become new" (2 Cor. 5:17). The old man is slain; the new man lives.

—HORATIUS BONAR

◆*Do you understand the language of Romans 6? What does it mean for the believer that they are a new man, a new creature in Christ Jesus?*

The Greatest Love

*But made himself of no reputation, and took upon him the
form of a servant, and was made in the likeness of men:
And being found in fashion as a man, he humbled himself,
and became obedient unto death, even the death of the cross.*

—PHILIPPIANS 2:7–8

The true extent of a man's friendship must be measured by his deeds. Tell me not what he says and feels and wishes. Tell me not of his words. Tell me rather what he does. "Friendly is that friendly does."

The actions of the Lord Jesus Christ for man are the grand proof of His friendly feeling toward him. Never were there such acts of kindness and self-denial as those which He has performed on our behalf. He has not loved us in word only but in deed.

For our sakes He took our nature upon Him and was born of a woman. He who was very God, and equal with the Father, laid aside for a season His glory and took upon Him flesh and blood like our own. The almighty Creator of all things became a little babe like any of us, and experienced all our bodily weaknesses and infirmities, sin excepted. "Though he was rich, yet for your sakes he became poor, that ye through his poverty might be rich" (2 Cor. 8:9).

For our sakes He lived thirty-three years in this evil world, despised and rejected of men, a man of sorrows, and acquainted with grief. Though He was King of Kings, He had nowhere to lay His head. Though He was Lord of Lords, He was often weary, hungry, thirsty, and poor. He took on Him the form of a servant and humbled Himself.

For our sakes He suffered the most painful of all deaths, the death of the cross. Though innocent and without fault, He allowed Himself to be condemned and found guilty. He who was the Prince of life was led as a lamb to the slaughter, and poured out His soul unto death. He "died for us" (1 Thess. 5:10).

—J. C. RYLE

◆*Spend some time reflecting on the sacrifice Christ paid for you if you are in Him.*

Our Father's Precious Thoughts

How precious also are thy thoughts unto me, O God!
how great is the sum of them! If I should count them,
they are more in number than the sand.

—PSALM 139:17–18

God's thoughts are precious *in themselves*; they are essentially precious. They must be so, since they are a Father's thoughts. How precious are His thoughts of eternal love toward us! Is there no preciousness in this truth to your soul, dear reader? I trust the honey from the comb is not half so sweet. "I have loved thee with an everlasting love: therefore with lovingkindness have I drawn thee" (Jer. 31:3). Is there no sweetness in this truth, in comparison of which all carnal sweetness is as gall? You have tasted the gracious stream and found it sweet; but have you followed that stream to the fountain whence it flowed—the everlasting love of your covenant God—and tasted yet more sweetness there?

Be assured of this, not one drop of honey drops into your cup but it comes from the heart of God. It exudes from that Tree of Life which He planted in this sinful, sorrow-stricken world, which was scathed and wounded by His own hand of justice. "Stricken, smitten of God, and afflicted.... It pleased the LORD to bruise him; he hath put him to grief" (Isa. 53:4, 10), that through this costly, touching, winning channel, the wounds of our Immanuel might flow into our souls His everlasting thoughts of love. Then you exclaim, "Did God love me from all eternity? Did He think of me then? Was He preparing all my future happiness and eternal blessedness, treasuring up for me all grace here and all glory here after? O God, *how precious* are Thy thoughts of love to me!" Yes, they are precious, because they are God's thoughts and not man's thoughts, divine and not human, thoughts of divine love and not of anger, of peace and not of wrath.

—OCTAVIUS WINSLOW

◆ *Who can even imagine the thoughts of God toward us, let alone understand their favor of us in Christ, if He had not told us Himself? If God has these thoughts toward us, what ought our thoughts be toward Him?*

Grow in Grace

But grow in grace, and in the knowledge of our
Lord and Saviour Jesus Christ.

—2 PETER 3:18

A person may deny himself in one thing, that he may seek himself in another. I may deny myself in meats and drinks, that I may have more money; deny myself in prodigality, that I may seek covetousness. A man may deny his pride in one thing, that he may be proud in another. But the sight of a crucified Christ will teach us to deny ourselves in everything. Therefore, the apostle Paul, pressing the Philippians unto humility and self-denial, opens before them the sufferings of Christ. By your knowledge of Christ crucified, you shall grow in grace, in one grace as well as in another, growing in assurance and yet in repentance. The sight of Christ crucified is a friend unto your repentance and a friend to your assurance. Said the apostle, "Grow in grace," not in this or that grace, but grace in general. "Grow in grace, and in the knowledge of our Lord and Saviour Jesus Christ" (2 Peter 3:18), so that the knowledge of Christ crucified is how you will grow in one grace as well as another.

In this way also your hearts shall be established in opposition to all sufferings and afflictions. It will encourage you to suffer, and it will enable you to suffer. Nicodemus came by night when he first came to Christ; but after he had seen Christ upon the cross, and saw the sufferings of Christ, how boldly did he own Christ then. The sight of a suffering Christ will both encourage to suffer and enable to suffer. All our sufferings are either outward or inward; if my sufferings and afflictions are outward, the sight of a suffering Christ will make me suffer; if my afflictions are inward and spiritual, what is there that will quiet the conscience of a poor trembling soul but Christ crucified? So you shall be established in opposition to all your sufferings and afflictions, inward and outward.

—WILLIAM BRIDGE

◆ *How can you have greater views of Christ and His sufferings?*
Are you growing in grace because of this?

Cross-Bearing

And he that taketh not his cross, and
followeth after me, is not worthy of me.
—MATTHEW 10:38

We have our cross to bear, and our whole life is to be a bearing of it. It is not Christ's cross that we are to carry; that is too heavy for us and, besides, it has been done once for all. But our cross remains, and much of a Christian life consists in a true, honest, decided bearing of it. Not to be nailed to it, but to take it up and carry it—this is our calling. To each of us a cross is presented when we assume the name of Christ. Strange will it be if we refuse to bear it, counting it too heavy or too sharp, too much associated with reproach and hardship. The Lord's words are very uncompromising: "If any man will come after me, let him deny himself, and take up his cross, and follow me" (Matt. 16:24). Our refusal to do this may contribute to our ease and reputation here; but it will not add to the weight of the glory which the resurrection of the just shall bring to those who have confessed the Master and borne His shame and done His work in an evil world.

In taking up our cross *daily* (Luke 9:23), our Lord connects the denial of self and the following of Him. He "pleased not himself"; neither must we, for the servant is not above his Master. He did not His own will; neither must we, for the servant is not above his Lord. If we endure no hardness, but are self-indulgent, self-sparing people, how shall we be followers of Him? If we grudge labor, or sacrifice, or time, or money, or our good name, are we remembering His example? If we shrink from the weight of the cross, its sharpness, or the roughness of the way along which we have to carry it, are we keeping the word: "Ye shall drink indeed of my cup, and be baptized with the baptism that I am baptized with" (Matt. 20:23)?

The cross on which we are crucified with Christ, and the cross which we carry, are different things, yet they both point to one direction and lead us along one way. They both protest against sin and summon to holiness.

—HORATIUS BONAR

◆ *What cross has Christ designated for you to carry? How can you carry it well by following His example?*

APRIL

◆

*The more frequently and seriously we think on Christ crucified
and what He did leave and forsake for us, the more willing
we shall be to leave and forsake worldliness for Jesus Christ.*

—WILLIAM PLUMER

Following Christ's Example

Whosoever will come after me, let him deny himself,
and take up his cross, and follow me.

—MARK 8:34

The lesson of self-denial is a hard lesson. You know that when a child is first taught, he complains that it is hard, and for a Christian it is the same. I remember Bradford the martyr said, "Whoever has not learned the lesson of the cross has not learned his ABC in Christianity." This is where Christ begins with His scholars, and those in the lowest form must begin with this. If you desire to be Christians at all, you must submit to this or you can never be Christians. Just as no one can be a scholar unless he learns his ABC's, so you must learn the lesson of self-denial or you can never become a scholar in Christ's school and be taught the mystery of contentment.

This is the first lesson which Christ teaches any soul: self-denial, which brings contentment, which humbles a man's heart. You know how when you hit something soft, it makes no noise, but if you hit a hard thing, it makes a noise; so with the hearts of men who are full of themselves and hardened with self-love. If they receive a stroke, they make a noise, but a self-denying Christian yields to God's hand, and makes no noise.

No one ever denied himself as much as Jesus Christ did: He gave His cheeks to the smiters. He opened not His mouth. He was as a lamb when He was led to the slaughter. He made no noise in the street. He denied Himself above all and was willing to empty Himself, and so He was the most contented that ever any was in the world. The nearer we come to learning to deny ourselves as Christ did, the more contented we will be.

—JEREMIAH BURROUGHS

◆ *Why is self-denial so difficult for you? Consider the ways that God is calling you to a life of self-denial.*

Our Supreme Friend

Herein is love, not that we loved God, but that he loved us,
and sent his Son to be the propitiation for our sins.

—1 JOHN 4:10

God is a loving friend. "God is love" (1 John 4:16). He is said to have engraved us on the palms of His hands (Isa. 49:16), that we may be never out of his eye, and He carries us in His bosom (Isa. 40:11), near to His heart. There is no stop or pause in His love; but as the River Nile, it overflows all the banks. His love is far beyond our thoughts. O the infinite love of God in giving the Son of His love to be made flesh, which was more than if all the angels had been made worms! God, in giving Christ to us, gave His very heart to us; here is love drawn in all its glory and engraven as with a point of a diamond. All other love is hatred in comparison with the love of our friend.

He is a careful friend. "He careth for you" (1 Peter 5:7). He minds and transacts our business as His own. He accounts His people's interests and concerns as His interest. He provides for us grace to enable us, glory to enrich us. It was David's complaint, "No man cared for my soul" (Ps. 142:4), but a Christian has a friend that cares for him.

He is a compassionate friend. We read in Scripture of the yearnings of His bowels (Jer. 31:20). God's friendship is nothing else but compassion; for there is naturally no affection in us to desire His friendship, and no goodness in us to deserve it; the loadstone is in Himself. When we were full of sin, He was full of compassion; when we were enemies, He sent an ambassador of peace; when our hearts were turned back from God, His heart was turned toward us. O the tenderness and sympathy of our friend in heaven! We ourselves have some relentings of heart to those who are in misery, but it is God who begets all the mercies and compassions that are in us, therefore He is called "the Father of mercies" (2 Cor. 1:3).

—THOMAS WATSON

◆ *Meditate on the magnitude of God's love and compassion for sinners, and let these thoughts give you courage to press on to know the Lord more than you do.*

Praise the Lord

Let every thing that hath breath praise the LORD.
Praise ye the LORD.
—PSALM 150:6

Praise and magnify the Lord Jesus Christ for of Him and from Him and by Him and through Him and to Him are all things. Praise Him on the Sabbath, for since His resurrection it is "the Lord's day." Praise Him the whole week, for His mercies flow down continually. Praise Him at night, for His goodness runs through the day. Praise Him in the morning, for those who seek Him early shall find Him. Praise Him at midnight, for at that hour David gave thanks. Praise Him seven times a day, for every day He fills you with food and gladness. Praise Him in sickness and in health, in joy and in sorrow, in life and in death.

Crown Him with songs, for He crowns the year with His goodness. Let His praise be continually in your mouth. Praise Him even more when others maintain silence or murmur against Him and blaspheme His holy name. Let their failure to do their duty arouse you to do yours. Whoever is found among the ungodly or profane, you should rather be numbered with the grateful. Would you make your burdens light? Extol the Son of God. That night cannot be very dark in which He "giveth songs" (Job 35:10). Who would not magnify and honor such a Savior?

Saints owe Him a debt of gratitude for living, for reason, for immortality; but for His grace they owe Him a song that should never end. To say nothing against Him, at the best, evinces a very low grade of virtue. To have a disposition to praise Him and to suppress it is not enough. Let the feeling be indulged; let the song be sung; let the shout be uttered. Let all the saints cry, "Hosanna to the son of David" (Matt. 21:9). Let them laud Him saying, "Alleluia." He that has a praising heart has a continual feast. Praise Him in the highest.

—WILLIAM PLUMER

◆ *How can you be a more joy-filled Christian so that your example would be seen by those around you? Why are you often not as joyful as you are called to be?*

The Sympathy of Christ

When Jesus therefore saw her weeping, and the Jews also weeping which came with her, he groaned in the spirit, and was troubled.

—JOHN 11:33

The whole history of Jesus's life is full of unmatched examples of His heart of sympathy. Jesus's bowels were moved before His arm was exerted; He stooped to mingle tears with mourners and wept over distresses which He intended to relieve. He is still the same in His exalted state; compassions dwell within His heart. In a way inconceivable to us but consistent with His supreme dignity and perfections of happiness and glory, He still feels for His people. When Saul persecuted the members on earth, the Head complained from heaven. Sooner will the most tender mother sit insensible and inattentive to the cries and wants of her infant than the Lord Jesus be an unconcerned spectator of His suffering children. With the eye and the ear and the heart of a friend, He joins to their sorrows. He counts their sighs, puts their tears in His bottle; and when our hearts are overwhelmed within us, He knows our path and adjusts the time and measure of our trials, and everything that is necessary for our present support and suitable deliverance.

Besides His care, He has an experiential sympathy. He knows our sorrows, not merely as He knows all things but as one who has been in our situation and who, though without sin Himself, endured when on earth inexpressibly more for us than He will ever lay upon us. He has sanctified poverty, pain, disgrace, temptation, and death by passing through these states. In whatever states His people are, they may by faith have fellowship with Him in their sufferings, and He will, by sympathy and love, have fellowship and interest with them in theirs.

What then shall we fear, or of what shall we complain, when all our concerns are written upon His heart, and their management, to the very hairs of our head, is under His care and providence; when He pities us more than we can do ourselves and has engaged His almighty power to sustain and relieve us?

—JOHN NEWTON

◆*Can you empathize with others better when you have experienced the same or similar things yourself? Do you believe Christ is able and ready to do the same with you? Entrust all your cares to Him.*

The Power of the Cross

*For though he was crucified through weakness, yet he liveth
by the power of God. For we also are weak in him, but we shall
live with him by the power of God toward you.*

—2 CORINTHIANS 13:4

It is not merely that we glory in the cross, but we draw strength from it. It is the place of weakness, for there Christ was "crucified through weakness" (2 Cor. 13:4); but it is, notwithstanding, the fountain-head of power to us; for as out of death came forth life, so out of weakness came forth strength. This is strength for activity or for endurance, for holiness as well as for work. He that would be holy or useful must keep near the cross. The cross is the secret of power and the pledge of victory. With it we fight and overcome. No weapon can prosper against it, nor enemy prevail. With it we meet the fightings without as well as the fears within. With it we war the good warfare; we wrestle with principalities and powers; we "withstand" and we "stand" (Eph. 6:11–13). With it we fight the good fight; we finish the course; we keep the faith.

Standing by the cross we become imitators of the crucified One. We seek to be like Him—people who please not themselves, who do the Father's will, counting not our life dear unto us, who love our neighbors as ourselves. We love the brethren as He loved us; pray for our enemies; revile not again when reviled; threaten not when we suffer; but commit ourselves to Him that judges righteously. We live not to ourselves and die not to ourselves; are willing to be of "no reputation" but to "suffer shame for his name," to take the place of and name of "servant," and to count the reproach of Christ greater riches than the treasures in Egypt (Phil. 2:7; Acts 5:41; Heb. 11:26).

—HORATIUS BONAR

◆ *In what ways does the Christian life seem like a paradox? Do you glory in the cross? Are you carrying your cross after Christ?*

Suffering Reproach

For therefore we both labour and suffer reproach,
because we trust in the living God, who is the Saviour
of all men, specially of those that believe.

—1 TIMOTHY 4:10

Jesus Christ was content to be reproached for us; He despised the shame of the cross (Heb. 12:2). It may amaze us to think that He who was God could endure to be spat upon, to be crowned with thorns in a kind of jeer; and when He was ready to bow His head upon the cross, to have the Jews in scorn wag their heads and say, "He saved others; himself he cannot save" (Matt. 27:42). The shame of the cross was as much as the blood of the cross; His name was crucified before His body. The sharp arrows of reproach that the world did shoot at Christ went deeper into His heart than the spear. His suffering was so ignominious, that, as if it is blush to behold, the sun withdrew its bright beams and masked itself with a cloud; and well it might when the Sun of righteousness was in an eclipse. All this abuse and reproach did the God of glory endure, or rather despise, for us. Let us then be content to have our names eclipsed for Christ. Let not reproach lie at our heart, but let us bind it as a crown about our head. Alas, what is reproach? This is but a small shot; how will men stand in the mouth of the cannon?

Are not men contented to suffer reproach for maintaining their lust, and shall we not for maintaining the truth? Some glory in that which is their shame, and shall we be ashamed of that which is our glory? Be not troubled at these petty things. He whose heart is once divinely touched with the loadstone of God's Spirit will account it his honor to be dishonored for Christ and does as much despise the world's censure as their praise. Let us be contented while we are in God's scouring house to have our names sullied a little. The blacker we seem to be here, the brighter shall we shine in glory.

—THOMAS WATSON

♦*How are you bearing the reproach and shame of following Christ? Are you content knowing Christ bore the greatest shame and reproach?*

Hindrances Removed

I can do all things through Christ which strengtheneth me.
—PHILIPPIANS 4:13

From those angelic appearances at the tomb of our Redeemer on His resurrection morn, we may gather some cheering lessons. When the anxious Marys were on their way to that tomb with their spices, the thought flashed into their minds, "Who will roll away for us that rock at the sepulcher?" But the difficulty is solved in a way that they had not dreamed of. An angel from heaven had already been there and had opened the gate of rock to let the King of Glory out. So God often sends an angel of help to roll away our hindrances. Some of them are real obstacles; some of them are created by our fears. The Christian often encounters difficulties in a stubborn will or in long-formed habits or in obstinate appetites. As soon as he submits to Christ, he finds these difficulties give way; divine power achieves for him what his own unaided weakness could not accomplish.

God always has an angel of *help* for those who are willing to do their duty. How often have we been afraid to undertake some difficult work for Him, but as soon as we laid hold of it, the rock of hindrance was removed. The tempter told us that if we attempted to save some hardened soul, we should encounter an immovable obstacle. We had faith enough to try, and prayer brought the power which turned the heart of stone to flesh. Evermore the adversary is busy in frightening us from labors of love for our Master. Yet if our single aim is to reach Jesus and to honor Jesus, no hindrance is immovable.

—THEODORE CUYLER

◆ *Are there "stones" in your life that you can identify? How can these hindrances be removed?*

Our Compassionate High Priest

Wherefore in all things it behoved him to be made like unto his brethren, that he might be a merciful and faithful high priest.
—HEBREWS 2:17

C hristian, if you would disclose your sorrows to One who sorrowed as none ever sorrowed; if you would weep on the bosom of One who wept as none ever wept; if you would bear your wound to One who was wounded as none ever was wounded, then, in your affliction, turn from all creature sympathy and succor to your "merciful and faithful High Priest." He is prepared to embosom Himself in your deepest grief and to make your circumstances all His own. He *can* "be touched with the feeling of [your] infirmities" and your sorrow (Heb. 4:15). So completely, so truly is He one with you that nothing can affect you that does not instantly touch Him. Your temptation from Satan, your persecutions from man, your struggles with an evil heart, your tribulations and dangers and fears are all known to Him, and He feels for you. Tender to Him are you, as the apple of His eye. Your happiness, your peace, your necessities, your discouragements are all to Him subjects of deepest interest and of incessant care.

If only you would but lift the eye of faith, you might discover that He is with you now; and of His faithfulness that never falters, of His love that never changes, of His tenderness that never lessens, of His patience that never wearies, of His grace that never decays, you may sing in the storm-night of your grief. It is ever His delight to prove Himself the strength of your fainting heart and the support of your sinking soul, to visit you in the hour of sorrow and calamity, breathing music and diffusing calmness over your scene of sadness and gloom.

Trust in Him, and He will be with you in life, in death, and in eternity; for His word is, "Neither shall any man pluck them out of my hand" (John 10:28). "Almighty Savior, in whom all fullness dwells and who is our merciful and faithful High Priest, feeling with us in all our infirmities, we humbly beseech Thee to grant us out of Thy fullness grace sufficient for us."

—ASHTON OXENDEN

◆*Have you told the Lord all that has taken place in your life; your burdens and what gives you joy? Do you tell the Lord everything, laying it all at His feet and surrendering all, or do you hold back, thinking He will not care or understand?*

Peaceable Living

Behold, how good and how pleasant it is
for brethren to dwell together in unity!
—PSALM 133:1

Christians are under unspeakable obligations above all others to live peaceably one with another. What, shall not the children of God be at peace one with another? Shall there be contention in the family of heaven among God's dear children? God is the God of peace. Shall not we, who profess subjection to Him, be peaceable one with another?

We hope that God will be at peace with us, though we have wronged Him and dishonored Him and injured Him more than any man in the world ever did us. Shall not we, then, be at peace one with another? Christ Jesus came into the world and died to this very end, that He might make peace, not between God and us only, but between one man and another. "For he is our peace, who hath made both one, and hath broken down the middle wall of partition between us" (Eph. 2:14). The apostle here is not speaking of peace with God but of peace one with another. "So making peace; and that he might reconcile both unto God" (vv. 15–16); that is, He died to make peace between one and another, and reconciling both unto God (Col. 1:20).

Shall not we, who are the visible members of the body of this meek and peaceable Jesus, be peaceable one to another? Alas, we have enemies enough to fight with, without fighting one with another. We need to mutually assist each other against our common enemies. We are but a little handful; Christ has but a little flock; and shall His sheep devour one another?

Let us rather join our hearts and hands in worshiping our God and in serving our dear Savior, who died for the sake of peace. Let us be full of quietness and meekness. Let us bear each other's burdens and bear with each other's infirmities, and rather return good for evil. Let us do what we can to help each in duty, and not spare time to contend. Let us pray for each other and be full of benevolence, quietness, meekness, and a forgiving temper.

—JONATHAN EDWARDS

◆ *Is there anyone you are not at peace with in the family of God? What do you need to do to restore peace?*

Follow Me

Follow me. —JOHN 1:43

In what ways may we imitate and follow Christ?

1. We may imitate Him in His humility. He was lowly in Spirit. He washed His disciples' feet. What Christ taught us by washing their feet was that we should do the humblest acts of kindness to one another. We should not be proud nor above any service that will do good to others.

2. We should be like Christ in meekness. We should not be easily made angry or excited. When Jesus "was reviled, [he] reviled not again" (1 Peter 2:23). When He was smitten, He did not smite back again. When He was spit upon, He did not resent it. "When he suffered, he threatened not" (v. 23). When He was in the hands of those who mocked Him and treated Him basely, He never fell into a passion. "He was oppressed, and he was afflicted, yet he opened not his mouth: he is brought as a lamb to the slaughter, and as a sheep before her shearers is dumb, so he openeth not his mouth" (Isa. 53:7). Even when He was hanging on the cross and His enemies were shaking their heads and taunting Him, He prayed, "Father, forgive them; for they know not what they do" (Luke 23:34).

3. We may imitate Christ in His habits of devotion. Though He did not pray to be seen of men, yet He would not keep from praying for fear He should be seen of men. Having spent the day in teaching and preaching and walking over the dusty plains of Judea, He would rest at night in a fit place of prayer and spend much time in communion with God. Oh, that we had the like spirit.

4. We may be like Christ in deadness to the world. He had nowhere to lay His head. In His public life he lived very much on the charity of poor and humble people. Yet He never murmured. Oh, that all young and old ones too would follow this good example.

—WILLIAM PLUMER

♦ *Consider other ways than those mentioned in which Christ acted and spoke which you can follow.*

Encouragements for the Tempted

*For we have not an high priest which cannot be touched
with the feeling of our infirmities; but was in all points tempted
like as we are, yet without sin.*
—HEBREWS 4:15

Many a tempted believer has been greatly exercised with this thought, "Can I be a child of God, since Satan tries me so much?" Let me tell you a few things for your comfort:

1. God's children are *the very persons* whom Satan especially attacks. And perhaps it is because you *are* a child of God that he so tries you.

2. There is a great difference between *being tempted* and *yielding to temptation*. Our Lord nowhere says, "Be not tempted," but He does say, "Enter not into temptation" (Matt. 26:41). This one is our *sin*; the other is our *trial*. It is a sin to welcome the tempter; but it is not sin to be tried by him.

3. If temptation is permitted to reach you, *it is for your good*. Temptation is to faith what fire is to gold. The furnace not only discovers the true gold from the false, but it also makes the true gold purer. It becomes perhaps less in bulk, because everything worthless has been severed from it, but more in value. May your faith grow brighter and stronger by the trial! And "being much more precious than of gold that perisheth, though it be tried with fire," may it be "found unto praise and honour and glory at the appearing of Jesus Christ" (1 Peter 1:7).

Be cheered and encouraged. You have a Savior; and He knows well what temptation is; and He can and does feel for His tempted people. "We have not an high priest which cannot be touched with the feeling of our infirmities; but was in all points tempted like as we are, yet without sin" (Heb. 4:15). Satan may lay his snares for you; but there is an almighty One near who is watching over you and who can shield you from all evil. The struggle may be severe and long. But if the Lord is on your side, you need not fear; victory will be surely yours, for it is written, "The God of peace shall bruise Satan under your feet shortly" (Rom. 16:20).

—ASHTON OXENDEN

◆ *Sometimes speaking to others about our temptations provides us with
courage to fight against them even more. Speak with someone about the
temptations that you face and how you can pray for one another.*

Knowing Christ Crucified

But God forbid that I should glory,
save in the cross of our Lord Jesus Christ, by whom the
world is crucified unto me, and I unto the world.

—GALATIANS 6:14

The knowledge of Christ brings one into the possession of Christ; thereby you will be furnished and prepared for every good word and work. For what is the death and suffering of Christ but the shop of virtues? Do you want faith? Christ crucified is the object of your faith, and the cause of it. Are you full of fears? Are you afraid because of the law and the avenger of blood that is following you at your heels? Look upon Christ crucified, and there you see the city of refuge. Are you impatient and forward? The sight of a patient Christ will make you patient. Are you proud? The sight of a humble Christ, a crucified Christ, will make you humble. Though a man be proud of this or that good thing, yet if he sees Christ crucified, he will there be told that Christ has paid for all; and this will bring down his pride. Do you complain of a hard heart? The sight of a broken Christ will break your heart, or nothing will. The knowledge of Christ crucified is what will furnish you and prepare you to every good word and work. And therefore, O friends, who would not labor to know Christ crucified!

This knowledge is soul-humbling knowledge. Other knowledge puffs up; but if you know Christ crucified, you may glory in your knowledge without pride. "Let not the wise man glory in his wisdom, neither let the mighty man glory in his might, let not the rich man glory in his riches" (Jer. 9:23). If I glory in my wisdom, I am proud; if I glory in my strength, I am proud; but if I glory in that I know Christ crucified, the more I glory in that, the humbler I am. That is a soul-humbling knowledge. Therefore, I say what a blessed thing it is to know Christ crucified.

—WILLIAM BRIDGE

◆*Consider what you know about Christ, and share with others how knowing this makes you more prepared for every good work.*

The Fruit of Afflictions

*Who comforteth us in all our tribulation, that we
may be able to comfort them which are in any trouble,
by the comfort wherewith we ourselves are comforted of God.*
—2 CORINTHIANS 1:4

Afflictions are designed for the manifestation of our genuineness to ourselves and others. When faith endures the fire, we know it is the right kind; and others, who see us brought out safely and losing nothing but the dross, will confess that God is with us (Dan. 3:27–28). This thought should resolve us to suffer, not only with patience but with cheerfulness, if God may be glorified in us. This made the apostle rejoice in tribulation, that the power of Christ might be noticed as resting upon him and working mightily in him.

Many of our graces likewise cannot thrive or show themselves to grow without trials; such as resignation, patience, meekness, long-suffering. I have seen porters who do not appear very strong, and yet they trudge along under a heavy burden which another could not carry so well. The reason is that they are accustomed to carrying burdens and by continual exercise their shoulders acquire a strength suited to their work. In the Christian life, activity and strength of grace are not ordinarily required by those who sit still and live at ease, but by those who frequently meet with something which requires a full exertion of what power the Lord has given them. It is by our own sufferings we learn to pity and sympathize with others in their sufferings: such a compassionate disposition, which stirs our feelings for the afflicted, is an eminent branch of the mind which was in Christ. But these feelings would be very faint if we did not in our experience know what sorrows and temptations mean.

Afflictions, lastly, do us good as they make us more aware of what is in our own hearts, and so promote humiliation and self-abasement. There are abominations which, like nests of vipers, lie so quietly within, that we hardly suspect they are there till the rod of affliction rouses them; then they hiss and show their venom. This discovery is very distressing; yet, till it is made, we are prone to think ourselves much less vile than we really are.

—JOHN NEWTON

◆*Share some of the blessed fruits you have seen in yourself or others that
have grown because of afflictions.*

The Just for the Unjust

*For Christ also hath once suffered for sins, the just
for the unjust, that he might bring us to God, being put
to death in the flesh, but quickened by the Spirit.*

—1 PETER 3:18

How then is the Christian justified? What is the secret of that peace and sense of pardon which he enjoys? How can we understand a holy God dealing with a sinful man as with an innocent one, and counting him righteous in spite of his many sins?

Christ has *stood in the place* of the Christian. He has become his surety and substitute. He has borne all that was laid upon Him to bear. Hence the Christian is a justified man.

Christ has *suffered for sins,* the just for the unjust. He has endured our punishment in His own body on the cross. He has allowed the wrath of God, which we deserved, to fall on His own head.

Christ has *paid the debt* the Christian owed, by His own blood. He suffered in their place and paid it to the uttermost farthing by His own precious death. God is a just God and will not require His debts to be paid twice over.

Christ has *obeyed the law* of God perfectly. The prince of this world could find no fault in Him. By so fulfilling it He brought in an everlasting righteousness, in which all His people are clothed in the sight of God.

Christ in one word has lived for the Christian. Christ has died for him. Christ has gone into the grave for him. Christ has risen again for him. Christ has ascended up on high for him and gone into heaven to intercede for his soul. Christ has done all, paid all, suffered all that was needful for his redemption. Hence arises the Christian's justification—hence his peace. In himself there is nothing, but in Christ he has all things that his soul can require.

—J. C. RYLE

◆ *Believer, what does it mean to you that you are united to Christ by faith?*

The Heart of God

Casting all your care upon him; for he careth for you.
—1 PETER 5:7

The Lord cares for you! Little, obscure, despised, unworthy though you may be or deem yourself to be, the Lord has an interest in you, the nearest and tenderest that ever dwelt in a heart of love. Bought with the Savior's blood, a temple of the Holy Ghost, sealed with the earnest of the Spirit as a child of God and an heir of glory, there is not an angel in heaven who God cares for as He cares for you. Will you not respond to this care by casting all your care on Him in the exercise of a humble, unquestioning faith?

The heart of God, from which all other hearts kindle their affection, interlaces you with its thoughts, its sympathies, its love; and the eye that searches the universe with a glance gives you its never-ending look of love. When my father and my mother forsake me, when human love departs from its most sacred home on earth, then the Lord will take me up. The emptiness of widowhood shall claim His pity, the aloneness of being orphaned shall receive His protection, the suffering of sickness will be upheld by His grace, the grief of death shall be soothed by His love, and the valley of death shall be brightened with His radiant presence.

Confide in and lean on this divine, human, precious, ever-present Savior. He desires your infinite confidence and warmest love. He is most worthy of it. Will you withhold it? Take that anxious care which lies like lead upon your breast, and chases peace from your mind, joy from your heart, and slumber from your pillow, and lay it upon the heart pierced by the soldier's lance—the One who gave His last drop of life-blood on the tree—and peace shall enfold you beneath its balmy wing. "Be careful for nothing; but in every thing by prayer and supplication with thanksgiving let your requests be made known unto God. And the peace of God, which passeth all understanding, shall keep your hearts and minds through Christ Jesus" (Phil. 4:6–7).

—OCTAVIUS WINSLOW

◆*Are you casting every care on Jesus? What cares do you carry yourself, and why? Surrender them all to Him.*

God, the Hearer of Prayer

Let us therefore come boldly unto the throne of grace, that
we may obtain mercy, and find grace to help in time of need.

—HEBREWS 4:16

Nothing gives us such a blessed assurance in prayer as the feeling that we are drawing near to One who is our *Father*, and that if we approach Him in the name of Christ, we are always welcome. Have you never observed the knock of a stranger at your door? He comes with a low, timid, hesitating rap, which seems to say, "I have no claim on the kindness of this house; I may be told I come too often; I may be sent away, as a troublesome petitioner." But how different is the bold knock of a child on his return from school, as he rushes joyously into his father's presence, throws his arms about his neck, and reminds him of some promised favor.

But does God really hear *me* when I kneel down and pray to Him? I know that He is the almighty governor of the world. He sits upon His throne ordering everything in heaven and earth. He looks down on the kingdoms of this world and makes them great or brings them low according to His own will. He refreshes the earth with rain or withholds the fruitful showers as He sees best. But is it likely that so great a Being should care about *my* little wants, and concern Himself about *my* trifling affairs? He may care about kings and nobles, He may take an interest in nations and countries, but surely *my* concerns, the wants and happiness of one so insignificant as I am, must be beneath His notice.

This may be a wonder to many of us, because we cannot help judging God as we do men. A man often will not take the trouble to busy himself about the little affairs of others. But it is not so with God. The very poorest and humblest has not a single want that is beneath His notice. Our Lord Himself assures us that not even a sparrow, which we count so worthless, falls to the ground without our heavenly Father's knowledge and permission.

—ASHTON OXENDEN

◆*In what ways have you seen God's care for you? Does His welcoming char-*
acter encourage you in prayer?

A Heart for the Unsaved

*That utterance may be given unto me, that I may open my
mouth boldly, to make known the mystery of the gospel.*
—EPHESIANS 6:19

The gospel is good news to poor sinners, the proclamation of a full and free forgiveness of all sin through faith in a crucified Redeemer. The gospel is the most glorious revelation of God to man, the brightest display of His justice, holiness, and love. Here we see the love of the Father, Son, and Holy Ghost planning, executing, and applying the gracious work of human redemption.

How transforming are the doctrines of grace when applied by faith through the power of the Holy Ghost. They remove the burden of sin by revealing a sin-bearing Savior; they strip man of his boasted superiority by laying him low at the foot of the cross; they change him into the image of Jesus by shedding abroad the love of God in his heart; they destroy the weeds of selfishness and strife by sowing the gracious seeds of unity, peace, and harmony. The wilderness becomes the garden of the Lord; the desert rejoices and blossoms as the rose.

Have you seen that the Lord is gracious? Can you from the heart bless God for His unspeakable gift? Do you know anything of the joy, which is unspeakable, of the peace which passes understanding, of the love of Christ which passes knowledge?

Knowing where the root of all his privileges and comforts lay, the heart of Paul glowed with delight in making known to others these unspeakable riches of Christ. By blessed experience he had learned that where sin abounded, grace did much more abound; that as sin reigned unto death so now grace reigns through righteousness unto eternal life by Jesus Christ our Lord. Therefore, he could tell every weeping penitent these glad tidings of great joy, that Jesus is able to save to the uttermost all that come unto God.

—THOMAS READE

◆ *Share with others what great things God has done for you. Resolve in
your heart to speak with an unbeliever in the coming days about the
riches of Christ.*

The Servant of All

But he that is greatest among you shall be your servant.
—MATTHEW 23:11

There is one character in which Christians too seldom think of their divine Redeemer. It is that of a servant, ever serving our highest interest. We call ourselves Christ's servants. Do we constantly think of Him as ours?

At the last supper, we read that Jesus rose from the table and laid aside His robe. He takes a towel and girds Himself after the manner of an attendant in a guest chamber. Pouring water into a basin, He washes the disciples' feet and wipes them with the towel with which He was girded. After the surprising act of self-humiliation is over, He says to them, "Know ye what I have done to you? Ye call me Master and Lord: and ye say well; for so I am. If I then, your Lord and Master, have washed your feet; ye also ought to wash one another's feet. For I have given you an example, that ye should do as I have done to you" (John 13:12–15).

Then He tells His disciples what the rulers of the Gentiles desire—to lord over others. But His disciples were to aim at a nobler rule—the rule of love and devotion to the needs of others. "And whosoever of you will be the chiefest, shall be *servant of all*" (Mark 10:44).

Look, my friend, over the earthly life of our blessed Lord, and you will find in it a beautiful illustration of the truth that the highest post of honor is the lowliest post of service. Every word, every deed is inspired by love. He condescends to teach the most ignorant, for they have the deepest need of light; to feed the hungry and poor out of His miraculous basket; to sit at meat with despised publicans; to heal wayside beggars and outcast lepers, the children of the poor, heartbroken mothers, and the servants in the noblemen's kitchens. And so, all through those three years' pilgrimage of love—instructing the ignorant, comforting the afflicted, pardoning the guilty, healing the sick, stooping to wash disciples' feet and to cleanse their more polluted hearts—Jesus is everywhere the "servant of all."

—THEODORE CUYLER

◆*In what ways can you better serve others in love? How is Christ serving you?*

Being Willing to Suffer

In nothing I shall be ashamed, but that with all boldness,
as always, so now also Christ shall be magnified in my body,
whether it be by life, or by death.

—PHILIPPIANS 1:20

The more frequently and seriously we think on Christ crucified and what He did leave and forsake for us, the more willing we shall be to leave and forsake worldliness for Jesus Christ. If Christ did leave His heaven for me, should I not leave my earth for Him? Should Jesus Christ leave the bosom of His Father and that sweet relation for me, and shall I not leave the bosom of my relation for Him? Shall Jesus Christ suffer for me a cursed death, and shall I not be willing to suffer a blessed death for Him? Christ suffered a cursed death for us, and our death is made blessed by the death of Christ. Think much of what Christ left for you, and then you will be more willing to forsake any worldly interest for Him.

Whatsoever you do now in a way of service, do it because your Father wills it. If you serve God now because your Father wills it, then when you come to suffer, you will willingly suffer because your Father wills it.

If you would be willing to suffer for the name of Christ, then go to God in prayer, and pray for boldness; and go to your friends, and beg them to pray for you. I remember when Latimer was to suffer, he called upon his friends, "Pray friends; pray for me; for sometimes though I am as bold as a lion, yet at another time I am so afraid, as I could run into a mouse-hole." Therefore say, "Come, my friends, I have a cowardly heart of my own and am unwilling to suffer for the name of Christ; pray for me." Therefore, if you are afraid to suffer for the name of Christ, get together, and in the midst of your petitions pray, "O Lord, give us boldness."

—WILLIAM BRIDGE

◆ *How will learning to rest on Christ now in our small afflictions train us to be faithful when big ones come on us? What does it mean that God gives grace according to the need?*

Saints of God Persevere

Will ye also go away? —JOHN 6:67

In all times of temptation, in all times of trial, in all times of error, in all times of adversity, in all times of creaturely, worldly, sinful allurement, may the tender, touching, melting words of Jesus penetrate our innermost soul: "Will ye also go away?" (John 6:67). Whatever happens, forsake not Christ. Walk so near to Him that you may feel He is at your side in every path and circumstance of life; lean on Him so confidently that you may find yourself, with the disciple whom Jesus loved, reclining upon the very bosom of your Lord. Let your everyday life be a constant going to, rather than a going from, Jesus. Be humbled and mourn that you ever forsook, distrusted, wounded, and grieved Him. Times without number we have done this. Alas, our Christian profession of Christ has been checkered and uneven. Declension and revival, relapse and recovery, backsliding and restoring have made up so much of our spiritual history; who would or could have borne with us as Jesus has? We have never forsaken Him and returned—throwing ourselves at His feet deploring, confessing, bemoaning the sinfulness of our ingratitude, forsaking, and distrusting—but He has graciously received us, gently raised us to His bosom, and lovingly and freely forgiven all our sins.

How touching, then, is the sympathy of Christ with the difficulties, temptations, and progress of our Christian perseverance. "Will ye also go away?" He could not endure the thought that among the many who went away and walked not with Him, any of His own true disciples should prove cold, false, and apostate. With what power and tenderness must this appeal to their affection, fidelity, and love have pierced their hearts.

Let us then endure all self-denial, hardship, scorn, persecution, or loss, even death itself, rather than deny the Lord Jesus, crucifying Him afresh, and putting Him to an open shame by turning from our solemn profession of faith and love.

—OCTAVIUS WINSLOW

◆*Has Christ ever forsaken you? How then can we forsake Him? Renew your devotion and commitment to Him in prayer, asking also for daily grace to be faithful.*

Keep the Conscience Clean

And herein do I exercise myself, to have always a conscience
void of offence toward God, and toward men.

—ACTS 24:16

When you first saw the *cross* and understood the meaning of the *blood*, you got your conscience purged "from dead works" (Heb. 9:14); and it was this cleansing of the conscience that gave you peace. It was not that you ceased to be a sinner or lost the consciousness of being one, but you had found something which pacified your conscience in a righteous way, and made you feel toward the law and the Lawgiver just as if you had never been guilty.

It is by keeping constantly before your eyes this blood of propitiation that you will keep your conscience clean and your soul at peace. It is this blood alone that can wipe off the continual sins that are coming across your conscience and which, if not wiped off immediately, will effectually stain it and influence your peace. You know how the steel of the best sword may be rusted by a drop of water. Yet if the water is not allowed to remain but is immediately wiped away, it harms not the steel, and no rust develops. If, however, through neglect or otherwise, the water remains, rust will follow, destroying both the edge and brightness of the weapon. So it is with sin. The moment it falls upon the conscience, the blood must be applied; else dimness and doubting will be the consequence. Remember it is the blood—the blood alone—that can remove these.

If, when you sin, you do not go at once to this and be washed and pardoned, but go to anything else first, you will only make bad worse. Keep, then, the conscience clean by continual application to the blood; and you will find that this, instead of encouraging you to sin, will make you more ashamed and afraid of it.

—HORATIUS BONAR

◆ *Is there anything that you need to confess to God? Peace and a clean conscience are desirable things.*

Faith Sees Christ

Unto you therefore which believe he is precious.

—1 PETER 2:7

He who believes will be saved from the guilt of sin. He takes Christ as his bleeding Lamb, as his great sacrifice for sin and as his surety to answer for him before God. He will also be saved from the power of sin. Faith crucifies the flesh with its affections and lusts. Every day it puts sin to death. And he will be saved from misery. It is only by faith that we will have rest. Death will not have power to destroy one who relies on Jesus. He that believes will never die—never die as the wicked die. To him death has no sting. Over him the grave gains no victory. Heaven is his house not made with hands.

The reason of all this is that "a man"—the man Christ Jesus—is to everyone that believes in Him "as an hiding place from the wind, and a covert from the tempest; as rivers of water in a dry place, as the shadow of a great rock in a weary land" (Isa. 32:2). The fact is that to the child of God Christ is everything. He is all and in all. His blood is the fountain where the soul washes and is clean. He is the chief cornerstone on which all good hope for eternity is built.

From this time forward let Him be all your desire and all your salvation. If Satan tempts you to forsake Christ, cling to Him more closely than ever. If ungodly men laugh at you, remember there is a day coming when God will hold them in derision. Fight on. Fight bravely. Be strong in the Lord. Earnestly ask God to increase your faith. Even a weak faith shall save the soul; but the stronger faith is the better.

—WILLIAM PLUMER

◆*What is it about Christ that makes Him everything to you?*

Three Persevering Graces

By whom also we have access by faith into this grace
wherein we stand, and rejoice in hope of the glory of God.
—ROMANS 5:2

What means can we use that we may not wax weary in the Christian course? Let us shake off spiritual sloth which says, "There is a lion in the way" (Prov. 26:13). He who is slothful will soon grow weary; he is fitter to lie on his couch than to run a race. It is a strange sight to see a busy devil and an idle Christian.

If we would not grow weary, let us pray for persevering grace. It was David's prayer, "Hold thou me up, and I shall be safe" (Ps. 119:117). And it was Beza's prayer, "Lord, perfect what thou hast begun in me." That we may hold a Christian course, let us labor for three persevering graces.

Faith keeps from fainting. Faith gives substance to things not seen, makes them to be as it were present (Heb. 11). As a binocular makes those things which are at a distance near to the eye, so does faith; heaven and glory seem near. A Christian will not be weary of service that has the crown in his eye.

Hope animates the spirit; it is to the soul as cork to the net that keeps it from sinking. Hope breeds patience, and patience breeds perseverance. Hope is compared to an anchor (Heb. 6:19). The Christian never sinks except when he casts away his anchor.

The third persevering grace is *love*. Love prevents a man from becoming weary. Love may be compared to the rod of myrtle in the traveler's hand, which refreshes him and keeps him from being weary in his journey. He who loves the world is never weary of following the world. He who loves God will never be weary of serving Him; that is the reason why the saints and angels in heaven are never weary of praising and worshiping God; because their love to God is perfect and love turns service into delight. Get the love of God in your hearts, and you will run in His ways and not be weary.

—THOMAS WATSON

◆ *With which of these three graces are you most acquainted? How can you grow in the others?*

The Doctrine of the Cross

For the preaching of the cross is to them that perish foolishness;
but unto us which are saved it is the power of God.

—1 CORINTHIANS 1:18

Contemplate the wonders which happened at the cross of thine Emmanuel. A dying thief was saved; the sun was darkened; the earth did quake; the graves were opened; the bodies of the saints which slept arose; the veil of the temple was rent in twain; the kingdom of heaven was opened to all believers. When Jesus said, "It is finished," and bowed His head and died, the law was magnified, justice was satisfied, all heaven rejoiced, and hell trembled to its core.

While in the carnal state, *self* is the pivot on which the sinner moves; and the circle which he draws as his own is formed by selfish motives, selfish principles, and selfish aims. But when the Spirit, by an act of grace, places him upon Christ as *center*, how wonderful the change. On every side he sees nothing but infinite purity and unbounded glory. All the powers of his soul are absorbed in the greatness and grandeur of redeeming love. Self is abased and subdued. Christ is exalted and glorified. Pride is nailed to the cross; and humility clothes his spirit with the beauties of holiness. The sinner now lays down the weapons of his rebellion. Through faith in the blood of Jesus, he obtains pardon and peace. The stormy conscience is quieted. The rugged disposition is made smooth. And heaven, in all its foretastes of joy and purity, is brought down into the soul.

Can you meditate on your crucified, glorified Redeemer and not feel the deepest sorrow mingled with the greatest joy? Sorrow at the remembrance of your sins, which were the very nails that wounded, the very spear that pierced His spotless soul; joy at the assurance that He died for you, that He loved you, that He gave Himself for you notwithstanding your vile ingratitude and unbelief. Hasten to His cross, cast yourself at His feet; pour out your heart before Him; tell Him all your wants.

—THOMAS READE

◆*What a Savior! Do you not have reason to rejoice and worship Him?*
Meditate on this Savior and the sacrifice He made for sinners like you,
and resolve to serve Him more earnestly.

True Love

Marriage is honourable in all. —HEBREWS 13:4

There are many good husbands and many good wives. They fear God. They study His law. They keep His commandments. They look to Jesus. They love prayer. They love the house of God. They love one another. They honestly do their duty. They are happy in each other. They delight in serving each other. If they have good health, they give their strength to God. If one is sick, the other watches and mourns. Each wishes the other to enjoy as much as possible. If they have children, they are a joint care. In company they are not unkind to each other, and in private they are full of tenderness. When one dies, the other mourns sore like the dove and feels that a lasting wound is made. If they have lived together long, the death of one is often soon followed by the death of the other. Surviving relatives cherish their memories, rise up, and call them blessed. They may have been poor, but they have left a rich legacy to their heirs. Such a union between them was blessed indeed. Marriage is honorable in all.

—WILLIAM PLUMER

How blest the sacred tie that binds,
In union sweet according minds;
How swift the heavenly course
   they run,
Whose hearts, whose faith, whose
   hopes are one.

To each the soul of each, how dear!
What jealous love, what holy fear!
How doth the generous flame within
Refine from earth, and cleanse from sin!

Their streaming tears together flow
For human guilt and mortal woe;

Their ardent prayers together rise
Like mingling flames in sacrifice.

Together both they seek the place
Where God reveals His awful face;
How high, how strong their raptures
   swell,
There's none but kindred souls can tell.

Nor shall the glowing flame expire,
When nature droops her sickening fire;
Then shall they meet in realms above,
A heaven of joy, a heaven of love.

—BARBAULD

♦ *In what ways can you be thankful that the Lord has given you to be an example to others in marriage, and in what ways can you still improve?*

Willing to Suffer

But rejoice, inasmuch as ye are partakers of Christ's sufferings; that, when his glory shall be revealed, ye may be glad also with exceeding joy.

—1 PETER 4:13

All the virtue of a medicine is in the application. If we apply this to the blood of Christ, though the medicine be made of the blood of God, it will not heal unless applied by faith. As fire is to the chemist, so is faith to the Christian; the chemist can do nothing without fire, so there is nothing done without faith. Faith makes Christ's sacrifice ours. It is not gold in the mine that enriches but gold in the hand. Faith is in the hand that receives Christ's golden merits. It is not a cordial in the glass that refreshes the spirit, but a cordial drunk down. Without faith, Christ Himself will not avail us.

Let us love this bleeding Savior, and let us show our love to Christ by being ready to suffer for Him. Many rejoice at Christ's suffering for them but dream not of their suffering for Him. Joseph dreamed of his preferment, but not of his imprisonment. Was Christ a sacrifice? Did He bear God's wrath for us? We should bear man's wrath for Him. Christ's death was voluntary. "Lo, I come...to do thy will, O God" (Heb. 10:7). "I have a baptism to be baptized with; and how am I straitened till it be accomplished!" (Luke 12:50). Christ calls His sufferings a baptism; He was to be (as it were) baptized in His own blood; and how He did thirst for that time! "I am straitened."

Let us be willing to suffer for Christ. Christ has taken the venom and sting of the saints' sufferings; there is no wrath in their cup. Our sufferings Christ can make sweet. As there was oil mixed in the peace offering, so God can mix the oil of gladness with our sufferings. "The ringing of my chain is sweet music to my ears," said a martyr. Life must be parted with shortly; what if it is a little sooner, as a sacrifice to Christ, as a seal of sincerity, and a pledge of thankfulness!

—THOMAS WATSON

♦*How do you understand the connect between our suffering for Christ and our faith?*

Words of Wisdom

Incline thine ear unto wisdom, and apply thine heart to understanding.
—PROVERBS 2:2

If you fear the Lord and keep His commandments, you shall have the comfort of His promises. Be sure also that you give your first and best unto God, for God is the first and best of beings, and if you "honour the LORD with thy substance, and with the firstfruits of all thine increase: so shall thy barns be filled with plenty, and thy presses shall burst out with new wine" (Prov. 3:9–10). And why should you not give the first of your time and the best of your all unto God who has given His best and only Son to you?

If you serve God while you are young, God will bless you when you are old. And if you come unto Him when you are young, you may know that He will not forsake you when you are old.

Let your company be good, for every man is as the company of his choice is. Solomon said, "Remember now thy Creator in the days of thy youth" (Eccl. 12:1), which in the Hebrew is the days of choice or choices, because in the days of youth a man makes choice of trade or calling, he makes a choice of religion, of a wife, and of his company; be careful of these choices.

Let your conversation be always seasoned with salt, for "by thy words thou shalt be justified, and by thy words thou shalt be condemned" (Matt. 12:37), says our Savior; for words are the index of the mind.

As for the world and the things of it, though you may pray for much, yet you must be content with little. The way to have a mercy or blessing is to be content to go without it.

Of all books, study the Bible. Of all duties, be much in prayer. Of all graces, exercise faith. Of all days, observe the Lord's day. And of all things in heaven and earth, be sure that you get an interest in God by Jesus Christ.
—WILLIAM BRIDGE

◆*Knowledge of the truth is not enough; we need wisdom. Wisdom is knowledge put to good use. As you hear the words of wisdom, especially from Proverbs, how can you put these to practical and good use?*

Rejoice in the Lord

I will greatly rejoice in the LORD, my soul shall be joyful in my God; for he hath clothed me with the garments of salvation, he hath covered me with the robe of righteousness, as a bridegroom decketh himself with ornaments, and as a bride adorneth herself with her jewels.

—ISAIAH 61:10

How much more joyful would the saints of God be if they dealt less with themselves and more with Jesus! They look at their sins, pore over their unfitness, pine at their leanness, and succumb to their failures and infirmities, their poverty and emptiness, and so all sweet, sacred joy droops and dies within their souls. But "the joy of the LORD is your strength" (Neh. 8:10). "The meek also shall increase their joy in the LORD" (Isa. 29:19). And seeing that the Lord has "clothed [them] with the garments of salvation" and "hath covered [them] with the robe of righteousness," it is the privilege of their soul to "greatly rejoice in the LORD" and "be joyful in my God" (Isa. 61:10).

But, beloved, remember that Christ's joy can only remain in you, and your joy be full, as in childlike faith you look directly and only and constantly to Christ. "We also joy in God through our Lord Jesus Christ, by whom we have now received the atonement" (Rom. 5:11). Oh, for a higher amount of holy joy among the Lord's redeemed. Who in this vast universe have more reason to make the valley resound and the mountain echo with the glad notes of praise, as you who are freed from servitude, who are delivered from hell, and who are on your way to heaven to spend your eternity forever with the Lord?

Beloved reader, if you are saved, if in the exercise of the lowliest faith you can cherish the hope of acceptance as a poor sinner with God through Christ, you may rejoice in tribulation and glory in infirmity and count the sufferings of this present time not worthy to be compared with the glory that will be revealed in you. "Rejoice in the Lord always: and again I say, Rejoice" (Phil. 4:4).

—OCTAVIUS WINSLOW

◆ *How does looking at ourselves discourage us but looking at Christ encourage us?*

Continue Steadfastly

Therefore, my beloved brethren, be ye stedfast, unmoveable.
—1 CORINTHIANS 15:58

We depart from Christ when we fall into sin, especially when we sin against our own consciences. In doing so we turn our backs on the blessed Jesus and hearken to His enemy. Will you sinfully, basely, and ungratefully leave Christ for the sake of other things? Will you leave Him who has the words of eternal life for the sake of the world, vanities, and trifles? Will you leave Him who died for you for the sake of wicked examples and for fear of the loss of your credit and reputation? Will you leave Him who wrought so hard for you that He even sweat drops of blood? Will you not deny yourself for Him and take upon you His easy yoke and His light burden, who bore the heavy burden of God's wrath for you? Can't you kill your lusts for His sake, who Himself was killed for you?

Consider how constant and steady Christ was for you in the midst of all those great temptations with which He was assaulted. If He had not continued constant in resisting them, you would have perished without hope or remedy.

What would have become of you to all eternity, if Christ, when He came to look death in the face and saw that He was condemned and must be crucified, had repented that He had undertaken your salvation? He might easily have avoided His crucifixion, but He loved you constantly, steadily, and to the end. He patiently bore His agonies—the derision of men, the crown of thorns, the scourging—patiently bore His heavy cross, and patiently was nailed to it and died upon it.

But if you will not continue steadfast to your Redeemer for His sake, do it for your own; for He has not the benefit of it, but you do. For if you leave Christ, whither will you go? By departing from Him, you foolishly cast yourself off from a sure and safe rock into the tempestuous and boisterous sea. Wherefore, be persuaded to continue steadfast to Him, and do not depart from Him.

—JONATHAN EDWARDS

◆*Believer, meditate on the sufferings of Christ which He endured in order to give you life and demonstrate His love for you.*

Take Up Your Cross

Whosoever doth not bear his cross, and
come after me, cannot be my disciple.
—LUKE 14:27

Christians have one mark more peculiar than any others; they are all cross-bearers. This is the unfailing token by which each member may be recognized. They all bear a cross. Nor do they hide it as if ashamed of it. They make it their boast. "God forbid that I should glory, save in the cross of our Lord Jesus Christ, by whom the world is crucified unto me, and I unto the world" (Gal. 6:14). Sometimes it is lighter and sometimes it is heavier; sometimes it has more of shame and suffering, and sometimes less, but still it is upon them. They carry it with them wherever they go. And it is always a cross; not merely so in name, but in reality, a token of reproach and sorrow. Sometimes they are represented as carrying it, and sometimes as being nailed to it, but it is still the cross.

They took it up when they first believed in Jesus and owned Him as their all. Then it was that they forsook the world and went out the gate, bearing the reproach of the crucified One. He whom they follow both bore the cross and was nailed to it, and why should they shrink from similar endurance? Shall they be ashamed of Him? Shall they not rather count it honorable to follow where He has led the way and to bear for Him some faint resemblance of what He bore for them? Shall anything in the world be esteemed more precious, more honorable than the cross of their beloved Lord? The world derides and despises it, but it is the cross of Jesus; and that is all to them. A saint once said, "O blessed cross of Christ, there is no wood like thine." The cross, then, is the badge of discipleship, and no follower of the Lord can be without it. The two things are inseparable. God has joined them, and man cannot part them. No cross, no saint. No cross, no Son.

—HORATIUS BONAR

◆*While we are all called to carry a cross, does Jesus let us carry it alone?*
How does Christ Himself help us in this task?

MAY

◆

Many desire to be glorified with Christ,
but they are not content to suffer for Him

—THOMAS WATSON

God's Wisdom in Nature

The heavens declare the glory of God;
and the firmament sheweth his handywork.

—PSALM 19:1

The creation is both a monument of God's power and a looking-glass in which we may see His wisdom. None but a wise God could so curiously contrive the world. Behold the earth decked with a variety of flowers, which are both for beauty and fragrance. Behold the heaven bespangled with light. We may see the glorious wisdom of God blazing in the sun, twinkling in the stars. His wisdom is seen in marshaling and ordering everything in its proper place and sphere. If the sun had been set lower, it would have burned us; if higher, it would not have warmed us with its beams. God's wisdom is seen in appointing the seasons of the year. "Thou hast made summer and winter" (Ps. 74:17). If it had been always summer, the heat would have scorched us; if always winter, the cold would have killed us.

The wisdom of God is seen in checkering the dark and the light. If it had been all night, there had been no labor; if all day, there had been no rest. Wisdom is seen in mixing the elements, as the earth with the sea. If it had been all sea, we had wanted bread; if it had been all earth, we had wanted water. The wisdom of God is seen in preparing and ripening the fruits of the earth, in the wind and frost that prepare the fruits, and in the sun and rain that ripen the fruits. God's wisdom is seen in setting bounds to the sea, and so wisely contriving it, that though the sea be higher than many parts of the earth, yet it should not overflow the earth; so that we may cry out with the psalmist, "O LORD, how manifold are thy works! In wisdom hast thou made them all" (Ps. 104:24). There is nothing to be seen but miracles of wisdom.

—THOMAS WATSON

◆ *What a great God we have! Take time to meditate on all the wonders*
of nature that we take for granted and yet show God's great wisdom in
creation.

Living a Life of Repentance

Blessed are they that mourn: for they shall be comforted.

—MATTHEW 5:4

Nothing passes with God for true repentance but a thorough change of heart and life—ceasing to do evil and learning to do well. When we discover our sin, it is not enough to confess it and to mourn over it. We must forsake it utterly and put it clean away. We must not only stop it in our actions, but pursue it home to our inclinations and desires, and dislodge it there: otherwise it will be all to little purpose; for the root being still left behind, it will surely shoot out again. Pray that you may become "holy as God is holy."

Remember that you have *daily* fresh sins to be repented of. Your disease is forever breaking out anew. You have need to go again and again to the cross to seek forgiveness. Your life must be a *life of repentance*, a constant looking to Christ for fresh grants of pardoning mercy.

Some may possibly call this a spirit of bondage. But truly that is a blessed bondage, which looses us from the chain of sin and binds us closely to our Lord. You may be daily conscious of your sinfulness and mourn over it before God, and yet you may have the fullest assurance of acceptance. You may be brokenhearted by reason of your unworthiness, and yet you may enjoy a peace that passes all understanding from the happy knowledge that Christ has put away your sin. A child does not cease to be a child and become a slave because he feels a keen regret for every act of disobedience to his loving father.

Think often of your sins, to humble you, and to keep you low. But also think often, with thankfulness, of that "fountain opened...for sin and for uncleanness," where every stain can be washed away (Zech. 13:1). Then will you know the meaning of those words, "sorrowful, yet alway rejoicing" (2 Cor. 6:10) and "blessed are they that mourn: for they shall be comforted" (Matt. 5:4).

—ASHTON OXENDEN

◆*Do you know the experience that Oxenden lays out here? Why are we so reticent to confess our sins? Is it that we have wrong thoughts of God and His willingness to forgive our sins and unworthiness?*

Strength in Weakness

I was brought low, and he helped me.
—PSALM 116:6

I have noticed that the deaf often have an unusual quickness of eyesight; the blind are often gifted with an increased capacity for hearing; and sometimes when the eye is darkened and the ear is closed, the sense of touch becomes so sensitive that we are able to communicate with the sufferer through that sense alone. This law helps explain why God put so many of His people under a sharp regimen of hardship and burden-bearing in order that they may be sinewed into strength; why a Joseph must be shut into a prison in order that he may be trained for a palace and for the premiership of the kingdom. Outside of the Damascus Gate, I saw the spot where Stephen was stoned into a cruel death; but that martyr's blood was not only "the seed of the Church," but the first germ of conviction in the heart of Saul of Tarsus. This law explains the reason why God often sweeps away a Christian's possessions in order that he may become rich in faith, and why He removes many off the track of prosperity, where they were running at fifty miles per hour, in order that their pride might be crushed and that they might seek the safer track of humility and holy living.

God's people are never so exalted as when they are brought low, never so enriched as when they are emptied, never so advanced as when they are set back by adversity, never so near the crown as when under the cross. One of the sweetest enjoyments of heaven will be to review our own experiences under this law of compensations, and to see how often affliction worked out for us the exceeding weight of glory.

—THEODORE CUYLER

◆ *Recall an instance when you were brought low but God lifted you up. Did it go the way you expected? Give the Lord thanks for His kindness in bringing good out of evil.*

A Most Delicate Plant

And grieve not the holy Spirit of God, whereby ye are
sealed unto the day of redemption.

—EPHESIANS 4:30

Be not surprised if you have occasional doubts after you have assurance. You must not forget you are on earth and not yet in heaven. You are still in the body and have indwelling sin: the flesh will lust against the spirit to the very end.

Assurance is a thing that may be lost for a season, even by the most sincere Christians, unless they take care. Assurance is a most delicate plant. It needs daily, hourly watching, watering, tending, and cherishing. Watch and pray the more when you have received it. As Rutherford says, "Make much of assurance." Be always upon your guard. When Christian slept in *Pilgrim's Progress*, he lost his certificate. Keep that in mind.

David lost assurance for many months by falling into transgression. Peter lost it when he denied his Lord. Each found it again, undoubtedly, but not till after bitter tears. Spiritual darkness comes on horseback and goes away on foot. It is upon us before we know that it is coming. It leaves us slowly, gradually, and not till after many days. It is easy to run down a hill. It is hard work to climb up. So, remember my caution when you have the joy of the Lord—watch and pray.

Above all grieve not the Spirit. Quench not the Spirit. Vex not the Spirit. Drive Him not away by tampering with small bad habits and little sins. Little irritations between husbands and wives make unhappy homes; and minor inconsistencies known and allowed will bring in a strangeness between you and the Spirit.

Hear the conclusion of the whole matter. The man who walks with God in Christ most closely will generally be kept in the greatest peace. The believer who follows the Lord most fully will ordinarily enjoy the most assured hope and have the clearest persuasion of his own salvation.

—J. C. RYLE

♦ *Is your spiritual assurance being hindered in any way by bad habits and little sins? In what ways do you grieve the Spirit?*

Christ's Love Excels All

Then said Elkanah her husband to her, Hannah, why weepest thou?
and why eatest thou not? and why is thy heart grieved?
am not I better to thee than ten sons?

— 1 SAMUEL 1:8

Christian, you are the spouse of Christ. What? Married to Jesus Christ and yet troubled and discontent? Have you not enough in Him? Does not Christ say to His spouse, as Elkanah said to Hannah, "Am not I better to thee than ten sons?" (1 Sam. 1:8). Does not Christ your Husband say to you, "Am not I better to you than thousands of riches and comforts, such comforts as you murmur for lack of?" Has not God given you His Son and will He not with Him give you all things? Has the love of God to you been such as to give you His Son in marriage, and yet you are discontented and murmuring? Consider your relation to Jesus Christ, as a spouse and married to Him: His person is yours, and so all the riches in Jesus Christ are yours, as the riches of a husband are his wife's.

Though some husbands are so vile that their wives may be forced to file for divorce, certainly Jesus Christ will never divorce His spouse. You who are one with Christ and are His spouse, will you murmur now and be discontented in your spirit?

You may have observed in some newly married, when there is discontent between the wife and the husband, that their friends will shake their heads and say, "They are not meeting with what they expected; ever since they were married together, the man and woman's looks are not as cheery as they used to be. Surely it is likely to prove an ill match." But it is not so here; it shall not be so between you and Christ. Oh, Jesus Christ does not love to see His spouse with a scowling countenance. As no man loves to see discontent in the face of his wife, surely Christ does not love to see discontent in the face of his spouse.

—JEREMIAH BURROUGHS

◆ *How does Christ see your face toward Him? What would it look like to daily live with a face of love and contentment, knowing we are married to Christ?*

Spiritual Joy

Thou wilt shew me the path of life:
in thy presence is fulness of joy.
—PSALM 16:11

Spiritual joy has God for its object. Not only is He the bestower of it, but He is the great object of the believer's delight. We are disposed to look here and there and everywhere for happiness. Like the restless bee, we try one flower after another. But never can we say of any earthly thing, "Here will I dwell. Here will I find that which satisfies me."

It is very different with the Christian. He, too, perhaps has made many a fruitless search; but he has found peace at last. He has found it in Christ. He rests his weary soul in the Savior's bosom, and he is happy. He feels that they may take away my worldly goods, my friends may forsake me, they may persecute me, bear false witness against me, and take away my character, but they cannot rob me of my blessed hope. They cannot separate me from my Savior.

If then you ever feel uncomfortable and restless, do not imagine that you would be better anywhere else than where you are or be better under any other circumstances. Do not set your heart on this or that object and think that if you had it, it would bring you happiness. Do not say, "Who will show me any good?" but rather say, "Lord, lift Thou up the light of Thy countenance upon me." Look upward to Him, from whom alone comes real peace.

It may happen sometimes that you open your Bible and get little or no good. You may turn to religious friends, but there is no comfort there. You may even come to God's house and find it a barren wilderness. But go to God Himself. Go to the Savior. Rest your soul upon Him; and you are sure to find peace. "Then will I go," said the psalmist, "unto the altar of God, unto God my exceeding joy" (Ps. 43:4). Christ is "our peace" (Eph. 2:14). "The LORD is my portion, saith my soul" (Lam. 3:24).

—ASHTON OXENDEN

◆ *Does your life exude joyful living? If not, what do you think may be the cause? Do you allow your feelings to dictate whether you are joyful, or do you seek to rest by faith in Christ in spite of what your feelings might be?*

The Way Up Is Down

Before honour is humility.
—PROVERBS 18:12

L et us observe the different states of Christ on earth and in heaven. How is the scene altered? When He was on earth, He lay in a manger; now He sits on a throne. Then He was hated and scorned of men; now He is adored by angels. Then His name was reproached; now "God also hath… given him a name which is above every name" (Phil. 2:9). Then He came in the form of a servant, and as a servant, stood with His basin and towel, and washed His disciples' feet (John 13:4–5); now He is clad in His prince's robes, and the kings of earth cast their crowns before Him. On earth He was a man of sorrows; now He is anointed with the oil of gladness. On earth was His crucifixion; now His coronation. Then His Father frowned upon Him in desertion; now He has set Him at His right hand. Before, He seemed to have no form or beauty in Him (Isa. 53:2); now He is in the brightness of His Father's glory (Heb. 1:3). Oh, what a change is here! "God also hath highly exalted him" (Phil. 2:9).

Was Christ first humbled and then exalted? Hence learn that the way to true honor is humility. "He that humbleth himself shall be exalted" (Luke 14:11). The world looks upon humility as that which will make one contemptible, but it is the way to honor; the way to rise is to fall; the way to ascend is to descend. Humility exalts us in the esteem of men, and it exalts us to a higher throne in heaven. "Whosoever therefore shall humble himself as this little child, the same is greatest in the kingdom of heaven" (Matt. 18:4).

Christ first suffered and then was exalted. See here that sufferings must go before glory. Many desire to be glorified with Christ, but they are not content to suffer for Him. "If we suffer, we shall also reign with him" (2 Tim. 2:12). The wicked first reign and then suffer; the godly first suffer and then reign.

—THOMAS WATSON

◆*Do you grasp this paradox? In what ways did Christ humble Himself? In what ways do you humble yourself?*

The Wakeful Life

The wisdom of the prudent is to understand his way.
—PROVERBS 14:8

There are some Christians who work, but they do not work like men awake. They move forward in a certain track of duty, but it is with weary footsteps. Their motions are constrained and cold. They do many good things, devise many good schemes, say excellent things, but the vigorous pulse of warm life is wanting. Zeal, glowing zeal—elastic and untiring—is not theirs. They neither burn themselves, nor do they kindle others. There is nothing of the "star" about them save its coldness. They may expect some sharp stroke of chastisement, for they need it.

There are others who are only wakeful by fits and starts. They cannot be safely counted on, for their fervor depends upon the feeling of the moment. A naturally impulsive temperament, of which perhaps they are not sufficiently aware, and which they have not sought either to crucify or to regulate, renders them uncertain in all their movements. This intermittent wakefulness accomplishes but little. They do, and they undo.

There are others who seem to be always wakeful, but it is the wakefulness of bustle and restlessness. They cannot live unless they are stirring, planning, and moving about. Their temperament is that nervous, impatient kind that makes rest or relaxation to be felt as restraint and pain.

The true wakeful life is different. It is a thing of intensity and depth. It carries ever about with it the air of calm and restful dignity, of inward power and greatness. It is fervent, but not feverish; energetic, but not excited; speedy in its doings, but not hasty; prudent, but not timid or selfish; resolute and fearless, but not rash; unobtrusive and sometimes silent, yet all around feel its influence; full of joy and peace, yet without parade or noise; overflowing in tenderness and love, yet at the same time, faithful and true.

This is the wakeful life! But before it is thoroughly attained, how much we are sometimes called upon to suffer through the rebelliousness of a carnal nature that will not let us surrender ourselves up wholly to God and present ourselves as living sacrifices, which is our reasonable service.

—HORATIUS BONAR

♦ *If you confess Christ, how deep and intense is your wakefulness? Is there anything you can think of that may be hindering you from a more wakeful life?*

The Exercise of Self-Denial

And he said to them all, If any man will come after me, let him deny himself, and take up his cross daily, and follow me.

— LUKE 9:23

A spirit of self-denial is needed if we would grow in conformity to our Lord and ripen for His presence. But how feebly do we often run our race! How little exertion do we make to win our prize! What a soft, easy life do many Christians of the present day live! Many of us seem to think that if we know the truths of the gospel and believe them and embrace them, nothing more is needed and that our work is done. But can this be getting ready for heaven? Can this be the religion of Christ? Must we not have mistaken the gospel? For what says our Lord? "If any man will come after me, let him deny himself, and take up his cross daily, and follow me" (Luke 9:23).

Remember, then, the cross must be taken up; not once or twice, but *daily*. We must not shrink from it because it galls us, but be content cheerfully to bear it. We must daily exercise some act of self-denial. Instead of doing something because it is pleasing to flesh and blood, we must ask ourselves, "Is it pleasing to *God*?" And if not, we must at once put a yoke upon our own will. Our desires, our intentions, our actions must all be brought into captivity to the obedience of Christ.

In short, dear reader, there must be a daily course of self-denial, if you would reach heaven; a daily dying to self, that you may live to God; a daily renouncing your own pleasure, that you may please your Lord—thinking nothing too dear to give up, nor anything too hard to bear for Him who counted not His life too dear, nor the cross itself too heavy to bear for you.

And you must practice this self-denial in little things as well as in great things. For it is in the everyday acts of life that the true Christian should show himself; not so much on special occasions, but in the ordinary path of duty that he most honors God by a cheerful, happy obedience to His will. Without this we cannot be growing and ripening and becoming fit for our Master's presence.

—ASHTON OXENDEN

◆ *Would you agree that in order to live for Christ, self-denial must be practiced conscientiously and intentionally? Why? Are you doing this?*

Comfort for the Assaulted Christian

The God of peace shall bruise Satan
under your feet shortly.
—ROMANS 16:20

The ready access which Satan has to the imaginative powers of the soul, and the quickness with which he can dart his poisonous suggestions into the heart, are most astonishing. No season is too sacred to prevent his bold intrusion. The house of God and the table of the Lord do not give a reprieve from this enemy. The Christian's private quiet time is often greatly disturbed by this restless invader who tempted Jesus in the desert.

How precious then is prayer and the Word of God. The sword of the Spirit and prayer are the weapons which Satan cannot long withstand when wielded by the arm of faith. "Resist the devil, and he will flee from you" (James 4:7) is written for the encouragement of tempted pilgrims.

But who can prevent the assaults of Satan? I might as soon attempt to catch the whirlwind in its path or stop the flowing stream. Yet I can and must resist them by faith and prayer, or I shall perish by them. All-sufficient help is offered. Jesus has said, "My grace is sufficient for thee: for my strength is made perfect in weakness" (2 Cor. 12:9). The promise is "God...shall bruise Satan under your feet shortly" (Rom. 16:20). I must daily seek this promised aid by humble, persevering prayer. Then, as surely as the promise stands recorded in the Bible, so surely will I be more than conqueror through the blood of the Lamb. This is not the work of an hour. The believer's warfare ends only when his life ends, when he puts off his earthly tabernacle and his earthly troubles together.

Almighty Savior, when sin is working within me, and my soul is bowed down with sorrow; when Satan buffets me with his horrid assaults, and all seems darkness and despair; when unbelief would tempt me to give up all for lost—then may I hear Thee speak in cheering accents to my soul, "Is any thing too hard for the LORD?" (Gen. 18:14).

—THOMAS READE

◆*Do you know these assaults of the evil one and have you, by grace, resisted the devil? How can you assist others in this battle?*

Counsel for the Tempted

*There hath no temptation taken you but such as is common to man:
but God is faithful, who will not suffer you to be tempted above
that ye are able; but will with the temptation also make a way
to escape, that ye may be able to bear it.*

—1 CORINTHIANS 10:13

Here are a few words of counsel to those who are tempted.

1. Resist the devil, and he shall flee from you. Fight on. Be not terrified nor faint at his assaults. He is not almighty.

2. Do not attempt to outwit and outreason your adversary; but like Christ, quote the Word of God upon him. The metal of that sword is too great and its edge too keen for him. He hates to hear, "It is written" or "Thus saith the Lord."

3. Lay firm hold on the promises made to the tempted, and be strong in the Lord. He "will not suffer you to be tempted above that ye are able" (1 Cor. 10:13). With the temptation, He will make a way of escape. The promises when believed are fatal to Satan's proposals. "My grace is sufficient for thee" rendered harmless all the buffetings of Satan in the case of Paul (2 Cor. 12:9). Know God's Word.

4. Be on guard in times of spiritual fullness. Pirates let empty ships pass by but attack those which are full. "If thou comest to serve the Lord, prepare thyself for temptation."

5. Be on your guard in the day of fear and sadness. Satan loves to terrify those already frightened and to oppress those already sorrowful. Encourage yourself in the Lord.

6. When a Christian is beginning a service for God's glory, then will Satan lie like a serpent in the way or as an adder in the path to bite the horse's heels that the rider may fall backward. In all new and difficult situations, be vigilant.

7. If you have been led astray, hasten your return to God. Stay not away because you have sinned much or little. The message is the same to all who have erred: "O Israel, return unto the LORD thy God; for thou hast fallen by thine iniquity" (Hos. 14:1).

—WILLIAM PLUMER

◆ *What are your greatest temptations? How has God delivered you from temptation in the past?*

Bonds Loosed

Thou hast loosed my bonds. —PSALM 116:16

Do you ask what is the bondage from which the Spirit of adoption frees us? I answer it is that bondage which springs from looking within yourself for evidences, for comfort, and for motives which only can be found in looking to Jesus. It is that spirit of legality which prompts you to be incessantly poring over your works, instead of dealing simply and solely within the finished work of Christ. That is a spirit of bondage which makes a Christ of duties and labors and sacrifices, of tears and confessions and faith, rather than directly and supremely dealing with Him "who of God is made unto us wisdom, and righteousness, and sanctification, and redemption" (1 Cor. 1:30).

Dear reader, your works, your doing, your sacrifices as a means of comfort and as grounds of hope are nothing but filthy rags, the bones of a skeleton, the chaff which the wind scatters. Why don't you have joy and peace and hope in believing? Simply because, unsuspected by yourself, you are putting your own work in the place of Christ's work. May you be led to cast yourself more entirely upon the atoning sacrifice of Jesus; to believe that God looks not at a single work you do as justifying you in His sight, but that He looks only to the divine, sacrificial, flawless, perfect work of His beloved Son!

Oh, come and rest where God rests, in the crucified one! If He is pleased to accept you in His Son, are you not satisfied so to be accepted? If the blood and righteousness of Emmanuel are enough for God, are they not enough also for you? Away then with your fears and distrust and bondage and enter fully into Christ. Then shall you exclaim, "Thou hast loosed my bonds" (Ps. 116:16). A sealed sense of pardoned sin gives liberty to the soul. Many of the Lord's people walk in bonds from not seeing how fully and freely and entirely their sins are pardoned. If Christ has borne and has pardoned all your sins, then you have nothing to do with them.

—OCTAVIUS WINSLOW

◆*Do you know this deliverance from a slavish fear and bondage?*
Continue to look to Christ rather than fall back into trying to have
peace through performing works.

Gospel Conversation

*Only let your conversation be as it
becometh the gospel of Christ.*
—PHILIPPIANS 1:27

My brethren, the conversation of all the saints is that they should, in their lives, be the epistle of Jesus Christ, the mysteries of the gospel, the deep things of God. Would you know what Christ's mind is, and what the excellencies of Christ are, and of the gospel? Read it in the lives of the saints. See their ways, and you may know much of the mind of Christ is in them. Then let your conversations be such as may be a full epistle of Christ to the whole world, that the world may read what Christ is in you.

Take heed of blotting and blurring this epistle. If a letter was sent from a great man, a prince or a king, and those who brought it smeared it and blotted the letter so that it could not be read, it would be taken very badly. So, you who profess yourselves to be Christians, you do not *bring* the letter only, but you *are* the letter. Therefore, do not blot and blur this epistle of Christ, but keep it fair so that all with whom you speak, all in the family, may daily read something of the mind of Jesus Christ in your conversation so that you may be the glory of Christ.

In 2 Corinthians 8 it is said of Titus and other fellow helpers that they were the messengers of the churches and the glory of Christ. Christians, I appeal to your consciences. Do you live so that the glory of Christ shines in you through the course of your lives? As the shine of a candle goes through the lantern, so the shine and the glory of Jesus Christ should go through Christians in their conversations to amaze the eyes of the world. Do not darken the glory of Christ, but make it as bright as you possibly can, so that this blind world may be able to see something of the glory of Christ in your conversations.

—JEREMIAH BURROUGHS

◆*How can you bear greater witness than you presently do to the glory and beauty of Christ?*

Family Worship

*And ye shall teach them your children, speaking of them
when thou sittest in thine house, and when thou walkest
by the way, when thou liest down, and when thou risest up.*

—DEUTERONOMY 11:19

A person who lives in the exercise of faith and love, and who finds by experience that it is good for him to draw near to God, will not want to be told how often he must pray, anymore than how often he should talk with an earthly friend. Those whom we love, we love to be much with. Love to God either resolves or prevents doubts and questions which may perplex those who only serve God from principles of constraint and fear. A believer will have his happiest days when he has most leisure and liberty of spirit for the exercise of prayer. However, I think family prayer should be performed at least daily, and when unavoidable hindrances do not prevent, twice a day. Though all times and seasons are alike to the Lord, and His ear is always open whenever we have a heart to call on Him; yet there is profit in beginning and closing the day with prayer. In the morning to acknowledge His goodness in our preservation through the night and entreat His presence and blessing on our family and callings in the course of the day; and at night to praise Him for the mercies of the past day, to humble ourselves before Him for what has been wrong, to wait on Him for new displays of His pardoning love, and to commit ourselves and our concerns to His care and protection while we sleep.

You will, of course, choose times when there is the least chance for interruption and when the family can gather with the most convenience. I would say that it greatly preserves regularity and good order in a house to keep consistently the same hours for family prayer. I think it is proper to read a portion of God's Word as part of family worship and to sing a hymn or psalm. The chief thing is that it may be a spiritual service and that it is guarded against becoming a formality.

—JOHN NEWTON

◆*Does your household practice family worship? What things could be
improved, and what can you give thanks to God for?*

Christ Cleansing the Heart Temple

Know ye not that ye are the temple of God, and that
the Spirit of God dwelleth in you?
—1 CORINTHIANS 3:16

The soul of every Christian is a temple. It becomes such at the time of conversion. Formerly a habitation of the evil one, it becomes, by regeneration, a "habitation of God through the Spirit" (Eph. 2:22). As the stones on Mount Moriah were but common stones until they were consecrated to God's use, so the powers and affections of a sinner's heart become, through true conversion, a dwelling place for Jesus. "Know ye not," says Paul, "that ye are the temple of God, and that the Spirit of God dwelleth in you? If any man defile the temple of God, him shall God destroy; for the temple of God is holy, *which temple ye are*" (1 Cor. 3:16–17). What a glorious idea this presents of a faithful follower of Christ! His heart is a sanctuary of the Spirit, full of holy thoughts and devout aspirations. Not a gloomy convent; but a tabernacle of praise, with strains of praises pealing through the arches, and the sweet incense of gratitude ascending from the altars. The mercy seat of prayer is there; and the flames of love send forth the "odour of a sweet smell" (Phil. 4:18).

But alas! How often is this inner temple of the believer profaned by intruders. Selfishness brings its sinful schemes into the apartments which belong to Christ alone. Gradually, and under fair pretenses, self edges in, first into the outer courts and then into the very temple of the soul. Then into this temple how often does the loving Jesus come with His *scourge* of sharp chastisements! How often does He twist the very plans of our selfishness into a cord to smite us? Our pride, too, is often fearfully scourged by humiliation. It is to purify, and not to destroy, that the chastising Lord enters into our heart temples. And our pitying Savior, when He weaves out of our sins a scourge to punish us, only carries out His discipline of mercy. Whom He *loves* He chastens; and *scourges* every child whom He receives.

—THEODORE CUYLER

◆*How has God scourged you in order to purify your worship of Him?*

The Way of Obedience

And an highway shall be there, and a way,
and it shall be called The way of holiness.
—ISAIAH 35:8

We ought to seek heaven by traveling in the way that leads thither. This is a way of holiness. We should choose and desire to travel in this way and in no other; and part with all those carnal appetites, which as weights will tend to hinder us. "Let us lay aside every weight, and the sin which doth so easily beset us, and let us run with patience the race that is set before us" (Heb. 12:1). However pleasant the gratification of any appetite may be, we must lay it aside if it is any hindrance or a stumbling-block in the way to heaven.

We should travel on in the way of obedience to all God's commands, the difficult as well as the easy, denying all our sinful inclinations and inter- ests. The way to heaven is ascending; we must be content to travel uphill, though it be hard and tiresome and contrary to the natural bias of our flesh. We should follow Christ; the path He traveled was the right way to heaven. We should take up our cross and follow Him, in meekness and lowliness of heart, obedience and charity, diligence to do good, and patience under afflictions. The way to heaven is a heavenly life; an imitation of those who are in heaven, in their holy enjoyments, loving, adoring, serving, and prais- ing God and the Lamb.

We should travel on in this way in a laborious manner. Long journeys are accompanied with toil and fatigue, especially if through a wilderness. Persons, in such a case, can expect hardships and weariness. So, we should travel in this way of holiness, improving our time and strength, to surmount the difficulties and obstacles that are in the way. The land we must travel through is a wilderness; there are many mountains, rocks, and rough places that we must go over, and therefore it is necessary that we should lay out our strength; our whole lives being spent on traveling this road.

—JONATHAN EDWARDS

◆*What "rocks, mountains, and rough places" are you facing in your journey?*
Will navigating these difficult spots be worth it in the end?

Serving God in the Ordinary Duties of Life

*And whatsoever ye do, do it heartily, as to
the Lord, and not unto men.*
—COLOSSIANS 3:23

I wish you to consider that a simple desire to please God, to walk by the rule of His Word, and to do all to His glory consecrates the actions of everyday life and makes everything that belongs to our situation and responsibility in public and family life a part of our religion.

It is a sad mistake to think that all time is lost which is not spent in reading, hearing sermons, or in prayer. These are rightly called *means* of grace; they should be attended at their proper time; but the *fruits* of grace are to be evident in our common daily course of conduct. It would be wrong to neglect the house of God and equally wrong to neglect the wise management of one's own house. It is primarily as a wife and mother of a family that she let her light shine to His praise. Do not think that she could serve the Lord better in any other situation than in that which His providence has placed her. I know that family cares are apt to encroach too much, but perhaps we would be worse off without them.

At best, if a meditative life is quieter, an active life is more honorable and useful. We have no right to live to ourselves. I do not think our Lord blamed Martha for providing a dinner for Himself and His disciples, but I suppose she was too concerned to have things arranged very nicely and perhaps lost her temper. I imagine her storming in upon Him, with her face red with heat and passion, to rebuke her sister. This was her problem. Had she prepared the dinner quietly with a smiling face, I believe He would not have rebuked her for being busy in the kitchen while He was talking in the other room. Religion does not consist in doing great things, for which few of us have frequent opportunities, but in doing the little necessary things of daily events with a cheerful heart, *as to the Lord.*

—JOHN NEWTON

◆ *Is this your view of how to be active in the Lord's work? What would you need to change so that you view all things as doing them unto the Lord?*

In but Not of the World

Wherefore come out from among them,
and be ye separate, saith the Lord.
—2 CORINTHIANS 6:17

God's children are *in* the world, but not *of* the world. They are in the world, and therefore He would have them engage in its employments, discharge its duties, and take part in its occupations. In John 17 we find our Lord interceding for His people: "I pray not that thou shouldest take them out of the world, but that thou shouldest keep them from the evil" (John 17:15).

The Christian laborer may labor still; and all the more heartily, because he is in the way of duty. The religious tradesman may still stand behind his counter, but there will be no underhanded dealing, and all his business will be done in the fear of God. It must and will be so if he is a Christian man.

The Christian farmer too will still cultivate his land, still exercise the same watchful care, still exert the same industry and forethought. But he will do it in a different spirit. While he sows the seed or looks after his flock, he will remember from where comes his increase. His eye will be often turned to Him who can alone give the blessing.

The child of God is not *of* the world. He has lost his greediness for its pleasures; for he has tasted of something better. He has lost his eager desire for gain; for he has won a prize, which exceeds all earthly treasures. He has lost his love for the worldly company; for he has now a new and better friend than this world ever gave him.

The Christian is called to give up the world—that is, all that is sinful, all that is frivolous, all that draws the heart from God. You will say perhaps, "Give us some rules that we may follow as to what we must give up." The only thing like a rule that I can give you is this: do nothing on which you cannot kneel down and ask God's blessing. Go nowhere where you would not wish Christ to find you.

—ASHTON OXENDEN

◆*In what ways may you be drawn away from Christ by your interactions*
with the world? How can you prevent this and walk in ways that would
please God?

Seasons of Life

That ye may with one mind and one mouth glorify God,
even the Father of our Lord Jesus Christ.

—ROMANS 15:6

Are you young? Be not wise in your own conceit. Count not that you will have a long life. Don't let the thoughts of an early death dishearten you. Play the man. Be firm. Be true to yourself, to your friends, and to God. Strive for the best things. Live unto Him who has bought you with His blood. Set a godly example of devotion to Christ. Live by faith in the Son of God. Let your prayers be frequent and fervent. Be not overly anxious about anything earthly. Lay up your treasure in heaven. Walk as Jesus walked, and leave all the results with God.

Are you in middle life? Is the burden of cares heavy? Cast it upon the Lord. Be of good courage. Trust in the Lord and do good. Be not faithless but believing. Expect the fulfillment of every promise according to its real tenor. Be not shaken at the stern realities of life. Rise above the low and carnal view of things. Stand firm in your lot in life. Do your duty unflinchingly. Glorify Christ in your body and in your mind, which are His.

Are you aged? Give yourself much to devotion. Remember Zion and pray for the peace of Jerusalem. Set an example of sweet submission to the will of God. Be not moved from your steadfastness. Honor Christ in your soul, body, and mind, both in living and in dying. Be not gloomy, nor fretful, but charitable and contented. Let a grateful and cheerful spirit, with wise and kindly counsel, make your presence welcome and helpful to those around you. The nearer you draw to heaven, let its light and peace shine in your face more and more, cheer your heart, and make your life a blessing to others.

—WILLIAM PLUMER

◆*Read 1 John 2 and think about the different ages John speaks about.*
Consider what other lessons can be learned from these.

The Privilege of Prayer

The LORD is nigh unto all them that call upon him.

—PSALM 145:18

Prayer must be the living, enshrouding atmosphere of a saint of God. Not one moment could we live without it. *Prayer*, either breathed from the believer's heart on earth or from the lips of the Great Intercessor in heaven, sustains each moment the life of God in the soul of man. Friend, where could you go with those burdens, wants, backslidings, shortcomings, and sorrows which compose so large a part of your daily life but to the throne of grace? Where could you resort for mercy, for strength, for fortitude, for patience, for comfort and soothing but where the God of love and power meets you and talks with you through Jesus, as a man communes with his friend?

It is in this light we come to regard prayer, not merely as a divine command or as a Christian duty, but as the holiest, sweetest, and most precious privilege God has given to us on earth. Look at its grandeur—a mortal, sinful mortal, in audience with the God of heaven! And when we consider that mortal in the light of a *child* and that God in the character of a *Father*, the wonder becomes one of unsurpassed beauty and tenderness.

But look at prayer's preciousness. It understands all the intricacies of our daily life. "Casting all your care upon him" (1 Peter 5:7). "Be careful for nothing; but in *every thing* by prayer and supplication with thanksgiving let your requests be made known unto God" (Phil. 4:6). What a tender, loving rebuke is this of restraining in prayer and limiting God, which restricts our petitions to the major concerns of life, while it leaves unprovided for the minor ones. And yet, dear friend, God is deeply interested in your *small* cares as well as your large one. Those comparatively trivial events, those lesser circumstances of your history, are often those which you feel the most keenly, which chafe the most sorely, and upon which so much that is important and momentous in your life depends. Learn, then, the blessedness and appreciate the privilege of hallowing with prayer the minute details of daily life.

—OCTAVIUS WINSLOW

◆ *Before you bow your head in prayer, consider: what are some of the minute details of your day or your life that you can commit to God?*

Progressive Growth

He shall be like a tree planted by the rivers of water,
that bringeth forth his fruit in his season.

—PSALM 1:3

True grace is always progressive. The true Christian grows in sweetness. A poisonous weed may grow as much as the hyssop or rosemary; the poppy in the field as the corn; but the one has a harsh, sour taste and the other mellows as it grows. A hypocrite may grow in outward dimensions as much as a child of God. He may pray as much, profess as much, but he grows only in outward appearance because he brings forth sour grapes. His duties are leavened with pride. The Christian ripens as he grows. He grows in love, humility, and faith, which do mellow and sweeten his duties and make them come off with a better relish. The believer grows as the flower. He casts a fragrancy and perfume.

A true Christian grows in strength; he grows still more rooted and settled. The more the tree grows, the more it spreads its roots in the earth. A Christian is compared to the vine, an emblem of fruitfulness; he must bear full clusters. We are told to perfect that which is lacking in our faith (1 Thess. 3:10).

A Christian must never be so old as to be past bearing; he brings forth fruit in his old age. A heavenly plant is ever growing; he never thinks he grows enough; he is not content unless he adds every day one cubit to his spiritual stature. We must not be content with just so much grace as will keep life and soul together, but we must be still increasing with the increase of God. We have need to renew our strength as the eagle; our sins are renewed, our wants are renewed, our temptations are renewed; and shall not our strength be renewed? Be not content with the first embryo of grace—grace in its infancy. You look for degrees of glory; therefore be Christians of degrees. Though a believer should be contented with a little in his estate, yet not with a little in religion. A Christian of the right kind labors still to excel himself and come nearer unto that holiness of God, the pattern and prototype of all holiness.

—THOMAS WATSON

◆ *Progressive sanctification is when the believer grows in Christ's likeness.*
Are you progressively loving Christ more, living like Christ more, and
putting sin to death daily?

Lessons from Paul

Be ye followers of me, even as I also am of Christ.
—1 CORINTHIANS 11:1

Did the apostle Paul, as appears from the clearest evidence, ever seek to deceive others, or was he himself deceived? We can only answer no, and we must draw this conclusion: his faith in Jesus was the result of overwhelming conviction of the truth of Christianity, and his conversion was the work of God. The Christian religion is a divine revelation, and to reject the gospel is dishonoring to God and destructive to ourselves.

The life of Paul is full of instruction. His humility, his heavenly mindedness, his deadness to the world, his self-denial, are brought before us in all their excellence. How fervent was his desire for the salvation of sinners; how great his willingness to suffer for Jesus's sake. He was himself a bright exemplar of the doctrines which he taught.

Did he declare man to be a rebel, deserving eternal death? He acknowledged himself to be the chief of sinners.

Did he proclaim Christ as the Lord our righteousness? He renounced his own merits and sought for justification only through the righteousness of his Redeemer.

Did he warn the churches against the sins of the flesh? He disciplined his body and brought it into subjection; lest after having preached to others, he himself should be a castaway.

Did he oppose the vanities of the world and the sinfulness of worldly conformity? He confessed: I die daily, the world is crucified unto me and I unto the world through the cross of Christ.

Did he exhort believers to set their affections on things above? He expressed his desire to depart and to be with Christ. So, he lived under the influence of the truths which he preached to others.

This is practical Christianity, experiential religion. Oh, that in our daily walk we would so exhibit the power of the gospel and show to all around us the beauty of holiness by a growing conformity to the mind of Christ.

—THOMAS READE

◆*Read each of the statements above and see how you compare with the apostle Paul.*

God's Honor toward His Children

If any man serve me, him will my Father honour.
—JOHN 12:26

The Father is greatly pleased that we should serve the Son. And it is only by the Holy Ghost that we can call Christ Lord. Our text says, "If any man serve me, him will my Father honor" (John 12:26).

God gives titles of honor to all who serve His Son. He calls them chosen, His sons, His daughters, His heirs, His friends, His jewels, His peculiar treasure. The church is Christ's spouse. He calls her by pet names—My love, My dove, My undefiled. All saints are the sheep of the Lord's pasture. They are a fountain sealed, a garden enclosed, and the Lord's heritage forever.

The Lord puts His Spirit upon all them that serve His Son. David was highly honored when Samuel came and anointed him, a lad, to be king of Israel. But no anointing is so precious as the Spirit who teaches us all things. He is the author of the new birth, of the inner life, of all grace and purity. When He is in the heart, He is a well of water springing up into everlasting life. One of the greatest honors God gave His Son when on earth was when He opened the heavens and the Spirit of God descended like a dove and lighted upon Him.

God honors those that serve His Son. Many of them have worn a crown of martyrdom; and many have confessed and denied not that God was with them. God says to His beloved, "I have chosen thee in the furnace of affliction" (Isa. 48:10). Not one of the redeemed in heaven has any fault with God's providence while they were on earth.

God honors Christ's bride always, in all circumstances and forever. He honors them at death, often in a very gracious manner. What precious testimonies dying believers bear to the faithfulness of God.

—WILLIAM PLUMER

◆ *What honor are you seeking? Are you more concerned with honor from men or honor from God?*

Fullness in Christ

And of his fulness have all we received, and grace for grace.
—JOHN 1:16

If this doctrine is true that there is fullness in Jesus Christ alone, which may and can and does give comfort and relief in the worst of times and conditions, what a great encouragement is here for everyone to belong to Christ, to get an interest in Christ. You will then have relief in the worst of times and conditions, but without an interest in Christ, there will be no relief in the worst of times. Who would not get an interest in Christ? If there are any readers outside of Christ, be encouraged to get an interest in Christ.

If this doctrine is true that there is fullness in Jesus Christ, why should we complain? Why should we be discouraged in such times as these or at any time or in any condition that we face? "Wherefore doth a living man complain?" (Lam. 3:39). Shall we complain or be discouraged when we have Christ's sufficiency for our relief at all times?

If this doctrine is true that there is fullness in Jesus Christ, why should we not *own* Christ in the worst of times? Why should we not *confess* Christ in the worst of times? Shall Christ be our relief in the worst of times, and shall we not own and confess Him in the worst of times? Shall we not own His truth and ways and ordinances, and confess them before the sons of men in the worst of times?

If this doctrine is true that there is fullness in Jesus Christ, what an evil thing it is to sin against Him. It is to sin against our remedy, our relief; it is to sin against our succor; all those sins are worse than the remedy; therefore, as I used to say, adultery in married persons is worse than fornication in those that are unmarried, because it is against the remedy. Christ is our remedy, our relief, therefore, to sin against Christ is to sin against the remedy.

—WILLIAM BRIDGE

◆*Do you have an interest in Christ? Do you believe that He is able and willing to meet your every need? How is this reflected in your words and actions?*

Love to Christ

How excellent is thy lovingkindness, O God!
—PSALM 36:7

If any godly man's life is unpleasant to him, it must be because his love to Christ is but small and not vigorous and active enough, because it lies dormant and is not frequently put into exercise. For it is utterly impossible but that those who live in the lively exercise of love to Him should have those sweet meditations as to make his life far from unpleasant.

Those that have a fervent love to any person can with pleasure spend their time in thinking of that person and of their perfections and actions. So, with great delight may those that love Christ with an active love think upon His glories; with pleasure may they meditate upon those infinite perfections that He possesses and that make Him lovely in their eyes. How must it please them to find out continually new beauties and glories which they saw not before, because the excellencies of Christ are infinite, and we will make new discoveries to all eternity and yet not have discovered all. How it fills the soul with a kind of rapture when it has discovered something more of excellency in Him who is the object of his highest love.

If men have a dear love to any of their fellow creatures, they desire to see them yet more excellent; they delight to see them attain new perfections. But now those that are the dear lovers of Christ, they have the pleasure of thinking that He has all possible excellency already: there is no room for desiring that He should be yet more excellent, because there is no excellency or beauty nor any degree of excellency that they can possibly think of but what He already possesses, so that they have no new beauties to desire for Christ, but only new beauties to discover in Him. Now what a pleasure must it raise in those that love Christ to think that He is so perfectly amiable. This is a peculiar delight that is raised from no other love but love to Christ.

—JONATHAN EDWARDS

♦*Do you confess that Christ is altogether beautiful to you, that there is nothing more you could desire? If so, what are some of the beauties you have discovered?*

God's Family

*Behold, what manner of love the Father hath bestowed
upon us, that we should be called the sons of God.*

—1 JOHN 3:1

All that is beautiful in human relationship or tender in human affection or gentle in human intercourse, all that is lovable and precious in the movements of a human heart from its lowest depth to its uppermost surface, all these are wrapped up in the one word *family*. For close-knit bonds, for steadfast faithfulness in love, for depth in sympathy, for endurance in trial and danger, where shall we find anything that can be compared with the story of earth's family circles? Conjugal love, parental love, filial love, brotherly love, sisterly love—all are here. The many streams of human affection empty themselves into it or flow out of it for the fertility and gladness of the earth.

We need not wonder then that this name should be chosen as one of the church's peculiar names. God delights in it as the name by which His company of chosen ones is to be specially called. *The family of God*—that is the church's name. As such He dwells in the midst of it, cares for it, and watches over it. His dealings with it are those of a father, fond yet strict, loving yet wise, sitting among His children, having His eye on each, and ordering in His gracious wisdom all the concerns of His household.

His heart is there. It is in His church that God's heart may be said especially to be. There it unfolds itself in a way such as it can do amid no other order of His creatures. There it shows itself in all its manifold fullness, such as it has no scope for elsewhere. It is in the family alone that the one thing we call affection or love is divided and spread out, like a sunbeam into the rainbow's sevenfold hues, there to display itself in all the rich tints of hidden beauty. So, it is in the church alone that the love of God is fully seen, not merely in all its intensity, but in all its varied riches; all kinds of love are unfolded there.

—HORATIUS BONAR

♦*Loving homes are sources of happiness and blessings. How ought our
spiritual family supersede even our earthly family?*

Following His Footsteps

If we suffer, we shall also reign with him.

—2 TIMOTHY 2:12

B elievers are compared to earthen vessels, easily destroyed by a small blow; but they are so strengthened and tempered by the power and supply of divine grace that the fiercest efforts of their fiercest enemies against them may be compared to the dashing of waves against a rock. So that this may be known and noticed, they are exposed to many trials; but the united and repeated assaults of the men of the world and the powers of darkness show with greater power that the Lord is with them and that His strength is made perfect in their weakness. Surely this thought, my friend, will give you consolation, and you will be content to suffer if God is glorified by you and in you.

By enduring temptation, you, as a living member of the body of Christ, have the honor of being conformed to your Head. He suffered, being tempted; and because He loves you, He calls you to a participation of His sufferings and to taste of His cup; not the cup of the wrath of God; this He drank alone, and He drank it all. But in affliction He allows His people to have fellowship with Him; so they fill up the measure of His sufferings, and can say, "as He is, so are we in this world" (1 John 4:17). Marvel not that the world hates you, and that Satan rages against you. Should not the disciple be as his Lord? Can the servant expect or desire peace from the avowed enemies of his Master? We are to follow Christ's steps. Can we wish to walk in a path strewed with flowers, when His was strewed with thorns?

If we made peace with the world, the world would let us alone; if we could be content to walk in sin, Satan would not bother us; but because grace has rescued us from his dominion, and the love of Christ constrains us to live to Him alone, therefore the enemy roars against us. He roars but cannot devour; he plots but cannot prevail; he disquiets but cannot destroy. If we suffer with Christ, we shall also reign with Him.

—JOHN NEWTON

♦*How can the truth of this meditation help you continue to fight against temptations and to be willing to suffer for Christ?*

Loving the Person of Christ

Lovest thou me? —JOHN 21:17

If your heart is drawn out in love to the very person of Christ, then you have gained the heart of God the Father forever. John 16:27 says, "For the Father himself loveth you, because ye have loved me." Not because you have loved My *benefits*, but because you have loved Me; you have gotten the heart of My Father, He says. Therefore, My Father loves you, because you have loved Me, because you love My *person*. Is it not a blessed thing, friends, to have the heart of God the Father? If your heart is drawn out in love to the very person of Christ, you have gained the heart of the Father forever. The Father loves you, the Son loves you, and they will come and make their abode with you (John 14:23). What a blessed thing it is, then, to have one's heart drawn out in love to the very person of Christ. Certainly, it is infinitely better to have one's heart drawn out in love to the *person* of Christ than to have a love to Christ on account of *benefits*, even though they are spiritual benefits.

If these things be so, why would we not all labor for this love to the person of Christ; to love Christ not for the benefits but for Himself? Oh, that I could persuade people to fix upon the person of Christ in their love. Would that this day that I could persuade you to this divine fixation of your love upon the person of Christ. I fear our love is not rightly placed; I fear we have love for Christ beneath Christ Himself. It is the great work of a minister to woo for Christ. Can a soul be wooed unto Christ and won over unto Christ, and not love the person of Christ? If you desire to be married to Jesus Christ, set not your affections upon benefits, nor on your own concerns in your love to Christ, but fix your love upon the *person* of Christ Himself.

—WILLIAM BRIDGE

♦*Take time to reflect on Christ, who He is, and what He has done for His children. Pray that your heart would be drawn to love Him more.*

The Glory of a Christian

Having your conversation honest among the Gentiles: that, whereas
they speak against you as evildoers, they may by your good works,
which they shall behold, glorify God in the day of visitation.

—1 PETER 2:12

There is a saying of Seneca, a heathen, "When you go out into the woods and see the tallness of the trees and their shadows, it strikes a kind of awful fear of a deity in you, and when you see the vast rivers and fountains and deep waters, that strikes a kind of fear of God in you. But," he said, "do you see a man who is quiet in tempests and who lives happily in the midst of adversities, why do you not worship that man?" He thinks such a man is worthy of much honor who will be quiet and live a happy life, though in the midst of adversities.

The glory of God appears in this more than in any of His works of nature. There is no work which God has made—the sun, moon, stars, and all the world—in which so much of the glory of God appears as in a man who lives quietly amid adversity. That was what convinced the king when he saw that the three children could walk in the fiery furnace and not be touched. The king was mightily convinced that surely their God was the great God indeed, and that they were highly beloved of their God who could walk in the furnace and not be touched, whereas the others who came only to the mouth of the furnace were devoured.

So, when a Christian can walk in fiery trials without his garments being singed, and has comfort and joy in the midst of everything (as when Paul in the stocks could sing, which had an effect upon the jailer), it will convince men, as they see the power of grace in the face of afflictions. May Christians conduct themselves in a gracious and holy manner in their afflictions as would make others exclaim, "This is the glory of a Christian."

—JEREMIAH BURROUGHS

◆ *Reflect over your life. What has the unbeliever seen in you that would draw out this same conclusion as Seneca? How can you see this in each other?*

The Believer's Friend

A man that hath friends must shew himself friendly:
and there is a friend that sticketh closer than a brother.
—PROVERBS 18:24

The love of Christ is the love of a friend. How touchingly and pointedly He delighted to speak of this: "Greater love hath no man than this, that a man lay down his life for his friends. Ye are my friends, if ye do whatsoever I command you. Henceforth I call you not servants...but I have called you friends" (John 15:13–15). God has created in the human heart the desire for friendship.

Jesus meets this holy yearning of our renewed nature; He reveals Himself as our friend, the friend who loved us from eternity, who shed His blood for us, sacrificed His life for us, paid our great debt, delivered us from captivity, and has given us the title, freedom, and wealth of a heavenly citizenship, henceforth calling us friends. Oh, what a friend is Jesus. Cultivate Christ's friendship, love Him as your friend, confide in Him as your friend, confess Him as your friend, consult Him as your friend, be faithful to Him as your friend.

Your love delights Him, your faith honors Him, and your service glorifies Him. Every want or trial, every sin and infirmity that brings you to Him but tests His friendship and endears Him to your heart, making you better acquainted with your best, your only, friend. You may be called to learn this precious truth—the friendship of Christ—by painful discipline amid the fading of earthly friendships; by the breaking of ties once so close, sacred, and endeared, distance separating you, misunderstanding alienating you, and death sundering you from the friend your heart cherished as God's most precious earthly gift. Be it so, if the result is your closer intimacy with Jesus, the friend who "loveth at all times" (Prov. 17:17). He will in all the changing, checkered scenes and circumstances of life "shew himself friendly" (18:24). Seek to mold your earthly friendships like Christ's. Let His friends be your friends.

—OCTAVIUS WINSLOW

◆ *Who is your greatest friend? Always remember that in all your difficulties Christ promises to be a "friend that sticketh closer than a brother" (Prov. 18:24).*

Every Man's Work

Thus saith the LORD of hosts; Consider your ways.
—HAGGAI 1:7

The work of meditation is every man's work, it is every day's work, and it is that work that is consistent with every business and condition. It is the work of the wicked, and it is the work of the godly.

Meditation is the work of the wicked, for it is their first step unto conversion. The prodigal considered himself and returned to his father's house. The prophet Haggai, calling the Jew to repent, said, "Consider your ways" (Hag. 1:7). "I thought on my ways, and turned my feet unto thy testimonies," said David (Ps. 119:59). Consider your ways; or, as in the Hebrew, set your heart upon your ways. The work of meditation, therefore, is the first step unto conversion.

Meditation is the godly man's work, for either he is weak or strong. If he is weak, he has need of it that he may be strengthened. If he is strong, he has need of it that he may be enlivened. There is no one that needs not to meditate. If a man is a beginner, he ought to meditate that he may advance. If he be a proficient, he ought to meditate that he may be perfect. If he is perfect with gospel perfection, he ought to meditate that he may hold on to his perfection. Psalm 1:2 says of the godly, "His delight is in the law of the LORD; and in his law doth he meditate."

As it is every man's work, so it is every day's work. There are some special times which are more suitable for meditation. But this work of meditation is every day's work. "When I awake," said the psalmist, "I am still with thee" (Ps. 139:18). How? By prayer and meditation. "I have set the LORD always before me" (16:8). How? By meditation and prayer.

—WILLIAM BRIDGE

◆*Meditation is a spiritual discipline. How proficient are you in its use? How can it become a greater part of your life? What things hinder you from meditation and how can those hindrances be removed?*

JUNE

◆

Learn to be like Christ—gentle, patient,
charitable, and sympathizing.
—OCTAVIUS WINSLOW

Growing in Holiness

And that ye put on the new man, which after God
is created in righteousness and true holiness.
—EPHESIANS 4:24

If you would know whether you are holy or not, try yourselves by these five things:

1. Meditate on the holiness of God, and discern if you cannot see a conformity, a *likeness* in your mind. There is no likeness or comparison in degree, yet there is a likeness in *nature* between God and the soul of the believer. The holy soul, when it thinks and meditates upon God's nature, finds a pleasure and delight, because there is an agreeableness in his new nature to the divine perfections.

2. Can you see any resemblance in your life to the life of Christ? No copy can ever come near the original nor ever will; yet you may perceive whether the same spirit, the same temper and disposition in a lesser degree, be in you that was manifested by the life and conversation of Jesus Christ.

3. Is there an agreeableness between your soul and the Word of God? The Bible is the epistle of Christ that He has written to us; if the same epistle is also written in our hearts that is written in the Scriptures, it may be found out by comparing. Have you love to all God's commands and a respect to them in your actions? Is it your delight to obey and hearken to the will of God? Do you obey them of choice? Is it what you would choose to do if God had not threatened to punish those who broke them?

4. Do you find by comparison a likeness and agreeableness between your heart and the lives of those holy men that we are assured were such by the Word of God? Do you walk with God as Enoch did or distinguish yourself by your piety amid wicked examples as Noah did?

5. Do you in a measure imitate the saints and angels in heaven? They spend their duration to the glory of God; they love Him above all things. And those that are holy on earth have also a resemblance and imitation of them: they are of a heavenly temper, of heavenly lives and conversations.

—JONATHAN EDWARDS

◆ *Do you find evidence of holiness in your life based on the above five points? Rejoice, and thank God for His work within you. Strive for greater holiness, knowing that He who has begun a good work in you shall continue it until the day of His return.*

The Danger of Trusting in Riches

He that trusteth in his riches shall fall;
but the righteous shall flourish as a branch.
—PROVERBS 11:28

We all naturally love ease. We have a natural love of rest. Toil and pain are irksome to the brute and the wise alike. Those earthly possessions which promise the greatest portion of enjoyment are the most coveted by man in general. In civilized countries it may be said in the expressive language of Solomon, "Money answereth all things" (Eccl. 10:19). Riches are able to obtain for us those various conveniences which tend to smooth the path of life. It provides us with food and clothing; with innumerable elegancies and luxuries; with opportunities of expanding our knowledge, of visiting distant countries, and of treasuring up the labors of our dead benefactors. Money can command almost everything, but what is most essential to our happiness is peace of conscience, joy in God, and victory over sin and death.

Here, then, arises the danger of riches. They provide us with every requisite to earthly pleasure. They give us a commanding influence over our poorer neighbors and an importance in the circle in which we move. Hence, we secretly desire after their increase. They engross the affections, they fill the mind, they captivate the will, and they usurp the place of God in the soul.

Paul bears his testimony against this sin in our nature: "Charge them that are rich in this world, that they be not highminded, nor trust in uncertain riches, but in the living God, who giveth us richly all things to enjoy" (1 Tim. 6:17).

If true believers, we ought again and again to impress upon our hearts this sacred truth: real happiness consists in having God for our portion; in being satisfied, yes, thankful for the allotments of His providence; in feeling ourselves to be pilgrims and strangers upon earth, hastening along the stream of time to that blessed world, where every trial will be forgotten—or, if remembered, will only, by its recollection, enhance our everlasting joy.

—THOMAS READE

◆ *Are you in any way trusting in or coveting after the riches of this world? How could you use the riches that you have been given to further God's kingdom?*

Answered Prayer

In the day when I cried thou answeredst me,
and strengthenedst me with strength in my soul.
—PSALM 138:3

A re you struggling against sinful desires and habits? He has promised to make His grace *"sufficient* for thee" (2 Cor. 12:9). Are you cast down because you feel the law in your members warring against the law in your mind? He has assured you that "he which hath begun a good work in you will perform it until the day of Jesus Christ" (Phil. 1:6). Are you troubled and disquieted by the many changes and sorrows of life? He tells you that if you truly love Him, He will make "all things *work together* for *good*" (Rom. 8:28). The heaviest calamities, the sorest ills which may happen, shall only seem like passing clouds, casting their dark mantle over the surface of the lake, while they have no power to disturb the deep and settled tranquility of its waters. "Thou wilt keep him in *perfect peace*, whose mind is stayed on thee: because he trusteth in thee" (Isa. 26:3).

Blessed assurance! What child of God has not felt the need of his Savior's succor and his Savior's sympathy when the language of the soul was, "vain is the help of man" amid doubts and fears and sorrows, amid trial and sickness and distress (Ps. 60:11)? The best that man can do is to clean the wound; he cannot heal it. The best he can do is to make tears flow less bitterly; he cannot dry them up. The best he can do is to speak the word of comfort; he cannot carry it home to the heart. "Miserable comforters are ye all" (Job 16:2). But how different when the soul in its great need casts itself at the throne of grace, and the earnest, importunate supplication ascends to the hearer and answerer of prayer! Then comfort flows, and peace pervades the believer's heart; then faith rises with fresh vigor and the soul says, "O magnify the LORD with me, and let us exalt his name together" (Ps. 34:3).

If you desire to know now how *every* desire, *every* petition, *every* prayer is met by a divine promise, study your Bible carefully; and instead of *brooding* over your cares and troubles, your sorrows and perplexities, take them at once to the mercy seat, and you will find comfort, relief, deliverance, and hope.

—ASHTON OXENDEN

◆ *Compare how much time you spend brooding over your cares and troubles with how much time you spend in reading the Word and in prayer. Could this be the cause for your fears and anxiousness?*

An Earnest Appeal

Search the scriptures; for in them ye think ye have eternal life:
and they are they which testify of me.

—JOHN 5:39

I lay before you an earnest appeal to your judgment, conscience, and heart in favor of the Word of God. Whatever you neglect, neglect not the Bible. If you are a professing believer, be careful how you blend in your reading the chaff of human fiction and story with the wheat of God's Word. It is utterly impossible, reason as you may, that you can cultivate a spiritual and devout taste and desire for the truth of God and the fiction of man. The Bible and the novel can never stand side by side.

As a Christian, guard against the light, frivolous, frothy literature of the day. It will lessen your conviction of what is *true*, it will depreciate the value of what is *divine*, it will impair your taste for what is *spiritual*, and it will bring poverty, barrenness, and death into your soul. God speaks to you from every paragraph and sentence of this Holy Book. It is His voice that we hear, His signature that we behold, His ineffable glory that the more it is viewed in this bright mirror, the more powerfully it may command our wonder and praise. When we approach these divine oracles and hear the voice of God—sometimes speaking out of the midst of the fire, but more often from the blood of sprinkling which speaks of better things than the blood of Abel—we may well bend our knee, and take the shoes from off our feet, for the ground we stand on is holy.

Oh, that power might come down on us from the Spirit of truth and grace, and beams from the Sun of righteousness break in upon our minds as we contemplate the intrinsic glories of the Bible. Let the truth and weight of these revelations sink deep into your hearts.

—OCTAVIUS WINSLOW

♦ *Are there other things besides the Bible that you are reading or watching that need to be cut off or curtailed because they are impacting your view of and relationship to God?*

A Threefold Requirement

What doth the LORD require of thee, but to do justly,
and to love mercy, and to walk humbly with thy God?
—MICAH 6:8

What does the Lord require of you? Is it to make your own peace? Is it to keep your own soul? No, no more than He requires of the sun to keep in its course. His own arm has wrought salvation, and He will secure it. He requires none of your help. But this He requires of you: "to do justly, and to love mercy, and to walk humbly with thy God" (Mic. 6:8).

1. "To do justly." We are by nature attached to worldly goods and wholly influenced by selfish principles. But faith in Jesus communicates new motives, views, and aims to the soul: it teaches us to have our treasure in heaven; to live loosely in the world; to be satisfied with our place and competence which Divine Providence has allotted us; and to love our neighbors as ourselves, because they are fellow sinners and are capable of being called to a participation with us in the honorable relation and privilege of the children of God. Upon these principles the practice of justice is attainable.

2. "To love mercy." None can truly love it but those who have tasted it. When your hearts feel the comforts of God's pardoning love, you will delight to imitate Him. When you can rejoice that He has forgiven you that immense debt, which is expressed as ten thousand talents (Matt. 18:24), you will have no desire to take your fellow servant by the throat for a few pence.

3. "To walk humbly." "Can two walk together, except they be agreed?" (Amos 3:3). When Christ is your peace, you will delight in God; you will set Him before you, commune with Him, learn to please Him, and keep His commandments. This is to walk with God; and you will walk humbly, remembering how much you owe to free grace, and how far you fall short in your best endeavors. These thoughts, impressed by the Holy Spirit, will humble you and keep you from being high in your own esteem, wise in your own conceit, and from seeking great things for yourself.

—JOHN NEWTON

◆*How does your daily Christian walk measure up to God's call in Micah 6:8?*

The Giving Christian

Freely ye have received, freely give.
—MATTHEW 10:8

Whoever would become rich in spiritual treasure must give away *bountifully*. This is the truest paradox in Christian living. He that saves for self only loses; he that loses for Christ's sake is sure to save. Would you grow rich toward God? Then learn to give. God loveth a cheerful giver. We cannot limit this rule to the donation of money. The mere gift of money is but part of Christian charity, though by no means an unimportant part.

We must freely give of everything that we have freely received from the Lord. If we have the heart to pray, let us give of our prayers. No inheritance that a rich father could have left me would compare in value with my widowed mother's prayer for me at the mercy seat. You have acquired the wisdom of age and experience, and can give those counsels which are apples of gold in baskets of silver to the young, the inexperienced, and the poor. Give your personal labors for Christ. Many a rich man seeks to quiet his conscience by giving money in lieu of his own presence in the mission school, the prayer meetings, or to those who are suffering. O man of wealth! God gave thee that very leisure you enjoy in order to do the very work of charity which your poorer, hardworking neighbor has no time to give. Those that have not money or counsel or charitable deeds to offer can at least display a godly example.

And so, a godly life may be from first to last all expenditure; just as the temple lamps consumed themselves away in giving light. But the life and the heart will grow the fuller, the brighter, and the stronger, the more they give.

—THEODORE CUYLER

◆ *Think about how you can further die to self and serve others as Christ did. In what ways could you give of yourself rather than just giving money?*

Are You Happy?

Happy is that people, whose God is the LORD.
—PSALM 144:15

What do I mean when I say the true Christian is happy? Has he no doubts or fears? Has he no anxieties and no troubles? Has he no sorrows and no cares? Does he never feel pain and shed tears? Far be it from me to say anything of the kind. He has a body weak and frail like other men. He has affections and passions like every other human. He lives in a changing world. But deep down in his heart he has a mine of solid peace and great joy which is never exhausted. This is true happiness.

Do I say that all true Christians are equally happy? No, not for a moment. There are babes in Christ's family as well as old men. There are weak members of the spiritual body as well as strong ones. There are tender lambs as well as sheep. There are not only the cedars of Lebanon but the hyssop that grows on the wall. There are degrees of grace and degrees of faith. Those who have most faith and grace will have most happiness. But all, more or less, compared with the children of the world, are happy men.

Do I say that real Christians are equally happy at all times? No, not for a moment. All have their ebbs and flows of comfort. Their bodily health is not always the same. Their earthly circumstances are not always the same. The souls of those they love fill them at times with anxiety. They themselves are sometimes overtaken by a fault and walk in darkness. They sometimes give way to inconsistencies and besetting sins and lose their sense of pardon. But as a rule, the true Christian has a deep pool of peace within him, which even at the lowest level is never entirely dry.

—J. C. RYLE

◆*Are you drinking from the pool of peace, or are you not presently happy? Think about what Christian happiness can look like even during times of trial.*

The Example of Christ

If any man serve me, let him follow me.
—JOHN 12:26

How kind is God to have given us a perfect pattern to follow in His Son our Lord Jesus Christ. We greatly needed one whose footsteps we might safely follow. We have no such pattern anywhere else. The best of men have always been but men at best. If any man would know the way to the kingdom, let him walk as Christ walked. His example is right. There is no flaw in it. By following it, you will do good to others. By walking as He walked, you will best honor God. It is the sum of religion to imitate Him whom we worship. We may not follow others unless they follow Christ.

If Christ's life is the rule, what sinners we all are. How little are we like Him. This is our fault. It ought to be our shame and grief. In many things we offend. We cannot answer for one of a thousand of our failures. We come short in all things. Even when we know God, we do not give Him all our hearts. Vain thoughts lodge within us. Wordiness attracts us. We walk in a pretense or admire those who do.

In this life our great sin is that we do not live what we learn, or practice what we know. Where is a man who does better than he knows he should? We read, hear, think, promise, and resolve, but our shame is that we don't live up to what we know.

Our Father, have mercy on us; pity and bless and save us. We are poor sinners; grant us Thy rich grace. We are lost sheep out in the wilderness; O seek and find us. Make us like Thy dear Son, Jesus Christ.

—WILLIAM PLUMER

◆ *How can you relate to this meditation? How can we better "live what we learn" and "practice what we know"? What example of Christ could you seek to start following today?*

Intercessory Prayer

Pray one for another. —JAMES 5:16

Praying for others is a blessed and happy Christian duty. James expressly charges us to "pray one for another" (5:16). What a mercy that "the effectual fervent prayer of a righteous man availeth much" (v. 16). And how many instances have we in Scripture of this kind of prayer obtaining much from God! Abraham's intercession for Sodom was favorably received (Gen. 18). Moses was heard when he prayed for the people (Num. 11:2; 14:19–20). Elijah's prayer for Israel was answered (1 Kings 18:36–39). Peter was delivered from prison in answer to the prayers of his brethren (Acts 12).

The following anecdote is mentioned in a book on prayer. A weatherbeaten sailor on his homeward passage encountered a dreadful tempest. His mother, who expected his return, was waiting with deep anxiety to see her son. During the raging of the storm, she trembled as she prayed in her cottage for her beloved child's safety. And with strong faith in God, she earnestly prayed for his preservation. When night came, she and her husband retired—but not to rest. They were far too anxious to sleep. As the morning dawned, the winds were hushed and all was calm. Presently the little gate in front of their dwelling turned on its hinges, the door opened, and their son—their beloved son—for whose life they had trembled, stood before them. The vessel had been driven into one of the many harbors on the coast and was safe. "Mother," said he, as his tears ran down his rugged face, "I knew that you'd pray me home!" It seems that in the midst of his danger, he had thought within himself, "My mother prays for me—Christians' prayers are answered, and I may be saved." This gave him strength and courage. And truly her petition was heard and granted.

If this should meet the eye of any mother or father, I would say, go and do likewise. Pray for your child. Pray especially for their soul. There is danger of it being wrecked in the storm of life. Your prayers may save them.

—ASHTON OXENDEN

◆ *Do you know that your parents have prayed for you? Do your children know you are praying for them? Daily lay before the Lord each of your children and their needs with supplication and thanksgiving.*

Be Merciful Christians

Be ye therefore merciful, as your Father also is merciful.
—LUKE 6:36

Oh, have a merciful heart one toward another. Look with a merciful eye upon those who are in great misery. This is that which becomes the gospel of Jesus Christ. A harsh, rugged, and cruel disposition is infinitely unbecoming the gospel of Christ. To see a Christian, one who professes the gospel, who makes more profession of the knowledge of God and of the free grace of God in Christ than others, and yet, when it comes to dealing with such as are in misery, he has a hard heart.

Be merciful to your enemies, not only be willing to be at peace, but be merciful. Do you see any who have wronged you in misery? Do not let them perish, but let compassion work even toward them. Oh, that our hearts yearned toward all! Christ, when He came near to Jerusalem, wept over it. Oh, that the same spirit was in us as was in Jesus Christ!

There's no such argument for mercy to others as the consideration of the mercies of God in Jesus Christ. A heart of mercy becomes the gospel of Christ, and it should be manifested really! Do not let people who are in misery have only verbal mercies from you; that is, you seem to pity them in words. Let there be real mercies toward them. Open your hearts and let something drop from you for the relief of those who are in misery.

"Be...tenderhearted" (Eph. 4:32). God manifests the tenderness of His heart in the gospel. And this is becoming to the gospel, to set this forth as a pattern: the tenderness of God's heart to poor sinners in the depth of misery. Do you see any in misery, and do you not find your heart to break toward them? If you do not find your heart breaking, set before you this infinite tenderness of God's mercies in Jesus Christ, and "'tis that which will break your hearts, if anything in the world will."

—JEREMIAH BURROUGHS

◆*Consider in what ways Jesus was merciful as He walked on earth, and seek by grace to emulate Him. Consider also how you might not only with words but also in deeds be merciful to those around you.*

Benefits of Afflictions

Before I was afflicted I went astray: but now have I kept thy word.
—PSALM 119:67

If the trials of God's people were without any benefits, their case would be sad. But all their experience unites with God's Word in declaring that from all their sorrows come much of the peaceable fruit of righteousness.

Affliction leads us to pray as it did Jonah. He was asleep in the ship but at prayer in the whale's belly. An apostle says, "Is any among you afflicted? let him pray" (James 5:13). Through Asaph, God says, "Call upon me in the day of trouble: I will deliver thee, and thou shalt glorify me" (Ps. 50:15).

Affliction teaches us the vanity of this world and weans us from it. How effectively it does this. It writes vanity of vanities on all things on this earth. It made one exclaim, "What shadows we are, and what shadows we pursue."

Affliction is a great expounder of Scripture. Luther said, "Three things make a good theologian—meditation, temptation, and prayer." And more than twenty-five hundred years before Luther, David said, "It is good for me that I have been afflicted; that I might learn thy statutes. The law of thy mouth is better unto me than thousands of gold and silver" (Ps. 119:71–72).

Affliction's great object is to promote purity of heart. Paul expressly says that the Lord chastens us that "we might be partakers of his holiness" (Heb. 12:10).

Afflictions have a reclaiming effect on wanderers. David says, "Before I was afflicted I went astray: but now have I kept thy word" (Ps. 119:67).

Affliction teaches us quietness and submission. It gives us the calm demeanor of a weaned child. It quiets our distresses. It teaches us that God will have His way.

Affliction leads us to trust in God. It strengthens our faith, and faith is a great grace. As gold answers all things, so faith gives the soul propriety in all the rich consolations of the gospel, in all the promises of life and salvation, in all needful blessings; it draws virtue from Christ to strengthen itself.
—WILLIAM PLUMER

◆ *Are you tempted to lose sight of God in times of affliction? Keep in mind that God often removes earthly comforts to make us more Christlike and remind us of the hope of better things to come.*

Self-Examination

Let us search and try our ways, and turn again to the LORD.
—LAMENTATIONS 3:40

How are we to examine ourselves? We must look deep into our heart and try to discover its actual state before God. Go carefully into your different actions, feelings, and motives and weigh them well so as to discover what has been right and what has been wrong in you. Let nothing be hidden from yourself or kept back from God.

1. Examine yourself by the rule of *God's Word* and not by *man's opinions*. A thing may not be counted wrong by men, and yet God's Word may condemn it.

2. Look not merely into your actions but inquire from what *motive* they are done. Is it, for example, from a desire for man's praise or for worldly gain, or for God's glory?

3. Inquire closely if you have good grounds for believing that you are accepted in Christ and therefore safe for eternity.

4. If you are Christ's servant, are you bringing forth much fruit? Are you daily growing in grace?

5. Find out what is your *besetting sin*—pride, lust, worldliness, evil temper, etc.—and whether you earnestly desire to put it away, whatever it is.

6. See if you are using self-denial and ever keeping "the flesh subdued to the Spirit."

7. Find out not only the actual wrong that you have done, but also the good that you have left undone.

8. Look carefully into every thought, word, and desire.

9. See whether you are taking Christ for your example in all you do.

10. Inquire into your conduct toward your spouse, relatives, friends....

11. Find out what are your particular temptations, and prayerfully guard against them.

12. Examine yourself as to whether your Bible reading and devotions are a delight to you, and whether they are regular and solemn or hurried and trifling.

13. Ask yourself if you are doing *all you might do* for the glory of God and for the good of your fellow man.

Above all, ask God to help you in this searching into your heart.
—ASHTON OXENDEN

◆ *What things need to change in order for you to be more holy?*

The Sin of Murmuring

These are murmurers. —Jude 16

The evil of murmuring is such that when God speaks of wicked men or shows the character of an ungodly man or woman, He points out this sin especially. I could name many Scriptures, but that verse in Jude is a most remarkable one. In verses 14 and 15 it says, "Behold, the Lord cometh with ten thousands of his saints, to execute judgment upon all, and to convince all that are ungodly among them of all their ungodly deeds which they have ungodly committed, and of all their hard speeches which ungodly sinners have spoken against him." Observe how mention is made four times of ungodly ones: "all that are *ungodly* among them...all their *ungodly* deeds which they have *ungodly* committed, and of all their hard speeches which *ungodly* sinners have spoken." Who are they? "These are," he says, "murmurers" (v. 16).

Would you know who are ungodly? They are those whom God, when He comes with ten thousand angels, shall punish for all their ungodly deeds that they do and for speaking ungodly things against Him. These ungodly ones are murmurers. Murmurers in Scripture are put in the forefront of ungodly ones, and it is most dreadful that the Lord, when He speaks of ungodly ones, puts murmurers in the very forefront of all.

Look to your spirits; you may see that this murmuring, which is the vice contrary to contentment, is not as small a matter as you think. You think you are not as ungodly as others, because you do not swear and drink as others do, but you may be ungodly in murmuring. It is true there is no sin, although some seeds and remainders of it exist, in those who are godly; but when men are under the power of this sin of murmuring, it convicts them as being ungodly as much as if they were under the power of drunkenness or whoredom or any other sin. God will look upon you for this sin as well as for any sin whatever. This one Scripture should make the heart shake at the thought of the sin of murmuring.

—JEREMIAH BURROUGHS

◆ *Why does murmuring or grumbling sometimes seem so small of a sin? Ask those close to you whether you tend to complain about things, and seek to put off this sin which so hinders our contentment.*

All Scripture Is Profitable

I will meditate in thy precepts, and have respect unto thy ways.
—PSALM 119:15

The doctrines that exalt the Lamb of God and lay the glory, power, and boasting of the creature in the dust and that display the electing love and sovereign grace of God in His salvation are the most precious to the truth-experienced heart of the believer. No less precious to him is the discerning teaching of God's Word. When there is a real experience of the power of doctrine, there will be a love of the precept. You will desire to have your heart purified and your life molded by the holiness of the truth.

The precept that directs separation from the world—that teaches us to deny all ungodliness and to live soberly, righteously, and godly in this present evil world—that bids us to take up our daily cross and follow a crucified Savior and realize our resurrection life in Him and so to seek those things that are above, where Christ sits at the right hand of God, must be precious to a Christ-loving heart. The rebukes of God's Word, humbling though they are, are welcome to the believer. The Word that gently chides your backslidings, unveils your follies, checks your inconsistencies, and lays your pride, self-seeking, and self-boasting in the dust is precious to your soul.

The Christian feels that "*all* Scripture is given by inspiration of God, and is profitable for doctrine, for reproof, for correction, for instruction in righteousness: that the man of God may be perfect, thoroughly furnished unto all good works" (2 Tim. 3:16–17), and therefore he welcomes *all*.

Beloved, count no less dear to your heart, or as less than the tender unfolding of God's love, those parts of His truth which reprove, humble, empty, and lay you low. The rebukes and reproofs of God's Word are as valuable and precious in themselves as the promises, since both equally seek the sanctification of the believer, and both emanate from the same divine mind and flow from the same loving heart.

—OCTAVIUS WINSLOW

◆ *What a blessing if we are finding the Word to be profitable in all things and situations of life. Pray for humility and grace to apply these convicting truths, knowing that the desired end is that our lives would reflect Christ.*

Christ's Care

In all their affliction he was afflicted, and the angel of his
presence saved them: in his love and in his pity he redeemed them;
and he bare them, and carried them all the days of old.
—ISAIAH 63:9

Is it not a great expression of Christ's love and delight to have communion with His children in all their sufferings? So it is, they have communion with Him in His comforts, and He has communion with them in their sorrows. Once He bore the curse of their sin for them, and now He bears the cross of their sin with them. They have the cedarwood and gold and silver from Him; He has the dirty cities from them. "In all their affliction he was afflicted" (Isa. 63:9). As a tender wife is afflicted with her husband and does care for him, so does Christ also; and therefore if you look at Song of Solomon 7:10, you will find that when the spouse says, "I am my beloved's, and his *desire* is toward me," it is the same words that is used for the wife in Genesis 3:16: "and thy *desire* shall be to thy husband." Why so? Not because Christ is subject to the will of the saints, as the will of the wife is subject to the will of her husband; but because (as the root word signifies to run up and down, to and fro, with attentiveness and care) this means the wife will run up and down and be busy looking to and caring for her afflicted husband, being afflicted with him in all his afflictions.

So Christ does carefully and tenderly, and is solicitous for the saints' good; His heart is as it were running up and down for them, and being afflicted with them in all their afflictions, and as the bride in Song of Solomon said, His desire or affection is toward me. What greater argument of delight and contentment can there be?

—WILLIAM BRIDGE

◆*How have you experienced the loving care of Christ in your life? Do you*
believe He always has your good in view?

God's Presence (1)

And he said, My presence shall go with thee,
and I will give thee rest.

—EXODUS 33:14

Reader, reflect on this high honor that He who reigns supreme amid the hosts of heaven, who is King of Kings and Lord of Lords, should condescend to become the friend, the companion of sinful erring man. Was ever a pilgrim more honored? Ever a traveler in better company? Yet God has ever been, and will be, the companion of them that fear Him. Enoch walked with God. Abram was addressed in these words: "Walk before me, and be thou perfect" (Gen. 17:1). Christian, have you not also realized the fulfillment of this gracious promise? "Yes," methinks I hear you say, "it has been the mainstay, the very life of my faith and trust. In the hour of trial, it has enabled me to lift up my head on high and to exclaim even from the deep waters, 'Yet I will rejoice in the LORD, I will joy in the God of my salvation'" (Hab. 3:18).

To the true believer, there is no promise so precious and encouraging that nerves him for conflict, fills him with peace, and animates him with hope. With God by his side, what enemy need he fear? What path refuse to enter? Is he stripped of worldly prosperity? He has one who can a thousandfold make up for the loss. Is he called to resign the loved and cherished, and to pass through the troubled waters of affliction? "I am still with thee" calms the anguish of his soul and is as balm to the wounded spirit. Whatever else may be taken from him, this he knows that if he keeps near to God, God will keep near to him and that amid flame and flood, amid storm and calm, in pain and health, in peril and safety, "the eternal God is thy refuge, and underneath are the everlasting arms" (Deut. 33:27).

—ASHTON OXENDEN

◆*How should the truth of God's presence change your view of the difficulty*
you are currently experiencing?

God's Presence (2)

And he said, My presence shall go with thee,
and I will give thee rest.

—EXODUS 33:14

Do you sometimes feel that God is not near to you, that your confidence, your faith, and your strength have failed you? May not this be the reason? You have wandered from God. His presence is near, but you perceive it not. The world—its joys and pleasures and cares—has come in between, and darkness is spreading all around and within you. Oh! Haste thee to thy Father and thy God; away from these passing vanities, and again He will take you by the hand and lift up upon you the light of His countenance. Let your past experience of the joy of His presence constrain you to "count all things but loss" (Phil. 3:8), and that you may have the fulfillment, the realization of this sweet promise. For if ever you have truly known what it is to have God by your side, then you know how precious and how delightful is the companionship. It can make the home bright and warm; it can sweeten the hard crust and make even a cup of water blessed; it can inspire the soul with peace and triumph in the dark night season of sorrow, and breathe sweet music over the scene of sadness and of gloom. Has it not in times past hushed the tempestuous billows with gentle command, "Peace, be still" (Mark 4:39)?

Christian, be it yours to walk with God. Strive to behold Him by faith amid your joys and sorrows, in the family, and in the world; in the secrecy of the closet and in the daily walks of life. See Him as He fills your cup and makes it run over. See Him as He dashed it from your lips not in anger but to draw you to Himself. See Him in the smiles of love of the unbroken family circle and in the sorrow and sadness which you must feel as you gaze on the empty chair or the picture on the wall. See Him leading you onward step-by-step, never failing nor forsaking you, but faithful unto all His promises.

—ASHTON OXENDEN

◆*Pause and consider what kind of conversation you would have with Jesus if He was sitting next to you. He has come so low as to tell us, "I am with you always" (Matt. 28:20). He must therefore desire that we would walk in the light of this truth day by day, rather than thinking we are all alone.*

One Thing Is Necessary

And Jesus answered and said unto her, Martha, Martha, thou art careful and troubled about many things: but one thing is needful: and Mary hath chosen that good part, which shall not be taken away from her.

—LUKE 10:41–42

One of the truths which Christ teaches a Christian is to understand what is the one thing that is necessary which he never understood before. You know what He said to Martha, "O Martha, thou cumberest thyself about many things, but there is one thing necessary." Before, the ungodly soul sought after this and that, but now he says, "I see that it is not necessary for me to be rich, but it is necessary for me to make my peace with God. It is not necessary that I should live a pleasurable life in this world, but it is absolutely necessary that I should have pardon of my sin. It is not necessary that I should have honor and promotion, but it is necessary that I should have God as my portion and my life hid in Jesus Christ. It is necessary that my soul should be saved. The other things are wonderful indeed, and I would be glad if God would give me them. A beautiful house and income and clothes and advancement for my wife and children—these are comforting things, but they are not necessary things. I may have these and yet perish forever; but the other is absolutely necessary." In this way Christ instructs the soul.

Many of you have had some thoughts about this, that it is indeed necessary for you to provide for your souls, but when you come to Christ's school, Christ causes the fear of eternity to fall upon you and causes such a real sight of the great things of eternity, and the absolute necessity of those things, that it fills your heart with fear, and this sight takes your eyes off all other things in the world.

—JEREMIAH BURROUGHS

◆ *Name the necessary things that you need from God in comparison with the comforting things you may desire. How can you better live with these necessary things in view?*

God's Marriage Covenant

I am married unto you. —JEREMIAH 3:14

Think upon the amazing goodness of God to enter into covenant with us. He never entered into covenant with the angels when they fell. It was much condescension in God to enter into covenant with us in a state of innocence, but much more so when we were in a state of enmity. In this covenant of grace, we may see the cream of God's love, and the working of His heart to sinners. This is a marriage covenant. "I am married unto you," says the Lord (Jer. 3:14). In the new covenant, God makes Himself over to us, and what more can He give? He gives us His promises, and what better bonds can we have?

Are you in covenant with God? God's covenant people are a humble people. "Be clothed with humility" (1 Peter 5:5). God's people esteem others better than themselves; they shrink into nothing in their own thoughts. David cries out, "I am a worm, and no man" (Ps. 22:6); though a saint, though a king, yet a worm. When Moses's face shined, he covered it with a veil. When God's people shine most in grace, they are covered with the veil of humility. Pride excludes from the covenant, for "God resisteth the proud" (1 Peter 5:5) and such are not in covenant with God whom He resists.

A people in covenant with God are a willing people; though they cannot serve God perfectly, they serve Him willingly. They do not grudge God a little time spent in His worship; they do not hesitate or murmur at sufferings; they will go through a sea and a wilderness if God calls. "Thy people shall be willing" (Ps. 110:3). This spontaneity and willingness is from the attractive power of God's Spirit; the Spirit does not force but sweetly draws the will; and this willingness in religion makes all our services accepted.

God's covenant people are a consecrated people. They have holiness to the Lord written upon them. "Thou art an holy people unto the LORD thy God" (Deut. 7:6). God's covenant people are separated from the world and sanctified by the Spirit. Holiness is God's stamp; if He does not see this stamp upon us, He will not own us for His covenant people.

—THOMAS WATSON

◆*What does it mean to be the bride of Christ? How should we then live when this can be said of us?*

Sanctified Afflictions

Many are the afflictions of the righteous:
but the LORD delivereth him out of them all.

—PSALM 34:19

The happiness of man consists not in an exemption from trials, but in having his will swallowed up in the will of God. For this we are taught to pray, "Thy will be done in earth, as it is in heaven" (Matt. 6:10). Just in proportion as we approximate to the unreserved obedience of the heavenly host, we shall be happy. Our trials are sent for this very purpose: to mold our will into the divine will, and consequently to make us holy and happy; for the benefits which believers derive from sanctified afflictions are many and great.

In affliction, we often detect the sin that most easily besets us. This is the most difficult sin to find out, though it is the most prevalent, on account of its blinding and deceiving nature. We have therefore cause to bless God for showing us our besetting sin and why He contends with us.

In affliction, we obtain clear views of the insufficiency of all earthly things. A dark shadow is thrown over the smiling scenes of a busy life. We discover how little value these possessions hold, the attainment of which once appeared so desirable.

In affliction, we learn to estimate, above all treasures, an assured interest in Jesus Christ. The blessedness of the believer is then felt and acknowledged. His peace of mind and hope of glory—the fruits of saving faith—are esteemed more precious than rubies.

In affliction, the promises of God's holy Word are sweeter than honey and the honeycomb. They are sacred cordials administered by infinite love to revive and strengthen the drooping saint.

Therefore, while the prosperous unbeliever in his abundance despises the "hidden manna" (Rev. 2:17), the believer in his heaviest trial can extract sweetness from the wormwood and the gall; for the Savior's love, experienced in the soul, renders all afflictions palatable, however distasteful to our nature.

—THOMAS READE

◆ *The psalmist said, "It is good for me that I have been afflicted" (Ps. 119:71). Can you agree with this statement? Look at your afflictions and ask, What "good" is God seeking to bring out of this trial?*

Learn to Be Like Christ

Let this mind be in you, which was also in Christ Jesus.
—PHILIPPIANS 2:5

If Christ patiently bears and tenderly sympathizes with your infirmities, you should be as patient and sympathizing toward the infirmities of your fellow Christians. "Let this mind be in you, which was also in Christ Jesus" (Phil. 2:5). Our brethren are encompassed with infirmity, each having his own and peculiar cross to carry, his burden to bear. Learn to be like Christ— gentle, patient, charitable, and sympathizing. The sympathy which the gospel instilled in the disciples of Christ toward our fellow disciples is great and full in its nature. The precept is, "rejoice with them that do rejoice, and weep with them that weep" (Rom. 12:15). The exhortation is, "we then that are strong ought to bear the infirmities of the weak, and not to please ourselves" (15:1). The feeling implied in these words is something more than sympathy, as it is commonly understood; something far exceeding ordinary pity or sympathy.

The family of God is one household, one brotherhood. The essential unity of this one family is in nothing more truly and touchingly displayed than in the oneness of sorrow and of joy which pervades alike each member of the sacred household. But, as if the Holy Spirit would define yet more clearly the nature of true sympathy, the church of God is presented under the similitude not of a family only but of *a body*. If one brother is wronged, wounded, slandered; or another is mourning, afflicted, tried; or yet another is weighed down by some heavy, clinging infirmity—I am to make that fellow Christian's wound, affliction, or infirmity *my own*. That blow is to be upon me as well as upon him, and that wound is to penetrate my heart as it penetrates his. "There should be no schism in the body; but that the members should have the same care one for another. And whether one member suffer, all the members suffer with it; or one member be honoured, all the members rejoice with it" (1 Cor. 12:25–26). "Bear ye *one another's burdens*, and so fulfil the law of Christ" (Gal. 6:2).

—OCTAVIUS WINSLOW

◆*Do you view the trials of other church members as your own? How can you be more helpful, caring, and loving to others?*

Those Besetting Sins

Who can understand his errors?
cleanse thou me from secret faults.
—PSALM 19:12

There are particular besetting sins in which each Christian could compose a list. Each one of us has some weak point. Each one has a thin spot in his wall of defense against the devil. Each one has a traitor in his camp ready to open the gates to Satan. He that is wise will never rest until he has discovered where this weak point is. This is that particular sin which you are here urged to watch against, to overcome, to cast out, to spare no means in keeping it under and bringing it into subjection that it may not entangle you in your race toward Zion. One is overcome with lust, another with a love of drinking, another with a temper, another with malice, another with coveteousness, another with worldly mindedness, and another with idleness. Each of us has some besetting sin which can hinder him far more than others and which he must keep an unceasing warfare or else he will never so run as to obtain the prize. Oh, these bitter besetting sins. How many have fallen in their full course and given God's enemies to blaspheme. They thought lightly of them, did not continually guard against them, and had a vain notion that they were altogether cut off.

Go, child of God, and search your heart, and see whether you can find there some seed of evil, some darling thing which you have tenderly spared because it was a little one. Away with it—there must be no mercy, no compromise, no reserve. It must be laid aside, plucked up, torn up by the roots, or it will one day cause you to fall, and prevent you from running your race toward Zion. The gates of heaven are broad enough to receive the worst of sinners, but too narrow to admit the smallest grain of unforsaken sin.

—J. C. RYLE

◆*What are some of your besetting sins? Confess these sins before the Lord,*
and pray for help to overcome.

Being Useful

Whatsoever thy hand findeth to do, do it with thy might.
—ECCLESIASTES 9:10

D id you ever watch a swarm of bees on a warm summer's day? All the members of that busy throng are employing themselves. Some may be seen flying quickly through the air in search of flowers from which to gather their harvest. Others are seen returning homeward with a goodly store of gathered honey. They enter the crowded hive and deposit their burden; but there is no confusion. Others, again, may be seen building up the little cells, each one beautifully shaped according to the truest rule. And a few are posted near the entrance, fanning the air with their wings for the sake of those within, who would otherwise be exhausted with their labor.

Here is a picture of God's church or family on earth. He would have us all to be workers, busy in His service, laboring for Him, employed in the great work of His kingdom.

Why are we sent here? Is it to be idlers? Is it to do our own work and to follow our own ways? Is it to labor only for the meat that perishes, to toil here for a few years for this world's pay, and then to pass away and be forgotten?

We have a nobler calling, a better portion than this. We must not leave the work of this world undone. Thank God, He is not a hard Master. He bids us labor and makes our very labor a means by which we may truly serve Him. We need not go out of the world to do His work. We shall serve Him most effectually if we carry out our Christianity into the everyday occupation of life. How many there are in the world who are always wishing to be useful, always *intending* to do something for God, often dreaming what they *might* do, if they were in such and such circumstances. If we would but begin by doing something that is *close to our hands*, it would be well. There is work enough before us, without looking elsewhere.

—ASHTON OXENDEN

♦ *Think of some specific ways you can live more for God. If you have been living mostly for yourself, do you need to seek repentance before you devote yourself by grace to Him more fully?*

Living above the World

They are not of the world, even as I am not of the world.

—JOHN 17:16

Faith is a daily preservative from a conformity to the corrupt customs and principles of the world. The believer, though in the world, is not of it; by faith he triumphs over its smiles and enticements; he sees that all that is in the world which is intended to gratify the desires of the flesh or the eye is not only to be avoided as sinful, but as incompatible with its best pleasures. He will mix with the world as far as is necessary in performing the duties of the occupation in life which the providence of God has placed him, but no further. His leisure and inclinations are involved in a different pursuit.

They who fear the Lord are the Christian's chosen friends; and the blessings he gets from the Word, the throne of grace, and the ordinances of grace make him look upon the poor pleasures and amusements of those who live without God in the world with a mixture of disregard and pity. He will obey God rather than man; he will "have no fellowship with the unfruitful works of darkness, but rather reprove them" (Eph. 5:11). And if, for this reason, he would be despised and hurtfully treated, whatever loss he suffers in such a case he counts his gain, and esteems such disgrace his glory.

I am not aiming to draw a perfect character, but to show the proper effects of that faith which justifies, which purifies the heart, works by love, and overcomes the world. A persistent effort to have such a frame of spirit, and so to adorn the gospel of Christ with growing success, is what I am persuaded you are not a stranger to; and I am afraid that they who can content themselves with aiming at anything short of this in their profession are too much strangers to themselves and to the nature of that liberty which Jesus has promised to make His people free. May you go on from strength to strength, increasing in the light and image of our Lord and Savior.

—JOHN NEWTON

♦*Does this experiential description of a child of God explain your life and desires? If so, go on in His strength, making mention of His righteousness; but if not, repent of your selfish living and turn to the Lord today.*

Strong in Grace

Be renewed in the spirit of your mind.
—EPHESIANS 4:23

If you would be strong in grace and abundant fruitfulness, you must often be comparing your heart and life with the rule of God's Word. There must be a continual watching over your own heart every now and then, examining and searching to see if you can't find some wicked way in you. Try your heart: see if you can't find some instances where it is unchristian and contrary to the rule of God's Word. This should be done frequently. If it be done every day, it is not too often. We should be continually as David, thinking on our ways and turning our feet to God's testimonies (Ps. 119:59).

Be most intent in fighting against that sin that most easily besets you. There are some sins that men are more apt to fall into. One is most apt to fall into greed; another into unclean thoughts and desires; another into passionate anger; another into evil speaking. Whatever it is, let that sin be especially opposed and resisted by you; fight against that sin that most easily besets you, but aim especially at the life of the sin. This is the direction the apostle gives: "Let us lay aside every weight, and the sin which doth so easily beset us, and let us run with patience the race that is set before us" (Heb. 12:1).

Be most intent on increasing the foundation graces, such as the knowledge of God, the understanding of His Word, the truths of the gospel, and a realizing sense of a future state of rewards and punishments. Labor to get your heart inflamed with love to God and abased by humility and a sense of your own unworthiness.

Above all things, you must do the utmost diligence and application of mind. The work of a Christian is compared to running, wrestling, fighting, and these exercises require the greatest labor. You must press forward "toward the mark for the prize of the high calling" (Phil. 3:14), and in all things you must go forth in God's strength. —JONATHAN EDWARDS

◆*Do you regularly examine yourself? Some examine themselves wrongly and too much without looking to Christ; others too little and minimize their sin. What is a sin that easily besets you, and how can you overcome?*

The Inward Conflict

For the flesh lusteth against the Spirit, and the Spirit
against the flesh: and these are contrary the one to the other:
so that ye cannot do the things that ye would.

—GALATIANS 5:17

Reader, take comfort about your soul if you know anything of an inward fight and conflict. It is not everything, I am aware, but it is something. Do you find in your heart of hearts a spiritual struggle? Do you feel anything of the flesh lusting against the spirit and the spirit lusting against the flesh, so that you cannot do the things you would? Are you conscious of two principles within you, contending for the mastery? Do you see anything of war in your inward being? Well, thank God for it! It is a good sign. It is evidence not to be despised. Anything is better than apathy, stagnation, deadness, and indifference. You are in a better state than many. The most part of so-called Christians have no feeling at all. You are evidently no friend of Satan. Like the kings of this world, he wars not against his own subjects. The very fact that he assaults you should fill your mind with hope. I say again, take comfort. The child of God has two great marks, and of these two you have one. He may be known by his inward warfare, as well as by the mark of his inward peace.

Let no Christian's heart fail because his lot is cast in a day of constant strife and conflict. Let us rather gird up the loins of our minds and be always ready to do battle. Let us remember there is nothing new and strange in the state of things we see around us. Our fathers did battle for the truth, and handed it down to us undefiled by sheer, hard fighting. Let us do as they did, and fight.

—J. C. RYLE

◆ *Do you recognize your life pictured in this meditation? In what way specifically? How does this give you cause for thanksgiving?*

Christianity in the Home

Train up a child in the way he should go: and when
he is old, he will not depart from it.
—PROVERBS 22:6

The most effective religious influence you have upon your sons and daughters does not come from the books you teach them but from the example you set before them. Your character streams into your children; it enters through their eyes and through their ears every hour. How quick they are to imitate! No photographic place is more sensitive to the images which lodge there. Your irritations irritate them; your dissimulations make them tricky and deceitful; your malicious gossip sets "their teeth on edge." If you talk "money-money," they will conclude that the primary purpose of life is to get rich. If you prefer life's amusements to prayer meetings, they will become lovers of pleasure more than lovers of God. If you give your child a dollar for the toy shop or a place of amusement, and only a dime for the contribution box, you teach them that self-indulgence is ten times more important than Christian benevolence.

If you live for the world, your children may die in worldliness and be lost forever. Just as certainly as you provide the clothes for their bodies, you weave the habits of their lives and the thoughts of their minds that they will be living with after you are dead. As clothes are made stitch by stitch, so you weave their character by numberless little things and by your unconscious influence. The Christian or unchristian atmosphere of every house is created by the parents.

—THEODORE CUYLER

◆ *What are you teaching your children by your actions more than your words? As parents, reflect on how you might be subtly teaching something you had no intention of conveying, and resolve to correct it.*

He Changes Not

For I am the LORD, I change not.
—MALACHI 3:6

Everything around us is given to change. Sickness casts a shadow on our health; adversity dampers the prospect of pleasant years; earthly friends may differ in their thoughts toward us—at one time showering us with affection, at another grieving us by a chilling slight—but in the Word of God our heavenly Father gives the sweet assurance that He changes not. His love, His faithfulness, and His power are infinite. To all His adopted children, His promises in Christ are yea, and in Him, amen; for Jesus is "the same yesterday, and to day, and for ever" (Heb. 13:8); having loved His own, He loves them to the end. What a blessed truth! How uplifting, how supporting to the tempest-tossed believer. O friend, are you resting on this unchangeable Rock? Is the unchangeableness of Jehovah Jesus your sure foundation? What can disturb your peace beneath the smiles of everlasting love? Nothing but sin, *indulged in the heart,* ought to trouble you. If Jesus dwells within you by His Spirit; if you are united to Him and are abiding in Him by a living faith; if your guilt is removed through the merit of His blood and the power of His intercession, then fear not, for nothing can harm you; be not afraid, for nothing can separate you from His love. He who saved you is unchangeable and will not forsake you. He who has redeemed you is omnipotent, and none can pluck you out of His hand.

There is no situation in which a believer can be placed—however dark or intricate, however slippery or dangerous—but in the Bible you can find appropriate guidance and adequate support. How strengthening, how comforting is the Word of God. With this spiritual armory, this divine treasury, we are fortified for the conflict, equipped for our pilgrimage, and upheld amid the dangers of this evil world.

—THOMAS READE

◆ *What aspects of God's character give you courage to press on in the face of challenges in your relationships or daily circumstances? Remember, nothing can separate His children from His love.*

Following Christ Fully

Turn not aside from following the LORD,
but serve the LORD with all your heart.
—1 SAMUEL 12:20

To follow a crucified Christ, to follow Him in the bloody paths of His sufferings, is to follow Him fully indeed. When one came and told Christ that he would follow Him wherever He went, Jesus said unto him, "The foxes have holes, and the birds of the air have nests; but the Son of man hath not where to lay his head" (Matt. 8:20). As if He should have said, "You must not expect great things in following Me, but you must be content to suffer hard things." Christ told the young man who came running, asking Him what he should do for eternal life, that if he would be perfect, he must sell all, and then come and follow Him.

Many think they desire to follow God, but when they meet with some trouble in their way, they seek to go around it, and yet hope to come to God safely at last. They would be loath *not* to be accounted followers of God. But let such know that this which they think to be their wisdom is a departing from righteousness. Many follow God as the dog follows his master. When he discovers a piece of meat, he then lets his master go and turns aside to it. Many seem to be forward in their profession of religion until they meet with some opportunity to satisfy their lusts; then they leave off their profession and turn aside to the enjoyment of their lusts. The heart that fully follows God is not only willing to deny every lust for Christ, but it gives itself up to God so that whatever will come of his home, credit, liberty, comforts, and life, it is agreeable to him if that is what would please God. It is not concerned about these things. The business he has to do is to follow the Lord. He knows that it is the work of the Lord to take care of his things while he is following Him.

—JEREMIAH BURROUGHS

◆*What has it cost you to follow the Lord? What are you willing to sacrifice to follow Him more fully?*

Knowing and Doing Good

Therefore to him that knoweth to do good,
and doeth it not, to him it is sin.
—JAMES 4:17

Let me beseech all who have been hearers of the Word and have gotten a great measure of knowledge, that as you know how to do good, you would do it. This is the soul of religion. Luther said, "I had rather do the will of God than be able to work miracles."

Firstly, to do what you know evidences your relation to Christ. You would count it an honor to be near allied to the crown, but it is more an honor to be akin to Christ.

Secondly, to know to do good and do it sets a crown upon the gospel. "Your obedience is come abroad unto all men" (Rom. 16:19); not your knowledge, but your obedience. To know to do good and not do it hardens others in sin, scandalizes religion, and makes people ready to turn atheists. When some of the Spaniards came to Hispaniola, the Spaniards' carriage being loose and profane, the Indians asked them what God they served. They answered, "The God of heaven." The Indians replied, "Surely your God is not a good God that has such bad servants." So, to know to do good and yet do it not puts a scar in the face of religion and brings an evil report upon it; but to do what we know trumpets forth the fame of the gospel and makes them that oppose it to admire it.

Thirdly, to know to do good and to do it entitles you to blessedness: "This man shall be blessed in his deed" (James 1:25), not for the deed, but in the deed.

Therefore, he who knows to do good and does it not is of all others most guilty. To him it is crimson sin; that is, it is heinous sin, capital sin, sin emphatically, sin with a witness and punished with a vengeance.

—THOMAS WATSON

♦ *Is there anything which you know God is calling you to do and yet you are not doing it? Why are you resisting?*

JULY

◆

If we would have a lasting and joyful assurance of acceptance with God, we must die unto sin; we must be crucified unto the world, and the world must be crucified unto us.

—WILLIAM PLUMER

A Thing to Be Desired

*But unto every one of us is given grace according
to the measure of the gift of Christ.*
—EPHESIANS 4:7

He that has much grace has much of the divine likeness. He has much of God's beauty imparted to him. He has much of the Holy Ghost dwelling in his heart. He has much of God. What else could be a greater and more desirable thing?

As it is most desirable to have much of the habit of grace, it is likewise to bring forth much of the fruits of grace. As the fruit of a tree is the most excellent part, so is the fruit of the Christian. It is the greatest honor and excellency of a Christian to be abundant in bearing fruit, as it is the greatest dishonor to be barren or to bear but little fruit. Grace abounding in the heart causes good works to abound. It tends to be, as much as the goodness of the ground and good tillage tends to fruitfulness.

But consider that it is a certain sign if you have no grace, if you don't desire and strive to grow in grace and fruitfulness. It is self-evident that he that loves holiness and is sensible about that which is above all things precious and desirable must desire much of it and not be content with a very imperfect degree of it; and he that truly hates sin as the most loathsome thing in the world, if he sees any of it in his heart, must desire and strive to get rid of it.

If you are a Christian, you already know that a great degree of grace is something earnestly to be desired, and you do hunger and thirst after righteousness. You are longing for more love to God, for a more unmoved faith in Jesus Christ, for more communion with God, for more of a Christian spirit and attitude, for more of a spirit of charity and a spirit of humility and thankfulness. And you are longing to bring forth more fruit, to walk more holily, to live more to God's honor and well-pleasing, and to do more good in the world.

—JONATHAN EDWARDS

♦ *What graces and fruit of grace are evident in your life? Consider sharing this with a fellow Christian, since others often see graces in us more than we see in ourselves.*

Are You Sinning Presumptuously?

But the soul that doeth ought presumptuously, whether he be
born in the land, or a stranger, the same reproacheth the LORD.

—NUMBERS 15:30

The man that sins against conscience presumptuously and will not be reclaimed does in effect say, "What care I for the commandment? It shall be no check upon me, but I will go on in sin and let God do His worst." A godly man fears the commandment (Prov. 13:13). He dares not sin because the law of God stands in his way; but the presumptuous sinner does not value the commandment; he will sin in spite of God's law. Oh, disparaged madness, to dare God to His face. Do we provoke the Lord to jealousy? Are we stronger than He (1 Cor. 10:22)? Good reason then that we should take heed of presumptuous sin. Let us examine ourselves if we are not guilty of sinning so presumptuously.

1. Is it not to sin presumptuously when we live in total neglect of duty? We know we ought to pray in our families yet do it not. To live in the neglect of family duties—is not this to sin presumptuously?

2. Is it not to sin presumptuously when we will do the same sins which we condemn in others (Rom. 2:1)? You condemn another for pride, and yet you live in that sin yourself. A father condemns his son for swearing, yet he himself swears. Is not this to sin presumptuously when we live in those sins which we condemn in others?

3. Do not they sin presumptuously against conscience who will sin in spite of heaven? Though they see the judgments of God executed on others, yet will venture on the same sins?

4. Do not they sin presumptuously who labor to stifle the convictions of their conscience and will not let conscience speak freely to them? This the Scripture calls holding "the truth in unrighteousness" (Rom. 1:18).

5. Do not they sin presumptuously who after they have felt the smart of sin, it has bred a worm in their conscience, a moth in their estate; and yet, after all this, they again embrace their sins?

Let these things be seriously laid to heart since presumptuous sins do much harden the heart.

—THOMAS WATSON

◆*Are you sinning presumptuously? Confess and forsake this sin, and you*
shall find mercy.

Christ Only

For ye are all the children of God by faith in Christ Jesus.
—GALATIANS 3:26

Beware of making a Christ of your faith, precious as it is. If you are staying away from the Savior because your faith is weak, you are substituting your faith for Christ, the channel for the fountain of comfort, peace, and salvation. If I have a mission to a king in the world, some petition to ask, and I linger on the steps that bring me to the royal presence or in the hallway that leads me into the royal chamber, should I marvel that I have no audience and, consequently, no response to my request? The lofty flight of steps, that magnificent corridor, are but introductions to my approach to the king, not the king himself. Such is faith! Divine and precious as it is, faith is but the path that leads us to the King. And although it is often with hesitation and weakness we tread this royal pathway, yet each new step upon which we place our foot brings us nearer to Jesus.

We must, however, beware of lingering upon the steps or of loitering in the side rooms, substituting our *going* to Christ for our having actually *come* to Christ. Onward we must press, not discouraged by our slow, nor elated by our rapid, progress; counting nothing of our faith but as a means to an end; and that end is our full reception of the Lord Jesus Christ, when we find ourselves in the royal presence, beholding "the king in his beauty" (Isa. 33:17).

It follows then that faith does not save you, it being but the instrument of salvation; that your weak faith is no reason why you should stay away from Christ, and that your strong faith is no plea recommending you to Christ. It is *Christ*, and Christ only, from first to last, that saves; and your faith is precious and valuable only as it brings you to Him.

—OCTAVIUS WINSLOW

◆ *Has faith brought you to the presence of Christ, or are you lingering by the way? In Him, you will find One ready and willing to help you in all your need. Do not rest in your faith, but rather in the author of faith.*

The Duties of Husbands and Wives (1)

*Wives, submit yourselves unto your own husbands, as it is fit in the Lord.
Husbands, love your wives, and be not bitter against them.*

—COLOSSIANS 3:18–19

What are the duties of husbands and wives? This is a great question which should be considered.

Husbands and wives ought to love each other. This love ought to be sincere, tender, strong, and constant. It must have its root in solid esteem. There is nothing that can take the place of love. On this point the Scriptures are clear and plain, "Husbands, love your wives, and be not bitter against them," and "Husbands, love your wives, even as Christ also loved the church, and gave himself for it.... So ought men to love their wives as their own bodies" (Col. 3:19; Eph. 5:25, 28). If a man fails here, he cannot possibly live joyfully with his wife all the days of the life of his vanity. Paul exhorts Titus so to teach and train the church, that the older women may teach the younger women to "love their husbands, to love their children" (Titus 2:4). Whatever, therefore, decreases the love of husbands to their wives or the love of wives to their husbands is wrong and should be put away. He who would draw the heart of husband or wife from each other is an enemy to both.

Husbands and wives owe to each other honor in their respective positions. No rude man can be a good husband, and no ill-tempered woman can be a good wife (1 Sam. 25; Prov. 21:19; 25:24). When honor ceases, love and peace depart. Both are commanded to give honor to each other.

Husbands and wives should endeavor in all lawful ways to please each other. Paul mentions as a mark of a good husband and a good wife that they try to please each other. If they do not try to serve and please each other, they will certainly be most unhappy.

—WILLIAM PLUMER

◆ *Are you loving, honoring, and pleasing one another as you are called?
Ask your spouse where you can grow.*

The Duties of Husbands and Wives (2)

Wives, submit yourselves unto your own husbands, as it is fit in the Lord.
Husbands, love your wives, and be not bitter against them.
—COLOSSIANS 3:18–19

Husbands and wives should try to carry each other's burdens. The cares of life are very crushing. They have been too heavy for many a strong spirit. If a husband cannot get help from his wife or a wife from her husband, who shall care for either of them?

Husbands and wives should tenderly sympathize with each other and stand up for each other. It is honorable for a husband or wife to cling to that one who has been chosen as their dearest of earthly friends.

Husbands and wives must be faithful to each other. They have promised to be so. It is shameful to break their vows. When a man prefers the company of another to that of his wife, he is already half ruined. When a woman prefers the company of another to that of her husband, she is on the road to disgrace.

The husband as the stronger owes to his wife protection in her person, reputation, health, and comfort. He is not a good husband who leaves his wife to fight against the billows of sorrow alone. The wife, as the weaker vessel, owes to her husband respect and obedience. She does not owe him the obedience as of a worker nor a child but of a friend and companion. The Bible is clear, "Wives, submit yourselves unto your own husbands, as unto the Lord. For the husband is the head of the wife" (Eph. 5:22–23). "Wives, submit yourselves unto your own husbands, as it is fit in the Lord" (Col. 3:18).

—WILLIAM PLUMER

♦*As a couple are you one another's best friend? If not, why not? Take time to talk about how you can be more so than you already are.*

Keeping Your Heart

Keep thy heart with all diligence; for out of it are the issues of life.
—PROVERBS 4:23

Our blessed Lord has told us that out of the heart proceed evil thoughts; the heart is the fountain of all wickedness. Evil thoughts are the springs of evil actions. Until the fountain is cleansed, all the streams which issue from it are therefore impure.

The heart undergoes a wonderful change when renewed by the Spirit of grace. But as man is renewed only in part, it becomes the constant duty and work of every believer to keep his heart with all diligence. Sinless perfection is the glory and blessedness of heaven. Here on earth, the most holy Christian finds daily need of deep humiliation.

Are you striving to maintain a conscience void of offense both toward God and toward man? Is "the thought of foolishness" distressing to you (Prov. 24:9)? Can you with Christian sincerity join in this prayer of the psalmist: "Search me, O God, and know my heart: try me and know my thoughts: and see if there be any wicked way in me, and lead me in the way everlasting" (Ps. 139:23–24)? The Scriptures declare: "As [a man] thinketh in his heart, so is he" (Prov. 23:7). This habitual inward state of the thoughts determines his character before God.

In order that our thoughts may please God, they must be brought into captivity to the obedience of Christ. The Word of Christ must dwell in us richly, in all wisdom and spiritual understanding, that out of the abundance of the heart, our mouth will speak to His praise and glory (Col. 3:16; Matt. 12:34). "Thy word," says David, "have I hid in mine heart, that I might not sin against thee" (Ps. 119:11). "Whatsoever things are true, whatsoever things are honest, whatsoever things are just, whatsoever things are pure, whatsoever things are lovely, whatsoever things are of good report; if there be any virtue, and if there be any praise, think on these things" (Phil. 4:8).
—THOMAS READE

◆*Reflect on the past twenty-four hours of your thought life. Have there been patterns you need to be aware of or sinful thoughts you must confess and repent of? What are some ways to keep your thoughts pure?*

Living Selflessly

*Look not every man on his own things, but
every man also on the things of others.*
—PHILIPPIANS 2:4

Selfishness is an evil root which grows naturally in the soil of man's heart and chokes the beautiful seeds of grace as they spring up. Of this the heart must be cleared. Worldly men are mostly selfish. Why are they so eager after *pleasure*? It is to gratify *self*. Why do they make money their pursuit? It is to enrich *self*. The comfort, the advancement, the well-being of *self* is the one great end for which they live.

"Every man for himself" is a maxim which we hear very commonly from the lips of worldly men. But how utterly opposed this is to the spirit of the gospel! There we are taught the very opposite principle, "Let no man seek his own, but every man another's wealth," or welfare (1 Cor. 10:24). The Christian should live no longer to himself, but unto Him who redeemed him. He has been "bought with a price" and therefore he is no longer his own, but God's (6:20). He should lay himself out for the glory of God and for the good of his fellow creatures. He should be *un*selfish.

How blest will your life be if spent not seeking merely *your own* happiness, but trying to make *others* happy, and to do *others* good; not selfishly asking, "How can I secure my own interest in the world?" but "How can I live to God? What can I do for Him? How can I add to the happiness of my neighbor, my friend, or my spouse?" This is blessedness indeed! An unselfish spirit has its own reward. The feeling that we are denying ourselves for the sake of others; the hope that by a little effort we may be of use to our brethren; the yielding up of something that we may have set our hearts on, in order that we may do some act of kindness to another, is in itself delightful. It may cost us something, but who can tell what a plentiful harvest of joy the heart is sure to gather by it? Beg of God to give you the heart to feel and the will to act, and you may be a real blessing to many.

—ASHTON OXENDEN

◆ *Why is it more blessed to give than to receive? What are you giving up in
order to better serve others?*

The Lord Is My Strength

The LORD is my strength and my shield; my heart trusted in him, and I am helped: therefore my heart greatly rejoiceth; and with my song will I praise him.

—PSALM 28:7

One of the principal purposes of our divine religion is to teach man where to find his indispensable element of *strength*. The divine Word, coming from the very Maker of man, who knows us completely, declares that "he that trusteth in his own heart is a fool" (Prov. 28:26). We have no spiritual strength in ourselves. Just as our bodies derive all their strength from the surrounding earth and air, so our souls obtain all spiritual power from a source outside of us. King David, whose native weaknesses were deplorably visible, was only strong when in alliance with God. His declaration is, "The LORD is my strength" (Ps. 28:7). This is the only strength which the Bible recognizes. Who are the Bible heroes? Men of talents, intellect, speakers, philosophers? No. They are Enoch who walked with God, Joseph who conquered sensual temptation because God was with him, Elijah who stood like a granite pillar against the tides of idolatry, and Daniel who never flinched at the lion's roar. Daniel gives us the secret of his strength in his three-times-a-day prayers with God. The Lord fed his inner soul as the subterranean springs feed a well and keep it full during summer droughts.

God's strength is "made perfect in weakness" (2 Cor. 12:9). This means that the divine power is most evident when our weakness is the most thoroughly felt. We first have to be emptied of all self-confidence. A bucket cannot hold air and water at the same time. As the water comes in, the air must go out. The meaning of some hard trials is to get the accursed spirit of self out of our hearts. When we have been emptied of self-trust, we are in the condition to be filled with might in the inner man by the power of the Holy Spirit.

—THEODORE CUYLER

♦ *Why is self-emptying so painful? In what ways is God emptying you so that you can rely on His strength?*

Christt Our Head

For the husband is the head of the wife, even as Christ is the head
of the church: and he is the saviour of the body.

—EPHESIANS 5:23

C hristian, you know that Christ is the Head, and we are the members. Then do not dishonor your Head. When there is a temptation to sin, ask yourself, Will not this be a dishonor to my Head? Do I receive blessings from the Head only to act after a sinful course?

Do not be a crown of thorns to your Head, Jesus Christ. The union is very great, for it is not only that we are members of Christ, and so we are in Christ, but Christ is in us. The root is not in the branch, but the branches are in the root; and the head is not in the members, though the head is joined with the members. But Christ is in us as we are in Him, and so the union is very glorious and mysterious. You complain of weakness, but is there not strength in Christ? Are you not joined to Christ thus, and a member of Him, and a branch in Him? Whatever infirmities you have which bow you down, there is enough power in Jesus Christ to give to any to enable them to walk in a holy conversation before the Lord, to renew their strength as the eagle. Manifest, then, the virtue of your Head, from where all the sinews of every member's strength arises.

And then you know the relation we have to Christ: He is the Husband; we are the spouse. Do not discredit your Husband. Any virtuous wife would make a mighty argument against walking in any evil way, "It will disgrace my husband." Especially if her husband is a public man in place of authority. Let this be an argument against every sin, even the appearance of evil. It will be dishonorable to the Lord Jesus, who is my Husband. How can I do this wickedness against my Lord and my God, who has betrothed me to Himself so that I am bone of His bone and flesh of His flesh?

—JEREMIAH BURROUGHS

◆*Do you honor Christ? Do you view temptations to sin as invitations to dis-*
honor Christ?

The Fruit of Faith

The just shall live by his faith.
—HABAKKUK 2:4

Faith is a wonderful plant in the garden of the soul. It yields all manner of precious fruits, and like the tree amid the streets of the New Jerusalem, it bears fruit all the year. Dear reader, there is no holiness in the soul except faith is its root. Springing from, resting in, and looking to Jesus, from whom it is found, faith produces love, joy, peace, patience, holiness, humility, and every grace that adorns the character and beautifies the walk of a believer in Jesus.

Faith is preciousness, too, in its wonder workings. It has a powerful ability of sight and extraction. It can see both sides of the guiding pillar—the cloudy and the bright. It can get a smile from God's frown, love from God's displeasure, mercy from God's judgment, encouragement from God's refusal, hope from God's delays. It can find a door of hope in the valley of Achor and can sing as sweetly in the dreary night seasons as in the bright and sunny day. It is a wonderful triumph of faith that can say, "The LORD gave, and the LORD hath taken away; blessed be the name of the LORD" (Job 1:21). So faith, laying one dispensation over against another, placing in the scales apparent opposites and contradictions in God's government, can see light in darkness, can produce harmony from discord, and can gather encouragement from defeat; and dipping its pencil in the darkest colors of sad and gloomy providences, can trace upon the canvas of the Christian's life some of its most brilliant and cheerful pictures.

Peace is a blessed fruit of faith. The peace which God gives, which the Holy Ghost creates, which the atonement of Christ secures, and which in its nature and blessedness "passeth all understanding" (Phil. 4:7) is only received from precious faith dealing with a precious Christ. Beloved, bring all your sin and guilt to the atoning blood of Jesus, and the "God of peace" will give you peace.

—OCTAVIUS WINSLOW

◆*How has looking at something by faith changed your perspective of the situation? Why and how does faith yield the fruit of peace?*

The Good Shepherd

I am the good shepherd, and know my sheep,
and am known of mine.

—JOHN 10:14

You who are tried and buffeted with difficulties in your way toward heaven, difficulties from without and from within, difficulties from afar and from at home, grief for your own sins and for the sins of others: the Good Shepherd knows you well, though you may not think so. You never shed a secret tear over your own corruption, never breathed a single prayer for forgiveness and helping grace, never made a single struggle against wickedness which He did not mark and note down in the book of His remembrance. You need not fear His misunderstanding your wants, you need not be afraid your prayers are too simple to be listened to. He knows your specific needs far better than you do yourselves, and your humble supplications are no sooner offered up than heard.

You may sometimes sigh and mourn for lack of Christian friends; you may sometimes grieve that you have not more around you with whom you might talk about salvation. But remember there is a Good Shepherd who is ever about you day and night. His eyes are on all your activities, and no husband, wife, brother, father, mother, sister, friend could take more tender interest in your soul's welfare than He does. If you transgress, He will grieve but will chasten and take you back. If you bear good fruit, He will rejoice and give more grace. If you sorrow, He will bind up your broken heart and pour in balm. He is ever watching and observing and listening.

What a blessed thing to be known of Christ, known and marked as His friends, His relations, His dear children, His beloved family, His purchased possession! Here we are often cast down, discouraged, persecuted, spoken against, and misunderstood, but let us take courage, our Lord and Master knows all. A day shall come when we shall no longer see through a glass darkly but face-to-face.

—J. C. RYLE

◆*How has Christ demonstrated His care over you, especially in times of loneliness or when friends forsook? Study to learn more of Christ's character of love toward His friends, and emulate that among your friends.*

The Jewels in the Cup

The cup which my Father hath given me, shall I not drink it?
—JOHN 18:11

There was a touch of poetry as well as Christian philosophy in the cheerful words of a young Christian who was near his last hour. "When I have the most pain in my body," said he, "I have the most peace in my soul. I do not doubt but that there is love in the bottom of the cup, though it is terribly bitter in the mouth." It was at the *bottom* of the cup that God had placed the precious blessing; and it was needful that he drink the whole bitter cup in order to reach it.

"The cup which my Father hath given me, shall I not drink it?" (John 18:11). These were the submissive words of the Man of Sorrows in Gethsemane. Thousands of His followers have faltered out the same words through their tears, when a heartbreaking trial was trying their faith to the utmost. But the sweet breath of Jesus has been on the cup and made it more palatable. And the lips that tasted the cup of sorrow have uttered such prayers as they had not made and could not make in seasons of prosperity.

The richest jewels of grace often lie at the bottom of sorrow's cup. Jesus could not push from Him the bitter agony of Calvary; redemption was at the bottom of that cup. He could not save Himself and yet save a guilty world of sinners. Either He must drink the cup of suffering, or we must drink "the wine of the wrath of God" (Rev. 14:10).

Looking down into the cup of sorrow which God mingles often for His children, what precious jewels glisten in the depths! Promises are there, sparkling like pearls: "As thy days, so shall thy strength be" (Deut. 33:25). "As many as I love, I…chasten" (Rev. 3:19). "My grace is sufficient for thee" (2 Cor. 12:9). What afflicted child of God would fling from him a cup which contains such priceless gifts as these?

—THEODORE CUYLER

◆ *Has God given you a cup of difficulty or sorrow to drink at this time? Embrace that cup, knowing that mingled with it are many precious promises which you may claim and gain strength from. He who gave it to you will help you through.*

Wholehearted Devotion

*And the work of righteousness shall be peace; and the effect
of righteousness quietness and assurance for ever.*
—ISAIAH 32:17

If we would have a lasting and joyful assurance of acceptance with God, we must die unto sin; we must be crucified unto the world, and the world must be crucified unto us. Sin must die, or our souls must die. Our obedience to God's law must be prompt, sincere, and universal. So says David, "Then shall I not be ashamed, when I have respect unto all thy commandments" (Ps. 119:6). Jesus Christ taught the same when He said, "If ye love me, keep my commandments" (John 14:15). "Happy is he that condemneth not himself in that thing which he alloweth" (Rom. 14:22). Are you walking in any way condemned by God's law or your own conscience? Turn from it; forsake it completely.

Practice entire consecration to God's service. Keep back no part of the price. Give Him all your abilities. Hear Paul, "I beseech you therefore, brethren, by the mercies of God, that ye present your bodies a living sacrifice, holy, acceptable unto God, which is your reasonable service" (Rom. 12:1). Again, "Abstain from all appearance of evil. And the very God of grace sanctify you wholly; and I pray God your whole spirit and soul and body be preserved blameless unto the coming of our Lord Jesus Christ" (1 Thess. 5:22–23). Our duty, our comfort, and our usefulness all urge us to lives of holiness—scriptural holiness, not superficial holiness whose rules are made by men.

In all this we must use great diligence. We have a great undertaking on our hands. Let us say so to ourselves and act accordingly. The Christian's life is a race, and a race well run is not easy. It is a wrestling with flesh and blood; and more than all, with spiritual wickedness in high places. It is a fight—a good fight, but a fight; and fighting is never easy. The prize set before every Christian is a crown of life, a crown of righteousness, a crown that fades not away.

—WILLIAM PLUMER

♦ *What areas in your own life are not entirely devoted to God? What changes do you need to make going forward to live a consecrated life?*

Earnest Prayer

Always in every prayer of mine for you all making request with joy.
—PHILIPPIANS 1:4

Look around you, Christian, and if you are truly one who has realized the preciousness of union with the Father and the Son and the Holy Spirit, you will soon discover many for whom it is your duty and your privilege to pray. You will pray for the members of your own family, that the love of God may be more abundantly shed abroad in their hearts, that they may follow the example of their Savior Christ and be made like unto Him, and that they may be refreshed with the dew of His blessing and may walk in love, as Christ also hath loved them.

You will pray for your relatives and friends, that they may be kept steadfast in the faith and zealous in the cause of their God. You will pray that the blessed Spirit may, in all things, direct and rule their hearts, and that their path may be as the shining light, which shineth more and more unto the perfect day. You will pray for those of your acquaintances who are afflicted or distressed in mind, body, or estate, that it may please God to comfort and relieve them according to their needs; giving them patience under their sufferings, and a happy issue out of all their afflictions.

You will pray for your ministers, that it may please God to endue them with heavenly gifts, that they may be wise to win souls and may themselves shine as the brightness of the firmament and as the stars forever and ever. You will pray for the prosperity of Zion and the peace of Jerusalem, that it may please God to guide and govern it by His good Spirit, and that all who profess and call themselves Christians may be led into the way of truth and hold the faith in unity of Spirit, in the bond of peace and in righteousness. The sorrow, affliction, distress, anxiety, and misfortune of others all will be made subjects of prayer by you, and you will entreat the Lord to sanctify His dealings with them, that they may learn the lessons He designs to teach.
—ASHTON OXENDEN

◆*Make it your practice to ask family members or those in your church family how you can pray for them. Be earnest in making notes of these needs and remembering them in your daily prayers.*

A Good Soldier

Thou therefore endure hardness, as a good soldier of Jesus Christ.
—2 TIMOTHY 2:3

Believers are soldiers. All soldiers, by their profession, are engaged to fight if called on; but who will be called to sustain the hottest service and be most frequently exposed on the battlefield depends on the will of the general or king. Some soldiers are in hard service abroad, while others are stationed round the palace and seek the king's face daily and have no dangers or hardships to encounter. These, however, are as likely to be called to arms as the others; but if not called upon, they may enjoy with thankfulness the more easy post assigned them.

So, the Captain of our salvation allots to His soldiers such stations as He thinks proper. He has a right to employ whom He will and where He will. Some are comparatively at ease; they are not exposed to the fiercest battles but live near His presence; others are, to appearance, pressed above measure, beyond strength, so that they despair even of life; yet they are supported, and in the end made more than conquerors through Him who has loved them.

Long observation convinces me that the temptations which some endure are not chastisements brought on them by unfaithfulness or for anything greatly wrong in their walk or talk. I rather consider that, in His warfare, as in worldly wars, the post of danger and difficulty is the post of honor and, as such, assigned to those He has favored with a peculiar measure of His grace. Possibly some suffer for the instruction of the rest, that we may learn to be more thankful to Him for the peace we enjoy and to be more humbly dependent upon Him for the continuance of it. The Lord's way is in the deep, and His path in the great waters, but faith brings in a good report. We need not doubt that He does all things well, and in due time we shall see it.

—JOHN NEWTON

◆*In reflecting on this meditation, which kind of soldier are you? Are you satisfied with the deployment He has for you?*

Weeping and Working

Jesus wept. —JOHN 11:35

The smallest verse in the Bible is one of the largest and deepest in its heavenly pathos. "Jesus wept." What mysterious meanings may have lain behind those tears, no one need try to fathom; but, for one, I prefer to see in them the honest expression of grief for a friend who was dead and of sympathy for two heartbroken women. Christ's power displayed at that sepulcher overwhelms me; it was the power of God. But His pity touches me most tenderly; it was the pity of a man. Those moistened eyes are my Elder Brother's. The sympathy that walked twenty miles to Bethany, that drew Him to those desolate women, that started the tears down His cheeks and choked His voice with emotion—that sympathy links us to Him as the sharer and the bearer of our own sorrows.

But it was a practical sympathy. Had our Lord come to Bethany and taken the two bereaved sisters into their guest-chamber and had a "good cry" with them and then gone away and left Lazarus in his grave and them in their grief, it would have been all that our neighbors can do for us when we are in a house of bereavement. But it would not have been like Jesus. He did not come to Bethany simply to weep. He came there to work a marvelous miracle of love. He wept as a man; He worked as the Lord of power and glory. He pitied first and then helped. The same love that moistened His eyes moved His arm to burst open that tomb and bring the dead Lazarus to His feet.

Is there no lesson for us in this? What are tears of sympathy worth if we refuse to lift a finger to help the suffering or to relieve distress? It is only when we "bear ye one another's burdens" do we "fulfil the law of Christ" (Gal. 6:2).

—THEODORE CUYLER

◆ *What things have you wept over? How can you practically not only weep when others weep but then help as Christ did? Is there someone right now who needs you to not only weep with them but "work" by helping them?*

The Ties Which Bind

For the love of Christ constraineth us.
—2 CORINTHIANS 5:14

We hardly need to remind the reader that the ransomed of the Lord make up the one church of Christ, the one family of God. What a uniting, sanctifying, and heaven-helping truth this is. The divisions which divide and separate the church of God are human; the ties which bind and unite the church of God are divine. The many variations of church polity and methods of worship which present to the eye the church as a "house divided against itself" (Matt. 12:25) are of man; but the affections and care and doctrines and the hopes that create a vital oneness in the family and control the habits and conversation of its members are of God and, because they are of God, shall never be destroyed. This truth is a heaven-helping truth. That which promotes our holiness, promotes our heavenliness; and growing in heavenly mindedness brings us nearer to heaven.

If we walked more in love and fellowship and compassion with the Lord's people, with each part of the body of Christ, we would have a sweeter cross and a lighter burden to carry. Are we not making more sure and steady progress in our heavenly course and in readiness for heaven itself when by love we are serving one another, rather than when in the bitterness and intolerant and rigid spirit we quarrel and dispute, bite and devour one another? Try the power of love, dear reader; lay aside the prejudice, suspicion, and coldness which divide you in fellowship and labor from other Christian relationships than your own, and see if you may not by godly communication, mutual faith, prayer, service, and compassion gather the strength and the encouragement that shall hasten and smooth your heavenward way. No grace advances the soul with greater power toward a heaven of love than love itself—whether it be love to man or love to God who redeemed man. "The love of Christ constraineth us" (2 Cor. 5:14).

—OCTAVIUS WINSLOW

◆*Do you have any acquaintances outside your immediate church whom you may call brother or sister? If not, could it be because you do not speak of the things of God with others or because you are judgmental? How could you foster more love with others?*

Purge Your Lusts

But those things which proceed out of the mouth
come forth from the heart; and they defile the man.
—MATTHEW 15:18

There is a mystery to contentment that consists not in bringing anything from outside to make my condition more comfortable, but in purging out something that is within. The men of the world, when they desire contentment and are lacking, must have something from outside to content them. But a godly man says, "Let me get something out that is already in, and then I will have contentment." Suppose a man has an illness that makes what he drinks taste bitter. He asks his wife to put some sugar into his drink, but it still tastes bitter. Why? Because the bitterness comes from this sickness within him. But let the doctor come and give him medicine to help him recover, and then he can taste his drink again. The same is true with the unbelieving in the world whose circumstances are bitter. They think if they could only be shown more mercy, it would be sweet instead of bitter, but even if God would put a spoonful of sugar in it, it would still be bitter.

The way to contentment is to purge out your lusts and inward bitterness. "From whence come wars and fightings among you? come they not hence, even of your lusts that war in your members?" (James 4:1). They are not so much from things outside but from within. I have said sometimes that all the storms around us cannot make an earthquake, but the vapors that come from within can. So, if those lusts that are within your heart were cast out, your condition would be a contented one. These are the mysterious ways of godliness that the ungodly men of the world never think about. Have you ever thought of such a way as this, to seek contentment by purging out the diseases of your heart that are within?

—JEREMIAH BURROUGHS

♦ *The Christian is called to put off and to put on. By simply putting off, we leave a void; therefore we must also put on. What is God calling you to put off and to put to death, and what is He calling you to put on?*

A Humble Reader

I am thy servant; give me understanding,
that I may know thy testimonies.
—PSALM 119:125

When we read the Bible, let us do so with earnest prayer for the teaching and help of the Holy Spirit. Here is the rock on which many make shipwreck at the very outset. They do not ask for wisdom and instruction, and so they find the Bible dark and carry nothing away from it. Pray for the Spirit to guide you into all truth. Beg the Lord Jesus Christ to open your understanding, as He did that of His disciples. The Lord God, by whose inspiration the book was written, keeps the keys of the book and alone can enable you to understand it profitably. Nine times over in this one psalm David cries, "Teach me" (Ps. 119). Five times over in the same psalm does he say, "Give me understanding." Well says Owen, "There is a sacred light in the Word; but there is a covering and veil on the eyes of men, so that they cannot behold it aright. Now the removal of this veil is the peculiar work of the Holy Spirit." Humble prayer will shed more light on your Bible than all the commentaries that were ever written. Remember this and say, "Oh God, for Christ's sake, give me the teaching of the Spirit."

Read the Bible with childlike faith and humility. Open your heart as you open your book and say to the Lord, "Speak; for thy servant heareth" (1 Sam. 3:10). Resolve to receive heartily every statement of truth, whether you like it or not. Beware of that habit of receiving some doctrines because you like them and rejecting others because they are damning to yourselves or to some lover or relation or friend. At this rate, the Bible is useless. Settle it down in your mind that you will receive all, and believe all, and that what you cannot understand you will take on trust. Remember, when you pray, you are speaking to God and God hears you. But remember, when you read, God is speaking to you, and you are not to answer again but to listen.

—J. C. RYLE

◆ *Do you ever take certain parts of the Bible to heart but seem to ignore or reject other parts? Seek to have a heart like Samuel that can say, "Speak; for thy servant heareth" (1 Sam. 3:10).*

Honoring God

Them that honour me I will honour.
—1 SAMUEL 2:30

If you are in covenant with the Lord, then God has honored you. He has exalted you and honored you greatly; and if God has honored you, why should you not honor God?

The more you fall down at the feet of the fullness of Christ, in the sense of your own unworthiness, inability, and insufficiency, the more you honor God. "One mightier than I cometh," said John, "the latchet of whose shoes I am not worthy to unloose" (Luke 3:16). The more you lift up the decrees and ways of God that are rejected by the world, the more you honor God. The more you keep close to God in declining times, the more you honor God. The more you trust God entirely, when all means fail and when there is not hope upon the means, the more you honor God. The more you serve God contrary to your own disposition and reach the service of God above your own disposition, the more you honor God. The more you prefer the things of God in time of competition, above other things, the more you honor God. The more you part with your much for God's less, the more you honor God.

What is honor? Honor is a testimony of another's excellency. When I can part with my much for God's little, I do testify an excellency in God, and the more I honor God. And the more you keep close to the name and faith of God in Christ, even where Satan's throne is, the more you honor God.

Now then, has God honored you and taken you into covenant with Himself? Surely then it is your duty to honor God, and by these aforementioned ways, you may honor God.

—WILLIAM BRIDGE

◆*How are you honoring God in private, in public, in your marriage, in your family, in your church, in your community? Are you consciously desiring to honor Him everywhere you go, in whatever you do?*

Sinful Impatience

The patient in spirit is better than the proud in spirit.
—ECCLESIASTES 7:8

Discontent and impatience are like two twins. "This evil is of the Lord; what should I wait for the Lord any longer?" (2 Kings 6:33), as if God were so tied that He must give us the mercy just when we desire.

Impatience is no small sin and arises from a lack of faith. Faith gives a right concept of God; it is an intelligent grace; it believes that God's wisdom tempers and His love sweetens all the ingredients; this works patience. Shall I not drink the cup which my Father gives me? Impatience is the daughter of unbelief. If a patient has an ill opinion of the physician and believes that he comes to poison him, he will take none of his medicine. When we have a prejudice against God and conceive that He comes to kill us, then we storm and cry out through impatience.

Impatience is lack of love to God. We bear the reproofs of whom we love, not only patiently but thankfully. Love "thinketh no evil" (1 Cor. 13:5). It puts the fairest and most candid gloss upon the actions of a friend; love covers evil. Love takes everything in the best sense; it makes us bear any stroke, it "endureth all things" (v. 7). Had we love to God, we should have patience.

Impatience is from lack of humility. The impatient man is not humbled under the burden of sin. He that studies his sins, the numberless number of them, how they are twisted together and sadly accented, is patient and says, "I will bear the indignation of the LORD, because I have sinned against him" (Mic. 7:9). The greater noise drowns the lesser; when the sea roars, the rivers are still. He that lets his thoughts expatiate about sin is both silent and amazed; he wonders it is not worse with him. How great then is this sin of impatience, and how excellent is contentment, which is a counter poison against this sin. The contented Christian, believing that God does all in love, is patient and has not one word to say unless to justify God.

—THOMAS WATSON

♦ *Is there any area of impatience that needs to be subdued in you? How does contentment breed patience in your relationship?*

The Bow in the Cloud

I do set my bow in the cloud, and it shall be for a
token of a covenant between me and the earth.
—GENESIS 9:13

The rainbow is a token of God's covenant with His people. "For this," says He, "is as the waters of Noah unto me; for as I have sworn that the waters of Noah should no more go over the earth; so have I sworn that I would not be wroth with thee, nor rebuke thee. For the mountains shall depart, and the hills be removed; but my kindness shall not depart from thee, neither shall the covenant of my peace be removed, saith the LORD that hath mercy on thee" (Isa. 54:9–10). Here, and here alone, is the security of the Christian, the unalterable purpose of a covenant God. He has given them a "bow in the cloud" to which in every season of impending danger, they may direct the eye of faith.

Reader, is yours a dark and cheerless day? Is your horizon obscured by the threatening clouds? Remember, there is the "bow in the cloud," the token of the unalterable covenant of God. Like the mariner in a stormy sea, you may be appalled at the indications of a coming tempest, you may be listening with alarm to the roar of the angry waves and the howling of the wind. Lift up the eye of faith; see yonder opening in the cloud, yonder faint ray of light, yonder splendid "bow…in the cloud." It is to you the covenant-token that relief is at hand, for the Lord "will look upon it" (Gen. 9:16). It is His own promise. Your sorrowing eye and the eye of your Father in heaven will meet in one spot, on Jesus Christ, and then, as the Lord remembers His covenant and thinks upon you for good, you will be enabled to "trust in the name of the LORD, and stay upon [your] God" (Isa. 50:10). Yea, the darker the cloud, the more brilliant will be the reflection; the heavier the trial, the sweeter the promise; for amid God's most mysterious dealing, you may discover marks of His power, His love, and His faithfulness.

—ASHTON OXENDEN

◆ *Think about your everyday disappointments or any trial you are experiencing. What "bow in the cloud" has God placed there for your encouragement?*

The Principle of True Love

By this we know that we love the children of God,
when we love God, and keep his commandments.
—1 JOHN 5:2

The principle of true love to the brethren is the love of God which produces obedience. "By this we know that we love the children of God, when we love God, and keep his commandments" (1 John 5:2). When people are free to form their connections and friendships, the ground of their communion is a sameness of inclination. The love spoken of is spiritual. The children of God, who stand in the relation of brethren to each other, though they have too many unhappy differences in points of less importance, agree in the supreme love they have to their heavenly Father and to Jesus their Savior. They agree in disliking and avoiding sin, which is contrary to the will and command of the God they love and worship. Upon this foundation they love one another; they are like-minded. And they live in a world where the bulk of mankind is against them, having no regard to their Beloved, and living in the sinful practices which His grace has taught them to hate. Their situation, therefore, increases their affection to each other. They are washed by the same blood, supplied by the same grace, opposed by the same enemies, and have the same heaven in view; therefore, they love one another with a pure heart fervently.

The properties of this love, where not hindered by ignorance and intolerance, have heavenly origins. It extends to all who love the Lord Jesus Christ in sincerity. It cannot be confined within the pale of a denomination, nor restricted to those with whom it is more immediately connected. It is gentle and not easily provoked; it thinks the best, makes allowances for weaknesses, and is easily entreated. It is kind and compassionate, and not in words only, but sympathizes with the afflicted and relieves the poor as enabled. And as it respects the image of Christ in others, it feels more attachment to those who are more spiritual without undervaluing or despising the weakest attainments of the true grace of the gospel. They are happy who so love the brethren.

—JOHN NEWTON

◆*Does your "love for the brethren" enable you to focus on your love to your heavenly Father and overlook things of less importance? Think about tangible ways you can demonstrate this and how it can be practiced more.*

Christian Conversation

Set a watch, O LORD, before my mouth; keep the door of my lips.
—PSALM 141:3

How delightful would the company of Christians be if the humble, loving, gracious, improving spirit, so much spoken of in the Holy Scriptures, filled every circle? How needful, then, is the prayer of David, "Set a watch, O LORD, before my mouth; keep the door of my lips" (Ps. 141:3). The following suggestions may tend to better our conversation with each other.

1. We ought never to speak critically, not even by insinuation, of absent people, except when duty requires it; and even then there should be a marked and sincere regret that the occasion calls for such an exposure of character.

2. We must guard against attributing wrong motives to the actions of others, even when appearances may seem contrary, remembering that God alone knows the heart—and who are we, that we should judge our brother?

3. We should avoid all talk that borders on flattery especially toward those who are present, knowing how destructive praise is to a fallen creature and how few are able to withstand its influence. This does not exclude a fitting commendation or a suitable encouragement when dictated by Christian simplicity and prudence.

4. We must not indulge in exaggerations or overstatements, which seem to give force to conversation but which destroy its delicacy and beauty. This way of speaking, by stretching it too far, borders on lying. Truth appears most beautiful in its own native simplicity.

5. Christian conversation is marked by love, humility, and purity. These are the peculiar features by which it is known. Although so attractive from its nature and excellence, yet how few know how to appreciate or relish its charms.

Love leads us to speak with delight on all subjects connected with the glory of God and the good of man. Humility draws a veil over her own graces and delicately discovers the excellencies of others. It frankly confesses our own faults and carefully conceals the failings of others. Purity, like the refreshing rose, sheds a fragrance peculiarly its own over our whole conversation and, like that lovely flower, leaves its reviving scent when we are gone.
—THOMAS READE

♦ *What areas of the first four points listed above do you struggle with? Repent and ask forgiveness for these sins.*

Your Bosom Friend

It is better to trust in the LORD than to put confidence in man.
—PSALM 118:8

L et God be your companion, your bosom friend, your instructor, your counselor. Take Him into the closet with you, into the study, into the kitchen, into the shop, into the marketplace. When you make a feast and call guests, invite Him as one of them. He is always willing to come; and there is no company like His. When you are in perplexity and are taking advice from friends, let Him be one of your "friends in counsel." When you feel lonely, make Him the "companion of your solitude."

If you know this divine companionship, you will be saved from much idle and wasteful company and conversation. You will not feel at home with worldly men, nor they with you. You will not choose the half-hearted Christian or the formalist for your friend; nor will any of those seek your fellowship. When thrown into worldly company, from your business or your relationships, as you may sometimes be, do not cease to be the Christian nor try to make excuses for the worldliness of those with whom you are obliged to associate; for that is just making excuses for yourself in associating with them. Do not try to make yourself or them believe that they are religious when they are not; but show them whose disciples you are; not necessarily in words, but by a way of conduct more expressive and efficacious than words. Do not conform to the world to please men or to save yourself from their taunt or jest. Be not afraid to ask a blessing at meals, have family worship, or enter into religious conversation because a worldly person is present. Keep constant company with the great God of heaven and earth; and let every other companionship be regulated by His. Go where you desire, if you can take Him with you; go nowhere if He cannot be admitted or if you must hide or disguise your divine discipleship.

—HORATIUS BONAR

◆*How can you practice this kind of discipleship every day? What would this look like from day to day?*

Worldly Evils

And fear not them which kill the body, but are not able to kill the soul.
—MATTHEW 10:28

A godly man may look down on all the whole army of worldly afflictions (evils) under his feet with a slight and disregard, and consider with himself and be joyful that however great they are and however numerous, let them all join their forces together against him and put on their most rueful and dreadful habits, forms, and appearances, and spend all their strength, vigor, and violence with endeavors to do him any real hurt or mischief, and it is all in vain. He may triumph over them all knowing this: these light afflictions, which are but for a moment, shall work out for him a far more exceeding and eternal weight of glory and, although sorrow continue for a night, yet joy comes in the morning as he remembers God's promise that all things shall surely work together for his good, and nothing shall offend.

If he loses all the worldly good things he has—his estate, friends, and family—or if his body is put to the greatest tortures and pains imaginable, he may consider that it is all best for him that it should be, and that all the hurt they can do to him is only to his body. Our Savior has commanded us not to fear them that kill the body and after that have no more that they can do; and whatever the world does against him, he has that to comfort him, that Christ has overcome the world.

How happy, then, must the condition of such a man be! Let any man now ask himself, Should he not think himself happy if he were delivered so from all those evils, that he was assured they would never trouble him more; if he were sure that he should never feel any more pain in his body, never have any want of any good things the world can afford, and never have any care and trouble for them? Although good men are often grieved and troubled by worldly afflictions, yet the godly have no reason to be troubled any further about them.

—JONATHAN EDWARDS

◆*Are you consciously a happy Christian? Do you face this world's evils with this attitude?*

Our Savior's Pledge

There is no want to them that fear him.
—PSALM 34:9

C hristian, you have all the *encouragement* you could possibly desire to attract you to a throne of grace; and, amid the varied experiences of life, there is not a grief which may not be assuaged, not a danger which may not be averted, not an anxiety which may not be lessened, not a pang which may not be alleviated, not a need which may not be supplied out of the inexhaustible fountain of grace to which you are *invited* and where you are *ever welcome.* "O fear the LORD, ye his saints: for there is no *want* to them that fear him" (Ps. 34:9). "He shall *cover* thee with his feathers, and under his wings shalt thou trust: his truth shall be thy *shield* and *buckler*" (91:4). "The LORD shall *preserve* thee from all evil: he shall *preserve* thy soul. The LORD shall *preserve* thy going out and thy coming in from this time forth, and even for evermore" (121:7–8).

That blessed Savior through whom you are encouraged to draw near has *pledged* Himself to intercede in your behalf and to obtain an answer to your prayers. Trust Him with your whole heart, for He is *"faithful* who had promised" (Heb. 11:11). The love He has already manifested and proved and sealed with His precious blood is a pledge that He will still be your friend and intercessor with the Father; that He will continue to display that love, in every cross you have to bear, in every cup of sorrow you have to drink, in every treasure you are called to relinquish, in every lonely and dreary path of duty or of trial by which you are journeying onward to your heavenly home.

He will be your "saviour thereof in time of trouble" (Jer. 14:8). His grace is yours to strengthen and sustain you; His Spirit is yours to guide, enlighten, and comfort you. His intercession is yours to secure for you all needed blessing; His promises are yours to cling to in your saddest and darkest hours; His power is yours to defend you from injury, to secure you against defeat; His heart is yours into which you may pour all your sorrows and feel sure of true sympathy; His home is yours to be your everlasting abode; and where He is, there you may be also.

—ASHTON OXENDEN

◆ *Can you think of one thing that you need that Christ is not able to supply? If there is not one thing, trust Him for all your needs. He is able and He is faithful!*

Fully Devoted

A double minded man is unstable in all his ways.
—JAMES 1:8

The entire surrender of the heart to God is the work of the Spirit, for "a man can receive nothing, except it be given him from heaven" (John 3:27). Nothing short of this will bring us to glory. Nothing short of this can give true assurance, peace, and joy. I can never taste the real comforts of religion until I follow the Lord fully. It is the lack of this undivided state of heart which causes so much unsteadiness in the walk and so much discomfort in the experience of many who profess Christ. These, who maintain with warmth the doctrines of grace, at the same time esteem of small importance the social and relative duties of the gospel. Such people seem to forget that to be really holy is to be relatively holy, that no truth can do us any personal good except it influences and purifies our hearts and lives. What should we think of those who, while they appear saints outside of their home, are fiends at home? Can it be a matter of surprise that they should feel no real satisfaction in either religion or in the world?

How great is the happiness of the true follower of Jesus! His sins are blotted out. His soul is beautified with salvation. He has not double aims. All his intentions are simple and single: his one desire is to promote the glory of his God and Savior. His heart is the abode of peace. His house is a home of joy and gladness. He has conflicts, and he has comforts. He has sorrow, and he has support. God is his Father. Angels minister to him, and all things work together for his good. He may be hated of men, but he is beloved of God. He may have to pass through deep waters, but underneath are the everlasting arms. He may often groan, being burdened, but in heaven all his tears will be wiped away. He shall there experience the eternal blessedness of that glorious promise: "He that overcometh shall inherit all things; and I will be his God, and he shall be my son" (Rev. 21:7).

—THOMAS READE

◆ *Identify the competing interests in your heart that hinder you from being fully devoted to God. Pray for a life driven with one purpose, to glorify God.*

Lasting, Unselfish Joy

I will rejoice in the LORD, I will joy in the God of my salvation.
—HABAKKUK 3:18

S piritual joy is a joy that lasts. Can this be said of earthly joy? No, we may have it today, but we cannot reckon upon it tomorrow. It is like the summer's sun, which often disappears as soon as we begin to bask in its warmth. Our mind is bent on it for weeks and months. At last we obtain it, and our heart is content. But how long does it remain? Perhaps it is soon taken away again. Or, if it remains, we discover that it does not give us the pleasure we expected. And then we turn to something else, in the hope of finding enjoyment in it.

But the joy we are speaking of, when it once enters the soul, remains there. We can reckon it as our own. Yes, once we gain this prize, it becomes ours. It may for a time be dampened and smothered in the soul; but it is planted there by the hand of God Himself. Satan may disturb it now and then. Sometimes it is so weak within us that it is hardly felt. But nothing can steal it away from that heart which God has blessed. "Your joy no man taketh from you" (John 16:22).

Spiritual joy is also unselfish. Worldly joy, on the other hand, too often has self for its center. What flatters and pleases and exalts self is what alone rejoices the worldly heart. But the Christian's joy has its center in God. He finds delight in God's service. He rejoices when God is honored. And he takes pleasure, too, in the welfare and happiness of others.

The Savior seems to have found His chief joy in doing good, in relieving the sick, in comforting the mourner, and in saving souls. And we are told that a thrill of delight is felt by the very host of heaven when a lost sheep is received and brought home to the fold. Such, too, is the Christian's joy. It is unselfish. To see his Father honored, to see his fellow man saved and happy, this brings the purest joy to his soul.

—ASHTON OXENDEN

◆ *Where are you finding your greatest joy, in worldly things or the things of God? How can you foster godly joy more than selfish happiness?*

The Benefits of Meditation

I will meditate also of all thy work, and talk of thy doings.
—PSALM 77:12

Meditation is a great help to knowledge; the more you think and meditate on what you read and hear, the more you know. If you would read much and hear much but not meditate, it will amount to little and you will never be wiser; but if a man meditates, he proves the wiser.

As meditation is a great help to knowledge, so it is a great friend to memory. Meditation strengthens memory; it stores the things that we hear or read in the memory. Many complain that they have bad memories and cannot remember. What is the reason but that we do not meditate on what we hear or read?

As meditation is a great help to memory, so it is a heartwarming work, a friend to warm the heart. If a man's body is cold, you chafe it and rub it, and by doing so you put life and warmth into it. Meditation chafes the soul and rubs the soul with truth.

As meditation is a heartwarming work, so it is that which will keep your hearts and souls from sinful thoughts. When the vessel is full, you can put in no more. If the vessel be full of puddle water, you cannot put in wine; if the vessel be full of wine, you cannot put in puddle water. If the heart is full of sinful thoughts, there is no room for holy and heavenly thoughts; if the heart is filled with holy and heavenly thoughts by meditation, there is no room for evil and sinful thoughts. What is the reason that men's hearts are so full of sinful and evil thoughts but because their hearts are not more filled with God? They think little and meditate little of God.

As meditation will keep you from sinful thoughts, so it will fit and tune your hearts for every duty, for prayer, for thanksgiving, and for holy communication of good things to those around you.

—WILLIAM BRIDGE

♦ *Take time to meditate today, and begin by resolving to meditate more, reflecting on and adding to the reasons above.*

Our Family Badge

If ye be without chastisement, whereof all are partakers,
then are ye bastards, and not sons.

—HEBREWS 12:8

It is very remarkable that the apostle fixes on affliction as a mark of true sonship. He makes it the family badge. Chastisement is, then, really one of the chief marks of our lawful and honorable birth. Were this characteristic not to be found on us, we should be lacking in one of the proofs of our sonship. Our legitimacy might be called into question. It might be said that God was not recognizing us as His true-born sons, and that either He had never received us as such or had rejected us. There must be the family badge to establish our claim of birth and to be a pledge of paternal recognition on the part of God our Father.

It is a solemn thought. Flesh and blood shrink from it. We look around to see if there is any way of escaping and ask if it must be so—yes, it must be. Yet it is also a cheering thought. It cheers us under trial to remember that this is the Father's seal set upon His true-born children. How it lightens the load to think that it is really the pledge of our divine adoption.

We need not count, then, upon bright days below nor expect to pass lightly over the pleasant earth as if our life were but the "shadow of a dream." Joy *within* we may expect, "joy unspeakable and full of glory," for that is the family portion (1 Peter 1:8). But joy from *without*, the joy of earth's sunshine, the joy of the world's ease and abundance, the joy of unsevered bonds and unweeping eyes is not our lot in this vale of tears.

Still in the ever-wakeful storms through which we are passing to the kingdom, there is peace—deep peace, too deep for any storm of earth to reach. In the world we have tribulation, but in Jesus we have peace. "Peace I leave with you, my peace I give unto you: not as the world giveth, give I unto you" (John 14:27).

—HORATIUS BONAR

♦ *Do you bear the family mark? Afflictions come in many forms, and we should not desire them, but must also be very careful not to resist when our Father lays them upon us. Let not your trials be wasted, but rather seek to profit from them.*

AUGUST

◆

*To be in the world and yet not of the world
is a high Christian attainment.*

—THOMAS READE

You Are Bought with a Price

*For ye are bought with a price: therefore glorify God
in your body, and in your spirit, which are God's.*
—1 CORINTHIANS 6:20

You are bought with a price; and *what* a price, O Christian! "Ye were not redeemed with corruptible things, as silver and gold…but with the precious blood of Christ" (1 Peter 1:18–19). Take with you the vivid remembrance of this truth, so that your whole life may be a holy life, a pleasant psalm of thanksgiving and praise to God. How powerful the argument, how touching the motive! I am a ransomed being; I am the price of blood, the blood of the incarnate Deity; therefore, from this time forward I am to glorify Him in my body, soul, and spirit, who redeemed, charmed, and saved me.

How can it be that we feel the power and live out the practical effect of this amazing, all-commanding truth so faintly? Oh, the anxious depravity of our nature! Oh, the deep iniquity of our iniquitous hearts. Will not the blood drops of Jesus move us? Will not the unknown agonies of the cross influence us? Will not His dying love constrain us to a more heavenly walk? Ransomed from the curse, from sin, and from Satan, brought out of Egypt as it were with a high and outstretched arm, surely this should speed us onward and hasten our progress heavenward and constrain us, with Moses, "esteeming the reproach of Christ greater riches than the treasures in Egypt: for he had respect unto the recompence of the reward" (Heb. 11:26). How should we then "lay aside every weight, and the sin which doth so easily beset us, and let us run with patience the race that is set before us, looking unto Jesus" (12:1–2), and so speed our way to the heavenly city.

—OCTAVIUS WINSLOW

◆*Believer, ponder the cost that was paid to redeem you. What would a life of gratitude look like in your life and in your relationships?*

Are You Fighting?

Fight the good fight of faith.
—1 TIMOTHY 6:12

What are the reasons why the Christian fight is a "good fight"? What are the points in which his warfare is superior to the warfare of this world? Let me examine this matter. I want no one to begin the life of a Christian soldier without counting the cost. I would not keep back from anyone that the Christian fight, though spiritual, is real and severe. It needs courage, boldness, and perseverance. But I want you to know that there is abundant encouragement if you will only begin this battle. The Scripture does not call the Christian fight a "good fight" without reason and cause.

The Christian's fight is good *because it is fought under the best of generals.* The leader and commander of all believers is our Divine Savior, the Lord Jesus Christ—a Savior of perfect wisdom, infinite love, and almighty power. The Captain of our salvation never fails to lead His soldiers to victory. The humblest servant in His army is not forgotten. The weakest and most sickly is cared for, remembered, and kept unto salvation. The souls whom He has purchased and redeemed with His own blood are far too precious to be wasted and thrown away. Surely this is good!

The Christian's fight is good because it is also *fought with the best of helps.* Weak as each believer is in himself, the Holy Spirit dwells in him, and his body is a temple of the Holy Ghost. Chosen by God the Father, washed in the blood of the Son, renewed by the Spirit, he does not go to war with his own weapons and is never alone. The Holy Ghost daily teaches, leads, and directs him. The Father helps him by His almighty power. The Son intercedes for him every moment. A threefold cord like this can never be broken!

—J. C. RYLE

◆ *What battles are you fighting personally in your life? What battles are you fighting together? What is the armor given to you to help you fight these battles?*

Rules for a Happy Home

Thou shalt love the Lord thy God with all thy heart,
and with all thy soul, and with all thy strength, and
with all thy mind; and thy neighbour as thyself.
—LUKE 10:27

As truth is always ordered toward godliness, so it will produce its fruits under all circumstances. The rules of right are few and simple. Yet how little are they followed except when impressed and taught by the power of God's Spirit. Then they are mighty. Who can but admire the effects produced in a Christian home by such principles and precepts as these?

1. Be humble. "Only by pride cometh contention" (Prov. 13:10).
2. "Keep thy tongue from evil, and thy lips from speaking guile" (Ps. 34:13).
3. Find your own happiness in trying to make others happy.
4. Mind your own business. Meddle not. Be not overbearing.
5. Beware of a fretful, suspicious, or judgmental attitude.
6. Overcome evil with good. Bless and curse not.
7. "Love is the fulfilling of the law" (Rom. 13:10).
8. Try daily to speak some useful knowledge in your family.
9. Do not magnify the trials or afflictions of life.
10. Beware of laziness. There is no greater enemy of peace and happiness.
11. Make it your business to serve God.
12. Keep out of debt. "Owe no man any thing" (Rom. 13:8).
13. "Remember the sabbath day, to keep it holy" (Ex. 20:8).
14. Keep the end of life in view. This will repress many vain wishes and restrain immoderate desires.
15. Let your prayers be frequent and fervent.
16. Never listen to scandal or backbiting.
17. Set the Lord always before you. Seek His glory. Do His will willingly.
18. Let Christ be all and in all. He is everything to us poor sinners. He is the chief among ten thousand.
19. Grieve not for things which cannot be helped.
20. Trust in the Lord forever.

—WILLIAM PLUMER

◆ *Select three of the above that by God's grace you are doing. Select three which you are very lax in doing. How can you help each other to press forward?*

Tempted Saints

The Lord knoweth how to deliver the godly out of temptations.
—2 PETER 2:9

The moment, dear friend, that a text of God's Word is suggested to your thoughts in favor of sin, of distrust of God, of disbelief of Christ, of self-injury, resist it with the holy indignation of a believer in Christ from the threshold of your mind, as coming from the evil one, prompting you to evil and seeking to slay you with the very arms God graciously provided for your defense. God's Word will fortify, strengthen, and help you in temptation. The Bible is the book of the tempted. Like its author, it is divine, invincible, and holy. It is the history of saints tempted like you, but from whose temptation God rescued them. "The Lord knoweth how to deliver the godly out of temptation" (2 Peter 2:9).

The most gracious souls, the most eminent saints, have been *tempted* saints. Abraham was tempted, David was tempted, Job was tempted, Peter was tempted, Paul was tempted, Luther was tempted, and above all Christ was tempted; and all from the same foe—Satan, "the accuser of our brethren" (Rev. 12:10). All passed through this heated crucible, all were taught in this painful school, all bore to heaven the scars of the wounds in this battle with the devil, but out of all, God delivered them. Do not think that some strange thing has happened to you, that you tread a peculiar solitary path, a path untrodden by the saints of God. No, you are one of the "great cloud of witnesses" (Heb. 12:1) of whom it is recorded "they...were tempted" (11:37), and with them you shall testify to the power of faith in giving you the victory over all the assaults of the world, the flesh, and the devil. Fly, tempted one, to the precious Scriptures. They are your grand arsenal, richly stored with every kind of weapon with which to vanquish your powerful, sleepless, subtle foe. But above all, fly to the Christ of the Scriptures and nestle your tempted spirit beneath His sheltering wing.

—OCTAVIUS WINSLOW

◆ *Where are you being tempted at this moment in your life? How does the Word of God give you examples to follow or promises of grace to overcome this temptation?*

Cleaving to a Living, Loving Savior

I am the vine, ye are the branches: He that abideth in me,
and I in him, the same bringeth forth much fruit.
—JOHN 15:5

There are some plants which we see growing against our walls whose branches are nourished from the parent stem. But in addition to that, they will, wherever they can, send out little roots of their own and so draw nourishment for themselves in more ways than one. Sometimes we see this very thing taking place among professing Christians. They are not satisfied with the support they obtain from the true Vine; but they are forever sending out little roots of their own to draw nourishment from other sources.

Carefully destroy all such roots wherever you find them shooting forth, and see that all your support comes from Christ. Let there be a constant chain of prayer linking you to Him and drawing you nearer and nearer to Him. Let your "life [be] hid with Christ in God" (Col. 3:3). Rest on His promises. Feed on Him as your spiritual food. Draw constantly from His fullness and ever be looking to Him as the deliverer and sustainer of your soul. Cling to Him, as closely as the limpet clings to the rock, both for safety and sustenance.

After all, what is true religion? It is not so much a belief in certain truths, or a holding of certain opinions, as it is a *cleaving of the soul to a living, loving Savior*. This is the religion that lasts. This is the religion that sustains the soul and gives it peace and joy. This is the secret of a really happy Christian life. Here is the spring of all growth and progress. Why do so many *begin* well, and nothing more? They get to a certain point, and there they stop. They have fled to Christ, perhaps, and have found peace in Him. But they do not *go on to live upon Him*; and therefore, there is no progress. They sink down wearied instead of running the Christian race.

Remember, then, Christ is *your* Savior and *your* friend. He is on your side, and through Him you will be sustained under every trial and will overcome every difficulty.

—ASHTON OXENDEN

◆*Consider whether you are drawing all your strength from Christ. Do you*
have other sources of seemingly secret strength which is really your weakness?

Forbearance

By long forbearing is a prince persuaded,
and a soft tongue breaketh the bone.
—PROVERBS 25:15

I am persuaded that love and humility are the highest attainments in the school of Christ, and the brightest evidence that He is indeed our Master. If any should seem inclined to treat you with less regard because you are a Christian, you will find forbearance, meekness, and long-suffering the most prevailing means to conquer their prejudices. Our Lord has not only taught us to expect persecution from the world, though this alone is a trial too hard for flesh and blood; but we must look for what is much more grievous to a renewed mind, to be in some respects slighted, censured, and misunderstood even by our fellow Christian. This can, perhaps, happen in times where we are really striving to promote the glory of God and the good of souls and cannot, without the reproach of our consciences, change our course, however glad we would be to have their approval.

Therefore, we are required not only to resist the world, the flesh, and the devil, but likewise to bear one another's burdens; which plainly intimates there will be something to be borne with by everyone's hands; and happy is he that is not offended. You may recall what unjust reports and surmises were received, even at Jerusalem, concerning the apostle Paul. It seems he was condemned unheard, and that by many, but we do not find that he was at all ruffled or that he sought to retort anything upon them. Doubtless, had he been so disposed, he might have found something to have charged them with, but he calmly and willingly complied with everything in his power to soften and convince them. Let us be followers of this pattern, so far as he was a follower of Christ; for even Christ pleased not Himself. How did He bear with the mistakes, weakness, intemperate zeal, and imprudent proposals of His disciples while on earth; and how does He bear with the same thing from you and me and every one of His followers now? Is it therefore too much to bear with each other for His sake?

—JOHN NEWTON

♦ *What does it mean to esteem others better than ourselves? Is there anyone whom you are not esteeming in such a way? Consider how you can change this.*

Trusting in God's Providence

And we know that all things work together for good to them that love God, to them who are the called according to his purpose.
—ROMANS 8:28

In no way do we observe more wonderful unfolding of God than in what we call His providence. This is a department of God's school in which we are learning fresh lessons every day. In providence, divine wisdom is married to divine love. All things work together for good to them who love God and trust Him. The skeptic jeers at this, but the trusting Christian knows it from actual experience. It is often a dear-bought experience, for some of God's truths are knocked into us by hard blows, and some lessons are spelled out through eyes cleansed with tears. Our perverse mistake is that we demand that God shall explain Himself at every step, instead of waiting for Him to unfold His intricate purposes at His own time and in His own way. Why one is set up and another (who seems equally deserving) is cast down; why the only little crib in one Christian home is emptied by death, and the nursery in another home is full of happy voices; why one good business prospers and another one is bankrupt—all such perplexing puzzles shake terribly the faith that is not well grounded on the Rock.

To all these pitiable outcries, the calm answer of our heavenly Father is: "Be still, and know that I am God.... I will bring the blind by a way that they know not.... What I do thou knowest not now; but thou shalt know hereafter" (Ps. 46:10; Isa. 42:16; John 13:7). These are the voices of love which come to us from behind the cloud. If we wait patiently, the cloud will break away or part asunder, and our eyes will behold the rainbow of mercy overarching the throne.

—THEODORE CUYLER

◆ *List a providence in which you were able to accept God's way and a providence in which you complained. Why has it been said that God's providence is like Hebrew, it must be read backward to understand it?*

The God of Peace

The God of peace shall be with you.
—PHILIPPIANS 4:9

A godly heart being enlarged to be capable of knowing God and enjoying something of Him can be filled by nothing in the world; it must only have God Himself. Therefore, whatever God might give to a godly heart, unless He gives Himself, it will not do. This heart will not only have mercy, but the God of that mercy as well.

We read in Philippians 4:7, "And the peace of God, which passeth all understanding, shall keep your hearts and minds through Jesus Christ." In verse 9 we read, "Those things, which ye have both learned, and received, and heard, and seen in me, do: and the God of peace shall be with you." The peace of God shall keep you, and the God of peace shall be with you. What I observe is that the peace of God is not enough to a godly heart, unless it may have the God of that peace. A carnal heart could be satisfied if he may have outward peace, though it is not the peace of God; peace in the world and in his work would satisfy him. But see how a godly heart goes beyond a carnal heart. All outward peace is not enough. I must have the peace of God. But if you have the peace of God, will that quiet you? No, I must have the God of peace. As I have the peace of God, so I need the God of peace. That is, I must enjoy God who gives me the peace; I must have the cause as well as the effect. I must see where my peace comes and enjoy the fountain of that peace as well as the stream of my peace. Have I health from God? I must have the God of my health or else I am not satisfied. It is not life, but the God of my life; it is not riches, but the God of those riches that I must have; the God of my preservation, as well as my preservation.

—JEREMIAH BURROUGHS

◆*Have you ever found yourself resting in the peace of God rather than in God Himself, or resting in His gifts rather than in the giver of the gift? How can you prevent this from happening?*

Two Common Errors

Work out your own salvation with fear and trembling.
For it is God which worketh in you both to will
and to do of his good pleasure.
—PHILIPPIANS 2:12–13

There are two fatal errors which, it is to be feared, abound among Christians. The one considers the divine as disrobed of its glory by insisting upon the necessity of human endeavors in the great work of salvation. The other declares that the absolute necessity of divine grace to the production of everything that is spiritually good in man is injurious to morality.

If a father, for instance, should pray for the conversion of his children and yet allow them to run wild, without presenting any checks to their evils, under the impression that God in His good time will save them if they are to be saved, and if they are not among the elect, would no blame be attached to him should they finally perish? Would he not, by such erroneous views of the work of salvation, actually be aiding the cause of Satan and the destruction of his unhappy child under the false notion of glorifying the sovereignty of God and the freeness of divine grace?

On the other hand, if a father should endeavor to train up his children in virtuous habits and be careful to guard them against the seductions of the world, and base all his hopes of success on his own efforts and paternal instructions without once feeling the power of that all-important declaration of the Savior, "Without me ye can do nothing" (John 15:5), would he not by such behavior manifest great impiety? And could not the Almighty withhold His spiritual blessing to show how easily He can ruin the most powerful human endeavors?

To trust God with all our hearts in the diligent use of the appointed means is the path which infinite wisdom has marked out for man as a moral agent. To be enabled to do this in a right spirit is the work of divine grace and is the way to obtain divine blessing.

—THOMAS READE

◆ *Have you viewed your children in either way described here? If so, what would repentance from this look like, and how will you rectify it with your children? How can you balance between these two extremes?*

The Warnings of Affliction (1)

*And be not conformed to this world: but be ye transformed by
the renewing of your mind, that ye may prove what is that good,
and acceptable, and perfect, will of God.*

—ROMANS 12:2

Affliction is full of warnings. It has many voices of various kinds. It
speaks counsel, rebuke, and affection. But it speaks warning too. Let
us hear some of its words of warning.

It says, "Love not the world, neither the things that are in the world. If
any man love the world, the love of the Father is not in him" (1 John 2:15).
There is no enforcement of this warning so solemn as that which affliction
gives. It exposes the world's hollowness and says, "Love not." It points out to
us its hastening doom and says, "Love not." It declares the utter impossibility of loving both the world and the Father. "If any man love the world, the
love of the Father is not in him" (v. 15). "Know ye not that the friendship of
the world is enmity with God?" (James 4:4). There can be no companionship between God and the world. They cannot dwell together under the
same roof or in the same heart.

It says, "Take heed, and beware of covetousness" (Luke 12:15). Riches
cannot help; neither can earthly comfort avail us in the hour of grief. They
cannot dry up tears nor reunite broken bonds. They cannot heal the living
nor bring back the dead. They do not profit in the day of darkness. Their
vanity and emptiness cannot then be hidden. "Thou fool, this night thy soul
shall be required of thee: then whose shall those things be, which thou hast
provided?" (v. 20). It is then we find that we need a "treasure in the heavens
that faileth not" (v. 33). "I counsel thee to buy of *me* gold tried in the fire,
that thou mayest be rich" (Rev. 3:18).

—HORATIUS BONAR

◆*Ask your spouse if they detect any "love of the world" in your life. Ponder
your afflictions, and ask yourself if they are speaking any of the warnings
in today's meditation.*

The Warnings of Affliction (2)

*And be not conformed to this world: but be ye transformed by
the renewing of your mind, that ye may prove what is that good,
and acceptable, and perfect, will of God.*

—ROMANS 12:2

L et us hear more of affliction's words of warning. Affliction says, "Abstain from all appearance of evil" (1 Thess. 5:22). Hate even the garments spotted by the flesh. It is not the flesh merely that we are to hate, but even its garments. It is not merely to abstain from evil, but from all appearance of evil. Suffering teaches us to shrink from sin—even from the remotest and most indirect connection with it. It says, "Do not this abominable thing that I hate" (Jer. 44:4).

It says, "Grudge not one against another" (James 5:9). Let there be no half-hearted affection in the family of God. Let there be no envy, no jealousy, no misunderstandings among the brethren. Why should we be less than friends who are both fellow sufferers and fellow soldiers here? Why should we not love one another with a pure heart fervently? Yet it often needs affliction to teach us this, to remove our jealousies, and to draw us together in love and sympathy.

It says, "Keep yourselves from idols" (1 John 5:21). If there be one remaining idol, break it in pieces and spare it not. Nothing is so fruitful a cause of suffering as idolatry. Nothing so forcibly displays the vanity of our idols as suffering. It is with this whip of cords that Christ scourges out of us the buying and selling, allowing no earthly traffic to proceed in His Father's house.

I give these warnings merely as examples; a few out of many which might be addressed. The two great points against which the warnings of chastisement are directed seem to be selfishness and worldliness. To scourge these thoroughly out of us is God's design.

—HORATIUS BONAR

◆ *Has affliction had its perfect work in you? Can you think of other ways than those mentioned in these two meditations in which God might be warning you through afflictions?*

Godly Living in a Wicked World

*Who knoweth whether thou art come
to the kingdom for such a time as this?*
—ESTHER 4:14

It is indeed sad when Christians are mixed with the wicked. David "beheld the transgressors, and was grieved" (Ps. 119:158), and Lot—who was a bright star in a dark night—was vexed or, as the word in the original may bear, wearied with the unclean conversation of the wicked. He made the sins of Sodom spears to pierce his own world. We ought, if there be any spark of divine love in us, to be very sensible of the sins of others and to have our hearts bleed for them; yet let us not break forth in murmuring or discontent, knowing that God in His providence has permitted it, and surely not without some reasons.

The Lord makes the wicked a hedge to defend the godly. The wise God often makes those who are wicked and peaceable a means to safeguard His people from those who are wicked and cruel. The king of Babylon kept Jeremiah and gave special order that he should be well looked to and lack nothing (Jer. 39:11–12). God sometimes makes brazen sinners to be a brazen wall to defend His people.

God mingles the wicked with the godly, that the godly may be a means to save the wicked. Such is the beauty of holiness, that it has a magnetic force in it to allure and draw even the wicked. Sometimes God makes a believing husband a means to convert an unbelieving wife, or a believing wife an unbelieving husband. "For what knowest thou, O wife, whether thou shalt save thy husband? or how knowest thou, O man, whether thou shalt save thy wife?" (1 Cor. 7:16).

The godly living among the wicked, by their prudent advice and pious example, have won them to the embracing of religion; if there were not some godly among the wicked, how, without a miracle, can we imagine that the wicked should be converted? Those who are now saints in heaven sometimes served diverse lusts. Paul once a persecutor; Augustine once a Manichaean; Luther once a monk; but by the holy walk of the godly, they were converted to the faith.

—THOMAS WATSON

◆ *Has God used your life as a witness to any so that they have been won to Christ? Is this your desire? How could you be a better witness?*

Joy in Suffering

But none of these things move me, neither count I my life dear unto myself, so that I might finish my course with joy.

—Acts 20:24

True spiritual joy depends but little on outward things. Think of those who lived in the days of the apostles. There was everything in their situation to cast them down. All outward things were against them. But there was that within them which enabled them to rejoice in their tribulation. Instead of being filled with alarm and sadness, they were "filled with joy, and with the Holy Ghost" (Acts 13:52). So it was in all their persecutions: they rejoiced that they were counted worthy to suffer shame for the Savior's name. See how they bore their troubles at Philippi. What do we hear under those prison walls? Is it the dismal sound of moaning and distress? No, we hear amid the clank of chains the voice of joy and gladness, the song of thankfulness and praise. Again it is said of others that they "took joyfully the spoiling of [their] goods, knowing…[they] have in heaven a better and an enduring substance" (Heb. 10:34). Think of the martyrs, too, who suffered so nobly, so patiently, so cheerfully for Christ's sake. They welcomed the very flames that took away their lives. How was this? Were they not filled with a joy from heaven, which man could not take from them?

And I would ask you if you know what Christian joy is. When have you felt happiest? When have you drunk deepest of this heavenly joy? Not perhaps when prosperity has shone full upon you, but in some hour of trial, when the world was nothing to you, but God was everything. Then you felt the Savior near you; you saw religion to be a real thing; your heart leaped with joy; you then experienced a happiness which you cannot describe.

—ASHTON OXENDEN

◆ *Do you know Christian joy in your suffering? How can you intentionally practice joy during suffering?*

Sing Praises

Sing praises to God, sing praises:
sing praises unto our King, sing praises.
—PSALM 47:6

Those who have been made partakers of the free and glorious grace of God are called to spend their lives in much praise and hallelujahs to God for the wonders of His mercy in their redemption. To you, O redeemed of the Lord, does this doctrine most directly apply itself; you who have been made partakers of all this glorious grace. It is you that God entertained thoughts of restoring after your miserable fall into dreadful depravity and corruption and into danger of the dreadful misery that unavoidably follows. It is for you, in particular, that God gave His Son, His only Son, and sent Him into the world. It is to you that the free application of the fruit of these things is made: all this is done perfectly and altogether freely, without any of your desert, without any of your righteousness or strength; wherefore, let your life be spent in praises to God. When you praise Him in prayer, let it not be with coldness and indifferency; when you praise Him in your closet, let your whole soul be active. When you praise Him in singing, don't just barely make a noise, without any stirring of affection in the heart, without any internal melody. Surely, you have reason to shout, cry, "Grace, grace, be the top stone of the temple!" Certainly, you do not lack mercy and bounty to praise God; you only lack a heart and lively affections to praise Him with.

If the angels are astonished at God's mercy to you and even shout with joy and admiration at the sight of God's grace to you, you yourself, on whom this grace is bestowed, have much more reason to shout.

Consider that a great part of your happiness in heaven, to all eternity, will consist in praising of God for His free and glorious grace in redeeming you. If you would spend more time about it on earth, you would find this world would be much more of a heaven to you than it is. Wherefore, do nothing while you are alive, but speak and think and live God's praises.

—JONATHAN EDWARDS

◆*How can you praise the Lord more than you currently do? Lift your voice in a song of praise.*

The Greatest of These

And now abideth faith, hope, charity, these three;
but the greatest of these is charity.
—1 CORINTHIANS 13:13

Charity is called the greatest of graces because it is the one in which there is some likeness between the believer and his God. God has no need of faith. He is dependent on no one. There is none superior to Him in whom He must trust. God has no need of hope. To Him all things are certain, whether past, present, or future. But "God is love" (1 John 4:8), and the more love His people have, the more likeness they have to their Father in heaven.

Charity is also called the greatest of the graces because it is most useful to others. Faith and hope, however precious, have special reference to a believer's own private individual use. Faith unites the soul to Christ, brings peace with God, and opens the way to heaven. Hope fills the soul with cheerful expectation of things to come and, amid many discouragements of things seen, comforts with visions of things unseen. But charity is preeminently the grace which makes a man useful. It is the spring of good works and kindnesses. It is the root of missions, schools, and hospitals. Charity made apostles spend and be spent for souls. Charity raises up workers for Christ and keeps them working. Charity smooths quarrels and stops strife and, in this sense, covers "the multitude of sins" (1 Peter 4:8). Charity adorns Christianity and recommends it to the world. A man may have real faith, and feel it, and yet his faith may be invisible. But a man's charity cannot be hid.

Finally, charity is the greatest of graces because it is the one which endures the longest. In fact, it will never die. Faith will one day be swallowed up in sight, and hope in certainty. But love will live on through the endless ages of eternity. Heaven will be the place of love. The inhabitants of heaven will be full of love, and in every heart and mind will be charity.

—J. C. RYLE

◆*When you think of love in the world to come, why is it so attractive to you?*

Winning by Example

Be thou an example of the believers, in word, in
conversation, in charity, in spirit, in faith, in purity.
—1 TIMOTHY 4:12

Next to God comes *your own family.* You have a most important and interesting duty to discharge to them. It is a happy thing for you if the other members of your family are of the same mind as yourself, if they feel with you on religious subjects and are seeking with you the way to heaven. Then there is a stronger cord that binds you together than even that of nature. And, in this case, your difficulties will be few.

But suppose it is otherwise. Perhaps you stand alone in your family: the rest are for the world; you are for God. Those to whom you would naturally look for a helping hand are rather disposed to check you. Those whom you have before regarded as your counselors in everything seem now to be a little alarmed at your earnestness and would put a clog upon your wheels instead of urging you onward.

If this be the case, do not fly off from them and take a solitary course of your own. Try to act in accordance with their wishes as far as you are able without wounding your own conscience. Let it be your earnest endeavor to win over every member of your family to the Lord's side. Try by gentle means to lead them into the same pleasant path into which you, through God's mercy, have been brought. It is far better to attract them by holiness and blamelessness of your actions, and to draw them with the silken cords of love, than to try to force them by heated arguments and by condemning them for what, perhaps, they do not yet see to be wrong. Endeavor to *win* them to Christ, for you cannot *drag* them into His service against their will. There are a thousand little acts of kindness you may daily show them, and a thousand ways in which the beautiful fruits of religion may display themselves. Be cheerful and kind to them. Love your home, and try to make it happy to all.

—ASHTON OXENDEN

◆*Does your family join with you in serving Christ? If so, praise God and seek ways to collectively be an example. If not, what can you do or change, considering the call of this meditation?*

Christians Persuaded to Fruitfulness

The root of the righteous yieldeth fruit.
—PROVERBS 12:12

This is the emblem of a good Christian: he is never without fruit, either blooming in his affections or being produced in his conversation. That I may persuade Christians to fruitfulness, I ask you to weigh these five things.

1. Fruit is that which God *expects* from us. We are His plantations; and "who planteth a vineyard, and eateth not of the fruit thereof?" (1 Cor. 9:7). Let us not be as Pharaoh's cows, which devoured the fat and yet were still lean; let us not be still devouring sermons, yet never the fatter.

2. Fruitfulness is one of the most distinctive characteristics of a Christian. "The root of the righteous yieldeth fruit" (Prov. 12:12). Fruitfulness differs a saint from a hypocrite! The hypocrite is all for show and pretense; he has fair leaves, but the "root of the righteous yieldeth fruit" (v. 12). It is the very definition of a branch in Christ that it "beareth fruit" (John 15:2). As a man differs from an animal by reason, as an animal differs from a plant by sense, and as a plant differs from a stone by vegetation, so a good Christian differs from a hypocrite by fruit.

3. Fruitfulness *adorns* a Christian as the fruit adorns the tree. A fruit-bearing Christian is an ornament to religion; the more fruitful the branch is, the fairer to look on. A dead tree, as it is unserviceable, so it is uncomely. A Christian decked with the fruits of righteousness is beautiful and glorious.

4. Fruitfulness is a *good evidence to show for heaven*; the fruits of love, humility, and good works are (as Bernard said) "seeds of hope, signs of predestination, the happy presages (foreshadows) of future glory." The righteousness of faith is always accompanied with the fruits of righteousness. He that can show good fruit goes full sail to heaven.

5. God *delights* in His fruitful trees; when His garden flourishes, He will walk there; He who curses the barren tree will taste of the fruitful tree. "I am come into my garden, my sister, my spouse: I have gathered my myrrh with my spice" (Song 5:1).

—THOMAS WATSON

◆*Sometimes we need the help of others to discern fruit in our lives. Ask someone close to you for an honest report concerning your fruitfulness. Take this report and your own consideration to the Lord.*

Godly Conversation

Seeing then that all these things shall be dissolved, what manner of persons ought ye to be in all holy conversation and godliness.

—2 PETER 3:11

If you profess that God has begun to work upon you by the gospel, what change has it wrought in you? Can those who live with you see your conversations so changed as to make them stand and admire the work of the gospel upon your hearts—husband to stand and admire the work of God upon the heart of the wife as if she were another woman, and so the wife to admire the grace of God upon the heart of her husband as if he were another man, and so your children not the same as before? What honor this would be to the gospel that, in places where it is preached with power, there might appear a change that becomes the gospel of Christ.

If your conversations do not show a mighty change that God has wrought in you, then it is not such as becomes the gospel of Christ. It may be you are somewhat better than you were before. You are more understanding and not as profane and worldly as you used to be but live somewhat better. This change is not that change which holds forth the work of the gospel, for when the gospel prevails, it makes the greatest change that ever was in the world. We may boldly assert this, that since the creation of the world, there was never such a change made in the world as the gospel makes. And, therefore, a conversation becoming the gospel must be a changed conversation. It must be mightily different from what it was before.

Sometimes we see it through the mercy of God that when men and women hear the Word, they are so changed that their friends stand wondering at them, What shall we have of them now? Such have cause to answer and say, "Blessed be God it is so. It is the gospel that has made such a change in me." This then becomes the gospel when your conversation is so changed, so holy, godly, and gracious, more than it was before.

—JEREMIAH BURROUGHS

♦*Paul calls the person born again a new creature. Pause a moment and reflect over the past year(s), and seek to discern what changes the Lord has worked in you if you have laid claim to His salvation.*

Fervent Prayer

The effectual fervent prayer of a righteous man availeth much.

—James 5:16

How is it that we sometimes see a Christian growing in the knowledge and love of God; making rapid strides toward heaven; meek, gentle, and Christlike in all his conduct; walking humbly and closely with his God; and recommending religion to others by his holy and happy life? And we see another full of talk and profession but harsh and unloving in his spirit; with a great deal of knowledge and quick in detecting the wrong in others, but unwatchful and inconsistent in his own walk. He makes no progress in the path of holiness. There is no real growth in grace, but his state today is much what it was a year ago.

What makes the difference between these two men? They are both, perhaps, trusting to Christ alone to save them; they both love to come to God's house; they both choose God's people as their companions; they both pass for religious men. What can be the reason, then, that the one is so true and bright a Christian and the other is so much otherwise? It is that the one is *a man of prayer*; the other is neglectful of it. The one lives to God and holds daily and hourly intercourse with Him; the other knows of Him but lives at a distance from Him.

What unspeakable strength will prayer bring to you! Utterly weak in yourself, you will thus become "strong in the Lord, and in the power of his might" (Eph. 6:10). "A man of prayer," says one who is now with God, "is a man of power." A praying soul is a thriving soul. Our great adversary, the devil, is aware of this; he knows full well the secret of our strength. Hence the closet is the Christian's battlefield. There he conquers. Satan aims at this fortress. He triumphs when he has succeeded in baffling prayer; but he trembles when he sees the weakest saint upon his knees. Make it your practice *never* to rise in the morning without kneeling down and engaging at least for a few minutes in heartfelt prayer. And *never* think of going to rest at night without doing the same.

—ASHTON OXENDEN

◆ *Are you a praying Christian? Do you pray in private and with others? Do you believe in the power of prayer, or is it simply an obligation?*

The Comfort of the Scriptures

For whatsoever things were written aforetime were written for our learning,
that we through patience and comfort of the scriptures might have hope.
—ROMANS 15:4

The Bible, while it is a proclamation of mercy to the vilest sinner, is equally the book of the afflicted. As a system of consolation, Christianity has no equal. No other religion in the wild world touches the hidden springs of the soul or reaches the lowest depths of human sorrow but the religion of Christ. Saints of the living God! Suffering members of a suffering Head! We cite you as witnesses to this truth. When your hearts have been overwhelmed, when adversity has wrapped you within its gloomy pall, when the broken billows of grief have swollen and surged around your soul, how you have fled to the Scriptures of truth for succor and support, for guidance and comfort! Nor have you gone to them in vain. "The God of all comfort" (2 Cor. 1:3) is He who speaks in this Word, and there is no word of comfort like that which He speaks. The adaptation of His Word to the varied, peculiar, and personal trials and sorrows of His church is one of the strongest proofs of its divinity.

Take to the Word of God what sorrow you may, go with mental clouding, with depression, with heart grief—even if its character, complexion, and depth surpasses any in the history of human sorrow—there is consolation and support in the Word of God for your mind. There is in these sacred pages a voice of sympathy and soothing chiming with your grief; and so by the "comfort of the scriptures [you] might have hope" (Rom. 15:4) that God will not leave you in trouble but will sustain you in it, bring you out of, and sanctify you by it, to the endless glory and praise of His great and precious name. May we say of the Bible as David said of Goliath's sword, "There is none like that" (1 Sam. 21:9). Christian, let me once more direct your eye—too dimmed perhaps by tears to behold the precious truth—to this divine source of true, unfailing comfort.

—OCTAVIUS WINSLOW

◆ *Paul calls the Corinthians to comfort one another with the comfort wherewith they had been comforted of God. Recall God's comfort given to you through the Word, and now share this with others who are in need of comfort as well.*

A High Christian Attainment

Be perfect, be of good comfort.
—2 CORINTHIANS 13:11

In this life few like Caleb follow the Lord fully. Yet nothing is more abhorrent to our all-gracious Redeemer than a divided heart and a lukewarm spirit. As all our happiness in our lives now and in eternity is the fruit of His love to us; so all our holiness is the fruit of His Spirit, drawing our hearts and fixing them wholly on Himself. It is the work of the Holy Spirit to take the things of Christ and to show them to us. It is to convince us of the emptiness of every earthly thing and the foolishness of seeking our own happiness in a world which is filled with wickedness. When the heart is filled with the love and Spirit of Jesus, how weak are the temptations of Satan, how powerless are the allurements of the world, and how comparatively smooth is the path of sorrow. To be in the world and yet not of the world is a high Christian attainment which Paul possessed to an eminent degree.

God's Word reveals to us the art of divine contentment under every burden and hardship. To a spiritual mind, even nature is full of instruction. The squirrel, when disturbed, skips from bough to bough, continuing always near the ground, while the lark, when alarmed in her nest, flies upward with rapid wing, singing as she soars. Just so the worldling when troubled with grief goes from one person to another, while the Christian leaving all his earthly cares behind him rises on the wings of faith and prayer to seek his rest in God.

Do we seek for comfort from our God and Savior and find it in the hour of trial? Jacob wrestled and prevailed. May we be Israels with God and never cease to pray till He gives that kind of faith which lessens the weight of sorrow, that hope which carries the soul with steady flight to glory.

—THOMAS READE

◆ *How do you respond to trials and burdens? In our trials we either run to Christ or run away from Him. Are you drawing closer to Christ, or does your faith grow dim and you withdraw? What do you think is the remedy?*

Slow Growth

O Lord, hear; O Lord, forgive.
—DANIEL 9:19

There is much in ourselves of which we have truly to be ashamed and to be filled with profound self-abhorrence. We need to be ashamed of our unbelief, of our low thoughts of the Savior, of our little love to God, of our slow progress in spiritual life, of our imperfect conformity to Christ, of the power of indwelling sin, and of our small spiritual attainments in knowledge, personal holiness, and heavenly readiness. What shame should cover us that we are so ready to compromise, to falter, and to halt. How deeply humbled we should be that there still exists in us so much carnality, love of the world, and conformity to the world—so little of the crucified spirit, of a cross-bearing Savior!

What cause of shame that, with all our profession, the pulse of spiritual life beats in our souls so faintly, the spirit of prayer breathes in us so feebly, that we possess so little real, vital religion and follow Christ at so great a distance. Filled with self-abasement should we be that the fruits and graces of the Spirit are in us so sickly, drooping, and shadowed that we have so limited a measure of faith, love, and humility; that we are so defective in our patience and meekness, wisdom and gentleness that with all our blossom and foliage, there is so little real fruit to the glory of our Father.

May we, in view of all this, exclaim with Ezra, in his deep grief and humiliation for the sins of the people, "O my God, I am ashamed and blush to lift up my face to thee, my God: for our iniquities are increased over our head, and our trespass is grown up unto the heavens." Where shall we fly, where hide our blushing face but in the blood of atonement; sprinkled afresh with which, we may lift up our heads and not be ashamed.

—OCTAVIUS WINSLOW

♦*Come before God and confess coldness, unbelief, lack of love, or whatever hinders you from living for and enjoying Christ daily. "Whoso confesseth and forsaketh [his sins] shall have mercy" (Prov. 28:13).*

Sour Fruit

*Either make the tree good, and his fruit good; or else make the
tree corrupt, and his fruit corrupt: for the tree is known by his fruit.*
—MATTHEW 12:33

I have a word for those professing Christians who have no life or reality about their religion and are only nominal members of Christ's church. I need hardly say there are many people in this condition. They are not skeptics and would be offended if you called them unbelievers. Yet the truth is, except for going to church on Sundays, they show no sign of Christianity. If you mark their daily life, they seem neither to think nor feel, nor care for their souls or God or eternity.

I warn you who are in this state, and I say it with pain, that you are the true cause of a vast proportion of unfaithfulness. I remember hearing a skeptic say, "Do you think I am going to believe your Christianity when I see so many of your church-goers living as they do? Do you mean to tell me that they think their creed is true and that they really believe in a resurrection and a judgment to come? I will believe when I see your people really believing. Right now your Christianity seems a great sham and a mere form." Alas! Such talk as this is often justified by facts. Nothing, nothing, I am convinced, does so much to hinder the progress of religion as the utter absence of truth and earnestness among professing Christians.

Men and women who crowd churches on Sundays and then live worldly selfish lives all week are the best proponents of skepticism. "If you believed what you heard in church," the skeptic says, "you would never live as you live at home." Oh, that people would think of the harm done by their inconsistency. "Awake thou that sleepest, and arise from the dead" (Eph. 5:14). It is bad enough to ruin your own soul, but do not add to your sin by ruining others.

—J. C. RYLE

◆ *Pause and ask yourself if there is anything, in words or actions, that may
be giving ammunition to the skeptic of religion.*

What Is It to Serve Christ?

Knowing that of the Lord ye shall receive the reward
of the inheritance: for ye serve the Lord Christ.
—COLOSSIANS 3:24

What is it to serve Christ? We must make sure that we make no mistake here. If we serve ourselves or the world or the devil and think we are serving Christ, we shall perish. Be not deceived, God is not mocked. Christ will not allow Himself to be cheated with meaningless words and empty promises.

To serve Christ is to take Him as our Mediator in all His offices. We must accept Him as our Prophet, to teach us by His word and Spirit and example. We must find no fault with any lessons He gives us. We must own Him as our High Priest, who shed His most precious blood for us and "hath given himself for us an offering and a sacrifice to God for a sweetsmelling savour" (Eph. 5:2). It is He who must pray for us in the courts above. He ever lives to make intercession for us. The Father always hears Him. And we must take Him as our King to rule in us and over us, by His laws, His precepts, His example, and His authority. We must murmur at nothing which He does.

We must serve Christ to the exclusion of all others. He is our one Lord, our one Master, our one Mediator. He is the stone which was set at naught by the builders and is become the head of the corner.

The service we give to Christ must be out of love to Him. If we do not give Him our hearts, His service will be drudgery. No Israelite under an Egyptian taskmaster gave a more unwilling service than does the poor man who has never been born again, who has not the love of God in his heart. But when the heart is all aglow with love to Christ, His service is easy and delightful.

—WILLIAM PLUMER

◆ *Give some concrete examples of what it would look like for you to serve*
Christ fully and unconditionally.

Lovable Christians

For all the law is fulfilled in one word, even in this;
Thou shalt love thy neighbour as thyself.
—Galatians 5:14

If Jesus were now upon earth, the most wretched outcasts would be drawn to Him; the poorest child would be glad to climb upon His knee and to kiss that sad, sweet countenance of purity and love. There would be nothing in this belittling His dignity as the Son of God. Christ Jesus was love incarnate. As much as He abhorred sin, He loved sinners, and sought to save the guiltiest. He never kept the most sinful from His presence. When hard-hearted Pharisees scoffed at Him for eating with publicans and sinners, His reply was that He came into the world for that very purpose—to seek and to win and to save those who were lost. Let us copy Christ. Let us learn from Him how to combine the most unbending sense of justice, purity, and loyalty to God with a lovable face, kind words, and an unselfish sympathy toward the most sinful as well as the most suffering.

Who are the best-loved people in our community? I answer unhesitatingly they are the *unselfish*. They are those who have drunk deepest of the Spirit of Christ Jesus. They are those who have more effectually cut that cursed cancer of self out of their hearts and filled its place with that love that "seeketh not her own" (1 Cor. 13:5). This beautiful grace sometimes blooms in most unexpected places. It was illustrated by a poor boy in a coal mine when an accident occurred, and a man came down to help the suffering. The brave boy said to him, "Don't mind me; Joe Brown is a little lower down, and he's almost gone; save him first!" There are enough "Joe Browns" who are lower down in poverty and ignorance, in weakness and in want than we are, and a Christian's duty is to save them. It was to save sinners from sinking into the deeper pit of hell that Jesus died on Calvary. He who stoops the lowest to rescue lost souls will have the highest place in heaven.

—THEODORE CUYLER

◆*Consider how others around you are perishing. How can you deny yourself in order to be a greater witness to others of God's grace, so that their hearts would be drawn to Him?*

A Quiet and Still Heart

And that ye study to be quiet.
—1 THESSALONIANS 4:11

When a Christian has a quiet, still heart, he is a vessel fit to receive mercy from the Lord. If you want a vessel to take in any liquid, you must hold it still, because if it stirs and shakes up and down, you cannot pour in anything. But you will say, "Hold still," so that you may pour the liquid in and not lose any. So, if we would be vessels to receive God's mercy and would have the Lord pour His mercy into us, we must have quiet, still hearts. We must not have hearts hurrying up and down in trouble, discontent, and vexing, but still and quiet hearts.

If a child throws a fit and kicks for something, you do not give him what he cries for until he is quiet and is content without it, and then you will give it to him. And so does the Lord deal with us, for our actions toward Him are just like your contrary children are with you. As soon as you want something from God, if you cannot have it, you are distressed and all in an uproar, as it were, in your heart. God intends mercy to you, but He says, "You shall not have it yet, until you are quiet, and then in the quietness of your heart, come to Me."

You who know God, have you not found this to be the way of God toward you? When you were troubled for lack of some spiritual comfort and your hearts were troubled at it, you got nothing from God all that while; but if you quiet your heart and can say, "It is right that the Lord should do with me as He will. I am under His feet and am resolved to do what I can to honor Him. And whatever He does with me, I will seek Him as long as I live and will be content with what God gives, whether He grants my desires or not." Often it will be when we are in this frame of mind, God will grant you the mercy and give you comfort you seek.

—JEREMIAH BURROUGHS

◆*Are you in a quiet frame of mind? If not, why not? Think about how you can attain quietness before God.*

Walk Worthy of Your High Calling

I therefore, the prisoner of the Lord, beseech you that ye
walk worthy of the vocation wherewith ye are called.
—Ephesians 4:1

To those who are called, walk worthy of your high calling. "I…beseech you that ye walk worthy of the vocation wherewith ye are called" (Eph. 4:1). Walk compassionately. Pity such as are yet uncalled. Have you a child that God has not yet called, a wife, a husband? Weep over their never dying souls; they are in their blood under "the power of Satan" (Acts 26:18). Oh, pity them! Let their sins more trouble you than your own sufferings. If you pity an ox or ass going astray, will you not pity a soul going astray? Show your piety by your pity.

Yours is a holy calling (2 Tim. 1:9). You are called to be saints (Rom. 1:7). Show your vocation by a Bible conversation. Do not flowers smell sweeter than weeds? Shall not they who are ennobled with grace have more fragrance in their lives than sinners? "As he which hath called you is holy, so be ye holy in all manner of conversation" (1 Peter 1:15). Dishonor not your high calling by any sordid behavior! When Antigonus was going to defile himself with women, someone told him he was a king's son. Oh, remember your dignity—"called of God," of the blood royal of heaven. Do nothing unworthy of your honorable calling. Scipio refused the embraces of a harlot because he was general of an army. Abhor all motions to sin because of your high calling. It is not fit for those who are the called of God to do as others; though others of the Jews did drink wine, it was not fit for the Nazirite, because he had a vow of separation upon him and had promised abstinence. Though pagans and nominal Christians take liberty to sin, yet it is not fit for those who are called out of the world and have the mark of election upon them to do so. You are consecrated persons, your bodies are the temples of the Holy Ghost, and your bodies must be a sacristy, or holy of holies.

—THOMAS WATSON

♦ *What does it look like to treat your body and your soul as not your own but as belonging to Christ?*

The Preciousness of God's Word

Thy word is a lamp unto my feet,
and a light unto my path.
—PSALM 119:105

The Bible is the opening of the heart of God. It is God's heart unveiled, each throb inviting the mourner in Zion, the poor in spirit, the widow, the fatherless, the persecuted, the sufferer—yea, every child of affliction and grief—to take refuge and sympathy, to find the protection and soothing of His heart. Thank God for the comfort and consolation of the Scripture! Open it with what sorrow and burden and perplexity you may, be it the guilt of sin, the pressure of trial, or the burden of sorrow, it speaks to the heart such words of comfort as only God could speak.

Have you ever borne your grief to God's Word, especially to the Psalms of David, and not felt that it was written for your particular sorrow? You have found your grief more accurately portrayed, your state of mind more truly described, and your situation more exactly and fully met, probably in a single history, chapter, or verse, than in all the books that the pen of man ever wrote.

What a proof that the Bible is the Word of God. We believe that no Christian is thoroughly versed in the evidence of the truth of the Bible, or is in a right position to understand its divine contents, until he is afflicted. Luther remarks that he never understood the Psalms until God afflicted him. Fly to the Word of God, then, in every sorrow. You will know more of the mind and heart of God than you, perhaps, ever learned in all the schools before. Study to know God's Word from a heartfelt experience of its quickening, sanctifying, comforting power. Sit not at the feet of men, but at the feet of Jesus. His Word alone can instruct you in these sacred and precious truths. You must learn in Christ's school and be taught by the Holy Spirit.

—OCTAVIUS WINSLOW

♦ *John Calvin called the Psalms, "an anatomy of all parts of the soul; for there is not an emotion of which anyone can be conscious that is not here represented as in a mirror." How do the Psalms resonate with your soul?*

Everything in Moderation

Let your moderation be known unto all men.
—PHILIPPIANS 4:5

Religion sweetens temporal delights and pleasures. Religion does not only allow us to enjoy temporal comforts but adds a new sweetness to them beyond what wicked and sensual men can find in them. When the wicked man pursues sensual delights in a wicked manner, he does it against his reason and conscience; his flesh drives him on against his mind; his understanding consents not, but opposes him in it, so that he enjoys his pleasures while at war within himself; his own reason and conscience oppose him, which takes away the sweetness of the pleasure; and his body only is partaker of the pleasure and not his mind. He enjoys pleasures, but there is a sting in them, and conscience roars and will not give him peace. His own reason will not let him alone to enjoy them peaceably.

For the godly, taking those delights according to reason and conscience, his internal man consents to his external in the enjoyment of them and partakes with him therein, and it is a pleasant feast that the body and soul enjoy together. His reason—the highest faculty of the man—gives him leave, and his conscience commends him in it, and there is no such perplexing disturbance in his breast as the wicked have; but all is done with peace and without the sting of conscience. The reasonable creature never feels better and more at ease than when he acts reasonably and according to the nature of a man and consistent with himself.

So, the temporal delights of the Christian are much sweeter than the earthly pleasures of the wicked, because they are taken with moderation; also because they are taken in their own season and in the right manner. Everything is most beautiful and most pleasant in its season. Snow is not beautiful in summer, or rain in harvest. "He hath made every thing beautiful in his time" (Eccl. 3:11).

—JONATHAN EDWARDS

♦ *Is there anything in your life that is hindering you in your walk with God? What conflicts are you experiencing between your reason and your body?*

Fatherly Love

*Like as a father pitieth his children, so
the LORD pitieth them that fear him.*
—PSALM 103:13

We call the feeling which the Father entertains for each of His children, love; and well we call it so, but this is not all. There is a difference in the love He bears to His eldest and His youngest born, a difference in the case of each, called forth by the peculiar character of each. It is this minute and special love which is so precious. Were it not for this, we would feel as if we had only part of our Father's heart, as if we had not all of that which rightfully belongs to us. But, realizing this, we feel as if we had His whole heart, and yet our having the whole did not rob our brothers and sisters of any. It is with a family as with the sun in the firmament. It is the property of all, and yet each has the whole of it. Even so with Jehovah, our heavenly Father; even so with Jesus, our Elder Brother. His is a special, personal, peculiar love, just as if He loved no other but had His whole heart to spare for us. His is a minute and watchful care, bending over *each*, day and night, as if He had no other to care for.

How sweet to think that each of us is the special object of such personal attachment, the peculiar object of such unwearied vigilance. What manner of love is this! Now we believe and are sure that we shall be fully cared for, with not one want or sorrow overlooked. Now we know that "all things work together for good" (Rom. 8:28) and that the end of everything which befalls us here shall be light and glory forever! "I know the thoughts that I think toward you, saith the LORD, thoughts of peace, and not of evil, to give you an expected end" (Jer. 29:11).

—HORATIUS BONAR

◆*Meditate for a few minutes on the love of God as it has been shown to you. Ponder by faith what this means for you day by day, that Christ loves you as no one else!*

The Root Cause

*There is nothing from without a man, that entering
into him can defile him: but the things which come out
of him, those are they that defile the man.*

—MARK 7:15

A person may honorably serve God in his calling, though it is not enjoyable, and he may comfortably enjoy God in his calling although it is not pleasant. Maybe you wonder if you can lay down your calling because you meet with many temptations, provocations, and impediments which hinder you in the service of God; and if you were free from this calling, then you would be more free for God and be more free from those snares and provocations that you meet with.

Luther tells us of a certain man that was given to anger, and to avoid provocation, he would go live alone as a hermit, and when going to the well with his pitcher, something displeased him and he threw down his pitcher and broke it in his anger, which when he had so done and reflecting on himself and his own actions, he said, "Well, now I see it is not my situation, but in my heart and self that does cause anger and aggravation; therefore I will return to my calling in work again." When people speak against this objection, what do they do but lay the fault of their anger and aggravation upon their condition or situation and excuse themselves? But our Savior said, "That which comes from within, that defiles a man, not that which comes from without."

It is not your condition or your situation or employment that defiles you but that which comes from within which defiles you. Mr. Greenham, being asked whether a man might avoid doing something he is called to do because he feels corruption in himself, said, "In avoiding society, you shall cover but not cure your infirmities; and though you depart from men, you cannot go out of yourself. It is not the use of the creatures, but the love of the creatures, that hinders from good." Surely, therefore, our hindrance to good does not lie in our calling, place, or employment; but it lies within ourselves.

—WILLIAM BRIDGE

◆ *Have you come to realize that our words and actions arise from our hearts
so that when we repent we are to confess not only the outward sin but the
inward root from which it arose? Meditate on some of your sins, and try to
determine the root of them.*

SEPTEMBER

◆

Fear the least sin more than the greatest suffering.

—JEREMIAH BURROUGHS

Upper and Nether Springs

He that is faithful in that which is least is faithful also in much:
and he that is unjust in the least is unjust also in much.

—LUKE 16:10

The aim of every Christian should be to harmonize two areas of godly character; to be equally faithful to God, and kind, just, and faithful to our fellow man. Christ would have the higher and lower regions of our lives correspond with each other, and both of them patterned after His own example. He never overlooked any duty or came short in the least things. He paid His tribute to the Roman government as a loyal citizen. After He had raised the daughter of Jairus from death, He commanded the astonished mother to give the child something to eat. When He had conquered the powers of darkness in His own sepulcher, He carefully folded up the napkin that had bound His bruised head, and laid it in the corner.

Yet there are too many Christians who fail to pattern their lives after their Master. While they do not neglect the "upper springs" of worship and meditation and Bible study and communion with God, they seldom think much about the "nether springs." They are very spiritually minded, but not very humanly minded. Friends, let us all guard against this deplorable mistake. Let us see to it that the upper regions of our lives toward God are not more plentifully watered than those lower regions which cover our conduct and connection with our fellow creatures. Our prayer meeting hours ought not to be any more rich or fair or fruitful than those hours spent at our work or homes. People do not watch how we look for communion, but they do watch us to see how we behave in our daily walk and conversation. The lowly places in which we meet our friends and business associates are to be just as fruitful as those Sabbaths in which we "see no man but Jesus."

—THEODORE CUYLER

◆ *How can we keep a proper balance between our love to God and love to our fellow man? Why is it important to realize that the love of God will naturally flow out to those around us?*

Seek Peace and Holiness in Religious Differences

Follow peace with all men, and holiness, without which no man shall see the Lord.

—HEBREWS 12:14

The two great points we are called to pursue in this sinful, divided world are peace and holiness. These are the peculiar characteristics of a disciple of Jesus; they are the richest parts of the enjoyment of heaven; and as far as they are received into the heart, they bring down heaven upon earth. They are more inseparably connected between themselves than some of us are aware of.

The longer I live, the more I see of the vanity and sinfulness of our unchristian disputes; they eat up the very vitals of religion. I grieve to think how often I have lost my time and temper that way, in presuming to regulate the lives of others, when I have neglected my own; when the beam in my own eye has so altered my sight that I could discern nothing but the mote in my neighbor's. I am not desirous to choose a better part. Could I speak the publican's words with a proper feeling, I wish not for the tongue of men or angels to fight about notions or sentiments. I understand that gospel truth is precious, that errors are abounding, and that it is our duty to bear an honest testimony to what the Lord has enabled us to find comfort in, and to instruct with meekness those who would be instructed; but it is not our duty, nay, I believe it would be sin, to attempt to beat our ideas into other people's heads. Too often I have attempted this in times past; but now I judge that both my zeal and weapons were carnal. When our dear Lord questioned Peter, He didn't say, "Are you wise, learned, and eloquent? Are you clear and sound and orthodox?" But only, "Lovest thou me?" (John 21:15). An answer to this was sufficient then, why not now? Any other answer would have been insufficient. If Peter had made the most pompous confession of his faith and sentiments, still the first question would have recurred, "Lovest thou me?" This is a Scripture precedent in speaking with others.

—JOHN NEWTON

◆ *In your interactions with others who confess Christ, do you seek peace and holiness, or do you seek to impose your thoughts on them? How can you change this without compromising truth?*

Christ Our Friend

*Henceforth I call you not servants; for the servant knoweth not
what his lord doeth: but I have called you friends; for all things
that I have heard of my Father I have made known unto you.*

—JOHN 15:15

If Christ is your friend, you have great privileges and ought to walk worthy
of them. Seek every day to have closer communion with Him who is your
friend, and to know more of His grace and power. True Christianity is not
merely believing a certain set of dry, unrelated doctrines. It is to live in daily
personal communication with an actual living person—Jesus, the Son of
God. "To me," said Paul, "to live is Christ" (Phil. 1:21).

Seek every day to glorify your Lord and Savior in all your ways. He that
hath a friend should show himself friendly, and no man surely is under such
great obligations as the friend of Christ. Avoid everything which would
grieve your Lord. Fight hard against besetting sins, against inconsistency,
against backwardness to confess Him before men. Say to your soul whenever you are tempted to that which is wrong, "Soul, soul, is this thy kindness
to thy friend?"

Think, above all, of the mercy which has been shown to you and learn
to rejoice daily in your friend! So what if your body be bowed down with
disease! So what if your poverty and trials be very great! So what if your
earthly friends forsake you, and you are alone in the world! All this may be
true, but if you are in Christ, you have a friend, a friend that never fails. Oh!
Think much on your friend!

Yet a little time and your friend shall come to take you home, and you
shall live with Him forever. Yet a little time and you shall see as you have
been seen and know as you have been known. And then you shall hear
assembled worlds confess that he is the rich and happy man who has had
Christ for his friend.

—J. C. RYLE

◆ *What does it mean for you that Christ calls you His friend? How could you
mirror His love in your relationship with others?*

God Our Exceeding Joy

Great is the LORD, and greatly to be praised.
—PSALM 48:1

What a God and Father you have to rejoice in! This is a source of spiritual joy; the loveliest and surest. To have a God to go to in all difficulties, troubles, and fears; a Father to fly to with every stress, every sorrow, every want. His eye is ever hearkening; His hand ever outstretched; His power equal to His goodness; His ability to aid equal to His readiness to aid. Surely, with such a covenant God and such a loving Father as ours, our heart ought to rejoice more in "God [our] exceeding joy" (Ps. 43:4). There is everything in God to make us joyful all day long. All His perfections smile upon us in Christ, and all are pledged to defend us, to provide for us, to supply us, and to bring us through all and out of all the vicissitudes, trials, temptations, and sins of this present life into life eternal.

We rejoice so feebly in God because we are so imperfectly acquainted with Him. And we are so little acquainted with Him because we have so few dealings with Him. We run to other people, we rest in human wisdom, we rejoice in other people, until the Lord empties, embitters, or removes them; and then we learn that it is better to put confidence in God, even in our own God, than in the greatest ruler.

The disappointment we have found in the others has brought God more really, fully, and blessedly into our soul. And we have learned more of Him as our trust, our hope, our joy; more of His condescension, His faithfulness and love; more of Him as our Father and our God, in our earthly disappointment, than we have ever learned in all the fullness of the world's sufficiency.

Child of God, rouse you to the truth that, though the depths of your soul's distress or depression or temporal embarrassments may have never been so profound, too deep for human power to soothe or relieve, yet you may hope and joy in God. God can, God will, and God has promised to help you.

—OCTAVIUS WINSLOW

♦ *What does rejoicing in God look like in the Christian life? How can you conscientiously practice this more?*

The Only Sure Foundation

*For other foundation can no man lay than
that is laid, which is Jesus Christ.*
—1 CORINTHIANS 3:11

The man who has a good hope founds all his expectations of pardon and glory on the mediation of Jesus the Son of God. He knows his own sinfulness; he feels that he is guilty, wicked, and lost by nature. But he sees forgiveness and peace with God offered freely to him through faith in Christ. He casts himself with all his sins on Jesus and rests on Him. Jesus and His atonement on the cross, Jesus and His righteousness, Jesus and His finished work, Jesus and His all-prevailing intercession, Jesus and Jesus only is the foundation of the confidence of his soul.

Let us beware of supposing that any hope is good which is not founded on Christ. All other hopes are built on sand. They may look well in the summertime of health and prosperity but will fail in the day of sickness and the hour of death. "Other foundation can no man lay than that is laid, which is Jesus Christ" (1 Cor. 3:11).

Church membership is no foundation of hope. We may belong to the best churches, and yet never belong to Christ. We may fill our pew regularly every Sunday and hear the sermons of faithful preachers and yet never hear the voice of Jesus or follow Him. If we have nothing better than church membership to rest on, we are in a poor plight. We have nothing solid beneath our feet.

Christ Himself is the only true foundation of a good hope. He is the Rock; His work is perfect. He is the stone, the sure stone, the tried cornerstone. He is able to bear all the weight that we can lay upon Him. He that builds on Him shall not be confounded.

—J. C. RYLE

◆ *What does it mean that Christ is the foundation of hope?*

Press Forward

If these things be in you, and abound, they make you that ye shall neither be barren nor unfruitful in the knowledge of our Lord Jesus Christ.

—2 PETER 1:8

The apostle Paul, as holy a man as he was, pressed forward and did not rest in past attainments. If you are a true Christian, you do hunger and thirst after righteousness. It is as natural to a sanctified nature to desire grace and hunger for that, as it is for our bodies to crave food; wherefore, let this appetite be increased and pursued. Strive to be more like Jesus Christ, and be more as you hope to be in heaven. As God, who has called you, is holy, so strive to be holy.

Be more prayerful—more frequent and more earnest in your approaches to the throne of grace; and besides your set times of prayer, let your heart be frequently lifted up to God when you are about your ordinary activities.

Frequently and carefully read the Holy Scriptures. Endeavor to read them with understanding, in particular applying them to your own situation. Be more frequent in your meditations upon God and Jesus, the wonderful love and grace of God, and the blessedness of heaven.

Frequently examine yourself, searching and trying your hearts and your ways, to see if you have turned aside from the path of duty, and where your life needs amendment. Be more frequent in religious conversation, in speaking of the things of a spiritual and eternal nature: let your tongue speak often about the great things which God has revealed in the gospel.

Be more exact in your walk, more in acts of obedience. There is nothing that tends so much to increase grace as the exercise of it in good works.

Use all possible endeavors and improve all opportunities that God puts into your hands for promoting the kingdom and interest of Jesus Christ among men. Use all endeavors to be some way or other instrumental to bringing souls to Jesus Christ. This is the work which Christ is carrying on in the world; let Christians be fellow workers with Him; let them in all their places carry on the same design.

—JONATHAN EDWARDS

◆*In which of the above areas can you be more fervent? How will you do this?*

Suffering Grace

*For unto you it is given in the behalf of Christ, not only to
believe on him, but also to suffer for his sake.*

—PHILIPPIANS 1:29

If there are two things laid out before you, sin on the one hand, and on the other there is suffering for Christ, if you would rather take up suffering than to commit the sin, you do plainly suffer for the name of Jesus Christ. And therefore, whatever the reward is—which they shall have that suffer for the name of Christ—all that reward is yours. Be of good comfort, for if you are ever called to suffer for the name of Christ, go away rejoicing that you are counted worthy to suffer shame or anything for the name of Jesus Christ. What a great encouragement is here from this great rewarder—who would not be willing to suffer for the name of Jesus!

If you wonder what you shall do to be willing to suffer for the name of Christ, as you feel very backward and unwilling to suffer for His name, are you conscious of your unwillingness? I say that person is not far from grace that is conscious of a contrary evil. He is not far from humility that is conscious of pride. He is not far from faith who is conscious of unbelief. So, he is not far from being willing to suffer for the name of Christ who is conscious of his own unwillingness.

The willingness to suffer for the name of Christ is part of our suffering grace; and suffering grace is given upon suffering ground: "Unto you it is given...not only to believe on him, but also to suffer" (Phil. 1:29). The opportunity to suffer is the gift of God. The will and heart to suffer is the gift of God. And the strength to suffer is the gift of God. Suffering grace is given when you are on suffering ground; in that hour you will be willing and be given wisdom to suffer for the name of Christ; then you will have suffering grace.

—WILLIAM BRIDGE

◆ *What does suffering for Christ look like in your life? All who will live godly shall suffer persecution, so if we are not suffering, is it connected to our not living godly?*

Fruit-Bearers

Herein is my Father glorified, that ye bear
much fruit; so shall ye be my disciples.

—JOHN 15:8

I often picture to myself a little group of holy men and women in any church, a compact group, a loving group, a devoted group of consistent Christians—not mere professors, but possessors of Christ; not talkers, but workers; not hearers only, but doers of the Word—fruit-bearers, light reflectors, living epistles of Christ, known and read by all men. What a blessed influence would they have on others; like leaven spreading itself over the whole mass; like ointment, scattering around the perfume of godliness. This would give life to our churches. This would put to silence the gainsayer. This would attract and win over the unbeliever.

Paul instructs us to "adorn the doctrine of God our Savior in all things" (Titus 2:10). What a word that is—*adorn* the doctrine! Can we add anything to that which is in itself so pure and bright and lovely as the gospel? Alas, we more often throw a veil over it and dim its beauties; we cast upon many a blot, and so mar its charms. And yet we *may* adorn the gospel, we may add a luster to it, by living under its power. What lovelier picture is there in the world than to see a holy and happy Christian living out the gospel in all that he does?

Let us try to make religion attractive by the blamelessness of our lives. Let us show forth the character of Christ in our daily conduct. Why is it that our Lord exhorts us to "let your light so shine before men" (Matt. 5:16)? It is that they may be led, by seeing our good works, not to praise *us*, but to glorify *our Father* which is in heaven. Even the poorest and most humble may do this. We may all let our light shine for Christ. For do we not see the glorious sun reflected on the tiny little dewdrop, as well as on the boundless ocean? "Herein," says Christ, "is my Father glorified, that ye bear much fruit" (John 15:8).

—ASHTON OXENDEN

◆*Are you doing, saying, or thinking anything that would detract from the glory of God? How can you live conscientiously to point others to Christ?*

Bearing God's Image

Be ye holy; for I am holy.
—1 PETER 1:16

Our holiness consists in our suitableness to the nature of God. Hence the saints are said to partake of the divine nature, which is not partaking of His essence but His image (2 Peter 1:4). Herein is the saints' holiness, when they are the lively pictures of God. They bear the image of God's meekness, mercifulness, heavenliness; they are of the same judgment with God, of the same disposition; they love what He loves, and hate what He hates.

Our holiness consists also in our subjection to the will of God. As God's nature is the pattern of holiness, so His will is the rule of holiness. It is our holiness when we do His will (Acts 13:22); when we bear His will (Mic. 7:9); when what He inflicts wisely we suffer willingly. Our great care should be to be like God in holiness. Our holiness should be qualified as God's; as His is a real holiness, ours should be. It should not be the paint of holiness, but the life; it should not be like the Egyptian temples, beautified without merely, but like Solomon's temple, gold within. "The king's daughter is all glorious within" (Ps. 45:13).

How illustrious every person is. He is a fair glass in which some of the beams of God's holiness shine forth. We read that Aaron put on his garments for glory and beauty (Ex. 28:2). When we wear the embroidered garment of holiness, it is for glory and beauty. A good Christian is ruddy, being sprinkled with Christ's blood; and white, being adorned with holiness. As the diamond to the ring, so is holiness to the soul; as Chrysostom says, they that oppose it cannot but admire it.

It is the great design that God carries on in the world, to make people like Himself in holiness. What are all the showers of ordinances for but to rain down righteousness upon us and make us holy? What are the promises for, but to encourage holiness? What is the end of Christ's dying, but that His blood might wash away our unholiness? "Who gave himself for us, that he might…purify unto himself a peculiar people" (Titus 2:14).

—THOMAS WATSON

◆ *While our holiness is complete in Christ, how do we become more holy as the Holy Spirit transforms us? In what areas do you need greater measures of holiness?*

How Trials Are to Be Appraised

Not that we are sufficient of ourselves to think any thing as of ourselves; but our sufficiency is of God.
—2 CORINTHIANS 3:5

I think the greatness of trials should be appraised by the impressions they make on our spirits rather than by their outward appearance. The smallest will be too heavy for us if we are left to grapple with it in our own strength, or rather weakness; and if the Lord is pleased to put forth His power in us, He can make the heaviest trial light. A lively impression of His love or of His sufferings for us, along with a sense of the misery from which we are redeemed—these thoughts will enable us to be not only submissive, but even joyful in tribulations.

When faith is in exercise, though the flesh will have its feelings, the spirit will triumph over them. But it is necessary that we know that we have no sufficiency in ourselves, and in order to know it, we must feel it. Therefore, the Lord sometimes withdraws His sensible influence, and then the buzzing of a fly will be an overmatch for our patience. At other times He will show us what He can do in us and for us; then we can adopt the apostle's words and say, "I can do all things through Christ which strengtheneth me…. He said unto me, 'My grace is sufficient for thee'" (Phil. 4:13; 2 Cor. 12:9).

When our trials are great, we run immediately to our all-sufficient friend, feel our dependence, and cry in earnest for help; but if the trial seems small, we are too apt secretly to lean to our own wisdom and strength, as if in small matters we can do without Him. It requires the same grace to bear with a right spirit a cross word as a cross injury. And it requires the same grace to bear with a right spirit the breaking of a china plate as the death of an only son.

—JOHN NEWTON

◆*How is God's grace sufficient for you in your present trials? Do you recognize that the grace of God that you need is the same whether the trial be large or small?*

Precious Faith

*That the trial of your faith, being much more precious than of
gold that perisheth, though it be tried with fire, might be found unto
praise and honour and glory at the appearing of Jesus Christ.*

—1 PETER 1:7

Habitual lively faith in Christ's presence and readiness to help is the
secret of the Christian soldier fighting successfully. It must never be
forgotten that faith can waver. All men do not believe alike, and even the
same person has his ebbs and flows of faith and believes more heartily at
one time than another. According to the degree of his faith, the Christian
fights well or ill, wins victories or loses skirmishes, comes off triumphant or
loses a battle. He that has most faith will always be the happiest and most
comfortable soldier. Nothing makes the anxieties of warfare sit so lightly on
a man as assurance of Christ's love and God's protection. Nothing enables
him to bear the fatigue of watching, struggling, and wrestling against sin
like the indwelling confidence that God is on his side and success is sure. It
is the "shield of faith" which quenches all the fiery darts of the wicked one.
It is the man who can say, "I know whom I have believed," who can say in
times of suffering, "I am not ashamed."

He who wrote the glowing words, "We faint not" and "Our light affliction, which is but for a moment, worketh for us a far more exceeding and
eternal weight of glory," was the man who wrote with the same pen, "We
look not at the things which are seen, but at the things which are not seen:
for the things which are seen are temporal; but the things which are not
seen are eternal" (2 Cor. 4:16–18). The more faith, the more victory! The
more faith, the more inward peace! Reader, I think it impossible to overrate
the value and importance of faith. Well may the apostle Peter call it "precious" (2 Peter 1:1).

—J. C. RYLE

◆ *How has faith changed a thought or action for you recently? How is this a
comfort to you?*

Lessons for Christian Living (1)

*That ye might walk worthy of the Lord unto all
pleasing, being fruitful in every good work.*
—COLOSSIANS 1:10

Christians must live differently than those in the world, especially in the following ways:

In self-denial. You must show that you can deny your opinions, your desires, and your wills. Though you have a strong desire for something, though you have opportunities to enjoy your desires, yet if you see God may have more honor in any other way, you freely and readily, without trouble, deny yourself to honor Him. Many think it is a superior spirit to be self-willed, in the sense of being passionate, contrary, and boisterous. But, certainly, this comes from weakness of spirit. No excellency is required for this; every fool can be so. But it is excellency to be able to overcome, to have command of one's spirit, to subdue and bring in order passions and violent stirrings of our spirit. This is precious and honorable in the eyes of God and man. This is a well-tempered spirit that is unyielding in the cause of God and the church; meek, quiet, yielding, and self-denying toward its own cause. Those who usually are the most boisterous and passionate for themselves are the most ill-spirited men and the most unyielding when it comes to the cause of God.

Show the excellency of your spirit, which enables you to do what others cannot do, by loving your enemies, praying for them, and doing them all the good you can. This is what our Savior commands His disciples in Matthew 5 when He would have them do more than others do.

Fear the least sin more than the greatest suffering. Morality raises a spirit highest next to grace; yet merely moral men account it foolishness to yield in little things for the avoiding of great sufferings. But a gracious spirit thinks the smallest truth of God is worthy to be upheld, even if he would experience the loss of his dearest comforts and suffer the greatest evils. Yea, he accounts suffering for small things the most honorable sufferings of all, as testifying to the greatest love.

—JEREMIAH BURROUGHS

◆*Does your life show that you readily yield to what God is calling you to do?
In what areas do you struggle most?*

Lessons for Christian Living (2)

*That ye might walk worthy of the Lord unto all
pleasing, being fruitful in every good work.*
—COLOSSIANS 1:10

Christians must live differently than those in the world, especially in the following ways:

Prize opportunities for service more than all outward contentment in the world. A gracious heart thinks it honor enough that God would use their service. He is not only willing to go on in his work, though no outward contentment come of it, and he esteems increased service for God so great a good that he accounts the lack of outward things worth the sacrifice.

Make conscientious use of time. This few do. Few consider filling up of their time with God's service because their spirits do not have an excellency about them. They cannot make use of their time in any worthy employment for God, themselves, or others; but a man of an excellent spirit knows how to employ himself in things that are excellent, and therefore prizes the time he has to work and is conscientious in the spending of it wisely.

Be conscious of the thoughts and secret workings of the heart. Avoid secret sins, and perform secret duties. A man who has a precious spirit does not like to have it wasted in extravagant thoughts and affections that lead away from God.

Rejoice in the good of others, even though doing so eclipses your light; and even though your gifts, your abilities, and your excellencies become dim in the eyes of others. Were it not for the prominence of some above you, your gifts perhaps would shine more brightly and be highly esteemed. We ought to rejoice in this from the heart, to bless God from the soul for His gifts and grace in others, that His name may be glorified more by others than I can glorify them myself; to be able truly to say, "Though I can do little, yet blessed be God there are some who can do more for God than I, and in this I do and will rejoice."

—JEREMIAH BURROUGHS

◆*Believer, can unbelievers see that your life is different? How are you living differently than those in the world?*

Uncharitableness

Judge not, that ye be not judged.
—MATTHEW 7:1

To you, my reader, I would say whenever you find yourself about to indulge in uncharitable remarks toward another, whether a professing Christian or otherwise, just stop yourself and say, "Let me have a peep in my own heart first." Be very careful to avoid this fault of uncharitableness. It is a most hateful one to fall into, and even the world condemns it. Do we not ourselves have some grievous failings, which are hidden even from our nearest friends and are known only to God? And if these were brought out to light, would they not condemn *us*? Oh, then, let us deal very tenderly with our brother, and make every allowance for him. It is better, far better, to be as the lark that is ever rising upward, and hovers wistfully over his own little nest, than as the quick-eyed eagle which pounces so eagerly on its prey.

Let us take this for a rule, and a golden rule it is, to speak but little of *others* and but little of *ourselves*; and also to be very hesitant in saying anything of others, unless we have *something good* to say of them. Let the world, if it will, be open-mouthed in its harsh judgments. Let it be eagle-eyed in discovering faults and blemishes in others. But let *us* be anxious to look at home, remembering that good man's resolution who said that whenever he spied a fault in his neighbor, he was determined to look for two in himself; remembering also our Lord's precepts, "judge not, that ye be not judged" (Matt. 7:1). "First cast out the beam out of thine own eye; and then shalt thou see clearly to cast out the mote out of thy brother's eye" (v. 5). Let us seek to have much of that Christian charity or love which "shall cover the multitude of sins" (1 Peter 4:8), that is, which delights rather to cover them over than to expose them to view. If such is our spirit, we shall, I am sure, be much happier and more useful, and we shall much more "adorn the doctrine of God our Saviour" (Titus 2:10).

—ASHTON OXENDEN

◆*Consider your words and thoughts. Are you prone to look at others' faults rather than your own? With whom are you most prone to do this? How can you be less judgmental and more charitable?*

A Precious Privilege

*For where two or three are gathered together
in my name, there am I in the midst of them.*
—MATTHEW 18:20

How encouraging are the promises of Jesus: "When thou prayest, enter into thy closet, and when thou hast shut thy door, pray to thy Father which is in secret; and thy Father which seeth in secret shall reward thee openly" (Matt. 6:6). "Where two or three are gathered together in my name, there am I in the midst of them" (18:20). Thus, a blessing is pronounced on secret and on social prayer. If they who fear the Lord speak often one to another, how much more will they delight to hold communion with their heavenly Father through the Son of His love.

Christian reader, is prayer the delightful exercise of your soul? Are your refreshments sought for, and obtained, at the throne of grace? Have you access, by faith in the blood of Jesus, to the Father of mercies, through the power of the Holy Ghost? Oh! Value a throne of grace. Cherish the Spirit. Prize the privilege of prayer. It is the first evidence of the beginning of a religious life, and the last act of the expiring believer.

Many are the apostolic exhortations to pray: "Pray without ceasing" (1 Thess. 5:17). "Continue in prayer" (Col. 4:2). "Give yourselves to…prayer" (1 Cor. 7:5). "I will therefore that men pray every where" (1 Tim. 2:8). "The effectual fervent prayer of a righteous man availeth much" (James 5:16). This made Saint Paul very desirous to have the prayers of all the churches in his behalf.

To the true believer, prayer is a precious privilege. At the mercy seat, sprinkled with the blood of Jesus, he pours out his heart, makes known his wants, and derives renewed strength to perform his duties. There, he lays his burden at his Savior's feet, and there he is filled with peace and joy.

—THOMAS READE

◆*Prayer can be one of the hardest spiritual disciplines. Why do you think this is the case? How can we stir up ourselves and others to be more fervent in prayer?*

The Knowledge of Our Hearts

*The heart is deceitful above all things, and
desperately wicked: who can know it?*
—JEREMIAH 17:9

While we remain on earth, we are in the Lord's school, and a fundamental lesson we have to learn is a knowledge of ourselves, which can only be acquired by painful experience. Books, sermons, and letters cannot teach it, nor can the observations we make of other people lead us far beyond theory. To have some tolerable ideas of the human heart in general is one thing; to know our own hearts is quite a different thing.

The deceitfulness of the heart, which we allow in words, enables it to disguise, conceal, and cover its own emotions so that the supposed sense we have of its deceitfulness is often the very thing that deceives us. We say that the sea is deceitful, and for good reason. It sometimes looks so smooth and glossy that one not experienced with it would not think it dangerous; but this is only in a calm. A small breeze will ruffle it, and in a storm it roars and rages. But the heart is more deceitful than the sea. It will swell and rage when there seems no wind to put it in motion or to awaken any suspicion. If I feel impatience and discontent under the pressure of great troubles, I am apt to blame the tempest for all the commotion and to excuse my own heart, which tells me it would behave better in circumstances more favorable. But when circumstances are calm, when I have no trial worth mentioning, when I am surrounded with comforts, being judge in my own case, I am forced to confess that things are well and that I can think of no other person whom I would want to changes places with. But if small matters are sufficient to upset me and a cross word or look causes me to forget all my undeserved mercies, then I find that my heart is deceitful indeed. I wish we were better, but it is important to know how bad we really are. For they will prize the physician, and most readily comply with his prescription, who are most sensible of the extent of their disease.

—JOHN NEWTON

◆ *To what depths has the Holy Spirit led you into the reality of your own
deceitfulness of heart? How has this caused you to value Christ more?*

Hope in God

For in thee, O LORD, do I hope:
thou wilt hear, O Lord my God.
—PSALM 38:15

Hope thou in God. Why should I not? I need just such a friend. He has all power and strength, and I am very weak. I cannot even think a good thought myself. Nor do I know how to pray as I ought. If the Lord does not help my infirmities, I could do nothing right. But I can do all things if He will gird me with strength. I will hope in God.

He has all the knowledge to understand my whole life and all the wisdom necessary to direct everything concerning me. He makes no mistakes. He is never deceived. He is never overburdened. He knows all my weaknesses. He knows my sorrows. He knows my sincerity. And He is so wise that He takes the cunning in their own craftiness. His wisdom never fails. It is never perplexed. I will hope in God.

He has as much mercy and kindness as I need. His lovingkindness is so great that human belief has never seen the full scope of it. The ocean of divine love is boundless and inexhaustible. God's love is strong. It passes the love of women. It is infinite. It produces the most amazing results. It fills all pious hearts with joy. It fills heaven with hallelujahs. Oh, I will hope in God.

For if I hope not in God, I will be apt to look to myself, and I am a fool and a sinner, a worm and blind, and unworthy of the very least of God's mercies. Who has at any time trusted in himself that he was righteous or wise or strong, and has not come to shame? I dare not lean to my own understanding, nor rely on my own wisdom, nor put any hope in my own righteousness. *Lord God of hosts, Father, Son, and Holy Ghost, give me grace to hope in Thee.*

—WILLIAM PLUMER

◆ *Take one thought from today's meditation, and explain why it is helpful to you and what it means for you.*

Resisting Temptation

Resist the devil, and he will flee from you.
—JAMES 4:7

The Lord gives us in James 4 both a *command* which shows us what our duty is, and also a *promise* to encourage us. The command of God is "Resist the devil." And it is your wisdom to obey this command. To tempt is the devil's work; to resist is the Christian's duty. It is very important to *resist the first motions of evil*. When a temptation comes, look up to God instantly for strength; if you parley with the tempter, you are lost. Mark carefully the steps by which Eve was ensnared. First, *she stood near* the forbidden tree. Then, when Satan proposed to her to eat of it, *she argued with him*. Then, *she looked at the fruit* and "saw that [it] was good for food, and that it was pleasant to the eyes." The temptation gained upon her, and she *touched it*. And finally, she finished by *eating it*. Saint Paul charges us not to "give place to the devil" (Eph. 4:27). Oh, let us not yield a single point to him. We know that a beggar, who may seem to be very modest out of doors, will, if once let in, command the house. And so, if we yield only a little to the tempter at first, we are, in fact, giving away our strength, and shall have less to resist him afterward. When the hem is torn, the whole garment is nearly sure to unravel.

If you would keep the devil out of your life and actions, you must keep him out of your thoughts and desires, for that is where he commonly begins to enter. If you would conquer sin, you must nip it in the bud and not wait till it is fully formed within you. Have you sometimes allowed your thoughts to dwell on some sinful object and to brood upon it with delight, picturing it to yourself under its most pleasing forms? This is *most dangerous*. When temptation gets this far, it rarely happens that it is stopped. Hear what the wise apostle says, "Every man is tempted, when he is drawn away of his own lust, and enticed. Then when lust hath conceived, it bringeth forth sin: and sin, when it is finished, bringeth forth death" (James 1:14–15).

—ASHTON OXENDEN

♦*Are you in any way toying with sin in your thoughts? What must you do with such desires? Notice how James tells us we are tempted when we are drawn away by our own lusts. This means that temptations can arise from within, and we need to be on guard for this.*

Our Prayer-Hearing God

Trust in him at all times; ye people,
pour out your heart before him.
—PSALM 62:8

Nothing is too small for God that concerns you, His loved child. Study the life of Jesus while on earth. Was there a circumstance or want or temptation in the history of His disciples too small or unimportant for His notice? He who regards the minute things in nature, alike regards the minute things in providence and despises not the "day of small things" in grace (Zech. 4:10). God made the atoms that form the pyramids, the dust that dances in the sunbeam, the insect that swims in the ocean drop. Do you think then that He can be indifferent to, or regard as beneath His notice, the smallest care, the most delicate sorrow, the smallest want, the lowest interest, that relates to you? Impossible!

Learn then to entwine with your petitions your small cares, your trifling sorrows, your little wants of daily life. Whatever affects you, be it a cross look, an altered tone, an unkind word, a slight, a wrong, a wound, a demand you cannot meet, a charge you cannot see, a sorrow you cannot talk about; turn it into prayer and send it up to God. Disclosures you cannot make to another, you can make to the Lord. Man may be too little for your great matters, but God is not too great for your small ones. Only give yourself to prayer, whenever the event calls for it.

Send up your heart unto God *just as it is*. Send up a whole heart, and He will return it a broken heart. Send up a broken heart, and He will return it a healed heart. Send up a cold heart, and He will return it a loving heart. Send up an empty heart, and He will return it a full heart. Send up a praying heart, and He will return it a praising heart. Only send up your heart to heaven whatever its frame or condition, its desires or wants, and your heavenly Father's loving gracious heart will descend and meet it when it ascends in faith and prayer to Him.

—OCTAVIUS WINSLOW

♦*Have you ever wholly poured out your heart to God? Come to Him and tell Him all that is in your heart, knowing that He desires you to do so.*

Where the Success of Our Work Lies

Establish thou the work of our hands upon us;
yea, the work of our hands establish thou it.
—PSALM 90:17

Though you do the work of your hand with all your might, yet you must not look upon the success of your work as the fruit of your hand, but of God's hand. When Israel went out against Amalek, Moses lifted up his hands, and Israel prevailed; then Moses built an altar and called it Jehovah-nissi; for "the LORD hath sworn that the LORD will have war with Amalek" (Ex. 17:16). In the Hebrew, "hath sworn" means the Lord put *His hand* on the throne of the Lord. Said one, "This is to show that this victory was not from Moses's hand, though it was a praying hand, but from the Lord's hand."

You see how it is with a child; a father bids him to do something which he knows he cannot do; therefore he secretly puts his own hand to the work; he praises the child, and the child thinks that his hand did it. So here, God bids us to do His work, and we think the success is the fruit of our hand, whereas in truth it is the fruit of our Father's hand.

Solomon says, "Whatsoever thy hand findeth to do, do it with thy might" (Eccl. 9:10). But in the next verse he says, "I returned, and saw…that the race is not to the swift, nor the battle to the strong" (v. 11). Why did he add these words immediately, except to show us that though we do God's work with all our might, yet we must not look upon the success as the fruit of our own hand.

What man or woman is there whom God has not entrusted with some work? It is true, indeed, that he who had but one talent buried it in the earth (Matt. 25:14–30). Those are most apt to be idle that have least, yet everyone has some talent or other, some work in his ability. Now, therefore in the name of the Lord I say, "Whatsoever thy hand findeth to do, do it with thy might" (Eccl. 9:10).

—WILLIAM BRIDGE

◆ *What talents has God given to you, and how are you using them for His glory? Talk with someone close to you about what gifts you see in each other, so that these may be used profitably as well.*

Live Peaceably

If it be possible, as much as lieth in you,
live peaceably with all men.
—ROMANS 12:18

E very Christian should make it appear that he is so set upon peace that if the laying down of his life could procure peace, he should be willing to do it. If we may fill in the breaches by standing in the gap and offering ourselves as a sacrifice of atonement and pacification, let us thus prove ourselves to be the true followers of Christ our Lord and Master, who has left us His own example for our imitation. This would be an excellent thing, becoming the gospel which we profess. We should not only be willing to acknowledge peace but seek it. Seek it for our inferiors. Do not say that such a person has wronged me and, therefore, let him seek me. No! It becomes you who make profession of the gospel of Christ not to stay until he who has wronged you come to you, but for you who are wronged by another to seek those who have wronged you so that they would be at peace with you.

You might think it unreasonable that you who are wronged should seek out peace; aye, but it becomes the gospel of Christ that you should do so. God sought you; you never sought Him. If God had not begun the work of peace with you, God and your souls would have been eternal enemies; and therefore, remember that you are not to live according to reason. You think there's all the reason in the world that those who have wronged you should crouch at your feet rather than you seek them. Well, grant it, there is all the reason in the world for it; but what is there in the gospel to the contrary? You are not to live only in your conversation as becomes reason, but you are to have your conversations as becomes the gospel of Christ, remembering that his offense to you is not as great as your offense was to God, and yet God seeks to be at peace with you through Christ.

—JEREMIAH BURROUGHS

♦ *Who has wronged you and you are holding a grudge against them?*
You are to go to that person and seek reconciliation. Did not Christ do so?
We wronged Him, and yet He descended so low as to come to us and call us
to be reconciled.

Mighty Weapons

For the weapons of our warfare are not carnal, but mighty through God to the pulling down of strong holds.

—2 CORINTHIANS 10:4

Lukewarmness and faint-heartedness are traitors in the army of God and do more to weaken the cause of truth than the fiercest opposition from its determined enemies. Faith and love, patience and prayer are mighty weapons in the hand of the Spirit. The weakest Christian, when exercising these graces, will be more than conqueror over the powers of darkness. Spiritual joy was the sweet portion and strength of the early Christians. They were exhorted by the apostle Paul to rejoice evermore, for this was the will of God in Christ Jesus concerning them. To such an extent did they carry this precious privilege, that they took joyfully the spoiling of their goods, knowing that in heaven they had a better and an enduring substance. They counted it all joy when they fell into diverse temptations. They rejoiced that they were counted worthy to suffer shame for the name of Jesus. And with a joy unspeakable and full of glory, they went to the rack, the lions, the flames, that they might receive the crown of life and enter into the joy of their Lord.

Oh! That a spirit of faith and love, of joy and peace would be poured out on us. Then with Paul we will glory; yea, be exceeding joyful in all our tribulations.

The reason why so many shrink from suffering for Christ's sake is the coldness of their love. Their faith, being weak, cannot bear them up against that stream of persecution which so powerfully sets in against them. Through fear, they yield to the attacks of the enemy and bring distress into their consciences, as well as discredit the gospel.

Oh blessed Jesus, save us from ourselves; deliver us from this present evil world; make us alive by Thy grace; uphold us by Thy Spirit; make us ever active in Thy service and fearless in our confessions of Thee.

—THOMAS READE

◆ *How can you be more vibrant in life? Practically, what would that look like?*

Pleasant Living

*Better is an handful with quietness, than both the
hands full with travail and vexation of spirit.*
—ECCLESIASTES 4:6

The Christian partakes of the comforts of this life with an honest mind
and singleness of heart. Those things that are enjoyed with an honest
mind are much sweeter and more pleasant than the enjoyments of a wicked
heart. We read in Acts 2:46 that the primitive Christians "did eat their meat
with gladness and singleness of heart."

The wicked man, though he has the pleasures of this life, does them
with fear. He lives in a slavish fear all his days of death and hell. He eats and
drinks with fear, and this takes away much of the delight of what he enjoys.
Though a man be rich and fares sumptuously, yet if he eats and drinks in
fear of his life, this takes away all the comfort of his riches. If one lives in
the enjoyment of many good things, yet if he lives so that he is exposed to
the enemy continually, a man that lives in a cottage lives better than he.
Feed a criminal condemned to die with the richest meal, he will not have as
much comfort of it as one that eats only bread and water without fear. The
wicked man, he takes these things as a thief that is afraid of the shaking of
a leaf (Prov. 28:1; Job 24:17). But the Christian, he partakes of his delights
in safety and without fear, can eat and drink without terrors, with boldness
and confidence.

The earthly comforts of the Christian are also very much sweetened
by the consideration of the love of God. God is their Father and friend and
gives them these blessings from love to them, and He delights in them. But
the wicked can have no assurance that his enjoyments are not given to him
in anger and in judgment.

The temporal delights of the godly are also very much sweetened
because they are enjoyed in love and peace. He eats and drinks in love to
God and Jesus Christ, and in peace with his neighbors, and in charity toward
the whole world.

—JONATHAN EDWARDS

◆ *Is anything preventing you from living fully devoted to God? Pray for this
singleness of heart.*

Secret Sins

*Thou hast set our iniquities before thee, our
secret sins in the light of thy countenance.*

—PSALM 90:8

Secret sins—heart sins—are the worst enemies of God and of our own souls. The Romans said of a certain enemy, "Whether he is a captive or a captor, he is alike dangerous." So, they slew him. We must spare no sin, but pursue it till it's dead. In dealing with our secret sins, let us consider:

1. Think much of the all-seeing purity of God. His holiness is a flaming fire. In His sight, the heavens are not even pure. The darkness hides Him not.

2. Let us often compare our acts and words and hearts with the perfect law of God. It is exceeding broad. The commandments are spiritual. If you have wrong views of the law, you cannot have right views of sin, and you may lose your soul.

3. Hide no sin from your own eyes, and refuse not to confess it before God. He that confesses and forsakes his sins shall find mercy.

4. Be careful not to subject your principles to needless trial. Daily cry, "Lead me not into temptation." Yet if tempted, resist the devil. Martin Luther said, "You cannot prevent the birds from flying in the air over your head, but you can prevent them from building a nest in your hair."

5. Set a double guard against those sins to which you are very liable. Are you easily angry? Then avoid men who provoke you. Are you inclined to be gloomy? Then study the promises, and seek the company of cheerful Christians.

6. Remember that there is no danger of hating sin too much, or of being too watchful against it. If you are inclined to be selfish, find out some way of killing those feelings. Are your children your idols? Remember they may be taken from you in a moment.

7. When you have tried your best, remember you may have overlooked some sins. Earnestly pray, "Search me, O God, and know my heart: try me, and know my thoughts: and see if there be any wicked way in me, and lead me in the way everlasting" (Ps. 139:23–24).

—WILLIAM PLUMER

◆ *Why are we so prone to overlook sin in ourselves? How can we be more
aware of our secret sins so that we would repent of them?*

Christ's Filial Love

When Jesus therefore saw his mother, and
the disciple standing by, whom he loved, he saith
unto his mother, Woman, behold thy son!
—JOHN 19:26

Let us look at Christ's filial love to His earthly parents. It is said that He "was subject unto them" (Luke 2:51)—that is, He reverenced their parental authority, displayed toward them all dutiful respect, yielded an unquestioning and cheerful obedience to their wishes and commands, lived with them, labored for them, and clung to them until He reached the point of manhood. Nor did His devoted love end here. He bore it with Him to His death; breathed it in touching expressions from the cross. In that hour of woe, when the throes and throbs of agony were upon Him and His soul was travailing in sorrow beneath the weight of His people's sins and the inflictions of divine wrath, He beheld His mother. Forgetful of Himself, He thought only of her; and giving her a look of filial affection, He commended her to the care of the disciple whom He loved, who from that hour adopted her as his own. How holy and touching this example of filial love!

What a memorable and impressive carrying out of the divine law, "Children, obey your parents in the Lord: for this is right. Honour thy father and mother" (Eph. 6:1–2). Would you be Christlike? Then cherish the deepest affection for your parents, the profoundest reverence for their authority and regard for their wishes. And when grief and sorrow, age and infirmity, poverty and sickness overtake them, cherish them as the most costly and precious of earth's treasures. Rock the cradle of their old age as gently and watchfully as they rocked yours in infancy, through the silent watches of many sleepless, weary hours by day and by night. —OCTAVIUS WINSLOW

◆ *How can you demonstrate this attitude toward your parents more than you currently do, even in the face of difficult circumstances?*

The Benefits of Much Fruit-Bearing

They shall be fruitful and increase.
—JEREMIAH 23:3

The fuller Christians are of fruit, the more we are like Christ, who was "full of grace and truth" (John 1:14). He received the Spirit without measure (John 3:34). This tree of life was ever bearing; and He brought forth several sorts of fruit; wisdom, righteousness, sanctification, etc. The more we are filled with the fruits of righteousness, the more we resemble the Sun of Righteousness. We were elected to this end, to be made like Christ (Rom. 8:29). Then we are most like this blessed Vine when we bear full clusters.

The more fruit a Christian brings forth, the more will Christ love him. "Now," saith Leah, "this time will my husband be joined unto me, because I have born him three sons" (Gen. 29:34). When we bear much fruit, then will Christ's heart be joined to us. Christ will pardon a weak faith; He will honor a great faith. It was not a sparkle of faith Christ commended in Mary Magdalene, but love aflame: "she loved much" (Luke 7:47). Christians, would you be like that beloved disciple which leaned on the bosom of Jesus? Would you have much love from Christ? Let Him have much fruit from you.

Bearing much fruit will usher an abundance of comfort into the soul *in the hour of temptation*. Satan will be sure to besiege the weakest Christian; all his darts fly that way, and a strong temptation may overcome a weak faith. But a flourishing faith stands like a cedar and is not blown down by the wind of temptation. A strong faith can stop the mouth of the devil, that roaring lion (1 Peter 5:8).

A store of fruit will give comfort in the hour of death; a little grace will make us above the fear of death. O what joy will it be on the deathbed, when a Christian can bring his sheaves full of corn! When he can show his five talents that he hath gained by trading! When there is not only a drop or two of oil, but his lamp is full of oil! If the devil show God our debts, we can show Him our fruit. O how sweet will death be.

—THOMAS WATSON

♦*How are you bearing fruit unto Christ's glory? In which areas are you lacking?*

Strength through Dependence

Be strong in the Lord, and in the power of his might.
—EPHESIANS 6:10

Reader, do not think that only when in sore straits and pressing emergencies are you required to make religion your stay, and to exercise the spirit which it enjoins. Imagine not that in the time of sickness or the solemn hour of death you can lay hold of gospel promises at will, and derive from them consolation and support, if in the season of health and the day of your prosperity, they are not in all your thoughts. If you do, you will be miserably disappointed. To be "strong in the Lord, and in the power of his might" (Eph. 6:10) when the dark storm gathers overhead and the thunder is heard, you must have used the grace vouchsafed for past emergencies and exercised the powers which He has already graciously conferred.

Remember, growth "in grace, and in the knowledge of our Lord and Saviour Jesus Christ" (2 Peter 3:18) does not consist so much in extent of knowledge as in the depth of knowledge or knowing things better. It is not so much in new duties as in old duties better done; the drudgeries of life gone through in a brighter, happier, and more Christian spirit, knowing that life is made up in a great measure of little and common and trivial things, but still doing these little and trivial things with a more single eye to the Lord, with more self-distrust and therefore more dependence upon God, with greater humility, with more prayer so that self is gradually but surely extinguished and we become strong, both to do and endure the will of God. Yes, believer, you are insensibly, it may be, yet most assuredly increasing your spiritual strength by each single act of faith and charity and self-denial; by showing in your daily walk more love, joy, peace, long-suffering, gentleness, goodness, faith, meekness, temperance; by your Christian manner, in your family circle and in the troubles of business and amid all occupations and requirements of life.

—ASHTON OXENDEN

◆*Rather than looking at great experiences or large deliverances in your life, try to look at the small ways in which the Lord continues to teach, guide, and strengthen you, and take courage that through all these little ways He is preparing you for greater things.*

All Is Love

For whom the Lord loveth he chasteneth.
—HEBREWS 12:6

All is love. Affliction is the expression of paternal love. It is from the deepest recess of the fountain of love that sorrow flows down to us. And love cannot wrong us. It blesses but cannot curse. Its utterances and actions are all of peace and gladness. It wants a larger vessel into which to empty itself, and a deeper channel through which to flow. That is all. It seeks to make us more susceptible to kindness, and then to pour that kindness in. Yes, love is the true, the one origin of the sharpest stroke that ever fell upon a bleeding heart. The truth is, there is no other way of accounting for affliction but this. Anger will not account for it. Forgetfulness will not account for it. Chance will not account for it. No, it is simply impossible to trace it to any cause but love. Admit this is its spring, and all is harmonious, comely, and perfect. If you deny it, all is confusion, cruelty, and darkness. Chastising love is the most faithful, most pure, most true, most tender, and deepest of all. Let this be our consolation.

Dear friend, "it is well." It is *good* to be afflicted. Our days of suffering here we call days of darkness; hereafter they will seem our brightest and fairest. In eternity we shall praise Jehovah most of all for our sorrows and tears. So blessed shall they then seem to us that we shall wonder how we could ever weep and sigh. We shall then know how utterly unworthy we were of all this grace. We did not deserve anything, but least of all to be afflicted. Our joys were all of grace—pure grace—much more our sorrows. It is out of the "exceeding riches of his grace" that trial comes (Eph. 2:7).

—HORATIUS BONAR

♦ *Why do you so often fight against affliction? How can you not lose sight of love during affliction? Think through ways you have learned this.*

Practice and Teach

Let all your things be done with charity.
—1 CORINTHIANS 16:14

I will give you two simple words of instruction. They are these: *Practice* and *teach* the grace of charity.

Practice charity diligently. It is one of those graces which above all grow by constant exercise. Strive more and more to carry it into every little detail of daily life. Watch over your own tongue and temper throughout every hour of the day, and especially in dealing with workers, children, and near relatives. Remember the character of the excellent woman, "In her tongue is the law of kindness" (Prov. 31:26). Remember the words of Paul, "Let all your things be done with charity" (1 Cor. 16:14). Charity should be seen in little things as well as in great ones. Remember the words of Peter, "Have fervent charity among yourselves" (1 Peter 4:8)—not a charity which just keeps lit but a burning, shining fire which all around can see. It may cost pain and trouble to keep these things in mind. There may be little encouragement from the example of others, but persevere. Charity like this brings its own reward.

Teach charity to others. Press it continually on workers if you have any. Tell them the great duty of kindness, helpfulness, and considerateness, one for another. Press it, above all, on children if you have any. Remind them constantly that kindness, good-naturedness, and good character are among the first evidences which Christ requires in children. If they cannot know much or explain doctrines, they can understand love. Let children be taught texts and hymns; but let not such teaching be made everything in their religion. Teach them to keep their tempers, to be kind to one another, unselfish, good-natured, patient, gentle, and forgiving. Tell them never to forget that without charity, "I am nothing" (1 Cor. 13:2).

—J. C. RYLE

◆ *How can you show each other greater charity from day to day? Would others characterize you as charitable?*

Not Your Own

*What doth the LORD thy God require of thee, but to fear the LORD
thy God, to walk in all his ways, and to love him, and to serve the
LORD thy God with all thy heart and with all thy soul.*

—DEUTERONOMY 10:12

As Christians you may never act anymore as if you were your own. In
giving yourself to God, you have cast off all pretenses to a right in
yourself, and if you begin again to act like you were your own, you deny
what you have done. You give and take away again; you have given all your
strength and abilities to God, and yet you take them and make use of them
as if they were your own. If you don't give yourself to God entirely, it is not
worth it to pretend to give yourself to Him at all; for He will accept no other
self-dedication but what is entire. For what do you mean by giving yourself
to God except you devote all to Him to be used entirely for Him and not for
yourself, to live for the time to come as His and not as your own?

You act as if you were your own if you do anything but what is to the
glory of God, and don't make the glorifying of Him your chief business. If
you do anything for the devil, anything for your lusts, anything merely for
the world or yourself, you leave God and serve your old masters.

You act as if you were your own if you omit any duty or commit sin for
the sake of your own pleasure. You are no longer to look at your own ease
or pleasure or profit any further than they respect and help religion and
God's glory.

If you are uncharitable; if you neglect the welfare of your fellow creatures; if you are not ready, freely and without grudging, to distribute to the
needs and necessities of others; if you withhold your hand from doing good
to your fellow Christians for needless fear of hurting yourself, you act as if
you were your own. Remember that you have given yourself to God with
all that you have; for if you are God's, what you possess is His, too, and not
your own.

—JONATHAN EDWARDS

◆*Have you devoted all to God in gratitude for what He has done for you?
Is there anything you are holding back from Him?*

OCTOBER

———◆———

The divine doctrine of trust is a wonderfully restful one to weary disciples. It takes the tiredness out of the heart.

—THEODORE CUYLER

Persevering Grace

And I give unto them eternal life; and they shall never perish,
neither shall any man pluck them out of my hand.

—JOHN 10:28

Would you desire perfect peace in life? Then lay hold on the doctrine of perseverance. Your trials may be many and great. Your cross may be very heavy, but your life is carried out according to an everlasting covenant, ordered in all things and sure. All things are working together for your good. Your sorrows are only purifying your soul for glory. Your sorrows are only shaping you as a polished stone for the temple above, made without hands. From wherever the storms blow, they only drive you nearer to heaven. Whatever weather you must go through, it is only ripening you for the garner of God. Your best things are quite safe. Come what will, you will "never perish" (John 10:28).

Would you have a strong consolation in sickness? Then lay hold on this doctrine of perseverance. Think as you feel the pins of this earthly tabernacle loosening one by one, "Nothing can break my union with Christ." Your body may become useless. Your members may be unable to perform their duties. You may feel like an old useless log, a weariness to others, and a burden to yourself. But your soul is safe. Jesus is never tired of caring for your soul. You shall "never perish."

Would you have full assurance of hope in death? Then lay hold on this doctrine of perseverance. Doctors may have given over their labors. Friends may be unable to minister to your wants. Memory may be almost gone, but the lovingkindness of God shall not depart. One in Christ, you shall never be forsaken. Jesus shall stand by you. Death shall not separate you from the everlasting love of God in Christ. You shall "never perish."

—J. C. RYLE

◆Have you ever felt like you were going to perish? How can the truth of Christ persevering with you comfort you?

Looking above Earth's Troubles

God is our refuge and strength, a very present help in trouble.

—PSALM 46:1

Happy, thrice happy, is the man who receives with childlike simplicity the Word of God and lives it out. He seeks God in everything and can feed on the hidden manna. He finds the promises to be full of truth and comfort. On them, as on a rock, he rests in safety. With wonder he sees the raging tempest, which, sweeping over the nations of the earth, clears away deep-rooted prejudices and prepares a smoother path for the chariot of the everlasting gospel.

He knows that glorious days are coming and therefore is not discouraged, though they be preceded by a stormy night. He hears the voice of his almighty Father speaking in gracious accents to allay his fears, "Be still, and know that I am God" (Ps. 46:10), and he is kept in perfect peace.

Come then, dear Christian, and take courage. Fear not the face nor the frown of man. The Lord reigns, be the earth ever so unquiet. Sing with David, unite with Luther, and say, "God is our refuge and strength, a very present help in trouble" (Ps. 46:1). Do not be dismayed at the troubles of the earth. Tremble not at the convulsions of the empires. Only fear God; only believe in His promises; only love and serve Him; and all things shall work together for your good, as they assuredly will for His glory.

Life is hastening quickly away. Eternity is at the door. Live, then, for eternity, and leave with God the concerns of time. Leave in His hands the safety of His church and the security of His cause. Cleave to Him with childlike simplicity. Seek His glory. Aim at perfection. Look high and look forward; and soon you shall be removed out of the reach of evil and placed securely in the paradise above!

—THOMAS READE

◆*Recall several promises of God from Scripture that are precious to you, and explain how they give you rest.*

Be Gentle

But the wisdom that is from above is first pure, then peaceable, gentle, and easy to be intreated, full of mercy and good fruits, without partiality, and without hypocrisy.

—JAMES 3:17

Imitate Christ in His gentleness, and be gentle to others as He is gentle to you. "The servant of the Lord must not strive; but be gentle" (2 Tim. 2:24). The great apostle could say, "We were gentle among you, even as a nurse cherisheth her children" (1 Thess. 2:7). "The wisdom that is from above is first pure, then peaceable, gentle, and easy to be intreated, full of mercy and good fruits, without partiality, and without hypocrisy" (James 3:17), and it teaches us "to speak evil of no man, to be no brawlers, but gentle, shewing all meekness unto all men" (Titus 3:2). Be gentle to the lambs of the flock; be gentle to those whose grace is little, whose faith is weak, whose strength is small, whose infirmities are many, whose sorrows are keen, whose trials are severe, whose positions and paths in life are difficult and perilous.

I beseech you, by the meekness and gentleness of Christ, in this way to be Christlike. Be gentle to them that have fallen by the power of temptation; those who have traveled in the ways of the Lord with such a slow and tardy step that they have been overtaken by evil. Be gentle, very gentle, to the broken heart and the wounded spirit. Speak gently to those to whom shame and grief and sin have bowed them down to the earth. Speak gently of those who, through weakness and frailty, have erred in judgment or in practice. Learn of Jesus in the gentleness with which He leads the burdened, and consider yourself as never so closely conformed to Him as when meekness, lowliness, and gentleness clothe you as a garment and make beautiful your whole being with its luster.

—OCTAVIUS WINSLOW

◆ *How are you doing regarding gentleness toward one another, toward children, family members, and others? In what ways can you display this grace more?*

God's Fatherly Hand

In thee, O LORD, do I put my trust.
—PSALM 31:1

Jonah, although he was in the fish's belly and there was no manner of appearance of ever being delivered—for what hope can a man have of deliverance that is swallowed by a whale?—trusted in God. They that trust in God are certainly safe in whatever condition they are in; they are safe in affliction and safe in prosperity. Jonah was as safe in the fish's belly, down under the bottom of the mountains, as if he had been in a strong tower, for he trusted God, and he was in God's hand. God's mercy and love is a bulwark and defense, so strong that the forces of all the creation are not able to hurt us.

Whatever God does to those who are His children, He does as a Father. It is all from love and tender affection; wherefore, if they meet with affliction, they ought patiently to receive it, considering that their heavenly Father orders it out of love to them. And though they cannot see God's gracious design in it now, yet they will see hereafter and will break forth into singing praises to God for His merciful afflicting of them.

If God gives them prosperity, they ought to receive it joyfully and gladly, as a gift of their kind Father, knowing that God sends it to them as children. The wicked cannot have this comfort in their outward good things, because they do not trust in God. The godly are nourished and provided for of God, as children are provided for by a father; but the wicked know not but that they are fed as beasts are fed, and fatted for the slaughter.

Wherefore, whatsoever your state and condition be, throw off all other confidences, and resolve to trust in God, and cast your whole burden upon Him; for it is good for a man to hope and quietly to wait for the salvation of the Lord.

—JONATHAN EDWARDS

♦*Do you see God's fatherly hand in your afflictions? How should this comfort you if you can by faith lay hold of this truth?*

A Hard Lesson to Learn

For I have learned, in whatsoever state
I am, therewith to be content.
—PHILIPPIANS 4:11

For a man or woman to have a murmuring heart when an affliction first happens is an evil, but to murmur when God has been a long time exercising them with affliction is more evil. Though a heifer when the yoke is first put upon her wriggles and will not be quiet, if after many months or years it will not draw the plow quietly, the farmer would rather fatten it and prepare it for the butcher than be troubled any longer with it. So, though the Lord was content to pass by that discontented spirit of yours at first, yet now that God has for a long time kept the yoke on you—you have been under His afflicting hand maybe many years and yet you remain discontented still—it would be just if God were to bear your murmuring no longer and that your discontent under affliction were but a preparation for your destruction.

Mark that text in Hebrews 12:11, "No chastening for the present seemeth to be joyous, but grievous: nevertheless afterward it yieldeth the peaceable fruit of righteousness unto them which are exercised thereby." It is true our afflictions are not joyous but grievous. Though when our affliction first comes it is very grievous, afterward it yields the peaceable fruit of righteousness. When you have been long in the school of afflictions, you are a very dull student in Christ's school if you have not learned contentment. "I have learned," said Paul, "in whatsoever state I am, therewith to be content" (Phil. 4:11). Paul had learned this lesson quickly; perhaps, you have been learning it many years.

A new cart may creak and make a noise, but after it has been used a while, it will not do so. So, when you are first a Christian and newly come to the work of Christ, perhaps you make noise and cannot bear afflictions; but are you an old Christian, and yet will you be a murmuring Christian? It is a shame for any who are old believers, who have been a long time in the school of Jesus Christ, to have murmuring and discontent spirits.

—JEREMIAH BURROUGHS

♦*Are you able to discern growth in your contentedness over the years of*
your Christian life? Have you learned the art of contentment? If not,
what do you need to do?

Take Heed to Your Tongue (1)

I said, I will take heed to my ways,
that I sin not with my tongue.

—PSALM 39:1

The tongue is an unruly member; God has set a double hedge before the tongue—the teeth and the lips—to keep it within its bounds, that it should not speak vainly. O look to your tongue! When a city is besieged, he that keeps the gates of the city keeps the whole city safe; so if you keep the gates or doors of your mouth, you keep your whole soul. How can we order or regulate the governing of our tongue that we do not dishonor God?

If you would have a better tongue, labor for a better heart. It is the heart that has influence upon the tongue. If the heart is vain and earthly, the tongue will be so; if the heart be holy, the tongue will be so. Look to your heart; get a better heart and a better tongue. How can I get my heart bettered? Get a principle of grace infused.

If you would not sin in your tongue, call to mind how you have formally offended in your tongue, and that will make you more watchful for the future. Have not you spoken words that have savored of discontent or envy? Have you not been guilty of censuring and slandering? Have you not been disgusted with passion? Hath not your tongue outrun your discretion? Have you not spoken words that you have been sorry for afterward and have caused either shame or tears? Observe former failings, how you have sinned in your tongue, and that will be a good help for the future! David certainly made a critical observation on some of his words, wherein he had offended: words of pride. "In my prosperity, I said, I shall never be moved" (Ps. 30:6); and "I said in my haste, All men are liars" (116:11). David having observed how he had offended in his tongue made a strict vow with himself, that he would look better to them: "I said, I will take heed to my ways, that I sin not with my tongue" (39:1).

—THOMAS WATSON

♦ *Consider your tongue—your words, your tone, and the intent of your heart behind the unwise use of your tongue. Do you have reason to repent and take heed to your tongue that you would not sin?*

Take Heed to Your Tongue (2)

I said, I will take heed to my ways,
that I sin not with my tongue.

—PSALM 39:1

Watch your tongue; most sin is committed for want of watchfulness. As the tongue has a double fence set about it, so it has need to have a double watch. The tongue, when it is let loose, will be ready to speak loosely; watch it, lest it run beyond its bounds in frothy and sinful discourse, "If thou hast thought evil, lay thine hand upon thy mouth" (Prov. 30:32); that is, say some, to lay your hand upon your mouth in a token of repentance. But it may bear another sense: if you have thought evil, if angry malicious thoughts come into thy mind, lay your hand upon your mouth to stop your lips, that your thoughts come not into words.

If you would not offend in your tongue, ponder your words well before you speak. "Be not rash with thy mouth" (Eccl. 5:2). Some speak vainly, because inconsiderately they do not weigh their words before they speak them. A talkative man does not mind his words but gives his tongue liberty; he may speak not only inadvisably, but unholily and give just offense.

If you would not offend in your tongue, pray to God to guard your tongue, "Set a watch, O LORD, before my mouth" (Ps. 141:3). Set not about this work in your own strength, but implore God's help; "the tongue can no man tame" (James 3:8). But God can tame it; therefore, go to Him by prayer. Pray, "Lord, set a watch before the door of my lips; keep me, that I may speak nothing to grieve Thy Spirit or that may tend to Thy dishonor."

If you would be kept from evil speaking, accustom your tongue to good speaking. If you would not have your tongue run out sinfully, let it be used to good discourse; speak often one to another of Christ and the things pertaining to the kingdom of God. The spouse's lips dropped as a honeycomb (Song 4:11).

—THOMAS WATSON

◆*List some of the ways you resolve with God's help to keep a watch over*
your tongue. Share with someone close to you so you can hold one another
accountable.

One Name Greater Than All

Now therefore ye are no more strangers and foreigners, but
fellow citizens with the saints, and of the household of God.
—EPHESIANS 2:19

No doubt there are other names for the saints besides family. But none of them express what this is intended to do. God calls them His *flock*, which implies tender watchfulness on His part and dependent helplessness on theirs. He calls them a *vine*, denoting their oneness, as well as the unceasing nourishment that is ever circulating through them from the parent stem. He calls them a *temple*, signifying their compactness of structure, symmetry of design, beauty of form, and, above all, fitness for the inhabitation and worship of Jehovah. He calls them a *body*, to set forth not merely their comely proportions but their marvelous unity and conscious vitality of being, as well as the closeness of the binding tie and their various serviceableness to each other. He calls them a *city*, intimating their happy community of privileges and rights and well-ordered government; the security, peace, abundance which they enjoy, the comforts of neighborhood with all its cheerful greetings and mutual offices of love. He calls them a *kingdom*, as expressive of their high and honorable estate, of the royalty, the glory, the dominion of which they have been made heirs.

But various and expressive as these well-known names are, they are still imperfect. They describe as it were only the outer circles, each name a circle of its own. But the inner circle, the inner region of our spiritual being, they do not touch upon. It is that well-known word, that magic name, *family*, which alone can express all that God sees of what is comely and tender, loving and lovable in the church of Christ into which He is pouring His love, through which He delights to see that love circulate unhindered, and out of which He expects that love to flow abroad.

—HORATIUS BONAR

◆ *In what ways can your church function more like a family? What practical*
things can you do to contribute in your church? What comforts do you hear
when you understand that God calls His people family?

Our Load-Bearing Father

Cast thy burden upon the LORD, and he shall sustain thee:
he shall never suffer the righteous to be moved.

—PSALM 55:22

The most common cause of weariness is the attempt to carry an over-load of care. This is not a wise forethought for the future or a proper provision for life's "rainy day." It is sheer worry. The exhortation for such overloaded Christians who toil along life's highway is this: "Cast thy burden upon the LORD, and he shall sustain thee" (Ps. 55:22). If we will only drop everything that is sinful and unnecessary in the shape of worry, He will enable us to carry the legitimate load. Weary one, "[cast] all your care upon *him*; for he careth for you" (1 Peter 5:7).

Suppose that a weary, foot-sore traveler were trudging along an uphill road on a sultry day, and a wagon overtakes him. The kind driver calls out: "Ho! my friend, you look tired. Throw that pack into my wagon; I am going your way." But the silly wayfarer, eyeing him suspiciously, as if he wished to steal it, churlishly replies, "Go along with you. I can carry my own luggage." We laugh at this obstinate folly, and then repeat the same foolish sin against the God of love.

When God says to us, "Give me your load, and I will help you," He does not release us from our share of duty. No more does the atoning Savior, when He bears the guilt and penalty of our sins, release us from repentance of those sins or from obeying His commandments. God's offer is to lighten our loads by putting His grace into our hearts and underneath our load. He then becomes our strength. His all-sufficient grace is made perfect in our weakness, so that God really carries the load. It was the Christ *in* Paul who defied Nero and conquered the devil. This divine doctrine of trust is a won-derfully restful one to weary disciples. It takes the tiredness out of the heart.

—THEODORE CUYLER

◆ *What burdens are you trying to carry on your own, rather than laying them on the Lord in prayer? Bow down before Him in a humble, trusting way, laying them all at His feet.*

The Divine Order

But now being made free from sin, and become servants to God,
ye have your fruit unto holiness, and the end everlasting life.
—ROMANS 6:22

The sinner's *legal* position must be set right before his *moral* position can be touched. Condition is one thing; character is another. The sinner's standing before God, either in favor or disfavor, either under grace or under wrath, must first be dealt with before his inner renewal can be carried on. The judicial must precede the moral.

It is of pardon that the gospel first speaks to us, for the question of pardon must first be settled in us before we proceed to others. The adjustment of the relationship between us and God is a vital beginning, both on God's part and on ours. There must be friendship between us before He can give or we can receive His indwelling Spirit; for on the one hand, the Spirit cannot make His dwelling in the unforgiven; and on the other, the unforgiven should be so occupied with the one question of forgiveness that they are not at leisure to attend to anything till this has finally been settled in their favor. The man who knows that the wrath of God is still upon him or is not sure whether it has been turned away or not is really not in a condition to consider other questions, however important, if he has any idea of the magnitude and terribleness of the anger of Him who is a consuming fire.

The divine order then is first pardon, then holiness; first peace with God, and then conformity to the image of that God with whom we have been brought to be at peace. For as likeness to God is produced by beholding His glory (2 Cor. 3:18), and as we cannot look upon Him until we know that He has ceased to condemn us, and as we cannot trust Him until we know that He is gracious, so we cannot be transformed into His image until we have received pardon at His hands. Reconciliation is essential to resemblance; personal friendship must begin a holy life.

—HORATIUS BONAR

◆ *What is your legal standing before God? Will this ever change? How does this affect how you live? Why?*

Precious Trial

As for me, I will call upon God.
—PSALM 55:16

Trial stirs us up to *lay hold on God in prayer*. Nothing probably in all the Lord's means of grace and dispensations of providence so leads us to prayer as the pressure of affliction. And so high a privilege is access to God, so sweet a spot is the throne of grace, so great and holy the blessings that come from a waiting soul upon the Lord. It must be a wholesome discipline that leads to such results. Count it a precious trial, a golden affliction that brings your heart into a closer communion with Christ! Your Elder Brother's voice may, like Joseph's, sound harshly and alarmingly upon your ear, filling you with fear and foreboding; yet it is the voice of your Brother, the "voice of the Beloved," and it speaks but to rouse you to a more full, confiding opening of your heart in prayer. Oh, precious trial! Oh, heaven-sent affliction that breaks down the barriers, removes the restraints, thaws the hardening that intercepts and interrupts my fellowship with God and with His dear Son Christ Jesus.

Our heavenly Father loves to hear the voice of His children; and when that voice is still, when there is a suspension of heart communion, and the tones are silent which were wont to fall as music upon His ear, He sends a trial, and then we rise and give ourselves to prayer. Perhaps it is a perplexity, and we go to Him for counsel; or it is a want, and we go to Him for supply; or it is a grief, and we go to Him for soothing; or it is a burden, and we look to Him for upholding. Maybe it is an infirmity, and we ask Him for grace; or it is a temptation, and we fly to Him for comfort; or it is a sin, and we go to Him for pardon. Be its form what it may, it has a voice, "Rise, and call upon thy God," and to God it brings us.

—OCTAVIUS WINSLOW

♦ *When in need do you turn to God or turn away from God? How would your circumstances change if you first went to God for help before anyone else?*

Persuading by Your Walk and Talk

While they behold your chaste conversation coupled with fear.

—1 PETER 3:2

You may, by your good conversation, be a means to convert other men, to bring wicked men into the love of the ways of God. The exhortation in 1 Peter 3:1–2 is directed to wives who have wicked husbands, "Likewise, ye wives, be in subjection to your own husbands; that, if any obey not the word, they also may without the word be won by the conversation of the wives; while they behold your chaste conversation coupled with fear." Mark how the apostle urges wives to look to their conversations to the end that they may be a means to gain their husbands.

I am persuaded that there are many gracious women who would give, if they had it, a thousand worlds to gain their husbands to those ways of godliness in which they have found so much sweetness. But perhaps they cannot get them to come and hear the Word; and if they do, their hearts rise against it or they do not regard it. But you, by your conversations, may do that which the Word will not do! You may be converters of them, and in this sense, indeed, there may be women preachers; that is, preaching in their lives and conversations, and that's all the preaching the Holy Ghost allows women. Let them preach that way, in their lives and conversations, in their families, and preach a sermon every day. And neither God nor man will find fault with any such things, and this is the way for them to do great service for God.

Husbands should do likewise to convert their wives. You complain of one another, but do you labor to convince and convert one another by your holy conversations? I am confident that there are many who are able to say by experience, "The Lord struck my heart and conscience when I saw the holy conversation of my wife, and seeing the wisdom, humility, obedience, and walk of my wife struck my heart." There are many who have given glory to God and acknowledged this, both wives by their husbands and husbands by their wives.

—JEREMIAH BURROUGHS

◆*Have you been a faithful witness of Christ to your spouse? Discuss this together if you can, and discern where you can do more to encourage your spouse.*

All Things New

*Therefore if any man be in Christ, he is a new creature: old things
are passed away; behold, all things are become new.*
—2 CORINTHIANS 5:17

If we are new creatures in Christ Jesus, we shall have the following unde-
niable evidence of regeneration in our souls:

1. Our perceptions will be new. A divine light will break in upon our
minds. The darkness of error, which obscured the truth from our view, will
be dissipated.

2. Our principles will be new. We will act from pure, holy, unselfish
motives. Faith working by love will be the underlying motive. Self will no
longer be the pivot on which we turn, but Jesus will be our all in all.

3. Our practice will be new. We shall no longer live according to sinful
customs of the world or the powerful temptations of the flesh, but according
to the holy precepts of the Word. We shall delight in the law of God after
the inward man. It will be our food and drink to do the will of our Father
which is in heaven.

4. Our plans will be new. We shall dedicate ourselves, and all we have
and are, to the service of that Divine Savior who loved us and gave Himself
for us.

5. Our prospects will be new. The darkness being past, and the true
light now shining, we shall see the distant radiance of the heavenly Zion
and behold, with the telescopic eye of faith, the land which is very far off.

6. Our privileges will be new. God will now be our reconciled Father;
Jesus our Elder Brother, Savior, and friend; the Holy Spirit, our sanctifier
and comforter; angels, our ministering spirits; and heaven our eternal home.

7. Our portion will be new. All those exceeding great and precious
promises, which in Christ are yea and in Him amen, to the praise and glory
of God are ours. We shall be heirs of God and joint heirs with Christ. We
shall be the citizens of the New Jerusalem.

To sum up all this blessedness, we shall experience in this world a pro-
gression in holiness and in the world to come a permanence of bliss.
—THOMAS READE

◆ *If you find these marks in you, rejoice with thanksgiving; God rejoices over
you with singing!*

Setting Our Affections on Things Above

Set your affection on things above, not on things on the earth.
—COLOSSIANS 3:2

God is a jealous God; and though Christ be a loving Husband unto every soul that is espoused to Him, yet He is very jealous of our affections. What man is not jealous of his wife when he sees that her affections are toward another? Are our affections toward things on earth? What does that do but raise the jealousy of Christ against us? Jealousy is the rage of man, what is it then in Christ? Therefore, as you desire that the jealousy of the Lord Jesus may not be raised against you; that the ways of God may be made sweet and easy toward you; that you may never lose your affections or the object of them; that you may have relief in the day of your troubles; that you may have full assurance of things to come; and that you will forever be there, "set your affection on things above, not on things on the earth" (Col. 3:2).

What shall we do that we may raise and draw up our affections unto these things above? For our affections are indeed too much on things here below. How shall we draw them off from them, and draw them up to things above?

You must be sure to get a new heart, and you must get knowledge of these things that are above, for there is no desire of unknown things nor affections to them. Some desire knowledge and not affections; some desire affections, and do not labor after knowledge. Give me knowledge hearted with affections, and affections headed with knowledge; for as knowledge without affections makes wicked men secure, so affections without knowledge makes godly men scrupulous. Study therefore to know more, and that knowledge gained shall be a light and a lantern to the feet of your affections.
—WILLIAM BRIDGE

◆*Ponder and meditate on the reality that our God is a jealous God. Find a few Bible passages that state this, and reflect on what this means for you in your relationship with Him.*

The Practical Exercise of Faith

The just shall live by faith. —ROMANS 1:17

Faith, in its practical exercise, has for its object the whole Word of God, and forms its opinion of all things which it is daily concerned with according to the standard of Scripture. When our Lord was on earth and talked with His disciples, their eyes and hearts were fixed on Him. In danger He was their defender, their guide when in perplexity, and to Him they looked for the solution of all their doubts, and the supply of all their wants. He is now withdrawn from our eyes; but faith still sets Him before us for the same purposes, with the same effects as if we actually saw Him. His spiritual presence, held by faith, is a restraint from evil, an encouragement to every service, and a present refuge and help in every time of trouble.

The believer takes delight in worship and sacraments, because there he meets his Lord. His religion is not confined to public occasions; but he is the same person in secret as he appears to be in the public worship, for he worships Him who sees in secret, and dares appeal to His all-seeing eye for the sincerity of his desires and intentions. By faith he is enabled to use prosperity with moderation; and knows and feels that what the world calls good is of small value, unless it is accompanied with the presence and blessings of Him who his soul loves. His faith upholds him under all trials by assuring him that every affliction is under the direction of his Lord; that chastisements are a token of His love; and the time, amount, and duration of his sufferings are appointed by infinite wisdom and designed to work for his everlasting good; and that grace and strength shall be given him. So his heart is fixed, trusting in the Lord, to whom he has committed all his concerns, and knowing that his best interests are safe, he is not greatly afraid of evil tidings but enjoys a stable peace in the midst of a changing world.

—JOHN NEWTON

◆ *How does laying hold of Christ by faith, even though you cannot see Him, help you in your daily walk?*

Christ's Welcome

For he shall deliver the needy when he crieth;
the poor also, and him that hath no helper.
—PSALM 72:12

If Christ is grieved at our unbelief, what must be the joy that our faith gives Him! If our hardness of heart shades His countenance, how must that countenance gleam with holy delight over the soul subdued in penitent love at His feet! Think it not presumption then to go to Jesus with the withered hand, with a chilled love, with declension of grace, with weakness of faith, with low frames, with a tempted, tried, and wounded spirit. Jesus Christ makes you whole. Christ is for the poor and needy and them who have no helper. It is said of David, the type of Christ, that there gathered unto him within the cave of Adullam "every one that was in distress, and every one that was in debt, and every one that was discontented…and he became a captain over them" (1 Sam. 22:2).

Around the glorious antitype, Jesus the Son of David, there gathers— received and welcomed—all who are in spiritual distress; who are in debt to the law of God, having nothing to pay; who are discontented with the world, with others, and with themselves; and lo, Jesus becomes the Captain of their salvation. Christ is for the necessitous, the bruised, the outcast, the bankrupt; and withered though your spiritual strength and beauty may be, Jesus's heart expands and invites you to the refuge of its warm, fathomless, changeless love.

Be not weary nor discouraged in the Lord's service. As they did to your Savior, many will seek to thwart, impeach, and wound you in your work of faith and labor of love for Christ. Heed them not. Rejoice if you are counted worthy to be identified with your Lord and Master in suffering for righteousness' sake.

—OCTAVIUS WINSLOW

◆ *Can you name one condition of soul which Christ says is too difficult for Him? If you cannot, then go to Him with whatever your condition may be, and find rest at the foot of the cross. How can you encourage others toward this purpose as well?*

The Sweetness of Meditating on God

My meditation of him shall be sweet: I will be glad in the LORD.
—PSALM 104:34

It is a sweet thing for a godly person to meditate on God and the things of God, because it is natural for him. Natural works are pleasant works. It is a tedious and difficult thing to row against a stream; but natural works are pleasant works. It is a natural thing for a worldly person to think and meditate on the world, and the things thereof; so, it is natural to a godly person to think and meditate on God and the things of God. The reason that the wicked take so much delight in thinking and meditating and musing on their sins and sinful ways is because sin is natural to them. But a godly person, being partaker of the divine nature, feels it natural to think on God and the ways and things of God; it is pleasant and therefore sweet.

But as it is natural for the godly to think on God and the things of God, so it is suitable to them. It is a natural work, as it is a suitable work. The more suitable anything is to us, the more it pleases us; all pleasures and delights arise from it. If you have a very large estate but it is not suited to your heart, you will have not pleasure in it. If you have a small estate and it is suited to your heart, you are happy and satisfied in it.

What in all the world is so suitable to a godly person as God? Is the object of man's understanding truth? God is truth. Is the object of his will good? God is good. Is the object of his affections love? God is love. Are our desires infinite? God is infinite. What is there that the soul of man can want but it is found in God? A suitable good is He; therefore, it needs be that it is a sweet thing to meditate on God and the things of God.

—WILLIAM BRIDGE

◆ *What is your natural disposition, to think on God and His things or yourself and your things? Take the time to meditate on God, and see whether your heart is drawn to Him.*

A Life of Faith

He that overcometh shall inherit all things; and
I will be his God, and he shall be my son.
—REVELATION 21:7

Shall trials shake us? No, in all this we are more than conquerors through Him that loved us. Shall sorrow move us? Faith tells us of a land where sorrow is unknown. Shall the death of saints move us? Faith tells us not to sorrow as those who have no hope, for if we believe that Jesus died and rose again, them also that sleep in Jesus will God bring with Him. Shall the pains and weariness of this frail body move us? Faith tells of a time at hand when this corruptible shall put on incorruption, and death shall be swallowed up in victory. Shall hardship move us? Faith tells us of a day when the poverty of our exile shall be forgotten in the abundance of our peaceful, plenteous home, where we shall hunger no more, neither thirst anymore. Shall the disquieting bustle of this restless life annoy us? Faith tells us of the rest that remains for the people of God, the sea of glass like crystal on which the ransomed saints shall stand, no tempest, no tumult, no shipwreck there. Shall the lack of this world's honors move us? Faith tells us of the exceeding and eternal weight of glory in reserve. Have we no place to lay our head? Faith tells us that we have a home, a dwelling, though not in any city on earth.

Are we fearful as we look around upon the disorder and wretchedness of this misgoverned earth? Faith tells us that the coming of the Lord draws nigh. Do thoughts of death alarm us? Faith tells us that "to die is gain" (Phil. 1:21) and whispers to us, "What! Are you afraid of becoming immortal, afraid of passing from this state of death, which men call life, to that which alone truly deserves the name?" Such is the Christian life—a life of faith. We live upon things unseen. Our life is hid with Christ in God. It has been the way of the saints from the beginning. This is the way in which they have walked, leaning on their Beloved; and such is to be the walk of the saints till the Lord comes.

—HORATIUS BONAR

◆ *Are you walking by faith or sight? Do you not need to pray as the disciples did, "Lord, increase our faith"?*

Be on Your Guard

Wherefore let him that thinketh he standeth take heed lest he fall.
—1 CORINTHIANS 10:12

If you've been able to resist the assaults of the wicked one, be encouraged but not careless. "Be not highminded, but fear" (Rom. 11:20). "Let him that thinketh he standeth take heed lest he fall" (1 Cor. 10:12). "Satan's opportunity is—a soul off its guard," said Hewitson. "The saint's sleeping time is the devil's tempting time," says Gurnall. When we are in the grave, the wicked one will cease from troubling and the weary will have perfect rest; but here every step we take we are among lions and must stand on our watchtower, fearing always and working out our own salvation with that trembling and care which alone can secure it. A holy jealousy is a great preservative against falling. The moment we begin to sleep, our watchful adversary is ready to assault us; but blessed is the man whom His Lord, when He comes, will find watching.

Be greatly on your guard in quiet times or when called to work alone, without the help and encouragement of others. Watch closely your thoughts and ways. "Two are better than one; because they have a good reward for their labour. For if they fall, the one will lift up his fellow: but woe to him that is alone when he falleth; for he hath not another to help him up" (Eccl. 4:9–10). It seems to have been when Eve was alone that she was tempted and overcome, and so she was the first in the transgression. Satan knew what an advantage solitude would give him in plying the blessed Master with his wicked suggestions when He was in the wilderness. Doubtless our Lord felt this at that time. It is certain He felt His solitude in His last temptation as He came to His disciples and found them asleep.

Our great refuge in temptation is the throne of grace sprinkled with atoning blood. In vain will we pray, if we plead any goodness of our own. Let us make mention of Christ's righteousness, even of His only.

—WILLIAM PLUMER

◆*Pride and self-reliance are damaging to the Christian life. Who has the Lord given you to walk this path of life together? What can you do to be a better helper for others?*

Our Highest End

We know that, when he shall appear, we shall be
like him; for we shall see him as he is.

—1 JOHN 3:2

Heaven is that place alone where our highest end and highest good is to be obtained. God made us for Himself. "Of him, and through him, and to him, are all things" (Rom. 11:36). Therefore, we attain to our highest end when we are brought to God, but that is by being brought to heaven, for that is God's throne, the place of His special presence. There is but a very imperfect union with God to be had in this world, a very imperfect knowledge of Him amid much darkness, a very imperfect conformity to God, mingled with abundance of estrangement. Here we can serve and glorify God, but in a very imperfect manner; our service being mingled with sin, which dishonors God. But when we get to heaven (if that ever be), we shall be brought to a perfect union with God and have clearer views of Him. There we shall be fully conformed to God, without any remaining sin; for "we shall see him as he is" (1 John 3:2). There we shall serve God perfectly and glorify Him in an exalted manner, even to the utmost of the powers and capacity of our nature. Then we shall perfectly give up ourselves to God; our hearts will be pure and holy offerings, presented in a flame of divine love.

God is the highest good of the reasonable creature; and the enjoyment of Him is the only happiness with which our souls can be satisfied. To go to heaven fully to enjoy God is infinitely better than the most pleasant accommodations here. Fathers and mothers, husbands, wives, or children, or the company of earthly friends are but shadows; but the enjoyment of God is the substance. These are but scattered beams; but God is the sun. These are but streams; but God is the fountain. Therefore, we should spend this life only as a journey toward heaven; we should make the seeking of our highest end and proper good, the whole work of our lives.

—JONATHAN EDWARDS

◆*Do you view the comforts and joys of this world as shadows of your delight in God, or are they distractions that keep you from your highest end?*

Sweet, Submissive Silence

I opened not my mouth; because thou didst it.
—PSALM 39:9

When a Christian comes face-to-face with the tremendous fact that God is dealing with him, then trial assumes a totally different aspect. When he sees that it is God's hand which is put on his back, he is ready to put his own hand on his mouth and keep still. Then he is ready to quiet himself as a child that is weaned of its mother.

It is a glorious discovery that we make when we discern the hand of God in either the experience of a great joy or of a great sorrow. An injury inflicted on us by a fellow person may arouse our resentment; we may scold him for his carelessness or rebuke him for his unkindness. But when we recognize the fact that our heavenly Father has administered the chastening stroke, then our calling is to practice a sweetly submissive silence. Sharp questions will do us no good, for God keeps His own secrets. Rebellious murmurings will only chafe our already smarting heart.

Try as hard as we can, we cannot get beyond this tremendous truth—*God did it!* And when we reach that truth and open our eyes to it and look at it rightly, it teaches us why we ought to lock our lips in submissive silence. "Be still, and know that I am God" (Ps. 46:10). This is not blind fatalism; it is intelligent trust that knows *who* it is trusting. We cannot know this glorious and eternal truth about God unless we are "still"; and on the other hand, that knowledge will tend to keep us still. No human parent feels bound to explain to his child the reasons for his conduct; and our heavenly Father has never promised to answer all our questions; He has only promised to supply our needs, and faith must silently accept His word when He says that "all things work together for good to them that love God" (Rom. 8:28).

—THEODORE CUYLER

◆*Does the way you think about your circumstances in life indicate that you do not believe "God is in them"? Think about the things that weigh you down, and consider how God is actually in them.*

Kept

*Fear thou not; for I am with thee: be not dismayed; for I am
thy God: I will strengthen thee; yea, I will help thee; yea,
I will uphold thee with the right hand of my righteousness.*

—ISAIAH 41:10

Whatever may be the cup your heavenly Father prepares for you, keep firm hold of this truth, that He will never forsake you. He "forsaketh not his saints" (Ps. 37:28). Do not shrink from the suffering that seems inevitable, the cup which may not pass your lips untouched; God will be with you. You are, perhaps, anticipating a fiery trial, a dread crisis of your case; the flesh shrinks from the knife, the heart dies within you at the thought of that hour of silent agony which approaches. Oh, have faith now in your heavenly Father. Do you think that He will leave you to drink that cup alone? Will He leave you to endure that pain alone? Will He let you pass through that hour alone? No, He will be with you, Christ will be with you, the Comforter will be with you, and "as thy days, so shall thy strength be" (Deut. 33:25).

Has God ever yet been to you a wilderness? Has His promise ever failed? Has Jesus ever stood aloof from your sore, leaving your wound untouched, unsoothed, unhealed? Has not the Lord always been better than all your trembling anticipations, quelling your fears, reassuring your doubting mind, and bearing you gently and safely through the hour of suffering which you dreaded? Then Trust Him *now*! Never, *never* will He forsake you! Let His will be done in you and by you, and both in doing and suffering, you may sweetly sing:

> My Father, choose the path I tread,
> Midst drooping hopes and pleasures fled,
> Or with bright sunshine round me spread,
> But never let me go!

> Yes, Lord, Thy wisdom, love, and power
> Are my strong rock, my sheltering tower,
> And this shall soothe life's darkest hour,
> Thou wilt not let me go!

—OCTAVIUS WINSLOW

◆ *Recall those times when you thought you would sink beneath the waves
but He was there to lift you up, and let those times be a pleading ground
for future distresses as well.*

A Settled Matter

Let us draw near with a true heart in full assurance of faith.
—HEBREWS 10:22

None do so much for Christ on earth as those who enjoy the fullest confidence of a free entrance into heaven. That sounds wonderful, but it is true. A believer who lacks an assured hope will spend much of his time in inward searchings of his heart regarding his own state. Like a nervous hypochondriacal person, he will be full of his own ailments, his own doubtings and questionings, his own conflicts and corruptions. In short you will often find he is so taken up with this eternal warfare that he has little time for other things and little time to work for God.

Now a believer who has, like Paul, an assured hope is free from these harassing distractions. He does not vex his soul with doubts about his own pardon and acceptance. He looks at the everlasting covenant sealed with blood, at the finished work and never broken word of His Lord and Savior, and therefore counts his salvation a settled thing. Therefore, he is able to give an undivided attention to the work of the Lord, and so in the long run to do more.

As Thomas Watson said, "Assurance would make us active and lively in God's service; it would excite prayer and quicken obedience. Faith would make us walk, but assurance would make us run; we should think we could never do enough for God. Assurance would be as wings to the bird, as weights to the clock, to set all the wells of obedience running."

And as Thomas Brooks explains so well, "Assurance will make a man fervent, constant, and abundant in the work of the Lord. When the assured Christian hath done one work, he is calling out for another. What is next, Lord, says the assured soul; what is next? An assured Christian will put his hand to any work, he will put his neck in any yoke for Christ."

—J. C. RYLE

◆ *Are you an assured believer? How can you gain greater assurance which will naturally give rise to greater obedience and fewer doubts and fears?*

No Spots

Thou art all fair, my love; there is no spot in thee.
—SONG OF SOLOMON 4:7

When the believer looks at himself, his own duties and performances, he sees nothing at all but spots, all smeared and spattered over. Though you look on yourself as spotted, Christ looks on you without spot, and God the Father looks upon you through Christ without spot and says, "Thou art all fair...there is no spot in thee" (Song 4:7).

You think that if God would make a discovery of your heart to all your Christian friends and acquaintances, you would appear so foul that they would cast you out of their friendship and never have anything more to do with you. Yet, for all this Christ says, "Thou art all fair...there is no spot in thee." Justification has no degrees. No, not in heaven—you are not more justified there than you are here. You are now as perfectly justified as ever and as accepted of Christ as ever. Sanctification is renewed day by day, being a work of God in us. We increase in it daily. But justification is a work of God outside of us and so it perfected at once. This makes a pardoned soul blessed, because pardon of sin is of such a nature that it is a perfect work.

Here is abundance of comfort to a pardoned soul. Though you are weak in sanctification, and it troubles you to think how far you come short of Abraham's faith, Moses's meekness, David's love, Paul's zeal, Solomon's wisdom, and Job's patience, yet know that you are equal in justification with Abraham, Moses, David, and all the prophets, and this is a great comfort to you against the weakness of sanctification.

Is the mercy of God so rich and glorious to me, though I am a poor, wicked sinner, that I should be made equal to the greatest saints in justification? How I should labor to follow hard after them and get as near to them as I can in point of sanctification! How we should imitate Moses's meekness, David's love, Paul's zeal, and Job's patience!

—JEREMIAH BURROUGHS

◆ *Do you believe what Burroughs says regarding your justification? If you are uncertain, why is this? How would being sure of this truth fire our zeal for sanctification?*

Abounding Grace

And God is able to make all grace abound toward you.
—2 CORINTHIANS 9:8

The grace of God is your strength, as it is your joy; and it is only by abiding in it that you can really live the life of the redeemed. Be strong, then, in this grace; draw your joy out of it; and beware how you turn to anything else for refreshment or comfort or holiness. Though a believing person, you are still a sinner—a sinner to the end—and, as such, nothing can suit you but the free love of God. Be strong in His grace. Remember that you are saved by believing, not by doubting. Be not then a doubter, but a believer. Draw continually on Christ and His fullness for this grace. If at any time you are enticed away from it, return to it without delay; and betake yourself to it again just as you did at the beginning. To recover lost peace, go back to where you got it at first; begin your spiritual life all over again; get at once to the resting place. Where sin has abounded, let grace much more abound. Do not go back to your feelings or experiences or evidences in order to obtain from them a renewal of your lost peace. Go straight back to the free love of God. You found peace in it at first; you will find peace in it to the last. This was the *beginning* of your confidence; let it be both last and first.

This abounding grace, rightly understood, will not make you sin; it will not relax morality or make inconsistency a small matter. It will magnify sin and enhance its evil in your eyes. Your footing or "standing" in grace will be the strongest, as well as the most blessed that you can ever occupy. If your feet be "shod with the preparation of the gospel of peace" (Eph. 6:15), you will be able to "stand" and "withstand," not otherwise. Remember how Paul and Barnabas urged this upon the Jews of Antioch, and "persuaded them to continue in *the grace* of God" (Acts 13:43).

—HORATIUS BONAR

◆*Have you lost peace? Return again to the free grace that found you and saved you, and rest in Him. Amazing grace, how sweet the sound, that saved a wretch like me.*

Christian Warfare

Wherefore take unto you the whole armour of God, that ye may be able to withstand in the evil day, and having done all, to stand.
—EPHESIANS 6:13

Reader, *it may be you know something of the Christian warfare,* and are a tried and proved soldier. If that be your case, accept a word of advice and encouragement from a fellow soldier. Let me speak to myself as well as to you. Let us stir up our minds by way of remembrance. There are some things we cannot remember too well.

Let us remember that if we would fight successfully, we must put on the whole armor of God, and never lay it aside till we die. Not a single piece of the armor can be dispensed with. The girdle of truth, the sword of the Spirit, the helmet of hope, each and all are needful.

Let us remember that the eye of our loving Savior is upon us morning, noon, and night. He will never suffer us to be tempted above that we are able to bear. He can be touched with the feeling of our infirmities, for He suffered Himself, being tempted. He knows what battles and conflicts are, for He Himself was assaulted by the prince of this world. Having such a High Priest, Jesus the Son of God, let us hold fast our profession.

Let us remember that thousands of soldiers before us have fought the same battle that we are fighting and came off more than conquerors through Him that loved them. They overcame by the blood of the Lamb; and so also may we. Christ's arm is quite as strong as ever, and Christ's heart is just as loving as ever. He that saved men and women before us is one who never changes. He is able to save to the uttermost both you and me and all who come unto God by Him. Then let us cast doubts and fears away. Let us follow them who through faith and patience inherit the promises and are waiting for us to join them.

—J. C. RYLE

◆*Read Ephesians 6 and consider what it looks like to daily put on each piece of armor.*

Spiritual Conflict

For which cause we faint not; but though our outward man perish,
yet the inward man is renewed day by day.

—2 CORINTHIANS 4:16

The Christian has been compared to a boat placed on a rapid river, which, if it is not moving against the current, will be carried down by it. To oppose a stream would require a power not of its own. Just so it is with the believer. He must contend against a torrent of inward corruptions, known perhaps only to God and his own heart; and having lost, through the fall, all spiritual strength, he feels utterly unable of himself to resist them. He, therefore, looks continually unto Jesus and, being strengthened with might by the Spirit in the inner man, is enabled to stem the stream and so prove that he possesses spiritual life and vigor.

This inward conflict, which marks the true believer from those who are the captives of Satan, brings much joy or pain, in proportion to the strength or weakness of faith. The life of the Christian is a daily combat. Those who are little acquainted with it feel no inward struggle between nature and grace. It is true some Christians are less troubled than others with internal conflict; but every view which the Scriptures give us of a life of faith is connected with force and opposition both from within and without.

It is called a race, a warfare, a pilgrimage. Therefore, believers are exhorted to run that they may obtain the prize; to fight that they may gain the crown; to persevere that they may reach their promised rest. "The soul of the sluggard desireth, and hath nothing: but the soul of the diligent shall be made fat" (Prov. 13:4).

Sanctification is the gracious work of the Spirit, transforming the soul of the sinner into the likeness of Jesus Christ. Holiness is essential to our happiness, for joy springs out of that faith which works by love, purifies the heart, and overcomes the world.

—THOMAS READE

◆ *Are you resisting inward conflicts or allowing them to carry you downstream? Are your inward conflicts carrying over into your relationships?*

Permitted Temptations

Satan hath desired to have you, that he may sift you as wheat.

—LUKE 22:31

The temptations of Satan by which he is successful in drawing many Christians from the path of duty, in filling them with spiritual pride, or lulling them into carnal security are not what I now speak of. In these attempts he is often most powerful and prevalent when least perceived, as he seldom distresses those who he can deceive. It is when these endeavors fail that he fights against the peace of the soul. He hates the Lord's people, resents all their privileges and comforts, and will do what he can to trouble them, because he cannot prevail against them. And though the Lord sets boundaries to his rage that he cannot pass, and limits both his manner and duration, He is often pleased to allow him to discover his hatred to a considerable degree; not to gratify Satan but to humble and prove His children; to show them what is in their hearts; and to make them truly sensible of their immediate and absolute dependence on Him and hasten them to watchfulness and prayer.

Although temptations are painful and terrible, yet, when by the grace of God, they produce these effects, they deserve to be numbered among "all things [that] work together for good to them that love God" (Rom. 8:28). The light carriage, vain confidence, and backslidings of many Christians might perhaps (humanly speaking) have been somewhat prevented, had they been more acquainted with this spiritual warfare and had they drunk from the cup of temptation.

One gracious purpose that the Lord has in permitting His people to be tempted is for the prevention of greater evils, that they may not grow proud or careless, or be ensnared by the corrupt customs of the world. In this light, I am convinced that however burdensome your trials may at some times prove, you are enabled to rejoice in them and be thankful for them. You know what you suffer now; but you know not what might have been the consequence if you had never been smarted by the fiery darts of the wicked one.

—JOHN NEWTON

◆*Can you see the temptations of Satan as permitted by God to work out His good in you? Try to give an example of this in your life so you can begin to recognize it more.*

Sufficient Grace for the Day

As thy days, so shall thy strength be.
—DEUTERONOMY 33:25

Christian, mark these words. They do not give the pledge that we shall not feel the burden and heat of the day. All they promise is that we shall get safely through. They do not say that we shall not feel the weight of our duties, trials, temptations, and conflicts; all they say is that we shall have strength to bear their weight and to journey on with our load. The grace imparted will then be "sufficient" for us, not superabundant but sufficient for our actual necessities, strength equal to our day.

Christian, distress not yourself about impending evils. You think you have not strength for the hour of sickness. Use the strength you now have in the day of health, and the promise will not then fail you. You fear you have not strength for the thorny path of prosperity, tread humbly and thankfully the path of prosperity, and you will not then be refused consolation and support. You fear you are unprepared to meet the King of Terrors and enter the gloomy valley. Live to the glory of God and as beseems your Christian profession, and when you are summoned to depart, His rod and staff will then uphold and comfort you.

It is by putting forth the strength already gained that you may hope to stand your ground when greater exertion and more vigorous effort are demanded. Strength to encounter the tempest will be given when the tempest rages; strength to contend with the foaming surges will be given when the hurricane has actually come; so strength to grapple with the last enemy will be given when he comes forth to meet you. Yes, Christian, be assured, grace and strength will be imparted when you need them, as certainly as they will be withheld before you need them. He who guides you knows your needs and in the day of trouble will not leave you comfortless. Journey on, then, with firmness, relying on the promise of Him who is faithful and true!
—ASHTON OXENDEN

◆ *Are you worried about impending evil? Read this meditation again, and consider how it is by faith alone that the encouragements God sets before us can be a comfort. Cling to Him who has helped you till this hour.*

The Object of Spiritual Joy

He will rejoice over thee with joy.
—ZEPHANIAH 3:17

Christ delights in your joy, loves your joy, is glorifed by your joy; and when He sees you resting in His blood and righteousness, coming in your poverty to the unsearchable riches of His grace, in your emptiness to His atoning blood, "He will rejoice over thee with joy; he will rest in his love, he will joy over thee with singing" (Zeph. 3:17).

Spiritual joy is a holy, sensitive plant. It shrinks from the rude, ungentle touch, from every influence uncongenial with its heaven-born nature. Watch it with sleepless vigilance, shield it with every hallowed defense. There are many hostile influences to which it is exposed, any one of which will seriously injure it. Temptation courted, sin tampered with, worldliness indulged, the creature idolized, means of grace slighted, Christ undervalued—any one of these things will damp your joy, cause it to shrink, and compel it to retire. But nothing will sooner or more effectually do this than looking away from the object and source of joy—the Lord Jesus Christ.

Your joy is not only *of* the Lord, but it is a joy *in* the Lord. That which caused the Ethiopian eunuch to go on his way rejoicing was not his baptism, Christlike as it was, it was *Christ* Himself. He had found Christ the Messiah, Christ the sin-bearer, Christ the sin-atoning Lamb as preached by Isaiah (Isa. 53), and *this* is what sent him on his way rejoicing.

There is everything in Christ to make you a joyful Christian. There is all redundance of grace to subdue your corruptions; overflowing sympathy to soothe your sorrows; a sovereign efficacy in His blood to cleanse your guilt; infinite resources to meet all your wants; His ever-encircling presence around your path; His ceaseless intercession on your behalf in heaven; His loving cognizance of all you feel and fear and need. Is this not enough to make your heart a constant sunshine, and your life a pleasant song?

—OCTAVIUS WINSLOW

◆*Do you know this joy? Recall the times of joy you have experienced. Has your joy subsided? If so, reflect on this meditation, and seek to have the joy of your salvation restored.*

Justified by Faith

Knowing that a man is not justified by the works of the law, but by the faith of Jesus Christ, even we have believed in Jesus Christ, that we might be justified by the faith of Christ.

—GALATIANS 2:16

What is the meaning of the expression "we are justified by faith"? How are we justified by faith? Why are we never said to be justified by other Christian graces? Humility is an excellent grace, most commended in Scripture, and putting us where we ought to be, in the dust. Meekness bears with pity, and forgiveness reconciles outrageous wrongs piled upon us, and so makes us like Christ who was brought as a lamb to the slaughter, and as a sheep before her shearers is dumb, so He opened not His mouth. Hope is an anchor to the soul, both sure and steadfast, and being lively animates the soul in all times of trial. Charity with her broad mantle covers the faults of others, fills the world with the fame of her deeds, and never fails. Repentance sits at the feet of Jesus and bathes them with its tears. And the fear of the Lord is a fountain of life to depart from the snares of death.

Excellent as all these graces are, yet it is nowhere said in Scripture that a man is justified by fear, by charity, by repentance, by hope, by meekness, or by humility. But he is said to be justified by faith. God does not put this honor upon faith because it is greater than other graces, for it is not. Love is greater (1 Cor. 13:13). So are all graces, which shall flourish forever. But the reason why faith justifies is because it receives Christ. In the language of the Bible, to receive Christ is to believe on Him. "As many as received him, to them gave he power to become the sons of God, even to them that believe on his name" (John 1:12).

—WILLIAM PLUMER

◆ *Since faith is the gift of God, how do we properly understand Jesus's rebuke, "O ye of little faith" and not excuse ourselves when our faith is small?*

NOVEMBER

◆

*To have some tolerable ideas of the human heart in general is
one thing; to know our own hearts is quite a different thing.*
—JOHN NEWTON

God's Thoughts Toward the Depressed

From the end of the earth will I cry unto thee, when my heart is overwhelmed: lead me to the rock that is higher than I.

—PSALM 61:2

There are peculiar stages of Christian experience in which the soul experiences the preciousness of God's thoughts. We refer to the season of *mental disquietude and depression*, or it may be of *despondency and despair*. You cannot at that moment command your mental powers, control your thoughts, or fix and concentrate them upon any consecutive train of serious and devout reflection. Is it not then soothing and precious to be reminded that your heavenly Father has thoughts of you, that your High Priest in heaven has thoughts of you, that each divine person of the glorious Godhead has you in remembrance, breathing the words with which He once comforted His church in the wilderness, "I know the thoughts that I think toward you, saith the LORD, thoughts of peace, and not of evil, to give you an expected end" (Jer. 29:11)?

Oh, let no child of God, around whose mind thick clouds are hovering, walking in darkness and having no light, be tempted to doubt God, to cast away His confidence and abandon His hope in Christ, yield himself to the desponding reflection that he has no place in God's thoughts of peace.

Christian sufferer, child of the light walking in darkness! Your Father's thoughts of you never were more tender, compassionate, and faithful than at this season of mental gloom or of spiritual despondency. You may not behold Him through the cloud that shades Him from your eye, but He from whom no darkness hides sees you and knows the way that you take. Though you may have relaxed your hand of faith on Him, He has not withdrawn His hand of love from you but is leading you by a right way to bring you to your heavenly and eternal home. "I am poor and needy; yet the Lord thinketh upon me" (Ps. 40:17).

—OCTAVIUS WINSLOW

◆ *Have these thoughts of God during your times of despondency lifted you up? Is there someone you know who could use such a word of encouragement from you, so they know they are not alone in this condition? How can you minister to them?*

Sin Dies Hard

For if ye live after the flesh, ye shall die: but if ye through the Spirit do mortify the deeds of the body, ye shall live.

—ROMANS 8:13

Sin like a serpent dies hard. This is true of all sin, especially of a besetting sin. Therefore, you must make a business of killing sin. It will kill you if you do not kill it. Your eternal well-being is at stake. Use every means in your power. Some sins go out only by fasting and prayer. Try those means.

Highly esteem holiness. It is moral excellence. It is very beautiful. It makes one more like God. Nothing unholy will stand the test of perfect holiness in the fear of God. This is the will of God concerning you, even your sanctification: "Be ye holy; for I am holy" (1 Peter 1:16).

In subduing corruptions, some have found it helpful to devote special attention to one besetting sin. In some cases this may help. But let us not forget that one sin always argues the presence of other sins, and that while we are watching one thief, others may be close behind us.

Seek the constant aid of the Holy Spirit. He searches all things. He hates iniquity. He loves all purity. His indwelling will do more than a guard of angels in driving out sin. He is the Spirit of holiness. He is its author. "Not by might, nor by power, but by my spirit, saith the LORD" (Zech. 4:6).

Think much of Christ. Highly prize His honor. Let His name be an ointment poured forth. Walk in Him, walk with Him, live unto Him, and die for Him. Draw strength and motives from His teachings, His example, His death, His resurrection, His ascension to heaven, His sitting at God's right hand, and His everlasting kingdom.

—WILLIAM PLUMER

◆ *How are root sins behind visible ones? How does thinking of Christ help in putting sin to death?*

God's Cure for Worrying

*The LORD is my rock, and my fortress, and my deliverer;
my God, my strength, in whom I will trust.*

—PSALM 18:2

From beginning to end, a Christian life is a life of faith. The word *trust* is the keyword of Old Testament theology, and the word *believe* is the keyword in the New Testament. They both mean the same thing. When our heavenly Father says to us, "Give Me your load, trust Me; what you cannot do, I will do for you," He expects us to take Him at His word. He never consents to carry our burdens unless we entrust them to Him.

Worry is blind; but God sees into the future and often sees the coming relief just ahead. Worry is impatient; but the patient God bids us *wait* and *see*. Worry complains of the weight of the loads; but God's offer is to lighten them by putting Himself, as it were, into our souls and under our loads. He then becomes our strength—a strength equal to the day. This is a supernatural work. This is what is meant by "My grace is sufficient for thee" (2 Cor. 12:9). This is the result of having Jesus Christ dwelling in our souls as a light to cheer and a power to sustain. "Follow Me" implies that Christ leads us at every step, and He never means to lead us over a precipice or leave us in a lurch. Such an actual and constant trust is the only real antidote to worry. The more entirely and simply and implicitly we trust, the quieter we become. Remember that God never promises anything more than grace sufficient for the hour and strength equal to the day. God's love will outlast all your tomorrows; roll your anxieties over on that love; it will cure your worrying.

—THEODORE CUYLER

◆*How do worry and impatience impact your relationship with God?
How would trust and faith remove these sins?*

Moderation in Mourning

But I would not have you to be ignorant, brethren, concerning them
which are asleep, that ye sorrow not, even as others which have no hope.
—1 THESSALONIANS 4:13

If we consider that our life is a journey or pilgrimage toward heaven, this teaches us to have moderation in our mourning for the loss of loved ones who, while they lived, lived a godly life. If they lived a holy life, then their lives were a journey toward heaven. Why should we be immoderate in mourning, when they got to their journey's end? Death, though it appears to us with a frightful aspect, is to them a great blessing. Their end is happy, and better than their beginning. "The day of death [is better] than the day of one's birth" (Eccl. 7:1). While they lived, they desired heaven and chose it above this world or any of its enjoyments. For this they earnestly longed, and why should we grieve that they have obtained it? Now they have gotten to their Father's house. They have more comfort a thousand times, now that they are home, than they did in their journey.

We are ready to look upon death as their calamity and to mourn that those who were so dear to us should be in the grave, that they are there transformed to corruption and worms, taken away from their loved ones and enjoyments. But this is our infirmity; they are in a happy condition, inconceivably blessed. They do not mourn but rejoice with exceeding joy; their mouths are filled with joyful songs, and they drink from the rivers of pleasure. They find no mixture of grief that they have changed their earthly enjoyments and companions for heaven. Their life here, even in the best circumstances, was filled with trials and afflictions, but now there is an end to it all.

It is true, we shall see them no more in this world, yet we ought to consider that we are traveling toward the same place; and why should we break our hearts that they have gotten there before us? A degree of mourning when loved ones are departed is not inconsistent with Christianity, but we have just reason that our mourning should be mingled with joy.

—JONATHAN EDWARDS

◆ *How do we properly mourn those whom we love who have gone to be*
with the Lord? How does the believer show to the world that death is a
conquered foe?

Prescriptions for the Cured Soul

I will declare what he hath done for my soul.
—PSALM 66:16

Has Christ been your soul physician? Then *break forth into thankfulness*. Though sin be not quite cured, yet the reigning power of it is taken away. Those that were cured by the brazen serpent afterward died; but such as are healed by Christ shall never die. Sin may molest, but it shall not damn. What reason you have to admire and love your Physician! The Lord Jesus has removed the core of your disease and its curse. Publish your experiences: "I will tell you what God hath done for my soul" (Ps. 66:16). As a man that has been cured of an old disease, how glad and thankful he is. He will tell others of the medicine that cured him. So say, "I will tell you what God has done for my soul: He has cured me of an old disease, a hard, unbelieving heart, a disease that has sent millions to hell."

Beware of relapses. Men are afraid of a relapse after they are cured; beware of soul relapses. Has God softened your heart? Take heed of hardening it. Has He cured you from some measure of deadness? Do not relapse into a drowsy security lest you have such an uproar and agony in your conscience as may make you go weeping to your grave. Take heed of falling sick again! "Sin no more, lest a worse thing come unto thee" (John 5:14).

Pity your friends that are sick unto death; show your piety in your pity. Do you have a child that is well and lusty but has a sick soul? Pity him; pray for him. David wept and fasted for his sick child (2 Sam. 12:16). Your child has the plague of the heart, and you have conveyed the plague to him; weep and fast for your child. Do you have a wife or husband that though they are not sick in bed, yet the Lord knows they are sick, under the raging power of sin? Let your heart yearn over them! Pray for them; the prayer of faith may save a sick soul. Prayer is the best medicine that can be used in a desperate case; you that have felt the disease of sin and the mercy of your Physician, learn to pity others.

—THOMAS WATSON

◆ *If you know the saving power of Christ, how can you show pity to those who are outside of Christ? In what ways can you guard yourself against relapses?*

Fear Not, Tempted Saint

*Fear not, little flock; for it is your Father's good pleasure
to give you the kingdom.*

—LUKE 12:32

Are the children of God out of reach of the devil while journeying to
their eternal rest? No, for what says the Scriptures? Fear not, tempted
saint; Jesus, in whom you believe, has vanquished this roaring lion. Are you
helpless in yourself? John says, "Greater is he that is in you, than he that
is in the world" (1 John 4:4). Are you afraid of falling one day by the hand
of your spiritual foe? Paul said, "God…shall bruise Satan under your feet"
(Rom. 16:20). Then let us not despond. The Spirit of God, who dwells in
the heart of His people, will make us more than conquerors through Jesus
Christ. How gracious are the words of Jesus to Peter when Satan desired to
sift him: "I have prayed for thee, that thy faith fail not" (Luke 22:32). How
cheering His love to Paul when *buffeted* by Satan: "My grace is sufficient for
thee" (2 Cor. 12:9).

Can we now for a moment doubt His willingness to save? Did He die
for us, and will He not preserve us? Did He pray for us, and will He not hear
our prayers? Did He invite us to come, and will He forbid our approach?
His compassion is not diminished, because He is in glory. His love is not
abated, because the heavens have received Him out of our sight. His tenderness is not less susceptible now that He is removed from the infirmities
of our nature. He still can be touched with the feelings of our infirmities.
He still feels in heaven for His poor afflicted members upon earth. Though
Lord of all, having all power in heaven and in earth, He is not insensible to
the needs of His people. He is their friend who loveth at all times; and who,
when they are gathered together in His name is ever in the midst of them.
Let us trust and not be afraid of the fury of the oppressor, as if he were ready
to destroy. Jesus ever reigns!

—THOMAS READE

◆*Jesus is a friend of sinners. If He received you as a sinner when you came to
Him the first time, why do you think He will not have you now as you come
again with all your questions and need?*

Are You a Grateful Christian?

What shall I render unto the LORD for all his benefits toward me?
—PSALM 116:12

C hristian! Let us help you give an answer to the question. If you are truly grateful, you will love the Lord. This is the best return you can make for His innumerable blessings, His unmerited favors. It is what He chiefly demands, without which all other returns are valueless and of no account. This is "the first and great commandment," the sum and substance of all religious and grateful obedience, that you "love the Lord thy God with all thy heart, and with all thy soul, and with all thy mind" (Matt. 22:37–38).

If you are truly grateful to God, you will honor Him with your hope and trust; you will make Him the object of devout address and prayer for time to come. In nothing does God declare Himself more honored by His children than in being regarded with firm trust and confidence.

If you are truly grateful to God for His benefits, you will strive to walk before Him in the land of the living. It will be your effort to serve God in all the duties of a sincere and commendable, holy and grateful obedience. You will make pious regularity of your life, testifying your sincere and unfeigned gratitude.

If you are truly grateful, you will be careful to pay your vows unto the Lord. Such was the resolution of the psalmist, and surely it is an indispensable return for the countless benefits received. Reader, here is much room for a heart-searching. The promise made on a sick bed, where is its fulfillment? The resolution formed when the star of hope again glimmered on your pathway, where is it now? The secret purpose, awakened in the soul by some providential deliverance, has it ever reached its accomplishment?

Finally, gratitude to God for His benefits will tend to increase your delight in His service. Your gratitude and obedience are sure to rise and fall together. Christian, be this your prayer: "O God, endue me with a spirit of true and pious gratitude for all Thy benefits, temporal and spiritual."

—ASHTON OXENDEN

◆ *Recall times in your life when you were so overwhelmed with the goodness and kindness of God, should He have asked you to do anything, you would have done it. Then ask yourself why your heart is not in that same place today, when you know His love and kindness to you has not and does not change.*

True Contentment

Let it be the hidden man of the heart, in that which
is not corruptible, even the ornament of a meek and quiet spirit,
which is in the sight of God of great price.

—1 PETER 3:4

Spiritual contentment comes from the disposition of the soul. The contentment of a man or woman who is rightly content does not come so much from outward circumstances or from any outward help, as from the disposition of their own hearts. The disposition of their own hearts causes and brings forth this gracious contentment rather than any external thing.

Let me explain myself. Someone is upset, maybe a child or a man or a woman, and you bring something to please them, perhaps it will quiet them and they will be contented. It is the thing you brought that quiets them, not the disposition of their own hearts; not any good temperament in their own hearts but the material thing you brought them. But when a Christian is content in the right way, the quiet comes more from within the heart rather than from any external circumstance or from the possession of anything in the world.

To be content because of some external thing is like warming a man's clothes by the fire. But to be content through an inward disposition of the soul is like the warmth that a man's clothes have from the natural heat of his body. A man who is healthy puts on his clothes and perhaps at first on a cold morning, they feel cold. But after he has had them on a little while, they are warm. How did they get warm? This came from the natural heat of his body. So, when a sick man, whose natural heat of his body has deteriorated, puts on his clothes, they do not get warm after a long time. He must warm them first by the fire, and even then, they will soon be cold again. So are the different contentments of men. The warmth of the fire—that is a contentment that results merely from external circumstances and will not last long. But that which comes from a quiet spirit within the heart will last. When it comes from within a man or woman, that is true contentment.

—JEREMIAH BURROUGHS

◆ *How can one discern whether our contentment arises from within or from without? Where are you seeking contentment?*

A Ready Hope

*But sanctify the Lord God in your hearts: and be ready always
to give an answer to every man that asketh you a reason of the hope
that is in you with meekness and fear.*
—1 PETER 3:15

If you have a good hope, be zealous and watchful over it. Beware that
Satan does not steal it away for a season, as he did from David and Peter.
Beware that you do not lose sight of it by giving way to inconsistencies
and by conformity to the world. Examine it often, and make sure that it
is not becoming dim. Keep it bright by daily carefulness over your temper, thoughts, and words. Keep it healthy by hearty, fervent, and continual
prayer, and by diligent work for Christ. The hope of the Christian is a very
delicate plant. It is an exotic plant from above, not a plant naturally grown.
It is easily chilled and nipped by the cold frosts of the world. Unless watered
and tended carefully, it will dwindle away to a mere nothing and scarcely be
felt or seen. None find this out so painfully as dying believers who have not
walked very closely with God. They find that they have sown thorns in their
dying pillows and brought clouds between them and the sun.

And, if you have a good hope, keep it always ready. Have it at your right
hand, prepared for immediate use. Look at it often and take care that it is
in good order. Trials often break in upon us suddenly, like an armed man.
Sicknesses and injuries to our earthly body sometimes lay us low on our
beds without any warning. Happy is he who keeps his lamp well-trimmed
and lives in the daily sense of communion with Christ. If you have a hope,
keep it ready at hand.

—J. C. RYLE

♦ *Is your hope shining brightly or growing dim? If your hope has faded, where
did you lose it, and how can it be recovered?*

Profits of the Work of Meditation

This book of the law shall not depart out of thy mouth; but thou shalt meditate therein day and night, that thou mayest observe to do according to all that is written therein: for then thou shalt make thy way prosperous, and then thou shalt have good success.

—JOSHUA 1:8

As the work of meditation is profitable to a godly person, so it is very satisfying and brings contentment. What person in love is not satisfied thinking and meditating on the person loved? What child is not satisfied thinking of its father that is absent in another country? David said, "My soul shall be satisfied as with marrow and fatness." When? "When I remember thee upon my bed, and meditate on thee in the night watches" (Ps. 63:5–6). I shall not only be contented, but my soul shall be satisfied. How? In a way of meditation.

The work of meditation is a most delightful work. What greater delight than to think of that God who we most delight in? Is it delightful to a wicked man to sit and muse on his sinful ways; and will it not be delightful for a godly man to sit and think and meditate on the Lord? But how can it be so delightful when it is a hard work?

Though it is hard in its practice, yet it is sweet and delightful regarding its profit. Is it not a hard work to the laborer to labor, and yet delightful regarding its profit? Is it not hard work for a seaman at sea through all the storm, and yet it is delightful in regard of the profit?

Friends, the harder the work is, the sweeter it is when the work is overcome; it is a sweet thing to overcome. The harder the nut to crack, the sweeter the meat when it is cracked; the harder the Scripture is that is to be opened, the sweeter is the kernel of truth when it is opened. Though it is a hard thing to meditate on God and the things of God, yet do consider why the work is hard, and you will say that the difficulty of the work is no impeachment to the sweetness which comes from it.

—WILLIAM BRIDGE

◆ *Why does Bridge talk about meditation as a hard work? Do you find it so? How can you overcome this in some practical ways?*

The Family of God

I bow my knees unto the Father of our Lord Jesus Christ,
of whom the whole family in heaven and earth is named.
—EPHESIANS 3:14–15

If you really belong to the whole family of God in heaven and earth, count your privileges and learn to be more thankful. Think of what a mercy it is to have something which the world can neither give nor take away, something which is free of sickness or poverty, something which is your own forevermore. The family home will soon be cold and tenantless. The family gatherings will soon be past and gone forever. The loving faces we now delight to gaze on are rapidly leaving us. The cheerful voices which now welcome us will soon be silent in the grave. But thank God, if we belong to Christ's family, there is a better gathering to come. Let us often think of it and be thankful!

The family gathering of all God's people will far outweigh all that their religion now costs them. A meeting where none are missing, a meeting where there are no gaps and empty places, a meeting where there are no tears, a meeting where there is no parting; such a meeting as this is worth a fight and a struggle. And such a meeting is yet to come to "the whole family in heaven and earth" (Eph. 3:15).

Therefore, let us strive to live worthy of the family to which we belong. Let us labor to do nothing that may cause our Father's house to be spoken against. Let us endeavor to make our Master's name beautiful by our character, conduct, and conversation. Let us love as brethren and abhor all quarrels. Let us conduct ourselves as if the honor of the family depended on our behavior. By our lives, we shall recommend our Father's family to others, and perhaps, by God's blessing, incline them to say, "We will go with you."

—J. C. RYLE

♦ *As you think about this future family life, how is your family reflecting these things already now? Discuss what things you can together change to make it more reflective of the family of God.*

More Grace

He giveth more grace. —JAMES 4:6

Growth in grace is not to be expected from emotional highs but from the faithful exercise and display in your daily deportment—your deportment in the troubles of business, your deportment in your families, amid all the occupations and requirements of life. Your life may present much the same general features for years; but still it ought to be a *growing* life, abounding *more* and *more* in the service of God. You are not to expect that greater opportunities will be put in your way, but you should make opportunities out of ordinary things, having an eye more capable of discerning them in common things, and being more ready to seize upon them and use them.

This is the Christian principle, and what you should aim for. Do not expect that your opportunities of exercising the "grace" given you will be such as to attract the notice of others; rather, they will lie *chiefly* in common things, in your ordinary duties, in your home circle, in resisting and overcoming habits of self-indulgence, habits of harshness, fretfulness, anger, etc.

"Grace" may be brought into exercise, too, in bearing sickness, trial, unkindness, or reproach with a patient, uncomplaining spirit; in helping and encouraging your neighbor; in being more generous, more kind, more sympathizing; in showing more "love, joy, peace, longsuffering, gentleness, goodness, faith, meekness, temperance" (Gal. 5:22–23). Grace increases in delighting more in prayer and the Word of God, setting the Lord more and more before you, ever keeping Him in mind.

It is thus *grace* will truly grow and expand, so that every fresh duty becomes easier, every fresh trial less painful. By bringing it into the detail of daily life, so that it may elevate and consecrate human affection, sweeten earthly love with the deepest and tenderest sympathies, pervade duty, pleasure, and recreation, you will most surely promote the *growth* of that divine principle which the Spirit of God has implanted within you. But we must never forget that our ability for all this comes from above; as there is only one source from which "grace" comes to us first, so there is only *one* source from which we can obtain renewed supplies: "he giveth more grace" (James 4:6).

—ASHTON OXENDEN

◆*Do you notice the "little things" that God is placing on your path of life so that you might be faithful in them? Think about how God's grace has been shaping you.*

The Danger of Overattachment

Husbands, love your wives, even as Christ also loved
the church, and gave himself for it.
—EPHESIANS 5:25

I address this to you, husbands and wives, because the Lord has made you not only one in relation but in affection and heart. The object of my affection has been removed, the time is past, but the remembrance of what it once was is worth much more than anything else that this poor world offers. May the Lord maintain, yea, increase your mutual regard, but may He likewise sanctify it, that you may avoid any sin and suffering. For there is a danger in an overattachment. It has cost me many pangs; yet, when I think of the apostle's charge that husbands should "love their wives as their own bodies," "even as Christ also loved the church" (Eph. 5:28, 25); these strong expressions lead one to conclude that the danger is not in loving too much but in loving improperly.

When a wife gives her husband her whole heart, she still has room for all her friends and his; and should those friends be increased twentyfold, there is still room for them all. But there is a peculiar kind of regard which is due to her husband only. If she allows herself to transfer this regard to any other man, though it went no further, it would be wrong. So, while we love the Lord supremely, we may love our husbands, wives, children, and friends as much as we can. But all must be held in subordination and subserviency to what we owe to Him, otherwise they will be idols, and we shall be idolaters; and the Lord will, in one way or other, let us know that He is a jealous God and will not bear a rival. Thank God if He has called you both out of this world and given you the same views and desires of better things than can be possessed here, for great is the privilege of walking together in the way of the kingdom.

—JOHN NEWTON

◆ *Does your spouse have a rightful place in your heart and affections?*
How are you expressing this?

The Christian's Responsibility

*Arise, shine; for thy light is come, and the
glory of the LORD is risen upon thee.*
—ISAIAH 60:1

It is a great thing to be a Christian. The very name is a noble one, beyond all the noble names of earth. The thing itself is inconceivably blessed and glorious. To say, "I am a Christian" is to say, "I belong to God's nobility; I am of the nobility of heaven."

Much, then, is expected of you. Do not disgrace the family name. Do nothing unworthy of Him who represents you in heaven, and whom you represent on earth. He is faithful to you; be you so to Him. Let men know what a Lord and Master you serve. Be His witnesses; be His mirrors; be His living epistles. Let Him speak through you to the world; and you speak of Him. Let your life tell your fellow men what He is, and what He is to you. He has honored you by giving you His name; He has blessed you by conferring on you sonship and royalty and an eternal heritage; see that you do justice to His love and magnify His greatness.

Let your light shine. Do not obstruct it or hide it or mingle darkness with it. "Arise, shine; for thy light is come, and the glory of the LORD is risen upon thee" (Isa. 60:1). It is the light of *love* that you have received; let it shine. It is the light of *truth*; let it shine. It is the light of *holiness*; let it shine. And if you ask, How am I to get the light and to maintain it in fullness? I answer, "Christ shall give thee light" (Eph. 5:14). There is light enough in Him who is the light of the world. "The Lamb is the light thereof" (Rev. 21:23). There is no light for man but from the Lamb. It is the cross, the cross alone, that lights up a dark soul and keeps it shining, so that we walk in light as He is in the light; for "God is light, and in him is no darkness at all" (1 John 1:5).

—HORATIUS BONAR

◆*Since we are to be reflectors of Christ, what are others seeing? What can you do to better reflect Him in your words and deeds?*

The Christian Lives by Rules

All scripture is given by inspiration of God, and is profitable for doctrine,
for reproof, for correction, for instruction in righteousness.

—2 TIMOTHY 3:16

All Scripture is given by inspiration of God and is profitable in some way to further the divine life in the soul. The following rules would be very helpful to many:

1. Set the Lord always before you. Live as seeing Him who is invisible. Think often, "Thou God seest me." To God we must give account. In Him we live and move and have our being. From Him is our fruit found. He is our rock, our refuge, our high tower, our strength." Blessed is he who forms his actions to please his Master.

2. Know, believe, and practice the entire Word of God. Form no prejudices against any part of the Bible. All of it is truth—all of it is precious truth. The part of Scripture which you slight probably contains the very truth most needful for the correction of some of your faults. The threats warn, the precepts guide, the promises encourage, the doctrines instruct, the examples draw, the histories illustrate, and the poems delight.

3. Put a proper estimate on time and eternity; on time because it is so short, because its pursuits are so vain, because on the right use of it depends everlasting consequences. On eternity because it is eternity—it has no bounds.

4. Never make a mock at sin and never jest with sacred things. Let holiness to the Lord be predominant on His day, His Word, His worship, His name, His cause.

5. Never attempt to find out how near you can come to sin without sinning. He that loveth danger shall die in it.

6. Steadfastly set your face against needless delays in doing any work for the honor of your Master, for the good of your fellow man or for your own edification. A sluggish attitude is one of the most deceptive of all the temptations of the devil. Do this very day and hour the duties which this hour and day have need of.

—WILLIAM PLUMER

◆*How can you improve in each of these six points? What would it look like practically?*

The Eternal Result

For our light affliction, which is but for a moment, worketh
for us a far more exceeding and eternal weight of glory.
—2 CORINTHIANS 4:17

We are assured that "if we suffer, we shall also reign with him" (2 Tim. 2:12); oneness in suffering here is the pledge of oneness in glory hereafter. The two things are inseparable. His shame is ours on earth; His glory shall be ours in heaven. Therefore, let us "rejoice, inasmuch as ye are partakers of Christ's sufferings; that, when his glory shall be revealed, ye may be glad also with exceeding joy" (1 Peter 4:13).

Truly the sufferings of this present life are not worthy to be compared with the glory which shall be revealed in us. The incorruptible crown is so surpassingly bright, and the "inheritance of the saints in light" (Col. 1:12) so excellent, that we may well be ashamed even to speak of present sorrow. How the eternal light will absorb the darkness here! How will the blessedness of the kingdom swallow up our earthly calamities and complaints! One hour of eternity, one moment with the Lord will make us utterly forget a lifetime of desolations.

But more than this: Our troubles do but enhance the coming joy. Our affliction is not only "light" and not only "for a moment," but it works for us a far more exceeding and eternal weight of glory. Our sorrows here are but adding to the weight of our eternal crown. In what way they do so, we are not told. It is sufficient that we know upon God's authority that such is really the case.

The time is at hand. The Christian's conflicts are almost over. Its struggles and sorrows are nearly done. A few more years, and we shall either be laid quietly to rest or caught up into the clouds to meet our coming Lord. A few more broken bonds, and then we shall be knit together in eternal brotherhood with all the scattered members of the family.

—HORATIUS BONAR

♦ *Put all your suffering and trials on one side of a scale, and put the glory of God and His presence on the other. Which side pulls down under the weight? Notice Paul says that affliction is actually working out this glory. Have patience!*

Supreme Love

Whom have I in heaven but thee? and there is none
upon earth that I desire beside thee.

—PSALM 73:25

To follow the Lord fully, I must have a lively faith in the promises of God made to me in Jesus Christ. I must experience the love of God shed abroad in my heart through the Holy Spirit given unto me. I must have a good hope through grace, a hope of eternal life. I must feel the sweet drawings of the Spirit, uniting me closer to Jesus in heart and affection. I must renounce all self-dependence and all creature dependence. I must renounce both my sins and my own supposed righteousness; I must abandon the flattering vanities of the world, and labor to subdue the lusts of the flesh. I must be willing to bear the cross, to deny myself, and to do anything for Christ. I must submit to the righteousness of God, yes, esteem it so inestimably precious as to count all things else in comparison to it but dung and dross. I must have my will swallowed up in the holy, sovereign will of God. I must lie passive in His hand, while being actively engaged in His service, ever desirous, with childlike simplicity, to do and suffer at all times and in all places according to the will of my heavenly Father. If this is to follow the Lord fully, then, oh my soul, lie prostrate at His feet in shame and confusion of face.

God will not accept a divided heart. To follow Him fully, I must follow Him only. The language of the church is, "Whom have I in heaven but thee? and there is none upon earth that I desire beside thee" (Ps. 73:25). "The LORD is my portion, saith my soul" (Lam. 3:24). Oh, may this be the language of my heart! I can never know true peace until Jesus reigns as the unrivaled sovereign of my affections.

Blessed Savior, be my only Savior! Let me not trust in anything but Thee. Let me love nothing but Thee, or love it for Thy sake. May I love Thee supremely and love Thy people, because they belong to Thee.

—THOMAS READE

◆ *Are you taken back by "sold out" believers? Why? Are you "sold out" for Christ because of all that He is and has done for sinners like you?*

God Thinks of You

For I know their works and their thoughts: it shall come, that I will gather all nations and tongues; and they shall come, and see my glory.

—ISAIAH 66:18

God thinks of all your spiritual exercises through which you pass—your fears and hopes, your doubtings and your trustings, your high and low frames, your infirmities of prayer, your faith and love. There is not a throb of your heart, not a feeling of your soul, not a thought of your mind growing out of the work of divine grace within; all that elevates or depresses, that grieves or cheers, that shades or brightens—there is nothing that does not engage the thoughts of God.

The thoughts of God are occupied *with the returns His people make.* Nothing you do escapes His notice. Is there anything done by you, for God, to which He is indifferent? No! He thinks of all your sincere desires to love Him, your lowly endeavors to serve Him, your earnest efforts to obey Him, and your feeble, imperfect attempts to honor and glorify Him. He thinks of all the poor attempts you make of loving work, of patient endurance and familial obedience. Have you a passing thought of Him as you weave your way through a crowd? God thinks of it. Is there a gush of love welling up from your heart in secret communion? God thinks of it. Do you quietly bring to an unknown home a cup of cold water to moisten the fevered lips of some poor suffering saint? God thinks of it. Have you given up some cherished idol or mortified some darling sin or resisted some strong temptation or acted in a way of self-denial for the honor of His name? God thinks of it.

Every habit you lay down or cross you take up or burden you bear or yoke to which you bow for Jesus shall be treasured up in the thoughts of your God through eternity.

—OCTAVIUS WINSLOW

◆*His thoughts toward you are multiplied even as you read this meditation and your heart engages with its words. Let your heart settle down in rest upon Him as the Rock and be at peace.*

An Abiding Rest

There remaineth therefore a rest to the people of God.
—HEBREWS 4:9

The more we contemplate the holiness of God and the nature of our redemption by Jesus Christ, the more we must be convinced that sanctification is the beauty and health of the soul. The holy Christian is the happy Christian. He may and must have troubles as he journeys to his heavenly rest; but as long as Jesus is his guide and guardian, darkness may reign without, but all shall be peace and light within.

Had Adam remained innocent, this world would have been a place of rest. But sin has filled the earth with thorns. Man is born to trouble. Sighing and sorrow, disease and death fill the pages of history. Is there no hope, no resting place, no refuge for the weary and heavy laden? Yes! All praise to sovereign grace, there is! Jesus is the sinner's hope and hiding place. Listen to His voice, "Come unto me, all ye that labour and are heaven laden, and I will give you rest" (Matt. 11:28).

Blessed invitation! Let us hasten to the Savior, through the drawing of the Spirit. He alone can give us rest, He who bore our sins in His own body on the tree and places upon us the easy yoke of a willing obedience to His commands.

Delightful exchange! Truly that burden is light which Jesus lays upon us: rest for labor, holiness for sin, happiness for misery. This is the rest wherewith He causes the weary to rest, and this is refreshing. Well did the apostle say, "We which have believed do enter into rest" (Heb. 4:3), a precious rest in the covenant love of God in Christ. This rest, through faith, is preparatory to the rest in glory which is reserved for the people of God.

What a glorious rest that will be: the absence of all evil and the enjoyment of all good, a rest not in idleness but of activities, for the redeemed serve God day and night.

—THOMAS READE

◆ *Have you found that His burden is "light"? What would your earthly cares look like if you had a continual eye on the glorious rest to come?*

He Will Never Forsake

I will never leave thee, nor forsake thee.
—HEBREWS 13:5

The Lord Jesus is a friend who never changes. There is no fickleness about Him. Those whom He loves, He loves unto the end. Husbands have forsaken their wives. Parents have cast off their children. Human vows and promises of faithfulness have often been forgotten. Many are neglected in their poverty and old age who were honored by all when they were rich and young. But Christ has never changed His feelings toward one of His friends. He is the "same yesterday, and to day, and for ever" (Heb. 13:8).

The Lord Jesus never goes away from His friends. There is never a parting and goodbye between Him and His people. From the time that He makes His abode in a sinner's heart, He abides in it forever. The world is full of leavings and departures. Death and the passing of time break up the most united family. Sons leave to make their way in life. Daughters are married and leave their father's house forever. Scattering, scattering, scattering is the yearly history of the happiest home. How many have we tearfully watched as they drove away from our homes, whose pleasant faces we have never seen again! How many have we sorrowfully followed to the grave and then come back to a cold, silent, lonely home. But thanks be to God! There is one who never leaves His friends. The Lord Jesus is He who has said, "I will never leave thee, nor forsake thee" (Heb. 13:5). The Lord Jesus goes with His friends wherever they go. There is no possible separation between Him and those whom He loves. There is no place on earth that can separate them from the friend of their souls.

—J. C. RYLE

◆*Jesus is more faithful than our closest friends and relations on earth.*
So do you run to Him more than to them for your comfort and joy?

What Jesus Is to His People

*Keep me as the apple of the eye, hide me
under the shadow of thy wings.*
—PSALM 17:8

He who once bore our sins and carried our sorrows is seated upon a throne in glory and exercises all power in heaven and on earth. Thrones, principalities, and powers bow before Him. Every event and providence in the world is under His rule. His providence pervades and manages all and is minutely attentive to every part, as if there were only a single object in His view. From the tallest archangel to the smallest ant or fly, all depend on Him for their being, their preservation, and their powers. He directs the sparrows where to build their nests and to find their food. He overrules the rise and fall of nations and controls all events so that while many intend nothing less in the matter of their designs, all concur and coincide in the accomplishment of His holy will. He restrains with a mighty hand the fearsome efforts and powers of darkness; and Satan with all his hosts cannot exert their malice a hair's breadth beyond the limits of His permission.

This is He who is the Head and Husband of His believing people. Happy are they who are blessed by His good pleasure. Safe are they who He has engaged to protect. Honored and privileged are they to whom He is pleased to show Himself, and whom He enables and warrants to claim Him as their friend and portion! Having redeemed them by His own blood, He sets a high value upon them; He esteems them His treasure, His jewels, and keeps them as the pupil of His eye. They shall not want; they need not fear; His eye is upon them in every situation, His ear is open to their prayers, and His everlasting arms are under them for their sure support. On earth He guides their steps, controls their enemies, and directs all His ways for their good; while, in heaven, He is pleading their cause, preparing them a place, and communicating to them reviving foretastes of the glory that shall be shortly revealed.

—JOHN NEWTON

◆ *All things are in our Lord's hands. Try to list something in your life that is not in His hand. What should this mean practically for you?*

Seeming Contradictions

The LORD maketh poor, and maketh rich:
he bringeth low, and lifteth up.
—1 SAMUEL 2:7

God often seems to work in contrary ways. When He intends the greatest mercies to His people, He first usually brings them into a very low condition. If it is a bodily mercy, an outward mercy that He intends to give, He brings them physically low and outwardly low. If it is a mercy in their possessions that He intends to give, He brings them low in that and then raises them; in their reputations He brings them low there and then raises them up. If in their spirits, God ordinarily brings their spirits low and then raises their spirits. Usually the people of God, before the greatest comforts, have the greatest afflictions and sorrows.

Those who do not understand God's ways think that when God brings His people into sad conditions, He is leaving and forsaking them, and that God does not intend any great good to them. But a child of God who is instructed in this way of God is not troubled. "My condition is very low," he says, "but this is God's way when he intends the greatest mercy, to bring men under the greatest afflictions." When He intended to raise Joseph to be second in the kingdom, God cast him into a dungeon a little before. So, when God intended to raise David and set him upon the throne, He made him to be hunted as a partridge in the mountains. God dealt this way with His own Son—Christ Himself went into glory by suffering (Heb. 2:10)—and if God so deals with His own Son, much more with His people.

A little before daybreak you know that it is darker than it was anytime before, so God will make our conditions a little darker before the mercy comes. By being instructed in this way, that God is accustomed to lead, will greatly help us to be content.

—JEREMIAH BURROUGHS

◆*Can you recall a time when things seemed to be going against you,*
but God was actually working out some greater purpose than you could
see at the time?

Drawing Love

Who shall come unto me?
—JEREMIAH 49:4

If you desire that your hearts may be drawn out in love to the person of Christ Himself, stand still a little with me, and see how much Christ has loved you and your person. Shall Christ love you, and will not you love Him? Consider with me, that the more impediments that any love breaks through, the more it calls for love in return. What impediments has not Christ's love broke through to come to us? It broke through all our unworthiness, the law, the justice of God, the wrath of God, the grave, hell, and all our unbelief.

And the freer any love is, the more it calls for love in return. Three things there are that draw out love—likeness, benefit, love. Where none of these are, the love given is most free. Christ has loved you, but you were not like Him when He loved you. You could do Him no kindness; you had no benefits to bestow upon Him. You had no love for Him. In the day when He said, "Now is the time of love," there was no love in your hearts for Him. Therefore, His love must needs be free.

But the more patient that love is, the more it calls for love in response. Our Savior stands knocking at your door. If Christ came riding past and knocked only once at your door and said, "Hasten after me or you are damned forever," it would have been much. But to stand at your door and knock, day after day, and year after year, with the unwearied hand of His love—what unspeakable patience, inexpressible love! Yet so has Christ done for you, and so has Christ loved you and your very person; and shall Christ love you, and shall your love rest anywhere but in the person of Christ? Do but consider how He has loved you and your person, and then your heart will be drawn out to love the person of Christ.

—WILLIAM BRIDGE

◆ *Consider the unfathomable love of Christ. Why will it take an eternity to plumb the depths of God's love?*

Spiritual Darkness

*Why art thou cast down, O my soul? and why art thou
disquieted within me? hope thou in God.*

—PSALM 42:11

There are seasons of spiritual desertion and gloom through which many believers are called to pass. Apart from this peculiar stage of the divine life, we should lose a great deal of a portion of Christ's sympathy. Spiritual darkness is a part of the discipline of every child of the light. It is a distressing, dreary stage; nevertheless, there is light enough in it for faith to see the footprint of the Shepherd and the flock, and this alone were sufficient to provide the gloomiest path with sunshine and to awaken ten thousand echoes of love in the loneliest.

Let no child of God, who may be in spiritual darkness and desertion of soul, cast away his confidence or cease to hold fast firmly the profession of his faith. Our blessed Lord did not renounce His Sonship or loosen His hold of faith when in the hour of His deepest gloom He exclaimed, "My God, my God, why hast thou forsaken me?" (Matt. 27:46). Imitate your Lord and Master.

Is your soul in a spiritual eclipse, the light of God's countenance hidden, the visible presence of your Savior withdrawn, the strong consolations of the Spirit suspended, prayer distilling no dew, the promises speaking no comfort? Be it so. Yet what is the message of your God to you? "Who is among you that feareth the LORD, that obeyeth the voice of his servant, that *walketh in darkness* and *hath no light*? let him trust in the name of the LORD, and stay upon his God" (Isa. 50:10). Here is the true, the beautiful attitude of faith in spiritual darkness—the soul settling itself upon God the strong one, the unchangeable one, the reconciled one. The mental depression, the spiritual darkness, the soul desertion through which you are now passing does not touch your union with the Lord Jesus, nor affect your adoption into God's family. You are still one who fears the Lord; who obeys the voice of His Servant; a child of light, though in darkness; beloved of God; and dear to Christ.

—OCTAVIUS WINSLOW

♦*Meditate on what it means to be adopted into the family of God. How can reflecting on this help us in our walking in the darkness? How can you help others during spiritually dark times?*

An Important Examination

Examine me, O LORD, and prove me; try my reins and my heart.
—PSALM 26:2

Let us examine ourselves and determine what affliction has been doing for us and what progress we are making in putting off the old man and in putting on the new. Am I losing my worldliness of spirit and becoming heavenly minded? Am I getting rid of my pride, my passion, my stubbornness, and becoming humble, mild, and teachable? Are all my idols displaced and broken, and do I use my human comforts as though I used them not? Am I caring less for the honors of time, for man's love, man's smile, man's applause? Am I crucified to the world and is the world crucified to me by the cross of Christ; or am I still ashamed of His reproach, and am I half reluctant to follow Him through bad report and through good, through honor and shame?

Do I count it my glory and my joy to walk where He has led the way, to suffer where He suffered, to drink of the cup which He drank, and to be baptized with the baptism wherewith He was baptized? Or, while professing to seek the kingdom hereafter, do I refuse to go through that tribulation through which I must enter? While willing to secure the crown of glory, do I shrink back from the crown of thorns? Am I every day becoming more and more unlike the children of earth, more and more transformed after the likeness and reflection of my Elder Brother? Do I realize this earth is neither my portion nor my rest?

Is chastisement really purifying me? Am I conscious of its blessed effects on my soul? Can I look back and say, "There I learned most precious lessons; I got rid of some of the body of this death and arose to a higher level from which I am striving to ascend to one higher still"? Have I learned much of the sympathy of Jesus and known the blessedness of having Him weep with me in my days of sorrow? Have I wiped off my rebellious tears and been taught to shed only those of love and submissive fondness, tears of brotherhood and sympathy, tears of longing to be absent from the body and present with the Lord?

—HORATIUS BONAR

◆ *Have you answered yes to these questions? Take time to reread them and give a thoughtful answer.*

Cheerful and Thankful

*By him therefore let us offer the sacrifice of praise to God continually,
that is, the fruit of our lips giving thanks to his name.*

—HEBREWS 13:15

A contented spirit is a cheerful spirit. Contentment is something more than patience; for patience denotes only submission, while contentment denotes cheerfulness. A cheerful Christian is more than passive; he doesn't only bear the cross but takes up the cross. He looks upon God as a wise God; and whatever He does, though it be not pleasing, is in order to a cure; hence the contented Christian is cheerful and, with the apostle, takes "pleasure in infirmities,…in distresses" (2 Cor. 12:10). He does not only submit to God's dealings but rejoices in them; he does not only say, "The Lord is just in all that is befallen me," but *Good* is the Lord." This is to be contented. A sullen melancholy is hateful. It is said, "God loveth a cheerful giver" (2 Cor. 9:7); yes, and God loves a cheerful liver. We are told in Scripture not to be anxious, but we are nowhere told not to be cheerful. He that is contented with his condition does not abate his spiritual joy; and indeed, he has that within him which is the ground of cheerfulness—he carries a pardon sealed in his heart.

A contented spirit is a thankful spirit (Job 1:21). This is a degree above the other: "in every thing give thanks" (1 Thess. 5:18). A gracious heart sees mercy in every condition, therefore he has his heart bent on thankfulness. Others will bless God for prosperity; he blesses him for affliction. So, he reasons with himself, "Am I in want? God sees it better for me to want than to abound. God is now dieting me; He sees it better for my spiritual health." What a height of grace this is! It is a temple where the praises of God are sung forth, not a sepulcher wherein they are buried. A thankful Christian in the greatest straits has his heart enlarged and dilated in thankfulness. He often contemplates God's love; he sees that he is a monument of mercy, and therefore he desires to be a pattern of praise.

—THOMAS WATSON

◆*Are you a cheerful person to all those around you or only to some? Do you
see mercy in every condition? How can you be a cheerful liver?*

The Everlasting Arms

The eternal God is thy refuge, and underneath are the everlasting arms.
—DEUTERONOMY 33:27

There is something about deep sorrow that tends to wake up the *child-feeling* in all of us. A man of giant intellect becomes like a little child when a great grief smites him or when death enters his household. I have seen a stout sailor, who laughed at the tempest, come home when he was sick and let his old mother nurse him as if he were a baby. He was willing to lean on the arms that had never failed him. So a Christian in the times of trouble is brought to this child-feeling. He wants to lean somewhere, to talk to somebody, to have somebody to love him and hold him up. His extreme circumstances become God's opportunity. Then his humbled, broken spirit cries out:

> O Lord, a little helpless child
> Comes to Thee this day for rest
> Take me, fold me in Thy arms,
> Hold my head upon Thy breast.

One great purpose in all affliction is to bring us down to the everlasting arms. What new strength and peace it gives us to feel them underneath us! We know that, far as we may have sunk, we cannot go any farther. Those mighty arms cannot only hold us; they can lift us up. They can carry us along. Faith, in its essence, is simply a resting on the everlasting arms. It is trusting them, and not our own weakness. The supreme purpose of Jesus as our Redeemer was to descend to the lowest depths of human depravity and guilt and to bring up His redeemed ones from that horrible pit in His loving arms. Faith is just our clinging to those arms, and nothing more.
—THEODORE CUYLER

◆ *Imagine for a moment that the Father's loving arms are holding you; what are you carrying that needs to be surrendered to Him? Why is it difficult to surrender this very thing?*

A Spirit of Praise and Thanksgiving

I will praise the name of God with a song, and
will magnify him with thanksgiving.
—PSALM 69:30

Commune with your own heart to determine its state regarding the existence and exercise of the spirit of thanksgiving and praise. There is hardly any part of our religious experiences which receives less attention and insight than this. As the result of this, we lose much personal holiness and God loses much glory. Praise is as much an element of our Christianity and as distinctly a duty and privilege as prayer. How little of it do we live out. We are so absorbed by the trials and discouragements of the Christian pilgrimage that we overlook its blessings and helps. We think so much about the somber coloring of the daily picture of life that we are insensible to its brighter hues. But if we thought more of the good and less of the evil; if we weighed our mercies with our trials; if we were to reflect that if one sorrow is sent, how much heavier a sorrow may have been prevented; if one trial comes, how much greater that trial might have been; and that when the Lord sends us many comforts, and crowns our arms with many victories, how we should examine our hearts to uncover and expel the lurking spirit of complaining and rebellion and fretting against the Lord. We should lift every window and remove every curtain that would limit the beams of God's goodness entering and shining in every corner, lighting up the entire soul with the sunshine of mercy and making it sing with the music of praise.

So then, I am to cultivate a feeling of gratitude and to breathe a spirit of praise for all that my God and Father pleases to send me. I am always to be in a thankful, praising spirit for all the dispensations of His providence and grace. What a holy state will my soul then be in. What happiness will arise in my heart.

—OCTAVIUS WINSLOW

◆ *What does praising God look like? In what ways can you turn your gloomy thoughts into a spirit of gratitude and praise?*

Reflective Gratitude

Bless the LORD, O my soul, and forget not all his benefits.
—PSALM 103:2

The Christian, as he journeys onward in the pathway of life, ought frequently to look back, and standing, as it were, on the shadowy side of the hill, review the way by which God has led him. If we would keep alive our gratitude, if we would like to have it to increase more and more, till, like a holy flame, it burns within us, we must often in thought retrace the varied turnings and windings of our earthly pilgrimage. We are so prone, amid our daily duties and our converse with the world, to forget and overlook the benefits received, that only by a careful and frequent retrospect can we continue, from day to day, cherishing a spirit of true and ever-increasing thankfulness to God. But, the oftener we make the review, the greater cause will we have for saying with David, "Who am I, O Lord GOD, and what is my house, that thou hast brought me hitherto?" (2 Sam. 7:18).

Christian, you cannot indeed reckon all the benefits you have received from the hand of God, for they are as numerous as the stars of heaven or the drops of the mighty ocean. Your common mercies, alas, too lightly valued; the air you breathe, the return of gladsome sunlight, the succession of the seasons, and the quiet and gentle stillness and repose of night—all these, with their unnumbered host of attendant blessings, are scattered on your path. But select a few of the benefits you have received, if only to awaken fresh gratitude.

Reflect, too, on the manifold spiritual mercies you have enjoyed, mercies from so many withheld: the Word of God in your home, the house of God to attend, the means of grace, the hallowed rest on the Sabbath, seasons of communion, times of refreshing from the presence of the Lord. If you are truly grateful, you will love the Lord. This is the best return you can make for His innumerable blessings, His unmerited favors. It is what He chiefly demands, without which all other returns are valueless and of no account.

—ASHTON OXENDEN

◆ *Why would the Lord tell His people so often to "remember" if it were not an important spiritual exercise to engage in? As you remember His gracious deeds to you, is your heart moved to a greater gratitude to serve Him alone?*

The Furnace

Behold, I have refined thee, but not with silver;
I have chosen thee in the furnace of affliction.
—ISAIAH 48:10

God has a great many crucibles for His gold, where He may refine it. There is so much alloy of pride, self-will, covetousness, and sinful idolatry in genuine Christians that they require the "refining pot" and the furnace. Sometimes prosperity is tenfold more damaging to us than sharp adversity. A time of sickness may do more for soul health than years of bodily strength and comfort.

To all my readers who are wondering why a loving God has subjected them so often to the furnace, my only answer is that *God owns you and me,* and He has a right to do with us just as He pleases. If He wants to keep His silver over a hot flame until He can see His own countenance reflected in the metal, then He has a right to do so. It is the Lord; it is my loving teacher; it is my heavenly Father; let Him do what seems good to Him. He will not lay on one stroke in cruelty or a single cross that He cannot give me grace to bear. Life's school days and nights will soon be over. Pruning time will soon be ended. The crucibles will not be needed in heaven.

So, to all my fellow sufferers who are threading their way through the tunnels of trial, I would say: "Tighten your loins with the promises, and keep the strong staff of faith well in hand. Trust God in the dark. We are safer with Him in the dark than without Him in the sunshine. He will not suffer your foot to stumble. His rod and His staff never break. Why He brought us here, we know not now, but we shall know hereafter. At the end of the gloomy passage beams the heavenly light. Then comes the exceeding and eternal weight of glory!

—THEODORE CUYLER

◆*Reflect on the times God has placed you in the furnace. How have you profited from and grown spiritually through them so that you have become more like Christ?*

DECEMBER

---◆---

This world is all the hell that a true Christian will endure,
and it is all the heaven unbelievers shall ever enjoy.

—JONATHAN EDWARDS

No Abiding Place

For here have we no continuing city, but we seek one to come.
—HEBREWS 13:14

This world is not our abiding place. Our continuance here is but very short. Man's days on the earth are as a shadow. It was never designed by God that this world should be our home. Neither did God give us these temporal accommodations for that end. If God has given us ample estates and children, or other friends, it is with no such design that we should be furnished here for a permanent abode; but with a design that we should use them for the present and then leave them in a very short time. When we are called to any secular business, or charged with the care of a family, if we improve our lives to any other purposes than as a journey toward heaven, all our labor will be lost. If we spend our lives in the pursuit of a temporal happiness, riches or sensual pleasures, credit or esteem from men, delight in our children, and the prospect of seeing them well brought up and well settled—all these things will be of little significance to us. Death will blow up all our hopes and will put an end to these enjoyments. "The places that have known us, will know us no more" and "The eye that has seen us, shall see us no more." We must be taken away forever from all these things, and it is uncertain when; it may be soon after we are put into possession of them. And then, where will be all our worldly employments and enjoyments, when we are laid in the silent grave?

The future world was designed to be our settled and everlasting abode. There it was intended that we should be fixed; and there alone is a lasting habitation and a lasting inheritance. The present state is short and transitory; but our state in the other world is everlasting. Our state in the future world, therefore being eternal, is of so much greater importance than our state here, that all our concerns in this world should be wholly subordinated to it.

—JONATHAN EDWARDS

◆ *Ponder the realities of life and death. How should we live each day both by "planting a tree" as Luther said and as living with "eternity stamped" on our eyes as Edwards said?*

Encouragements in the Lord's Work

But ye, brethren, be not weary in well doing.
—2 THESSALONIANS 3:13

Would you have much joy and peace in believing? Try to do all the good you can in the world. There are always many living and dying in ignorance and sin, and no one goes near them and tries to save their souls. If all the communicants in all our churches laid themselves out to go among those who are without God in the world, with the Bible in their hands and Christlike loving sympathy in their hearts, they would soon be far happier than they are now, and the face of society would soon be changed. Idleness is one great cause of the low spirits of which so many complain. Too many, far too many Christians, seem quite content to go to heaven alone and care nothing about bringing others into the kingdom of God.

If you try to do good in the right way, you never need doubt that good will be done. Many a Sunday school teacher comes home on Sunday night with a heavy heart and thinks that his or her labor is all in vain. Many a visitor returns from his visits and thinks he is producing no effect. Many a minister comes down from his pulpit desponding and cast down, imagining that his preaching is of no purpose. But all this is disgraceful unbelief. There is often far more going on in the hearts and consciences than we see.

He that "goeth forth and weepeth, bearing precious seed, shall doubtless come again with rejoicing, bringing his sheaves with him" (Ps. 126:6). There are more being converted and saved than we suppose. Many shall sit down in the kingdom of heaven whom we never expected to see there. Let us read on, and pray on, and visit on, and speak on, and tell of Christ to everyone we can.

—J. C. RYLE

◆*Name some of those you know among your family, church, neighbors, work, etc. who have not trusted in Christ. Pray for them by name and ask God to open doors for you to speak with them.*

Serving God Fully

How long halt ye between two opinions?
if the LORD be God, follow him.
—1 KINGS 18:21

The soul that follows God fully will follow Him forever, because in fully following the Lord, it finds so much ease, peace, joy, and satisfaction that it is forever settled and confirmed in this way. There is never ease, sweetness, and full contentment in God's ways until the heart rests in Him fully. When we are distracted with jealousies, fears, and doubts and are longing after some other way, many temptations will pester the spirit continually. But when it is fully resting in God, then it goes on with ease; it is satisfied and blesses itself in this way. Temptations vanish and the soul is freed from much distraction and trouble.

The ship that is part in the mud and part in the water is battered up and down so that in a little time it beats itself all to pieces. But if it is taken off from the mud and put into the full stream, it goes with ease and safety. Thus, it is with a man's heart: while it sticks partly in the mud of the world or the filth of any lust, and when a conviction of conscience strives to remove the lust but it is not fully taken off, there is nothing but vexation and trouble in that soul. But when it is removed and gives itself fully to God in His blessed and holy ways, how sweet and blessed is the ease it finds. When a man stumbles on a path, the way is tedious to him. He is soon weary and gives up; but when he is whole, the way is easy, and he holds his way to the end.

So, when there is falseness in men's hearts, they halt in the ways of God. They quickly find them tedious. But others, who are of sound spirits, find them delightful, and they go on with strength and hold on to the end.

—JEREMIAH BURROUGHS

◆ *Are you familiar with the way God is leading you? How can you walk in that way with delight?*

The Lord Our God

For God so loved the world, that he gave
his only begotten Son, that whosoever believeth in him
should not perish, but have everlasting life.

—JOHN 3:16

God's greeting of love to Israel was "I am the LORD your God" (Lev. 11:44). It is no less now His salutation of grace to everyone who has believed on the name of His Son, Christ Jesus. God becomes our God the moment that we receive His testimony of His beloved Son. This new relationship between God and us, in virtue of which He calls us *His* and we call Him ours, is the simple result of a believed gospel.

If anyone reading these lines would ask, "How am I to become a child of God?" we answer in the words of Scripture, "Whosoever believeth that Jesus is the Christ is born of God." Nothing less than believing can bring about this sonship; and nothing more is needed. The joy and the peace and the love and the warmth—these are the *effects* of faith, but they are not faith. They are the fruits of a conscious sonship which has been formed by the belief of the divine testimony of Jesus as the Son of God and the Savior of the lost. "As many as received him, to them gave he power to become the sons of God, even to them that believe on his name" (John 1:12).

God's simple message of grace contains peace for the sinner; and the sinner extracts the peace therein contained, not by effort or feeling, but by the simple belief of the true words of God. Good news makes one glad by being believed, and they refuse to yield up their precious treasure to anything but to simple faith. Believe the tidings of peace from God, and the peace is all your own. It is not to him that works or feels or loves, but to him that believes that God says, "I am the LORD your God."

—HORATIUS BONAR

◆ *Have you believed this message from God? If so, thank God and rest in His love. If not, come to Him now, believing He is and that He is the rewarder of those who diligently seek Him (Heb. 11:6).*

Affections for Christ

For where your treasure is, there will your heart be also.
—MATTHEW 6:21

If you do not set your affections on Christ and the things of Christ, you are no fit match for Him; you will not be found marriageable unto Jesus Christ. A woman is not fit to be married to a man if her affections are not drawn out and knit to him; and if your affections are not drawn out to Christ and the things of Christ, you are no fit match for Christ. We must all be espoused to Christ and married to Him; as the church, so every believer is the true spouse of Christ.

As you cannot be married to Christ unless your affections be set on Him and the things above, so you will never own Him unless your affections are set on Him. It is the duty of all the saints to own Christ, His ways, His truths, His ordinances: "He that is ashamed of me before men, him will I be ashamed of before my Father which is in heaven," said Christ (see Mark 8:38). Now look at what a person cares much about, what he will not be ashamed of; but if he cares not, he will not own it, but will be ashamed of it. We must own Christ here, or He will not own us hereafter.

If your affections be not set upon things above, they will never be drawn away from things here below; it is gracious affections that mortifies carnal affections. Sin is mortified by the contrary good; the joy of the world, by the joy of heaven; worldly grief, by spiritual grief; the snow is not melted but by the warm beams of the sun, and the more your hearts are warmed and drawn out with love to Christ, the more your love and affections to the world will be mortified.

—WILLIAM BRIDGE

◆ *How do our choices influence our affections? Are you making choices that are affecting how you feel about Christ and His service? What changes must you make going forward?*

Stop the Spiritual Leak

And he said unto them, Take heed, and beware of
covetousness: for a man's life consisteth not in the
abundance of the things which he possesseth.
—LUKE 12:15

The comforts of life do not depend on having much, for it is Christ's maxim, "Man's life consisteth not in the abundance of the things which he possesseth" (Luke 12:15), but it is in being contented. Is not the bee as well contented with sucking from a flower as the ox that grazes on the mountains? Contentment lies within a man, in the heart; and the way to be comfortable is not by having our barns filled, but our minds quieted. "The contented man," says Seneca, "is the happy man." Discontent is a fretting humor which dries the brains, wastes the spirits, corrodes and eats out the comfort of life. Discontent keeps a man from enjoying what he possesses.

A drop or two of vinegar will sour a whole glass of wine. Though a man has the affluence and confluence of worldly comfort, a drop or two of discontent will imbitter and poison all. Comfort depends on contentment. Jacob went halting when the sinew upon the hollow of his thigh shrank; so when the sinew of contentment begins to shrink, we go halting in our comforts. Contentment is as necessary to keep the life comfortable as oil is necessary to keep the lamp burning. The clouds of discontent do often drop the showers of tears. Would we have comfort in our lives? We may have it if we will. A Christian may carve out what condition he will to himself. Why do you complain of your troubles? It is not trouble that troubles, but discontentment; it is not the water without the ship, but the water that gets within the leak which sinks it. It is not outward affliction that can make the life of a Christian sad; a contented mind would sail above these waters, but when there is a leak of discontent open and trouble gets into the heart, then it is disquieted and sinks. Do therefore as the mariners: pump the water out. Stop the spiritual leak in the soul, and no trouble can hurt you.

—THOMAS WATSON

◆ *Do you have a leak in the ship or some drops of vinegar in the wine of your life, allowing discontent to trouble you? Are you fostering discontent in others? What must you do?*

Denying Self

If any man will come after me, let him deny himself.
—MATTHEW 16:24

It is becoming the gospel of Jesus Christ for men and women to be emptied of themselves, no matter what becomes of us; to be willing to give up ourselves for public good; to venture our estates and lives and all our comforts; yea, to be swallowed up in the glory of God; to be nothing, that Christ may be all. In the gospel, we find that Christ was swallowed up with the glory of His Father; and He did not come to do His own will, but the will of His Father that sent Him. Though He was one who had infinitely more excellence than all men and angels in heaven and earth, yet He was content, for the honor of His Father, to be made as a worm and no man, to be trampled underfoot, to endure the greatest extremities of all sorts. So we, while we live in this world, should be taken off from ourselves.

It is a good lesson of the gospel, and the first lesson. Since our Lord and Master denied Himself and emptied Himself for good to us, what is becoming the gospel but that all Christians should deny themselves? It is very unbecoming for a Christian to be selfish, to have his self-ends and self-ways and self-interest in everything, as almost all men in the world are. But one who would live as for the gospel must be wholly emptied of himself. Whatever parts, home, wealth, and honors he has in the world must be melted into the glory of God.

Jesus Christ, for the glory of His Father, was infinitely content to deny Himself more than we can, for what have we to deny ourselves of? Then you or I live as becomes the gospel when all that we apprehend to have any excellency in, we have it all swallowed up in the glory of God; when we can dedicate and consecrate our lives, honors, liberties, houses, and comforts all to the glory of God, and be as nothing to ourselves and let God be all in all to us.

—JEREMIAH BURROUGHS

◆ *In what ways do you find your sinful nature resisting the call to deny yourself? In what specific ways can you deny yourself today and going forward for the sake of Christ?*

The Christian's Safety

*Commit thy way unto the LORD; trust also
in him; and he shall bring it to pass.*
—PSALM 37:5

Whatever difficulties you may be under, whatever trials and afflictions, you may say as Job did, "Though he slay me, yet will I trust in him" (Job 13:15). Let Him do with me what He pleases. Whatever afflictions He orders to me, I know I am His child, one of His family, and have an interest in His Son, and I will place my confidence in Him.

Surely a child of God, one that Christ died for, one that God dearly loves, one to whom God has promised that all things shall surely work together for his good may safely lay hold of this promise without any danger. God never yet failed any of His children that so trusted in Him. They that trusted in God have never yet found occasion to be ashamed because of their disappointments. "Commit thy way unto the LORD; trust also in him; and he shall bring it to pass" (Ps. 37:5). "Cast thy burden upon the LORD, and he shall sustain thee: he shall never suffer the righteous to be moved" (55:22).

Surely you can believe God when He so positively promises, "God is not a man, that he should lie; neither the son of man, that he should repent: hath he said, and shall he not do it? or hath he spoken, and shall he not make it good?" (Num. 23:19).

Certainly, if you were fully resolved to trust in God and to give yourself up entirely into His hands and let Him do as He will, trusting in His mercy through His Son, Jesus Christ, who died for you, you need not to afflict yourself, but you may lie down and sleep and wake, the Lord sustaining you. A child of God may come with boldness to the throne of grace and say, "Lord, surely I am Thy servant. I am Thy child; Thou hast made a covenant with me and with my dear Savior for me. I am a member of Thy Son and will trust in Thee, whatsoever Thou doest to me, whatever afflictions Thou layest upon me."

—JONATHAN EDWARDS

◆*How do you treat the promises of God? Do you believe God presents them
to us to be laid hold of by faith, or do you somehow push them away from
you for one reason or another?*

Trials Ought Not to Discourage Us

And God shall wipe away all tears from their eyes; and there shall
be no more death, neither sorrow, nor crying, neither shall there be
any more pain: for the former things are passed away.

—REVELATION 21:4

B e not greatly discouraged at the many tribulations, difficulties, and dis-appointments which lie in the path that leads to glory, seeing our Lord has told us before and has made a suitable provision for every case we can meet with. He Himself is always near to those that call upon Him. He is a sure refuge and almighty strength, a never-failing, ever-present help in time of trouble; likewise, He Himself was a man of sorrows and acquainted with grief for our sakes. He drank of the full cup of unmixed wrath for us; shall we then refuse to taste the cup of affliction at His appointment, especially when His wisdom and love prepare it for us and proportion every circumstance to our strength; when He put it into our hands, not in anger but in tender mercy, to do us good and to bring us near to Himself; and when He sweetens every bitter draught with those comforts which none but He can give? Let us rather say, "None of these things move us, neither do we count anything on this side of eternity dear," so that we may finish our course with joy, and run with patience the race which is set before us.

The time is short, the world is passing away, all its care and all its vanities will soon be at an end. Yet a little while, and "we shall see him as he is" (1 John 3:2). Every veil shall be taken away, every seeming frown be removed from His face, and every tear wiped away from ours. We shall be like Him. Even now, when we contemplate His glory as shining in the glass of the gospel, we feel ourselves, in some measure, transformed into the same image; what a sudden, wonderful, and abiding change shall we then experience when He shall shine directly, immediately, and eternally upon our souls without one interrupting cloud between!

—JOHN NEWTON

◆ *How does a focus on the eternal perspective help us when we suffer? How*
does it comfort you to know that your present trial has been measured by
the hand of your heavenly Father?

Two Eternities

The way of life is above to the wise, that
he may depart from hell beneath.
—PROVERBS 15:24

We are never dying creatures; we are shortly entering upon an eternal state, either of happiness or misery. Have serious thoughts about this. Examine your soul as to which of these two eternities is like to be your portion. We must shortly depart hence, and whither will you go, to which of these eternities, either of glory or misery? The serious meditation of the eternal state we are to pass into would work strongly these fruits within us.

Thoughts of eternal torments are a good antidote against sin. Sin tempts with its pleasure; but when we think of eternity, it may cool the intemperate heat of lust. Shall I, for the pleasure of sin for a season, endure eternal pain? Sin, like those locusts (Rev. 9:7), seems to have on its head a crown like gold, but it has in it a tail like a scorpion and a sting in its tail that can never be plucked out. Shall I venture eternal wrath? Is sin committed so sweet as lying in hell forever is bitter? This thought would make us flee from sin, as Moses from the serpent.

The serious thoughts of eternal happiness would very much take us off from worldly things. What are these sublunary things to eternity! They are quickly gone; they salute us and take their farewell. But I am to enter upon an everlasting estate; I hope to live with Him who is eternal; what is the world to me? To those who stand upon the top of the Alps, the great cities of Campania are small things in their eyes; so to him who has his thoughts fixed on his eternal state after this life, all these things seem as nothing in his eye. What is the glory of this world! How poor and contemptible, compared with the eternal weight of glory!

The serious thoughts of an eternal state, either of happiness or misery, should have a powerful influence upon whatsoever we take in hand. Every work we do promotes either a blessed or cursed eternity.

—THOMAS WATSON

♦*Spend a few moments considering this meditation; it may make an eternal difference.*

I Will Trust

I am with you always, even unto the end of the world.
—MATTHEW 28:20

One great secret during time of trouble is to be at peace with your conscience. It was not through Peter's fault but through his heroic faithfulness that he had reached that prison cell. It lay right in his path of duty, and he had kept that path unflinchingly. He had come there for Christ's sake, and his Master had once assured him, "Lo, I am with you always" (Matt. 28:20). How he should escape from that dungeon, or whether he should escape at all, he left entirely in that Master's hand. Faith was the pillow beneath that persecuted head, and so that midnight hour witnessed the sublime scene of tranquil slumber, while the executioner's axe or sword was sharpened for the impending blow.

Troubled child of God, go look at that most suggestive scene in that Jewish jail. Look at it until you get ashamed of many a peevish complaining you have uttered, and many a worry that has driven all sleep from your own eyes. Learn from it how to trust God, even in the darkest hour. Peter was simply practicing the same grace that his brother Paul did afterward, when from his prison in Rome he wrote to his son Timothy, "I know whom I have believed, and am persuaded that he is able to keep that which I have committed unto him against that day" (2 Tim. 1:12). Paul knew that his martyrdom was at hand, but he had made Jesus Christ his trustee, and he felt no more uneasiness than he did about the rising of tomorrow's sun.

Both these men were just what you profess to be, no more and no less; they were Christ's men. They had no more promises than you have, and no other arm to rely on than you have. And yet the watchword of their brave, fearless, composed, and compacted lives was, "I will trust!"

—THEODORE CUYLER

◆*Peter and Paul didn't know if the end of their trial would be death or deliverance, yet they trusted in God. How would your thinking change when going through difficulties if you would trust like Peter and Paul did in their circumstances? Reflect on God's faithfulness in the past so that you might have this confidence today.*

Two Christian Sayings

I must work the works of him that sent me, while it is day:
the night cometh, when no man can work.

—JOHN 9:4

There are two Christian sayings which I would recommend to your notice:

1. "Live while you live."
2. "Do what you can, while you can."

Dear reader, seek to live to some purpose. Work "while it is day," for your day is but a very short one, and then cometh "the night…when no man can work" (John 9:4). Let your humble prayer be that the world may be somewhat the better, and not worse, for your stay in it.

A Christian minister who was nearing death once said, "When I die, I shall have my greatest grief and my greatest joy. My greatest grief is that I have done so little for Jesus; my greatest joy is that He has done so much for me."

The fault of many Christians is that they are too much occupied with *self*. Their religion mainly consists in a doubting anxiety about their own spiritual safety. This continues week after week, and month after month; and all the while they are leaving undone, perhaps, some work which God has evidently appointed for them. If they were only doing their work, the doubts which harass them would, in all probability, speedily disappear.

Who is it that suffers most from fears about his *bodily* condition? Who is it that is forever complaining of pains and aches and alarmed at every little change in his pulse? Is it the laborer, whose time is well employed from morning till night? Is it the man of business, whose farm or merchandise keeps his hands and head constantly at work? No, it is generally the person who has no settled occupation, who has no fixed and definite work to do.

And so it is with Christians. The most constantly and usefully employed are generally the healthiest and strongest Christians. It is those who think they have no work to do for God, and who do none, that are usually distressed with harassing doubts and fears as to their condition. To such I would say, rouse yourselves to some active Christian duty. There is plenty of work to be done, and few ready to do it. It is a happy thing to labor for God.

—ASHTON OXENDEN

◆ *Which life described above is more like yours? In what ways could you labor more?*

The Christian Life Compared to a Race

So run, that ye may obtain.
—1 CORINTHIANS 9:24

If you desire to run the Christian race, remember the admonition, "so run, that ye may obtain" (1 Cor. 9:24). Your steps must be controlled by the Word of God, or you will wander far from the way. You must obtain your sufficiency and strength from Christ by faith and prayer, or you will faint and be unable to endure until the end. We read of some (Gal. 5:7) that ran well for a season but were afterward hindered and turned aside. Be on your guard; for there are many that will try to divert you from your course. Satan, the world, and your own evil hearts will combine and form various attempts to slacken your pace and to withdraw your attention from the one thing needful. Dread the thought of stopping short or turning back; the more you meet with opposition, be so much the more earnest to increase your diligence and to cry mightily to Him who can keep you from falling, to preserve you unblameable in love while here, and at last to present you faultless before the presence of His glory with exceeding joy.

Believers, why are we not as wise as the children of the world? We see how those who are entering a race are thinking and talking about it and preparing for it every day. Does not their diligence shame us, who are so cold, faint, and negligent in the most important and honorable race! Let us gird up the loins of our mind. Some of you have not far to run now; you have taken many weary steps since you were first called, but the end is near, the period of your complete salvation is now much nearer than when you first believed. Think of Jesus, the forerunner, and the judge: He has already entered within the veil for us, His eye is upon us, and He is near to assist and is waiting to receive us. May His Spirit and His example stimulate us to press forward to the prize of our high calling, to tread down every difficulty, and to be faithful unto death that we may receive the crown of life.

—JOHN NEWTON

♦ *What do you do when you become weary when running the race?*

We Are Travelers

But this I say, brethren, the time is short.
—1 CORINTHIANS 7:29

This life ought to be spent by us as only a journey or pilgrimage toward heaven. We ought not to rest in the world and its enjoyments but should desire heaven. We should *seek first the kingdom of God* and above all things to desire a heavenly happiness, to be with God and dwell with Jesus Christ. Though surrounded with outward enjoyments and settled in families with desirable friends; though we have friends whose society is delightful, and children in whom we see many promising qualifications; though we live by good neighbors and are generally loved where known; yet we should not take our rest in these things. We should be so far from resting in them that we should desire to leave them all in God's due time. We ought to possess, enjoy, and use them, with no other view but readily to leave them, whenever called to it, and to exchange them willingly and cheerfully for heaven.

A traveler does not rest in what he meets with, however comfortable and pleasing on the road. If he passes through pleasant places, flowery meadows, or shady groves, he does not take up his contentment in these things but only takes a glance at them as he goes along. He is not enticed by fine appearances to put off the thought of proceeding. No, his journey's end is in his mind. If he meets with comfortable accommodations at an inn, he entertains no thoughts of staying there. He considers that these things are not his, that he is but a stranger, and when he has refreshed himself or slept for a night, he is going forward; and it is pleasant for him to think about how much of the way he has already traveled.

So should we desire heaven more than the comforts and enjoyments of this life. The apostle mentions it as an encouraging, comfortable consideration to Christians, that they draw nearer to their happiness. "Now is our salvation nearer than when we believed" (Rom. 13:11). Our hearts ought to be loose from earthly things, as that of a man on a journey, that we may as cheerfully part with them whenever God calls.

—JONATHAN EDWARDS

◆ *Is there anything to which you find yourself so attached that it will prove difficult to leave this present world? How can you guard against driving your tent stakes too deeply?*

To Which World Do You Belong?

For what is a man advantaged, if he gain the whole world,
and lose himself, or be cast away?

—LUKE 9:25

A man living for the world is one that could be content if God would let him live here in this world and enjoy what he does. He would be content to live here forever and could be satisfied though he never enjoyed anything from God but what he has received here if he could always hold on to it. Here's an evident argument of a man of the world. He has for outward show as much as the world can afford any man—the comfort of his body, his comeliness, his health—he has as much as the world can give. He has a comfortable home with all comforts belonging to it, and he has in the world all that his heart can desire. He has wife and children about him, in whom he has great delight and contentment. Now I would say to this man, "What are you saying? Would not this satisfy your heart if you might be always here, always have your house, walks, riches, and goods of the world? Would it not satisfy your soul, though God should never give you anything else but this?" I beseech you in your own thoughts, answer to God this question and seriously look into your heart, for you may know very much the answer to this question. That man or woman whose conscience tells them this would satisfy, we may conclude that they are of the world, because the things of the world would be enough for his or her portion.

Now take a man or woman who is chosen out of this world, who is of the kingdom of Jesus Christ, who the Lord has revealed the things of another world and the excellencies of Jesus Christ, and such a one would say, "Lord, it is true, I am unworthy of the least crumb of bread that I eat or the least drop of water, but yet it is not all the world, nor ten thousand worlds, that can satisfy my soul, for the portion of it is nothing by Thyself."

—JEREMIAH BURROUGHS

◆*For what things are you living? Are you living for Christ or the things of this world? Will they stand the test of time and endure forever?*

The Benefits of Affliction

This is my comfort in my affliction: for thy word hath quickened me.
—PSALM 119:50

Afflictions lead us to prayer. It is a pity it should be so. Long periods of ease and prosperity without painful changes have an unhappy tendency to make us cold and formal in our secret worship, but troubles rouse our spirits and constrain us to call upon the Lord in earnest, when we feel a need of that help which we only can have from Him.

Afflictions are useful and, in a degree, necessary to keep alive in us a conviction of the vanity and unsatisfying nature of our present world and all its enjoyments; to remind us that this is not our rest; and to call our thoughts upward, where our true treasure is, and where our conversation ought to be. When things go on as we wish, our hearts are prone to say that it is good to be here.

A child of God will desire a greater and personal understanding of His holy Word, and this attainment is greatly promoted by our trials. Many promises in Scripture are made to and designed for those in affliction, and though we may believe they are true, we cannot know their sweetness, power, and suitableness unless we ourselves are in a state of affliction. The Lord says, "Call upon me in the day of trouble: I will deliver" (Ps. 50:15). Until the day of trouble comes, such a promise is like a city of refuge to an Israelite who, not having slain a man, was in no danger of the avenger of blood. But some can say, "I not only believe this promise upon the authority of the speaker, but I can set my seal to it: I have been in trouble; I trusted Him for relief and was not disappointed. The Lord truly heard and delivered me." So, afflictions give occasion of our knowing and noticing more of the Lord's wisdom, power, and goodness in supporting and relieving than we would otherwise have known.

—JOHN NEWTON

♦ *While we do not pray for more afflictions, can you see that your afflictions have led you to greater confidence in God's promises? If so, then should we not be more receptive to the afflictions God permits us to experience?*

God's All-Sufficiency for the Supply of Our Wants

But my God shall supply all your need according to his riches in glory by Christ Jesus.
—PHILIPPIANS 4:19

If God by the exercises of His common bounty toward men shows that He has an all-sufficiency for the supply of their wants, then what encouragement is here to look to God and trust in Him for whatever we stand in need of. God shows us every day, if we did but consider it, by His daily goodness to us, that He is able to do everything for us that we need to have done, and that He is wise enough to contrive for us in all difficulties, and good enough to give us sufficient provision for our needs. He shows that He delights in goodness and in providing for the good of man. We see the daily fruits of it, besides what we are taught about it in the Word of God.

Therefore, whatever your wants are, be directed to go to this fountain. If your wants are outward, if you are in need of things for your comfortable subsistence, go to Him who has promised that all those things should be added to you if you seek first the kingdom of God. If you want health, if you want ease, if you have needs for yourself, if you have needs for your children, go to that river of God's bounty that is full of water. Don't be anxious about these things, but go to God and leave your case with Him, and cheerfully wait in a way of well-doing for what He shall see fitting to provide for you.

If your wants are spiritual, here is encouragement to go to Him and trust in Him. The manifestations of power, as His plenty, abundance, constancy, and all-sufficiency, may convince us of His ability to redeem our souls from all adversity. May His wisdom in supplying for our wants convince us of the sufficiency of His wisdom to supply for us and guide us in the way of peace.
—JONATHAN EDWARDS

◆ *If God has provided for you in the lesser things, will He not provide for you in the greater? Have you found His promise ever unfulfilled?*

Beware of Unbelief

Take heed, brethren, lest there be in any of you an evil
heart of unbelief, in departing from the living God.
—HEBREWS 3:12

As faith is the uniting grace, so by unbelief we depart from God. There are good things in our life and evil things. The good things of life do lure men from God. The evil things of this life scare men from God, but faith will preserve from both.

If a man is tempted with the good things of this life, yet if he has faith, he will not depart from God, for by faith we live upon God in the use of the good things.

If a man is tempted to depart from God by the evil things of this life, yet if he has faith, he will not depart from God; for by faith we live above losses and above crosses, so that faith preserves us from both. Therefore, unbelief is the root and ground of all our apostasy or departing from God. We know how it was with the three friends of Daniel, what it was that kept them in the evil day; there was the music on the one hand, and the fiery furnace on the other; but between both, they were kept and preserved, for they believed. It was their faith that kept them from departing.

If unbelief be a mother sin, a parent sin, a breeding sin—the root and cause of other sins—then unbelief must be the root and ground and cause of apostasy. What is the cause of all our sins but our unbelief? What is the reason that men are so covetous and worldly but because of their unbelief? What is the reason when people are in trouble that they use indirect means to get out of trouble but because of their unbelief? What is the reason a spouse or child will tell lies? Because of unbelief. Unbelief is the mother sin, the parent sin, and therefore unbelief is the cause of departing from God. Take heed of departing from God; take heed of unbelief, and an evil heart of unbelief, whereby we depart from God.

—WILLIAM BRIDGE

◆ *Describe unbelief and what it looks like practically. Are you affected by unbelief in any way? What is the opposite of unbelief?*

God's Ways Are Good

It is good for me that I have been afflicted.
—PSALM 119:71

Contentment is taking pleasure in God's ways. This happens when I am well pleased in what God does, as long as I can see God in it, though I may desire that God in His due time would remove it and I may use the means to remove it. I am well pleased as long as God's hand is in it. To be well pleased with God's hand is a higher degree of contentment than the previous one. It comes from not only seeing that I should be content in this affliction, but seeing that there is good in it. There is honey in this rock, and so I do not only say, "I *must* or I *will* submit to God's hand," rather, the hand of God is good and therefore I can say, "It is good that I am afflicted." To acknowledge that it is just that I am afflicted is possible with someone who is not truly content. I may be convinced that God deals justly in this matter, He is righteous and just, and it is right that I should submit to what He has done. The Lord has done righteously in all ways! But that is not enough! You must say, "Good is the hand of the Lord." It was the expression of Eli, "It is the LORD: let him do what seemeth him good," when it was a hard word. It was a word that warned very difficult things to Eli and his house, and yet Eli says, "It is the LORD: let him do what seemeth him good."

Perhaps, some of you may say, like David, "It is good that I have been afflicted." Not just good when you see the good fruit it has produced, but to say when you are afflicted, "It is good that I am afflicted. Whatever the affliction, yet through the mercy of God, mine is a good condition." It is indeed the top and height of the art of contentment to be able to say, "My condition and afflictions are very difficult and trying; yet through God's mercy I am in a good state and the hand of God is good."

—JEREMIAH BURROUGHS

◆*Have you learned, as Paul, in whatever condition you find yourself to be content? Think of an example of a time when you could truly say, "It is good that I have been afflicted."*

Fix Your Eye on Christ

Lord, Increase our faith.
—LUKE 17:5

Do you belong to those who *really profess Christian faith and Christian obedience* and are trying, however weakly, to follow Christ amid an evil world? I think I know something of what goes on in your hearts. You sometimes feel that you will never persevere to the end and will be obliged someday to give up your profession. You are sometimes tempted to write bitter things against yourself and to fancy you have got no grace at all. I am afraid there are myriads of true Christians in this condition, who go trembling and doubting toward heaven, with Despondency and Much-Afraid and Fearing in *Pilgrim's Progress*, and fear they will never get to the Celestial City at all.

My advice to all such persons is very simple. Say every morning and evening of your life, "Lord, increase my faith." Cultivate the habit of fixing your eye more simply on Jesus Christ, and try to know more of the fullness there is laid up in Him for every one of His believing people. Do not be always poring over the imperfections of your own heart and dissecting your own besetting sins. Look up. Look more to your risen Head in heaven, and try to realize more than you do that the Lord Jesus not only died for you, but that He also rose again, and that He is ever living at God's right hand as your Priest, your Advocate, and your almighty friend.

Take courage, believer. The bolder and more decided you are, the more comfort you will have in Christ. You cannot have two heavens: one here, and the other hereafter. You are yet in the world, and you have a body, and there is always near you a busy devil. But great faith shall always have great peace.

—J. C. RYLE

◆ *Are these spiritual fears present in your heart? Why? Will you commit to pray each day, "Lord, increase my faith"?*

Which Road Are You On?

*Enter ye in at the strait gate: for wide is the gate, and broad is
the way, that leadeth to destruction, and many there be which go in
thereat: Because strait is the gate, and narrow is the way, which
leadeth unto life, and few there be that find it.*

—MATTHEW 7:13–14

What a painful consideration that, respecting the narrow way, "few
there be that find it" (Matt. 7:14), while of the wide gate our Lord has
said: "many there be which go in thereat" (v. 13). I am a dying creature walking on the verge of an awful eternity. Heaven and hell lie before me; to one
of those two places I am, at the close of every day, advancing a day's journey.

This day may bring me to my eternal abode of happiness or misery. The
sleep which I take this night may be the sleep of death—and should it be so,
where would my spirit, dislodged from earth, find itself? Oh, my soul, ask
yourself, with all the solemnity which becomes so great a question, where
am I going? Soon I must be called into the presence of my Judge, but what
reception shall I meet with there? What answer does conscience now make?
Have I believed with the heart unto righteousness? Is the life which I now
live a life of faith in the Son of God?

I find from the Word of God that these two roads lie through the
wilderness of this world. The one, at its beginning, is pleasant to carnal
nature, being strewed with forbidden pleasures, sensual delights, and materialistic gratifications; but growing darker and more crooked and thorny
as life advances, it ends abruptly in eternal misery. The other, difficult at
the entrance, requires many sacrifices and much self-denial; but gradually increasing in light and beauty, it terminates in the blissful regions of
immortal glory.

—THOMAS READE

◆*On which of these roads are you walking? What will be your final destination should you this moment meet God?*

Which Door Is Open?

*Behold, I stand at the door, and knock: if any man hear
my voice, and open the door, I will come in to him.*

—REVELATION 3:20

It shall not profit you to say the door of your heart has never yet been opened and you don't know how to do it. I shall show you this is not the case, and I shall prove that you have always admitted other guests most readily. Have not your own relations knocked? Parents, wife, and children; yes, and the door was at once opened, and they entered in and took up a large place in your affections. Has not the world knocked? Yes, and the door was at once opened, and in there came cares about the things of this life and anxieties about earthly matters and the love of money and excessive attention to business.

Has not sin knocked? Yes, long ago, and the door was at once opened, and there entered wickedness, polluted thoughts, abominable lusts, and fleshly dispositions, and they have dwelled there and filled up your thoughts. And lastly, Satan knocked and told you it was a mistake to think sin so very sinful. God would not be so very strict; ministers were too particular; it was not necessary to think about Christ and be watchful and attend church regularly and search the Scriptures and pray without ceasing. Only let him in and he would show you a better way. And at once the door was opened, and he entered in and dwelled there and took possession of your goods; and then your house was filled, and you have dared to be at peace.

But all this time Jesus has been standing, knocking, waiting, asking to be admitted, and so far, has it all been in vain? Think what an insufferable insult. The Lord Jesus Christ comes freely offering righteousness, peace, and joy in the Holy Ghost, and the door is not opened. He brings white raiment to cover your uncleanness and the water of life which He purchased with His own blood, and the door is not opened.

—J. C. RYLE

♦ *Has Jesus entered the door of your heart? What are you looking for that He is not able and willing to provide?*

The Value of Your Soul

*For what shall it profit a man, if he shall gain the
whole world, and lose his own soul?*

—MARK 8:36

You have a soul—a soul that will live forever in happiness or in misery.
And you have but one soul. You have two ears; though one of them
may be deaf, you may hear with the other. You have two eyes; in one of them
you may be blind, yet with the other you may see very well. Yet you have but
one soul. If you lose that, all is lost.

That soul is worth saving. It will exist as long as there is a heaven or
a hell, as long as there are men or angels or a God. That soul may be very
happy, as happy as an angel; or it may be very miserable, as miserable as a
devil. It can rise high and shine gloriously in the presence of God, or it can
sink to low vices, to deep ruin, yea, to the lowest hell.

Your soul needs to be saved if it is still lost. It is dead in trespasses and
sins. By nature, you were without Christ. Without divine grace no man
loves God, fears God, trusts God, obeys God, or lives unto God. God's Word
says you need salvation. Your conscience says you need salvation. Your best
friends know that you need salvation. And you need salvation more than
you need anything else. You may be weary and need rest; you may be poor
and need money; you may be sick and need medicine; you may be hungry
and need food; but you need salvation more than all these things.

It is possible for you to be saved. Salvation is provided. It is offered to
you by the Lord. Other sinners are entering the kingdom of heaven. Men
once as lost as you are have sought and found mercy. Many who are still on
earth were once in a secretly rebellious state, but God called them, and they
ran after Him. O you may be saved!

—WILLIAM PLUMER

◆ *Why is your soul so valuable? What does this mean for you practically,
since we often can know something to be true, but it never changes our
behavior?*

Eternal Life or Eternal Death

I call heaven and earth to record this day against you, that
I have set before you life and death, blessing and cursing:
therefore choose life.

—DEUTERONOMY 30:19

Death to the true Christian is an entrance into eternal pleasures and unspeakable joys, but the death of a sinner is his entrance into never-ending miseries. This world is all the hell that a true Christian will endure, and it is all the heaven unbelievers shall ever enjoy.

The sinner, when he dies, leaves all his riches and possessions: there is no more money for him to have the pleasure of fingering; there is no more fine apparel for him to be arrayed in, nor proud palace to live in. But the Christian, when he dies, he obtains all his riches, even infinite spiritual, heavenly riches.

At death, the sinner leaves all his honor and enters into eternal disgrace; but the Christian is then invested with his. The one leaves all his friends forever; when he sees them again at the resurrection, they will be either glorifying God in His justice in damning him or else ready to tear him. But the other, he goes to his best friends and will again meet his best earthly friends at the resurrection in glory, full of mutual joy and love.

The death of the believer is in order to gain a more glorious resurrection, but the death of a sinner is but only a faint shadow and prelude of the eternal death the body is to die at the great day and forevermore.

So great is the difference between the death of the one and the other, it is even as the difference between life and death, between death and a resurrection. Wherefore, now you have both before you—the glorious gainfulness of the death of a Christian and the dreadfulness of the death of a sinner—or rather you have life and death set before you, to make your choice; wherefore, choose life.

—JONATHAN EDWARDS

◆ *What shall your end be? What shall your family's end be? What must you do about this?*

Blessed Redeemer

For the wages of sin is death; but the gift of God is
eternal life through Jesus Christ our Lord.
—ROMANS 6:23

If you would view sin's darkest colors and most terrible effects, go to Bethlehem and ask, "Why did the King of heaven become an infant? Why was He who fills all space wrapped in swaddling clothes and laid in a manger?" Go to Gethsemane and ask, "Why did the incarnate God agonize and sweat great drops of blood?" Go to the judgment hall and ask, "Why did the sovereign Judge of men and angels submit to be judged? Why did the innocent suffer such indignities? Why was the guiltless condemned to die?" Go to Calvary and ask, "Why did the Lord of glory hang on the accursed tree? Why did the Lord of life condescend to pour out His soul unto death?"

It was to save you from your sin, to redeem you from the curse of the law by being made a curse for you, to deliver you from going down into hell by becoming your ransom. It was to merit heaven for you by His precious atonement and obedience unto death. It was to purchase for you the eternal Spirit by whose powerful aid you might believe and love and delight in this precious Savior, this adorable Redeemer, this almighty Deliverer, through whom your sins are pardoned and by whom you have access unto God as your reconciled Father. Oh, my soul, praise the Lord for His mercy, and never cease to speak good of His name!

Let this view of sin, and of a sin-bearing Savior, humble you in His presence and empty you of pride and vainglory. Let it, at the same time, fill you with gratitude to God for having provided such a remedy against the evils of the fall.

Sin—even your sin—nailed, pierced, and agonized the Lord of glory! Oh, then hate sin and avoid it as you would tremble to plunge a spear into your Savior's bosom, as you would shudder to trample under foot His sacred blood.

—THOMAS READE

◆ *Meditate on the price Christ paid to set His people free. Now take your*
most troublesome sin you struggle with, confess it, and put the sword
through it, or let the sword pierce your Savior.

A Life of Compassion

Weep with them that weep.
—ROMANS 12:15

It is the richest luxury on earth to share by compassion the sorrow, to soothe by gentleness the grief, to wipe away by kindness the tears of another. This Christ did, and we are to prove our discipleship to Him by imitating His example. "Remember them that are in bonds, as bound with them"—sharing their chain—"and them which suffer adversity, as being yourselves also in the body" (Heb. 13:3)—exposed to like weaknesses and assaults, calamities and griefs.

Oh aspire, beloved, to be a drier of human tears; to always have a hand ready to wipe them away. Who can estimate its worth? To have soothed one sorrowing person, to have met one pressing need, to have unbound one crushing load, to have dried one tear of grief, to have shed one beam of light on a dreary path, to have reclaimed one wanderer, to have made one widow's heart to sing for joy, to have befriended and comforted an orphan is a work to be measured in its importance and its blessedness only by a life. Let your life be an outflowing of compassion to the distressed and needy, the widow and fatherless. Be like Christ, "who went about doing good" (Acts 10:38); raise the fallen, strengthen the weak, comfort the feeble-minded; and if tears of compassion and sympathy will soothe and take away the tears of penitence and adversity, then be it your mission and your privilege to "weep with them that weep" (Rom. 12:15).

In heaven there will be no more tears! It is tearless, because it is sorrowless; it is sorrowless because it is sinless; it is sinless, because it is the dwelling place of the holy Lord God and of the "spirits of just men made perfect" (Heb. 12:23). How magnificent the description! "And God shall wipe away all tears from their eyes; and there shall be no more death, neither sorrow, nor crying, neither shall be there any more pain" (Rev. 21:4).

—OCTAVIUS WINSLOW

♦*Focus on Christ's compassionate character. Ask God to show you ways in which you can practically implement being compassionate to those around you.*

Eternal Rest

When thou passest through the waters, I will be with thee.
—ISAIAH 43:2

Believer, fear not the passage to that "rest." The apostle was willing to brave the swellings of Jordan because of the beauty of the land that lies beyond it. "[I have] a desire," he says, "to depart, and to be with Christ; which is far better" (Phil. 1:23). He was ready to pass through the fiery ordeal, because he was conscious of the truth that the skirts of his garment only should be injured, while the soul, safe as in the citadel of God, should only shine with greater lustre, rising on imperishable pinions and resting not till it should soar and sing with the seraphim beside the throne.

Journey on, then, child of God, grasping firmly the promise, "My presence shall go with thee, and I will give thee rest" (Ex. 33:14). Be calm in the contemplation of your departure; leave every future step of your earthly pilgrimage in the hands of Him who will lead you by "the right way" (Ps. 107:7). Seek to have more of the mind of Christ. Be earnest in prayer. Let the Word of God be your daily study: "a lamp unto [your] feet, and a light unto [your] path" (119:105). Live ever to the glory of God, and by the faithful, conscientious discharge of the duties of your calling, be "an example of the believers, in word, in conversation, in charity, in spirit, in faith, in purity" (1 Tim. 4:12). Thus, advance onward in the pathway of promise and when the close of the journey is reached, the voice of Him "whom having not seen, ye love" (1 Peter 1:8) will then whisper these encouraging words: "Fear not, for I am with thee.... I will not fail thee, nor forsake thee.... When thou passest through the waters, I will be with thee" (Isa. 43:5; Josh. 1:5; Isa. 43:2).

God of all grace, by whose good hand upon me I have hitherto been guided in my pilgrimage, hold Thou me up, and so I shall be safe.

—ASHTON OXENDEN

◆ *Think over the past years of your life and recall the mercies of God. As you reflect over these, be encouraged that He who has brought you to today will finish what He has begun; therefore, fear not the passage that brings you there.*

Are You Prepared?

And as it is appointed unto men once to die.
—HEBREWS 9:27

B e persuaded for your own safety to look a little forward and be concerned about your welfare for the life to come and not only what you will eat and what you will drink and wherewithal you will be clothed for the little time you are to remain here. Frequently ask yourself the question of what you intend to do if death comes and summons you out of the world and away from all your earthly good things. Even if you are not prepared to die, you cannot resist the summons from the King of Terrors. When death comes, he will take you from all your dear enjoyments, whether you will or not, never to set your eye on those things again. And as there will be no encountering death, so neither will there be any entreating it. He will not be wrought upon by cries and tears; he is altogether inescapable. He will not wait for you one minute, that you may have a little opportunity to be better fitted and prepared to go with him.

Consider whether you are in such a state that you need not fear to meet death. If he should come immediately, should you meet him with terror and horror under dreadful apprehensions of going into another world and leaving all these things forevermore? Or should you be able to look him cheerfully in the face, knowing that although you must be stripped of these enjoyments, yet death cannot take from you your heavenly happiness; knowing that although he takes you away from your earthly possessions, he cannot deprive you of your heavenly inheritance? Though he takes you from your earthly friends and family, yet he is not able to separate you from your heavenly Father, nor from Jesus Christ, the spouse and bridegroom of your soul.

How would it be with you if death should call you now? Would he find you asleep or diligent at your work, with your loins girt and your lamps burning?

—JONATHAN EDWARDS

♦ *Are you busy preparing for tomorrow's earthly cares, or are you preparing for an eternal future?*

Fear of Death Abolished

And deliver them who through fear of death were
all their lifetime subject to bondage.
—HEBREWS 2:15

Are you in bondage because of the fear of death? How this hinders your happy, joyful progress heavenward. Jesus can loosen and virtually has loosened these bonds. He reminds you that you are not to contemplate death but His personal and glorious coming. If your thoughts will wander from this bright and blessed hope to the more gloomy and repulsive object of your departure from Him, you are to remember that He has vanquished death and has passed through the grave as your substitute, your surety, your Head; that He has extracted the venom of the one and has irradiated the gloom of the other; and that you have no sting to apprehend and no shadows to dread, because He has passed that way before you.

Moreover, He has pledged His most loving and most faithful word that when you tread the valley, solitary and alone as you must be, you shall fear no evil, for He, your risen, living Lord and Savior will be with you. "Lo, I am with you always" (Matt. 28:20). Then, why hug these chains, why wear these bonds, when simple unquestioning faith in your Lord's assurance—and He is worthy of your love's absolute confidence—would deliver you?

Perhaps your life is ebbing, earth's toils and events are fading, and the ties that bind you here are breaking one by one, but that one fetter still enslaves you, the most painful and heaviest of all—the fear of death! Turn your eye to Jesus, with whom your soul is in a living and inseparable union; Jesus, your life-creating, life-keeping Head. One glance, one touch, and your fears are dissolved, and your fettered spirit is free. Is Christ enough for your life, its trials, its sorrows, its changes, its sins but not equal in the support of His grace, the comfort of His love, and in the sunshine of His presence for the sinking departures and throes of death? Away with such suspicion and distrust. How dishonoring to Him who so loved you as to part with the last drop of blood and the last pulse of life. Sick, sinking, dying believer, your Savior is near!

—OCTAVIUS WINSLOW

◆*Do you fear death? How can you be prepared to die without fear?*

Bearing Christ's Image

And as we have borne the image of the earthy,
we shall also bear the image of the heavenly.
—1 CORINTHIANS 15:49

Reader, as we draw our meditations to a close, we would earnestly and affectionately press upon you the solemn truth that if you would make progress in the divine life, if you would enjoy inward peace, comfort, and hope, if you would abide in Christ and glorify your Father in heaven by bearing much fruit, then you must cultivate the daily habit of revealing to your God and Savior at the throne of grace all your longings and desires. In this respect, it is not one act of faith that makes us "complete in him" (Col. 2:10). We grow up into Him. We are not molded all at once into the image of Christ, we must be "renewed day by day" (2 Cor. 4:16).

The divine life of the soul is a breathing life, and its breath is drawn from fellowship with Christ. Christ is as needful every moment as He is the first hour of conscious believing on Him. We need Him every night and morning, every struggling, toiling day, as much as at the beginning of our spiritual history. Strive to apprehend this glorious truth, to realize more of a personal, abiding union with Christ by living near to the throne of grace and by a daily conformity to His image. It is God's declared purpose to give you success in your effort. Rest upon this thought. Carry it ever in your heart. Forget not you are called to this glorious work—to go on from day to day into a more entire conformity to the Lord Jesus Christ. Your constant aim and effort must be to part with and to master every evil desire and passion till it might with truth be said of you, "He is a Christian because he is like Christ." This is your "calling" to always make progress in it till the last moment of your earthly existence.

—ASHTON OXENDEN

◆*It is the will of God that His people be sanctified. As you reflect back on this year, ask yourself if the image of Christ is being formed in you, so that it is being expressed more and more in your outer man through your words and actions.*

Are You in Christ?

Prepare to meet thy God.
—AMOS 4:12

And now, reader, before you lay down this book, *ask yourself whether you shall be found among the many* who shall "sit down...in the kingdom of heaven" (Matt. 8:11). The question demands an answer. I charge you to give your soul no rest until you can answer it in a satisfactory way. Time is passing quickly away, and the world is growing old. The signs of the times ought to set us all thinking. The distress of nations with perplexity seems to increase every year. The wisdom of statesmen seems utterly unable to prevent wars and confusion in every direction. The progress of art and science and civilization appears entirely powerless to prevent the existence of enormous moral evils. Nothing will ever cure the disease of human nature but the return of the Great Physician, the Prince of Peace—the second coming of Jesus Christ Himself. And when He comes, shall you be found among the "many" who shall "sit down with Abraham, and Isaac, and Jacob, in the kingdom of heaven" (v. 11)?

Why should you not be found among the many? I know no reason except your own lack of will, your own indolence and laziness, or your own determined love of sin and the world. An open door is before you: why not enter into it? The Lord Jesus Christ is able and ready to save you: why not commit your soul to Him, and lay hold on the hand which He holds out from heaven? I repeat that I know no reason why you should not be found amongst the "many" at the last day.

—J. C. RYLE

◆ *You must give your own account before God. Within which group will you be found? If you are not in Christ by faith, what holds you back? Repent today and believe the gospel before it is too late. If you can say by faith, "Come quickly, Lord Jesus," keep your garments unspotted and press on till the end.*

Biographical Sketches

Horatius Bonar (1808–1889). One of eleven children and coming from a long ancestry of ministers, Horatius Bonar was born at Old Broughton, Edinburgh, in 1808. He received a degree in divinity from the University of Edinburgh after which in 1838 he commenced a lifelong pastoral ministry that spanned over fifty years. In 1843 he married Jane Catherine. Although they were blessed with nine children, five of them died during childhood. In addition to preaching, Bonar wrote several influential books and over 600 hymns. Many of these hymns are still being used today including his best-known hymn, "I Heard the Voice of Jesus Say." Bonar has been affectionately called the "prince of Scottish hymn-writers." Bonar's preaching and writings portray his greatest burden which was the winning of souls. Horatius Bonar died at his home in July of 1889.

William Bridge (ca. 1600–1670). William Bridge was born in Cambridgeshire, England, around 1600. He entered Emmanuel College when he was sixteen years old and graduated with his MA in 1626. He was ordained in the Church of England in 1627 and then became rector of St. Peter Hungate in 1632. In 1636, Bridge came into conflict with Matthew Wren, bishop of Norwich, for nonconformity which forced him to flee into exile to Rotterdam where he co-pastored a church with Jeremiah Burroughs. In 1641 Bridge returned to England and was appointed a few years later as a member of the Westminster Assembly. He served several churches until his death in 1670. Bridge married twice, the name of his first wife is not recorded; his second wife was a widow. Bridge's *Works* have been printed in five volumes; one of his most well-known books is *A Lifting Up for the Downcast*.

Jeremiah Burroughs (1599–1646). Jeremiah Burroughs was born in 1599. He was tutored by Thomas Hooker and educated at Emmanuel College, Cambridge. After leaving Cambridge, he ministered to two congregations in East Anglia. In 1637 he took a call to Rotterdam, where he served for four years before returning to London, where he preached in various churches until his death. Grieving over the divisions of the church, Burroughs wrote *Heart-Divisions Opened*, in which he pleaded for the unity of all who loved the truth, and argued that what made comparatively minor differences into causes of rigid divisions was a wrong spirit and wrong motives. Of the many books that he authored, his most famous is *The Rare Jewel of Christian Contentment*. Burroughs died from complications as the result of a fall from his horse.

Theodore Cuyler (1822–1909). Theodore Cuyler was born in 1822 in the beautiful town of Aurora, New York. His father died when he was four years old, which left him as an only child with his mother. Together they moved back to her parents' home where he grew up on a farm, often spending time with his grandfather. Cuyler said of his mother that "she was one of the best mothers that God ever gave to an only son." He graduated from Princeton Theological Seminary in 1846. He then pastored a church in New Jersey before becoming the minister of the Market Street Dutch Reformed Church in New York City. In 1860 he accepted a call to the Park Presbyterian Church in Brooklyn where he pastored over four thousand souls for many years. Cuyler's contemporaries and friends included Horatius Bonar and Charles Spurgeon. Cuyler was no stranger to suffering as he lost two of his children in infancy and one daughter as a young adult. The Lord used these trials in his life to equip him for preaching and writing. One of his best-known volumes is *God's Light on Dark Clouds*, which is packed with direction and comfort for those who are suffering. He died at the ripe age of eighty-seven in 1909.

Jonathan Edwards (1703–1758). Jonathan Edwards was the only son of eleven children born to Timothy and Esther Edwards in Windsor, Connecticut. Entering Yale at the age of thirteen, Edwards loved natural history and was fascinated with the discoveries of Isaac Newton. Converted around the age of eighteen, Edwards grew to love the doctrine of God's sovereignty, which he used as the foundation of his theological teaching. In 1727 Edwards married Sarah Pierpont whose remarkable piety he had observed since she was the age of thirteen. Together they had twelve children. Besides being a great and ardent preacher, Edwards was a prolific writer. His most notable sermon preached during the revival of 1741 was *Sinners in the Hands of an Angry God*. This sermon and others that he preached have been used for the awakening and salvation of many. Jonathan and Sarah Edwards's legacy includes a vice president, many pastors, thirteen university presidents, sixty-five professors, and many other leaders. In 1758 Edwards died from the effects of the smallpox vaccine. He is buried in Princeton Cemetery.

John Newton (1725–1807). Born in London, John Newton lost his mother to tuberculosis before he was seven years old, yet her teaching stayed with him. At the age of eleven, after only two years at a boarding school he joined his father, a sea captain, on his first voyage at sea. Newton continued his sea life until he was thirty. During those years he worked with a slave-trader and suffered many hardships. including being flogged, captured, and treated as a slave. He nearly committed suicide. In 1748, Newton ended his seafaring days and worked in Liverpool where he first heard George Whitefield preach. God wondrously saved him and called him to preach the gospel. A major part of Newton's ministry was his letter writing where he could express his inmost thoughts on spiritual and practical subjects with great wisdom. He also wrote over 280 hymns, the most famous being *Amazing Grace*. In 1750 Newton married Mary Catlett and they adopted his two nieces. He died in December 1807. His self-penned epitaph says, "JOHN NEWTON. Once an infidel and libertine, a servant of slaves in Africa, was by the rich mercy of our LORD and SAVIOUR JESUS CHRIST preserved, restored, pardoned and appointed to preach the faith he had long laboured to destroy."

Ashton Oxenden (1808–1892). Ashton Oxenden was born the son of wealthy parents Sir Henry and Mary Oxenden. Sadly, Ashton hardly knew his mother as she died when he was just six years old, but he believed that he owed much to her prayers. At the age of nineteen he entered Oxford and was soon ordained into ministry although he says that he "lacked as yet that clear influence of the Holy Spirit, which can alone rightly and effectually mould the heart, and fit to engage in a work of such special solemnity and importance." Oxenden married when he was fifty-six years old and was blessed with one child. About this time, he received a call from Canada. Believing he was too old to leave England he declined but was unanimously called again. With his wife's blessing he accepted, and they left England for Canada. Here he ministered for nine years often traveling from church to church on horseback. During this time Oxenden took a special interest in the Canadian Indians and several of his writings have been translated into their native tongue. In 1879 Oxenden took a call back to England where he labored for several more years. He left a legacy of many practical writings including a children's hymn book and an autobiography.

William Plumer (1802–1880). William Plumer was born on July 26, 1802, in Greensburg, Pennsylvania. He attended college at Washington College in Virginia and upon graduation attended Princeton Seminary in New Jersey. He was licensed to preach in 1826 and officially ordained as a minister in 1827. In 1829 Plumer married Eliza Hassell who was a widow. Plumer not only was an able and gifted preacher, serving several churches throughout his life, but was also a prolific writer. He authored at least twenty-five books, as well as numerous tracts and newspaper articles. Some believe that his commentary on the book of Psalms excels that of any other expositor. Plumer also had a fervent prayer life. "His prayers," wrote Moses D. Hoge, "were the tender pleadings of a soul in communion with God." Besides preaching and writing, Plumer also taught at various institutions and founded Staunton's Institute for the Blind, Deaf and Dumb. In 1880, Plumer died due to complications that arose after having surgery to remove kidney stones. He is buried in Hollywood Cemetery in Richmond, Virginia.

Thomas Reade (1776–1841). Little is known of Thomas Shaw Bancroft Reade. He was born in Manchester, England. He married Mary Calverley Bladys and after her death, he married Saray Paley. He was blessed with five sons, Joseph, Robert, William, George, and Samuel. He is best remembered for two devotional titles he published in his lifetime: *Christian Experience as Displayed in the Life and Writings of Saint Paul* and *Spiritual Exercises of the Heart*. The latter volume, recently reprinted by Reformation Heritage Books, is full of experiential and practical wisdom. He died at the age of sixty-five.

John Ryle (1816–1900). John Ryle was one of the most influential evangelical pastors of the nineteenth century. Born to a wealthy family in 1816, he was sent to the prestigious Eton College, where he excelled in sports, and then went on to Oxford. It was during his time at Oxford, after a significant illness, that he first turned to the Bible and the Lord in prayer. Upon graduation he desired to follow his father's footsteps in the world of banking as well as being a member of Parliament, but a series of events prevented this from happening. Ryle then felt called to the ministry. It was also at this time that he married his first wife who, as well as his second wife, died young, after which he married for a third time. Ryle was known as a man of granite yet with the heart of a child. Over the span of his lifetime, he wrote several commentaries as well as many practical books. Although he desired to work until his death, a stroke and other physical complications compelled him to retire a few months before his death in 1900.

Thomas Watson (1620–1686). It is probable that Thomas Watson was born in Yorkshire. He studied at Emmanuel College in Cambridge. Around 1647 he married Abigail Beadle and together they had seven children, of which four died at a young age. Watson was a gifted preacher and had a great gift of prayer. One day after hearing him preach a man followed him home to ask for a copy of his prayer to which Watson replied, "That is what I cannot give, for I do not use pen for my prayers; it was no studied thing, but uttered, pro re nata, as God enabled me, from the abundance of my heart and affections." Watson was imprisoned in 1651 for one year for his Presbyterian views before being reinstated to his pastorate in 1652. A decade later, due to the Act of Uniformity in 1662, Watson was ejected from his pastorate. He continued to preach in private whenever he had the opportunity. In 1686 Thomas Watson died suddenly while in his closet in prayer.

Octavius Winslow (1808–1878). Born in Pentonville, a village near London, Octavius Winslow was one of thirteen children. The family decided to move to New York when Octavius was seven years old. Octavius sailed to America with his mother and siblings; his father died before he could join them. Winslow's God-fearing mother was left to raise the children alone and was used greatly in shaping the heart of Octavius who came to know the Lord at a young age. He was ordained into ministry in 1833. Winslow married Hannah in 1834 and they had ten children, although one died shortly after birth and one died in young adulthood. In 1839 Winslow moved back to England and became one of the leading nonconformist ministers of the nineteenth century who promoted Reformed experiential and practical theology. He wrote more than forty books, some of which went through several printings. Following his mother's death, Winslow published two books of her letters, diary, and thoughts, *Heaven Opened* and *Life in Jesus*. On March 5, 1878, after a short illness, Octavius Winslow died, and was buried in Abbey Cemetery, Bath.

Scripture Index

OLD TESTAMENT

Genesis
9:13   July 22
18:19   March 2

Exodus
33:14   June 16 & 17

Leviticus
11:44   February 5

Numbers
15:30   July 2

Deuteronomy
10:12   September 30
11:19   May 14
30:19   December 24
31:8   March 22
33:25   October 29
33:27   November 27

Joshua
1:8   November 10

1 Samuel
1:8   May 5
2:7   November 22
2:30   July 20
12:20   June 29

1 Kings
8:23   January 28
18:21   December 3

Nehemiah
6:9   January 26

Esther
4:14   August 12

Job
6:24   March 19
19:25   February 12

Psalms
1:2   January 10
1:3   May 21
9:2   March 13
16:11   May 6
17:8   November 21
18:1   March 1
18:2   November 3
19:1   May 1
19:12   June 22
25:14   March 21
26:2   November 25
28:7   July 8
31:1   October 4
34:9   July 27
34:11   January 8
34:19   June 20
36:7   May 25
37:5   December 8
38:15   September 17
39:1   October 6 & 7
39:9   October 21
42:8   January 29
42:11   November 24
46:1   October 2
46:10   January 11
47:6   August 14
48:1   September 4
50:15   February 17

Psalms (*continued*)

55:12–13	February 15
55:16	October 11
55:22	October 9
57:7	February 7
61:2	November 1
62:8	September 19
66:16	November 5
69:30	November 28
72:12	October 16
73:25	November 17
73:26	February 4
77:12	July 30
90:8	September 24
90:17	September 20
95:6	January 5
103:2	November 29
103:13	August 30
104:34	October 17
116:6	May 3
116:12	November 7
116:16	May 12
118:6	February 20
118:8	July 25
118:24	February 1
119:15	June 14
119:50	December 16
119:67	June 11
119:71	December 19
119:105	August 28
119:125	July 19
119:151	March 15
128:4	March 16
133:1	April 9
138:3	June 3
139:17–18	March 29
141:3	July 24
142:6	February 2
144:15	June 7
145:18	May 20
150:6	April 3

Proverbs

2:2	April 27
3:6	February 26
4:23	July 6
6:27	February 10
11:28	June 2
12:12	August 17
14:8	May 8
15:24	December 10
16:33	March 24
18:12	May 7
18:24	May 30
22:6	June 27
25:15	August 6

Ecclesiastes

4:6	September 23
5:4	January 3
7:8	July 21
9:10	June 23

Song of Solomon

4:7	October 24

Isaiah

32:17	July 13
35:8	May 16
40:11	January 20
40:29	March 8
41:10	October 22
43:2	December 27
43:7	January 19
48:10	November 30
48:17	March 4
60:1	November 14
61:10	April 28
63:9	June 15
66:18	November 18

Jeremiah

3:14	June 19
17:9	September 16
23:3	September 26
31:3	February 8
49:4	November 23

Lamentations

3:40	June 12

Ezekiel
18:32 January 15
36:26 March 27

Daniel
9:19 August 22

Amos
4:12 December 31

Micah
6:8 June 5

Habakkuk
2:4 July 10
3:18 July 29

Zephaniah
3:17 October 30

Haggai
1:7 May 31

Malachi
3:6 June 28

NEW TESTAMENT

Matthew
5:4 May 2
5:14 January 24
5:16 February 22
6:6 March 18
6:21 December 5
6:33 January 22 & 23
6:34 January 31
7:1 September 14
7:13–14 December 21
10:8 June 6
10:28 July 26
10:38 March 31
11:30 March 20
12:33 August 23
14:23 January 6
15:18 July 18
16:24 December 7

16:26 January 1
18:20 September 15
23:11 April 18
28:20 December 11

Mark
3:35 March 5
4:34 January 9
4:40 March 6
6:31 February 3
7:15 August 31
8:34 April 1
8:36 December 23
10:39 March 26

Luke
6:36 June 10
6:41 February 19
9:23 May 9
9:25 December 15
10:27 August 3
10:41–42 June 18
12:15 December 6
12:32 November 6
14:27 April 30
16:10 September 1
17:5 December 20
22:31 October 28

John
1:16 May 24
1:43 April 10
3:16 December 4
5:39 June 4
6:67 April 20
9:4 December 12
10:14 July 11
10:28 October 1
11:33 April 4
11:35 July 16
12:26 June 8
12:26 May 23
13:35 January 16
14:18 January 25
14:20 March 9

John (*continued*)

15:5	August 5
15:8	September 8
15:15	September 3
17:16	June 24
18:11	July 12
19:26	September 25
21:17	May 28

Acts

2:28	March 3
9:11	March 25
16:31	January 14
20:24	August 13
24:16	April 21

Romans

1:17	October 15
4:5	March 17
5:1	February 24
5:2	April 23
6:22	October 10
6:23	December 25
7:12–13	January 27
8:13	November 2
8:21	February 28
8:28	August 7
8:35	February 16
12:1	March 12
12:2	August 10 & 11
12:15	December 26
12:18	September 21
15:4	August 20
15:6	May 19
16:20	May 10

1 Corinthians

1:18	April 24
3:11	September 5
3:16	May 15
6:20	August 1
7:29	December 14
9:24	December 13
10:10	February 29
10:12	October 19
10:13	May 11

10:31	February 25
11:1	May 22
13:13	August 15
15:49	December 30
15:58	April 29
16:14	September 29

2 Corinthians

1:4	April 13
1:6	February 23
3:5	September 10
4:16	October 27
4:17	November 16
5:14	July 17
5:15	March 14
5:17	October 13
6:17	May 18
9:8	October 25
10:4	September 22
13:4	April 5
13:5	January 13
13:11	August 21

Galatians

2:16	October 31
3:26	July 3
5:14	August 25
5:17	June 26
5:25	January 21
6:14	April 12

Ephesians

2:19	October 8
3:14–15	November 11
3:19	February 14
4:1	August 27
4:7	July 1
4:23	June 25
4:24	June 1
4:30	May 4
4:32	February 11
5:2	February 13
5:15	February 27
5:23	July 9
5:25	November 13
6:10	September 27

6:13	October 26
6:19	April 17

Philippians

1:4	July 14
1:20	April 19
1:27	May 13
1:29	September 7
2:4	July 7
2:5	June 21
2:7–8	March 28
2:12–13	August 9
3:14	January 4
4:5	August 29
4:6	January 18
4:9	August 8
4:11	October 5
4:13	April 7
4:19	December 17

Colossians

1:10	September 12 & 13
2:10	January 2
3:2	October 14
3:10	February 18
3:11	January 17
3:18–19	July 4 & 5
3:23	May 17
3:24	August 24
4:5	January 7

1 Thessalonians

4:11	August 26
4:13	November 4
5:16	January 12

2 Thessalonians

3:13	December 2

1 Timothy

4:12	August 16
4:10	April 6
6:6	March 11
6:12	August 2

2 Timothy

1:12	January 30
2:3	July 15
2:12	May 27
3:16	November 15

Hebrews

2:15	December 29
2:17	April 8
3:12	December 18
4:9	November 19
4:15	April 11
4:16	April 16
9:27	December 28
10:22	October 23
12:1	February 21
12:2	March 10
12:6	September 28
12:8	July 31
12:14	September 2
13:4	April 25
13:5	November 20
13:14	December 1
13:15	November 26

James

1:8	July 28
3:17	October 3
4:6	November 12
4:7	September 18
4:8	March 7
4:17	June 30
5:16	June 9
5:16	August 19

1 Peter

1:7	September 11
1:16	September 9
2:7	April 22
2:12	May 29
3:2	October 12
3:4	November 8
3:15	November 9
3:18	April 14
4:13	April 26
5:7	April 15

2 Peter

1:4	February 9
1:8	September 6
2:9	August 4
3:11	August 18
3:18	March 30

1 John

3:1	May 26
3:2	October 20
3:14	March 23
4:10	April 2

4:19	February 6
5:2	July 23

Jude

v 16	June 13

Revelation

3:20	December 22
21:4	December 9
21:7	October 18